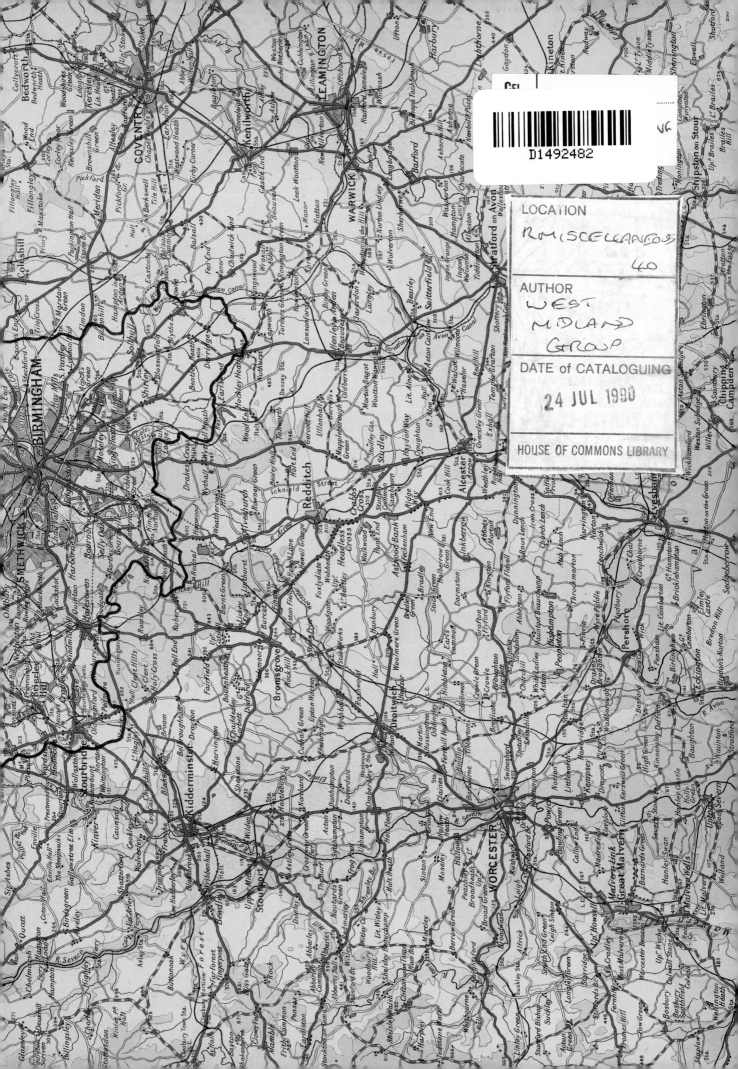

CONURBATION

A PLANNING SURVEY OF BIRMINGHAM
AND THE BLACK COUNTRY

CONURBATION

A PLANNING SURVEY OF BIRMINGHAM
AND THE BLACK COUNTRY BY THE
WEST MIDLAND GROUP

1948
THE ARCHITECTURAL PRESS, 9-13 QUEEN ANNE'S GATE, LONDON S.W.1

MADE AND PRINTED IN GREAT BRITAIN

Foreword

BY now the foreign observer has ceased to be astonished at the quality of the thought that has gone into the surveys and plans for the redevelopment of urban England. Even if a good part of this work had not been done under the difficult conditions of the war, it would still be remarkable. But the cause for his astonishment—and incidentally, for his envy—remains; and it is conspicuous in the present report.

The complex of towns, boroughs, urban spores, submerged villages, and open land which make up a conurbation is no easy field for study. One might consume a lifetime in its investigation without feeling that one had come to the bottom of its problems. By a combination of statistical analysis and shrewd observation, the West Midland Group have put together the essential facts upon which future planning policy must be based; and they have summed up the results in a series of recommendations. The relative compactness of this report is an indication of their mastery of these data.

Certain facts about this West Midland area set it off quite definitely from other parts of England, and give it an economic resilience that other areas have lacked, as shown by the prosperity of Birmingham itself during the period of the great economic depression. Even the most casual observer senses an old-fashioned confidence among its business men and industrialists; but the penalty for such prosperity has been, perhaps, that of retarding improvements in both living and working conditions that have been long overdue. Plainly, the moment has now arrived for facing those arrears and overcoming them; but, as the Group point out, the job is not made any easier by the fact that the repairs must be undertaken while the steam is up.

Birmingham, the regional capital of this area, was the centre of two critical events in the industrial revolution. The first was, of course, connected with the works of Messrs. Boulton & Watt, which provided the chief source of power for the new technical era. The second was the pioneer experiment in sound housing and community planning for the worker in direct relation to industry. Watt's engine set the pace for production; Cadbury's Bournville, equally, set a new level for consumption, though unfortunately it was not until after the First World War that this experiment bore full fruit in the standard design of the new housing estates throughout England.

Surprisingly, in view of the relative prosperity of the West Midland area, the Group states that "the Conurbation has been found to have a low proportion of workers rendering the services that mark a high standard of living"; and one of their conclusions is that " Shopping Centres, Hotels, Restaurants, Theatres, Concert Halls, Assembly Rooms, should be developed throughout the Conurbation ". In time, even more than this will be required; for under the terms of the new Education Act a considerable expansion of educational facilities must be provided for; indeed, one may well look forward to a turning point in planning, perhaps a generation ahead, when the present shortages and arrears have been overcome. At this point, capital outlays on education, culture, and recreation, that is, on durable consumption goods, may well over-balance those for renovating industry and transportation. For this reason the Social and Cultural Survey which the Group originally contemplated, but was not able to carry out, would seem to be the next item in the order of business; for without it neither the neighbourhood unit nor the Conurbation as a whole can be adequately planned.

On the need for a few comprehensive, all-purpose Authorities for this area, in order to overcome the isolations and needless conflicts of the present divisions, the Group seems agreed; and though this is a matter on which an outsider should perhaps speak warily, I should like to emphasize this need, for it is a universal one. Without such Authorities, there is no way of lessening disabilities and evening out advantages for the Conurbation as a whole.

Not least admirable about this report is the way with which the Group addressed itself to such a difficult problem as the redemption of the blasted sectors of the industrial landscape, with its mountainous slag-heaps; and Mr. Jellicoe's proposals form a significant contribution to this survey.

On my recent visit to England I found myself constantly repeating the admiring sentence that was on Emerson's lips when he came here during the great depression of 1847: " England is no country for faint-hearted people," and I find myself saying it again. Your burdens are heavy and must sometimes seem insupportable; but here, as perhaps no place else in the world to-day, are the political intelligence, the administrative skill, and the civic probity and courage, that will transform the old handicaps into fresh opportunities. The present study of the Conurbation points to a day when Birmingham and the Black Country will be as solvent in human terms as they have been, in the past, in industrial and financial terms. That hope " maketh not ashamed ".

Lewis Mumford

WEST MIDLAND GROUP ON POST-WAR RECONSTRUCTION AND PLANNING

5

T. O. Gray, Esq., J.P., (*Hon. Treasurer*),
  Formerly Manager, Westminster Bank Ltd., Birmingham.
  Hon. Treasurer, Birmingham Citizens' Society.

Herbert J. Manzoni, Esq., C.B.E., M.Inst. C.E., M.T.P.I.,
  City Engineer and Surveyor, Birmingham.
  Hon. Surveyor to the Midland Joint Town Planning Advisory Council.

Sir Wilfrid Martineau, M.C., T.D., M.A.,
  Solicitor.
  Alderman of the City of Birmingham ; Lord Mayor, 1940-41.
  Chairman of Education Committee, and Member of the General Purposes Committee of the Birmingham
    City Council.

Mrs. M. Morris, M.A.,
  Chairman, Council of Social Service for Stoke-on-Trent and North Staffs.
  Investigator for Nuffield College (for Stoke District).

Clive D. A. Powell, Esq., J.P., F.R.I.C.S.,
  Chartered Surveyor and Land Agent.
  Chairman (1944-45), Warwickshire, Staffordshire and Worcestershire Branch of the Chartered Surveyors'
    Institution.
  Member of Worcestershire War Agricultural Executive Committee.

Professor J. G. Smith, O.B.E., M.Com., M.A.,
  Formerly Vice-Principal of the University of Birmingham.
  Formerly Dean of the Faculty of Commerce and Social Science, University of Birmingham.

Professor L. Dudley Stamp, C.B.E., B.A., D.Sc.,
  Chief Adviser on Rural Land Utilisation, Ministry of Agriculture.
  Director of the Land Utilisation Survey of Britain.
  Professor of Geography, University of London.
  Vice-Chairman of the Scott Committee.

Sydney Vernon, Esq., LL.M.,
  Solicitor.
  Pro-Chancellor of the University of Birmingham.
  Member of the Provincial Hospitals Regionalization Council.
  Director of certain Industrial Companies.

Corresponding Members

G. W. Cadbury, Esq., M.A.,
  Chairman of Economic Advisory and Planning Board, and Chief Industrial Executive, Province of
    Saskatchewan, Canada.
  Director, British Canners, Ltd.
  Trustee, Bournville Village Trust.

Alderman G. W. Kenrick,
  Chairman of County Planning Committee of Worcestershire County Council.

Secretary

C. Bertram Parkes, Esq., M.B.E., L.R.I.B.A.,
  Chief Architect to the Bournville Village Trust.
  Member of the Council of the Royal Institute of British Architects, 1939-1946.

RESEARCH ORGANIZATION

The Group itself is the governing body, responsible for drafting the research programme and for all matters of policy and finance.

Various fields of research are allocated to the separate Committees whose titles and membership are set out below. The Committees discuss their particular sections of the programme and draw up detailed instructions for the conduct of investigations, some of which are dealt with in discussion among Committee members, while others are entrusted to members of the staff. In every case, the reports are drafted by sectional Committees before being passed to the Group for final consideration.

For the present survey a co-ordinating committee—the Conurbation Committee—was set up in order to collate the different branches of the survey at regular intervals.

The following formed the Committees which organized the survey and supervised its progress :—

CONURBATION COMMITTEE

Sir Hugh Chance (*Chairman*)

Professor P. Sargant Florence.
Mr. Sydney Vernon.
Mr. Paul S. Cadbury.
Professor J. G. Smith.

Mr. H. J. Manzoni.
Sir Wilfrid Martineau.
Mr. R. H. Kinvig.
Dr. R. E. Priestley.

Mr. C. B. Parkes (*Secretary*)

GEOGRAPHICAL COMMITTEE.

Dr. R. E. Priestley (*Chairman*)

Professor L. Dudley Stamp.
Mr. R. H. Kinvig.
Mr. W. Morley Davies.
Mr. Paul S. Cadbury.

Mr. A. Hudson Davies
Mr. G. Cadbury.
Mr. Clive D. A. Powell.

Mr. K. M. Buchanan† (*Secretary*)

INDUSTRIAL COMMITTEE.

Professor P. Sargant Florence (*Chairman*)

Major C. R. Dibben.
Mr. G. Cadbury.
Mr. Sydney Vernon.
Professor J. G. Smith.
Mr. Paul S. Cadbury.

Mr. A. Hudson Davies.
Mr. T. O. Gray.
Sir Hugh Chance.
Dr. R. E. Priestley.

Mr. C. B. Parkes (*Secretary*)

BUILDINGS COMMITTEE.

Mr. H. J. Manzoni (*Chairman*)

Mr. A. C. Bunch.
Professor J. G. Smith.

Mr. Paul S. Cadbury.
Dr. R. E. Priestley.

Mr. C. B. Parkes (*Secretary*)

COMMUNICATIONS COMMITTEE.

Mr. H. J. Manzoni (*Chairman*)

Mr. G. Cadbury.
Dr. R. E. Priestley.

Sir Wilfrid Martineau.
Mr. Paul S. Cadbury.

Mr. C. B. Parkes (*Secretary*)

LAND CLASSIFICATION COMMITTEE.

Mr. W. Morley Davies (*Chairman*)

Mr. G. Cadbury.
Mr. Clive D. A. Powell.
Professor L. Dudley Stamp.
Dr. A. W. McPherson.*
Mr. Paul S. Cadbury.
Dr. R. E. Priestley.
Mr. C. B. Parkes (Secretary until March, 1944).
Mr. R. H. Kinvig, M.A. (Head of Geography Department, University of Birmingham).
Mr. W. G. D. Walters, M.Sc., F.R.I.C. (Soil Survey of England and Wales).

Dr. D. A. Osmond, M.Sc., A.R.I.C., (University of Bristol Agricultural & Horticultural Research Station, Long Ashton).
Professor G. W. Robinson, M.A., Sc.D. (Professor of Agricultural Chemistry, University College of North Wales, Bangor).
Professor T. Wallace, C.B.E., M.C., D.Sc., F.R.I.C. (Director, University of Bristol Agricultural & Horticultural Research Station, Long Ashton).

Mr. K. M. Buchanan† (*Secretary*).

PUBLICATIONS COMMITTEE.

Sir Hugh Chance (*Chairman*)

Dr. R. E. Priestley.
Mr. Paul S. Cadbury.

Professor P. Sargant Florence.

Mr. C. B. Parkes (*Secretary*)

* Dr. A. W. McPherson died in July, 1946, after the work of the Committee had been virtually concluded.
† Lecturer in Geography, University of Witwatersrand, South Africa, since June, 1946.

STAFF

The staff which was engaged upon the survey and report worked under the direction of the Secretary, Mr. C. B. Parkes, M.B.E., L.R.I.B.A. The cessation of hostilities in the summer of 1945 and the rapid changes in conditions which have followed made the prosecution of this survey much more difficult than in the case of the survey of Herefordshire, the Group's first major planning survey, which was published in 1946 under the title of *English County*; this was particularly so in the case of the staff, none of whom worked continuously with the Group throughout the whole period of the survey and the preparation of the report.

The staff engaged upon the Conurbation survey and report were as follows :—

Mr. E. A. Avery.	Dr. A. W. McPherson, B.Sc.*
Mr. K. M. Buchanan, B.A.*	Mr. J. C. Massie.
Mr. Tom Burns, B.A.	Mr. A. L. N. Stephens, M.A.
Miss Janet Glaisyer, M.A.	Mr. Clive B. Williams, B. Com.†

* Of the Department of Geography, University of Birmingham—(Head of Department, Mr. R. H. Kinvig, M.A.).

† Working under the direction of Professor P. Sargant Florence, of the Faculty of Commerce and Social Science, University of Birmingham.

Mrs. F. L. Goodman acted as Assistant Secretary until January, 1947, and her place has since been taken by Miss G. E. Nottley.

ACKNOWLEDGEMENTS

In addition to the plans and reports prepared by Mr. G. A. Jellicoe, P.I.L.A., M.T.P.I., F.R.I.B.A., and Mr. Thomas Sharp, M.A., L.R.I.B.A., P.P.T.P.I., F.I.L.A., the reports upon which Chapters II and X and the Appendix are based were prepared at the invitation of the Group by persons not members of the Group or of its staff. The Historical Sketch which forms Chapter II was written by Professor W. H. Court, M.A. (Cantab.), M.A. (Harvard), and Chapter X, Smoke Pollution, is based on a report prepared by Mr. J. K. Best, F.R.I.C. The Appendix on The South Staffordshire and Cannock Chase Coalfields and Future Planning in the West Midland Conurbation is the work of Mr. M. J. Wise, M.C., B.A., of the Department of Geography, University of Birmingham, who, with the assistance of Mr. A. Wood, also carried out the survey of development on the edge of the Conurbation and in the surrounding countryside.

The Group gratefully acknowledges the part played by the Bournville Village Trust in all the work which preceded the publication of this Report. The Trust has provided staff to carry on the day-to-day administration of the affairs of the Group and a great deal of the work of research.

The Foreword is written by Professor Lewis Mumford, the well-known American sociologist, author of *Technics & Civilization, The Culture of Cities*, etc., who visited Birmingham during his tour of this country in the summer of 1946, and was able to meet members of the Group and see something of its work.

In order to overcome some of the difficulties encountered in the preparation of *English County* for the press, the Group invited Mr. T. C. Kemp, of *The Birmingham Post*, to undertake the task of editing the text of the Report before publication. Mr. Kemp attended all meetings of the Group and of the Conurbation Committee over a period of two years and also shared in the work of the Publications Committee. The Group would like to acknowledge the way in which he has carried through a difficult and protracted task.

The Group is again indebted to Mr. P. B. Redmayne, M.A., for his help in the publication of *Conurbation*, as of *English County* ; he has been responsible for the layout of maps and diagrams and for the visual presentation of the Report in its published form. Mr. F. T. Lockwood supervised the preparation of the illustrations for publication and the technical work of presentation. Mr. W. E. Cossons has been responsible for preparing the text of the report for the printer and for seeing the book through the press ; he also supervised the compilation of the Index.

It is clear that a report such as the present could not have been completed without the assistance and co-operation of a large number of people, especially those occupying official positions in the Regional Offices of Ministries and of Local Authorities throughout the area. To these people, many of whom have shown kindness, helpfulness and sympathy with the aims of the Group which have been of the greatest encouragement, the Group offers its very grateful thanks.

Special thanks are due to the Surveyors and Town Planning Officers of the twenty-four Local Authorities in the Conurbation. Besides providing the maps and information which formed the basis of the Surface Utilisation map, they and the staffs of their departments have assisted the work of the Group in a great many other directions, and particularly in the Housing and Open Space surveys.

The Group offers its grateful thanks to :—

Mr. Arthur Booth, F.R.I.B.A., M.I.Struct.E., F.R.S.A., M.Inst.M.&Cy.E., Borough Surveyor, Wednesbury.

Mr. R. H. J. Comber, M.Inst.M.&Cy.E., Engineer and Surveyor, Brierley Hill.

Mr. Clifford B. Eck, A.M.Inst.C.E., A.M.Inst.M.&Cy.E., Borough Engineer and Surveyor, Oldbury.

Mr. Roland Fletcher, M.Inst.C.E., Borough Engineer and Surveyor, Smethwick.

Mr. F. H. Gibbons, O.B.E., M.Inst.M.&Cy.E., Borough Engineer and Housing Director, Dudley.

Mr. M. E. Habershon, O.B.E., M.Eng., M.Inst.C.E., M.Inst.M.&Cy.E., Borough Engineer and Surveyor, Walsall.

Mr. H. N. Hughes, M.Inst.M.&Cy.E., Engineer and Surveyor, Darlaston.

Mr. C. R. Hutchinson, B.Sc., A.M.Inst.C.E., M.Inst.M.&Cy.E., Engineer and Surveyor, Solihull.

Mr. H. G. Jefferson, M.Inst.C.E., A.M.T.P.I., F.R.San.I., M.Inst.M.&Cy.E., Borough Surveyor, West Bromwich.

Mr. W. M. Jones, A.M.Inst.C.E., Engineer and Surveyor, Sedgley.

Mr. A. H. Lawrence, M.Inst.M.&Cy.E., M.R.San.I., Engineer and Surveyor, Wednesfield.

Mr. W. M. Law, M.B.E., A.M.Inst.C.E., M.Inst.M.&Cy.E., Borough Engineer and Surveyor, Wolverhampton.

Mr. N. D. Martin, M.Inst.M.&Cy.E., M.R.San.I., Engineer and Surveyor, Willenhall.

Mr. J. W. Mason, M.Inst.M.&Cy.E., M.T.P.I., Engineer and Surveyor, Tettenhall.

Mr. G. N. Maynard, A.M.Inst.C.E., F.S.I., A.M.T.P.I., Borough Surveyor and Architect, Stourbridge.

Mr. H. S. Onions, Engineer and Surveyor, Aldridge.

Mr. Harold Piper, M.S.I.A., Surveyor, Amblecote.

Mr. T. Porter, A.M.Inst.C.E., A.M.I.Mech.E., Borough Engineer and Surveyor, Sutton Coldfield.

Mr. A. F. B. Sidwick, M.Inst.M.&Cy.E., Borough Engineer and Surveyor, Bilston.

Mr. P. J. Stanton, Engineer and Surveyor, Coseley.

Mr. T. W. Tivey, M.Inst.M.&Cy.E., Borough Engineer and Surveyor, Halesowen.

Mr. S. G. Wood, M.Inst.M.&Cy.E., M.R.San.I., Borough Surveyor, Rowley Regis.

Mr. H. N. Woodard, M.Inst.M.&Cy.E., Borough Engineer and Surveyor, Tipton.

Mr. L. Abbott, M.B.E., M.T.P.I., P.A.S.I., Town Planning Officer, South East Staffs. Joint Planning Committee.

Mr. H. G. Avery, A.R.I.B.A., M.T.P.I., Town Planning Officer, Dudley and District Joint Planning Committee.

Mr. F. Greenwood, M.T.P.I., Superintendent of the Town Planning Department, City of Birmingham.

The Group acknowledges also the assistance and co-operation, over an equally wide field, of officials of the Regional Office of the Ministry of Town and Country Planning :—

Mr. E. H. Doubleday, M.T.P.I., A.R.I.C.S., M.I.Mun.E., County Planning Officer, Hertfordshire ; Regional Planning Officer, West Midland Region, 1942-1945.

Mr. R. K. Kelsall, M.A., Regional Office, Birmingham.

Mr. L. F. I. Wolters, L.R.I.B.A., M.T.P.I., Regional Office, Birmingham.

Many others have contributed their time, special knowledge and expert opinion, and the Group wishes to record its indebtedness to :—

Professor L. J. Wills, Sc.D., Ph.D., of the Geological Department of the University of Birmingham, for supervising the preparation of the Geological Map and Sections (Figures 1, 2 and 3) ;

Mr. A. J. Gardner, Public Relations Officer, National Association of Local Government Officers, for revising the contents of Table III, " Powers and Duties of Local Government Authorities ", in Chapter IV ;

Mr. F. J. Patrick, F.L.A., Birmingham City Librarian, for permission to reproduce the illustrations on pages 31-35 ;

Miss D. M. Norris, F.L.A., Assistant in Charge of Local Collection, for invaluable assistance in the work of tracing and selecting maps and illustrations used in Chapters II and IV ;

Trent Navigation Co., Weaver Navigation, and Severn Carrying Co., for kindly supplying information about their proposed future development ;

Professor Gilbert Walker, D.Litt., M.A., of the Faculty of Commerce, University of Birmingham, for supplying unpublished material used in Chapter VI.

Mr. F. Barnett, A.R.San.I., Sanitary Inspector, Bilston, for assistance with the Housing Survey.

Dr. A. Parker, Director of the Fuel Research Station, Department of Scientific and Industrial Research, for permission to reproduce figures published in *Nature* and elsewhere and for statistics hitherto unpublished.

Dr. A. R. Meetham, Superintendent of Observations on Atmospheric Pollution, Department of Scientific and Industrial Research, and Mr. G. W. Farquharson, Senior Smoke and Factories Inspector, Birmingham, for supplying information used in the Chapter on Smoke Pollution.

Mr. R. Fletcher, Borough Engineer and Surveyor, Smethwick, for providing the information for the maps of Smethwick showing the analysis of each main category of Surface Utilisation.

Mr. A. V. Williams, Town Clerk, Bilston until 1947, and Mr. A. F. B. Sidwick, Borough Surveyor, Bilston, for providing information on which an unpublished series of maps analysing Surface Utilisation in Bilston have been based.

Mr. W. G. D. Walters, M.Sc., A.R.I.C., of the Soil Survey of England and Wales, for carrying out most of the field work connected with the Land Classification survey of the area around the Conurbation and for correcting and revising the map on Plate 12.

The Ministry of Agriculture and Fisheries and Mr. E. Gittins-Jones, Deputy Regional Rural Land Utilisation Officer of the Ministry, for their assistance in the Land Classification survey.

Sir Ben Smith, Chairman, West Midlands Division, National Coal Board, for providing access to information contained in the Appendix on the South Staffordshire and Cannock Chase Coalfields, and to Mr. J. Griffith, M.A., LL.B., Legal Adviser, Mr. H. J. Crofts, Production Director, and Mr. J. C. Micheson, Assistant Production Director, all of the National Coal Board, West Midlands Division, for valuable assistance in the preparation of this section of the Report.

Miss M. J. Hawthorne, of the Department of Geography, University of Birmingham, for assistance in drawing the maps shown in Figures 55 to 61.

Acknowledgements of sources of photographs appear on page 288.

Contents

LIST OF ILLUSTRATIONS

Coloured Plates

Illustrated Sections

THE
WEST MIDLAND
CONURBATION AND REGION
IN RELATION TO
ENGLAND AND WALES

CLYDESIDE

TYNESIDE

WEST RIDING

HULL

MERSEYSIDE MANCHESTER

LIVERPOOL

SHEFFIELD

CREWE

STOKE

NOTTINGHAM

DERBY

STAFFORD

SHREWSBURY

LEICESTER

COVENTRY

WARWICK NORTHAMPTON

WORCESTER

HEREFORD

GLOUCESTER

OXFORD

CARDIFF

BRISTOL

LONDON

OTHER PRINCIPAL CONURBATIONS

CHAPTER I

Introduction

THERE are few activities in which a little knowledge may be more dangerous than in town and country planning. However urgent may be the immediate need for reconstruction and development, a long-term view is necessary if the permanent needs of men, agriculture and industry are fully to be met; and these needs can be related to present conditions only when the planners have all the facts before them.

It is the purpose of this Report to supply such basic facts as apply to the Birmingham and Black Country Conurbation. The term " conurbation " means an area of continuous urban development which includes and connects two or more towns. It was Professor Patrick Geddes who first drew attention to the need for studying the new groups of related urban communities which had grown up during the 19th century. With the increase in population and the industrialization of Britain, factories and people tended to be drawn into a few aggregates of inter-dependent towns, suburbs and townships, all of which had certain strong economic and social links and common characteristics; Patrick Geddes called such groupings " conurbations ". The term has since gained currency as a useful, though loosely defined, concept among planners, geographers and sociologists. The Birmingham and Black Country area forms a clear example of what is meant by a " conurbation ". Its towns and villages began to develop into their present size and state, and the rough extent and function of the whole area was decided, during the industrial revolution of the late 18th and the 19th centuries, when the whole area was appropriated by industrial enterprise. The Industrial Revolution brought material prosperity in its wake, but it left behind also a rapidly accumulating heritage of problems to be dealt with by the first generation with the energy and knowledge needed to face them.

This Report is not primarily a plan. The main objectives of the West Midland Group have been the assembly of facts and figures collected on the spot, and the examination of those bases on which the good life may be securely founded in the Conurbation area. At the same time the Group recognizes that even though the elementary conditions for decent living may be secured for the Conurbation as a whole, each district has its own particular problems which can be solved only by careful examination of local conditions: so that while the Group has made certain recommendations, these are, for the most part, of a general nature and have been arrived at as the result of surveying the Conurbation as a whole. These recommendations may have to be modified or expanded in detail to suit particular areas, but generally they may be taken as pointers to communal well-being. This overall view is particularly necessary in the Conurbation area as the close inter-dependence of industries, the varied nature of Local Authorities, and the value to the whole of the limited open space within the area, all demand that planning decisions should be taken with the greatest good of the whole area in mind.

The Conurbation forms the heart of the industrial Midlands and extends roughly from Birmingham in the south-east to Wolverhampton in the north-west, and from Walsall in the north to Stourbridge in the south. A population of over two millions occupies an area of approximately 270 square miles. Here, at the very hub of industrial England, lies one of the most patent problem areas in the country, an area in which arrears in planning can be wiped out only by concerted and comprehensive action on the part of the twenty-four Local Authorities which control its destiny.

The history of the Conurbation is a story of industrial acceleration in which the needs of man took second place to the demands of manufacture. Two hundred years ago, various industries sprouted simultaneously over the Midlands. The sword- and gun-makers of Birmingham, the smiths of Dudley, and the lorimers of Walsall, staked their claims without any thought for planning. Trades rose and flourished. Local coal pits supplied forge and furnace. The mine, the slag-heap and the quarry marred the surface of a pleasant countryside. Factories spread in ribbon development along the canal bank and the railway track. The iron-works displaced the plough, and the march of industry went relentlessly on, until, by the middle of the 19th century, thousands of acres had been consumed to satisfy the unending demands of factory, mine and workshop.

Today the planner is confronted with a gigantic sprawl of factories, houses, cities, towns and villages. Industry is too firmly rooted and widespread to be moved wholesale. The workers who serve it have been housed in dwellings that have sprung up in the shadow of the factories. Recent planning has taken definite steps to improve housing, but there still remains an inconvenient heritage from the past, and war has impeded the efforts made to meet current needs. Uncontrolled growth has sent towns stretching along main roads until it is now difficult to see where one ends and another begins. Yet among this new growth lie hundreds of acres of derelict land awaiting the reviving hand of the imaginative planner to restore them to fruitful use.

Industry is a permanent factor in the Conurbation. The cities, towns and villages cannot be moved: its old-established industries and the people who serve them cannot be transplanted whole to new areas. The machinery of this highly industrialized area is so complex that migration on a large scale is impossible, even if it were desirable. There can be no question of new towns for old in the Conurbation. The problem of the planner is, therefore, two-fold. He has concurrently to improve the old and develop the new. Repairs must be effected under steam. The contribution of the Midlands to the national economy is of such importance that the Conurbation must put its house in order with a minimum of interference to output.

Yet around these fixed features there still remains sufficient room for the planner to deploy; but his scheme of operations must be comprehensive. The Local Authorities within the Conurbation are such near neighbours that unity in purpose and co-operation in action are essential. The Group, therefore, favours large all-purpose Authorities, capable of a comprehensive outlook yet with sufficient discernment to retain those local interests and characteristics whose preservation is important. The appointment by the Ministry of Town and Country Planning of a team of experts to draw up a Regional Plan is welcomed by the Group as likely to foster co-operation between Local Authorities. The Group has always taken a keen interest in local government, and has set up two special committees which published their reports in 1944 under the title " Reports on the

Control and Use of Land, and the Administrative and Financial Problems of Town Planning, with a note on the Size and Functions of Local Government Units ".

The information contained in the following chapters is submitted as a foundation of fact on which Local Authorities can base their future plans. Communications are the common concern of all in so thickly populated an industrial area. Population in its turn is the complement of industry, and housing of both. There are thousands of cases of workers who are employed in one area and who live in another. The chapter on Housing discloses that one-third of the houses in the Conurbation should be replaced as soon as possible. The chapter on Population records the changing age-structure of the inhabitants, a factor which sooner or later will react upon industry. It is only by weighing these inter-related facts one with another that a balanced economy for the Conurbation and a good life for its people may be reached.

High importance is attached to the facts given in the chapter on Industry, which views the subject from the points of view of stable employment, high employment, use of the capacities of the population, the standard of living, and participation in national policies, as well as of efficiency. The diversity of industry in the Conurbation is already wide; and the Group is of the opinion that, if a planned balance of population and industry is to be maintained, there is no need at present to introduce into the Conurbation completely new industries. This conclusion is a corollary to the chapter on Population, which states that within the present area of the Conurbation, two million people can be housed at reasonable density and with good measure of open spaces and undeveloped land. If the population rises much higher than its present figure, encroachment on open land will reduce valuable assets in order to meet what may turn out to be merely a temporary or a local need. The chapter also emphasizes the dearth of those services which raise the standard of life within the Region. In distribution, in professional services, in hotels, in entertainment and sport, the proportion of workers is lower than the national average by 15 per cent. to 50 per cent. The Conurbation urgently needs more shopping centres, hotels, restaurants, theatres, concert halls and assembly rooms. For several years there has been a lack of services, amenities and cultural life in the industrial Midlands. War has aggravated the situation, and if the shortage continues it is likely that the Conurbation will suffer substantial economic loss in that potential buyers will be kept away, and positions on managerial and technical staffs will not attract the most suitable candidates.

Closely related to the chapter on Industry is that on Factory Buildings. A number of modern factories in the Conurbation are efficiently planned and enjoy a full measure of those amenities which men of wide outlook include in their plans. But a large proportion of industrial buildings are badly sited and poorly planned. Many huddles of houses and workshops survive from the period when everything was sacrificed to the manufacturing opportunities of the moment. The Group's survey of factories, while not comprehensive, indicates the lines which any detailed assessment should follow. Increasing recognition of the importance of planned buildings, making for efficiency and convenience, is apparent in such schemes as the proposed system of flatted factories for the Birmingham Jewellery District.

The importance of the chapter on Surface Utilisation cannot be overstressed. The prime object in all sound planning is to decide on the best use to which land may be put in the interests of the community. The Conurbation offers few geographical obstacles to full utility. There are very few areas for which a good case could not be made for more than one use. Land in the Conurbation area is precious, and its right use can only be

THE CHARACTER OF THE CONURBATION

The Conurbation, remote from natural communications, owes its creation to its mineral resources, but its structure to canals and railways. These remain after much of the industry which called them into being has died or gone. They became arteries of the new industries which spread out along them from the old centres.

Canal and railway, Smethwick. The centres of industrial towns become complex networks of rail and waterways. Adjacent land is covered with closely-packed factories. Around and in between live the workers.

Looking into the Black Country from Mucklows Hill, above Halesowen. The canal at the foot of the hill was originally cut through the countryside. Designed to carry coal and iron from the Conurbation, it is now lined with industrial development.

Canal, railway and road, Bilston. The twentieth century adds motor-ways to the network. They, too, become lined with development. Between the transport routes the land is often derelict.

THE CHARACTER OF THE CONURBATION

The southern part of the Black Country looking westwards from above Blackheath. Some of the Conurbation still shows evidence of the natural beauty which existed formerly. The town in the valley to the right is Old Hill. The houses on the left are the outskirts of Blackheath.

The environment of the Black Country towns. Hundreds of thousands of people who live and work in the middle of the Conurbation have to find their recreation and their contact with the open air in these polluted surroundings.

THE CHARACTER OF THE CONURBATION

Sporadic development from a background of closely-packed industrial plant, railways and offices. The terrace street extends into the country, which it has become impossible to farm and which lies idle awaiting the developer.

Looking across the western part of the Conurbation from Wollescote. The valley of the Stour fills the middle distance. On the left is Lye, with Quarry Bank and Brierley Hill beyond. The extreme left of the photograph is in the direction of Amblecote. In the centre distance lies Dudley. Cradley Heath and Old Hill are the large urban area extending across most of the right of the photograph. Towards the foreground, in the centre of the right-hand half, lies Cradley. The large area of industrial plant and workings and of derelict land between Cradley and Lye is clearly visible.

Houses—Factories—Derelict Land. The tips and spoil banks of the Black Country are now the habitual playgrounds of children.

THE CHARACTER OF THE CONURBATION

Quarries, cuttings, spoil banks and pit mounds have changed even the contour of the countryside. Factories and houses are spread loosely over the level ground in the valley and on the hill top.

*Prospect from a new housing estate.   Derelict land and factories.
The hill top in the distance is being removed by quarrying.*

Derelict land in the making.   A burning pit mound.

correctly assessed when the claims of housing, industry, agriculture and recreation are carefully weighed. A sound case for housing may have to take second place to a stronger agricultural claim to the good earth; playgrounds may oust workshops by their larger contribution to a balanced whole. But right decisions can only be taken when the planner has the whole of the present picture accurately in view. With this in mind the Group has prepared a Surface Utilisation Map of the Conurbation area. The survey is based on information supplied by Local Authorities, supplemented, wherever the need appeared, by field work, and great care has been taken in assembling this information on one map. The scale of 6 inches to the mile was adopted to show in sufficient detail the whole of the Conurbation. The main land uses are shown in eight categories. It has been found impossible, for technical reasons, to include a reproduction of the complete map in this book, although its separate publication in a useful size is under consideration. Sections of the map, however, have been included in this Report. The important point is that the survey has been made, the map exists and is available for use. Already it has revealed useful and sometimes surprising information about the Conurbation. Superficial observation might lead to the conclusion that the Birmingham and Black Country area is densely built up. The map reveals that " undeveloped " land, open spaces and derelict land represent 56.0 per cent. of the total. Excluding Birmingham, the map shows that more than one-tenth of the Black Country is derelict land, that is, land that has been spoiled by extractive industry and by industrial waste, or is cumbered by derelict buildings. In 1945 a survey of the derelict land in the area was undertaken by Mr. S. H. Beaver for the Ministry of Town and Country Planning. Since this survey was made about a thousand acres of derelict land have been developed as housing sites, and further large stretches are in process of being levelled. In 1944, schemes for the rehabilitation of two derelict areas were prepared for the Group by Mr. G. A. Jellicoe. The schemes are included in this Report and demonstrate how these unplanned places may be converted into assets for the future. Here again the importance of the comprehensive view emerges. Although the present drive for houses is converting much derelict land back to usefulness, the overall view will ensure that a wise balance is kept between the needs of the moment and the balanced layout of the future.

In addition to the Jellicoe scheme, the Group presents a scheme as a basis for the detailed planning of the Catshill area. This latter scheme has been prepared by Mr. Thomas Sharp, and is advanced as an example of right land use. The Catshill area is admirably suited to be one of the main market garden areas of the Midlands, but the gradual encroachment of Birmingham's outer suburbs is spoiling the agricultural pattern. The Sharp scheme would stop this process of attrition and develop the Catshill area in those uses which would contribute fruitfully to the Conurbation as a whole.

With a view to the prevention of similar encroachment in other areas, the chapter on Land Classification in the Area surrounding the Conurbation gives an assessment of the agricultural values of land which might be in danger of misuse, were its potentialities not fully recognized. The Group also regards as important the preservation of those green wedges which still keep open the marginal land surrounding the Conurbation. These strips of open country are vital to a healthy and balanced pattern. Once an open space is closed, it seldom, if ever, returns to its first state; and although the Birmingham and Black Country Conurbation has more open land than is apparent to the casual observer, the surge of industrial and economic life in the area is so strong that strict control is necessary if land is to be preserved from the unconsidered occupation which has done so much damage in the past.

The Mining Survey which is published as an appendix was actually planned as an integral part of the survey of the Conurbation. The death of Dr. A. E. W. McPherson, who was responsible for the research involved, unfortunately prevented any use being made of the material collected. In 1947, however, a survey was eventually carried out by Mr. M. J. Wise; its completion at so late a date has prevented the incorporation of its results into the Report as a whole.

The Group is aware that this Report might usefully have included other aspects of the Conurbation in its survey. A Social and Cultural Survey was considered, but the war-time conditions under which most of the field work was carried out placed severe limits on the recruitment of suitable research workers.

At the same time, the monthly meetings of the Group brought out many points upon which agreement was reached. The Group would like to see cultural and recreational centres included in any re-assessment of local needs. Provision should be made for the religious needs of each district. Community Centres are not only desirable but also necessary in the large housing estates which absorb thousands of working people at the end of each working day.

Planning is in the air. The object of this Report is to bring it down to earth in the Birmingham and Black Country Conurbation, a district which is by no means so black as it has been painted. The Group is of the opinion that by the reclamation of waste land, by the preservation of unspoiled land, and by the restoration of misused land, the Conurbation could become a more attractive and more efficient place. There is room in the area for its present industries to expand naturally; there is room for its inhabitants to be decently housed; and there is room for the preservation of those natural amenities so necessary to a population closely occupied in industry. There is room for everything that is needful, but there is no room to waste, and in economic and imaginative planning no authority can afford to ignore its neighbour. It is with a view to achieving co-operative and far-sighted planning that the information contained in the following chapters has been collected.

CHAPTER II

Historical Sketch

EARLY GROWTH OF MANUFACTURE

INDUSTRIAL OCCUPATIONS are old in the West Midlands; yet industrial town life, especially that of the large towns, is a comparatively modern development. This rapid modern growth, which took place to meet the demands of the moment, has been largely responsible for many of the problems which to-day face the inhabitants of the Birmingham and Black Country Conurbation.

The increasing concentration of many industries of highly varied character in the counties of the West Midlands, chiefly within the 270 square miles of the Conurbation, did not attract the serious attention of local historians until the late 18th and early 19th centuries. That they then began to think it worth writing about shows that the process must already have gone far[1]. But the origins of an industrial life which they thought remarkable can be traced back to a much remoter time; the industrialism of their day was the late product of a long and complicated social development.

William Hutton, the first historian of Birmingham, thought that the town's industrial importance dated from about the time of Charles II; but records of Midland industries go back to a period a hundred years earlier than this, and some of them, including characteristic metal trades, go back to medieval times. Developments of industrial occupation on the great scale came, however, as Hutton rightly guessed, in the 17th century, and above all in the century to which he himself belonged, the 18th.

The general causes of the growth of manufacture in the West Midlands during those two centuries are plain, although the details of their operation are often difficult to trace. They were, first, the presence of rich natural resources of coal and iron-ore; second, the acquisition of industrial skill by the inhabitants, in other words, the growth of an industrial wage-earning population; and, third, the accumulation of capital and its investment in industry. The growth of extensive markets for the Midland products kept pace with the advancing use of these natural and acquired resources.

These advances took place among a population previously given over to agriculture and the country crafts, a people without a tradition of industrial life. The early process of industrialization took place under conditions which have long passed away, and we shall not understand it well until the agrarian history of the Midland counties has been

---

[1] The best-known of the historians of Birmingham was also the first, William Hutton (1723—1815), whose book on the town was published in 1781. A much abler man, as an economic historian at any rate, was William Hawkes Smith, whose *Birmingham and its Vicinity* came out in 1836. For the early history of the Midland trades see now W. H. B. Court, *The Rise of the Midland Industries, 1600-1838* (1938); and for the period from 1860 onwards, G. C. Allen, *Industrial Development of Birmingham and the Black Country* (1929).

written; until we know much more of the rural communities, which, during those early times, were being broken up and flung into the mould of an industrial society.

Coal-mining and iron production took the lead, growing steadily in importance in Staffordshire, Warwickshire and Shropshire throughout the 17th and 18th centuries. Upon the heavy industries a mass of lighter manufactures, using coal and iron, was built up. The most widely distributed of these in the Black Country was nail-making. The coal-burning Stourbridge glass trade, established at the end of the 16th or beginning of the 17th century, is another good example of a characteristic, although highly localized, industry of the West Midland coal region. Other industries began to flourish in other towns. Belbroughton began to produce scythes and Walsall became known for harness and saddlers' ironmongery. Meanwhile, Birmingham was turning away from the tanning and clothiery trades which had formed its staple industries in the past, and was taking up various metal trades, such as sword- and gun-making, brass and copper products, and the manufacture of metal buckles.

All this had already taken place before the close of the 17th century. In the next hundred years industry went rapidly forward. A profound change in industrial technique began towards the end of the 18th century, caused largely by the partnership of James Watt and Matthew Boulton. The revolution in technical methods brought about by steam, however, came at a late stage in the development of the Midland trades, and took place comparatively gradually. There was hardly an Industrial Revolution in the Midland counties such as was produced in Lancashire by the relatively rapid transformation of the cotton industry. Much more notable than any single event was the steady and widespread expansion of Midland industrial activity, which had been going on for many generations and proceeded from a number of causes.

Many of these early industries were nothing more than country crafts which gradually came to serve a world market as the demand for their products spread from their immediate neighbours to London and the rest of the kingdom; a demand which spread also from Great Britain to the Continent, North America, India, Africa and the West Indies. Technical methods were often primitive in the extreme, without being romantic, and the work of the Black Country craftsman was carried on under bad conditions. Technical developments were slow; but developments in financial methods were forced by the need of more capital to meet contracts of ever greater size by the extended use of credit and by the central control and organization which this capital brought with it. Wealthy investors and skilful managers were coming forward, familiar with the problems of industry on the large scale. Their method of meeting growing demand was to organize the marketing of the products of a multitude of independent industrial craftsmen. Often they organized the supply of raw materials too, and were in a position to grant to purchasers whatever credit might be required. The craftsman increasingly lost his independence, and became in time a paid industrial employee.

Industrial occupations organized in this way, of which the old Black Country nail trade might be taken as the outstanding example, could be carried on anywhere. They led not so much to urban life as to the industrialization of the countryside, of innumerable villages, hamlets, and comparatively remote localities. The widespread industrial sprawl, begun in this way, survives in the Black Country today. Urbanization was not the concomitant of industrialization before the 19th century.

Yet the big industrial unit, with its tendency to concentrate population in a particular place, was not absent. It was to be found quite early in the heavier trades supplying raw materials. The coal-pit increased in size and the iron-works, especially, tended to become a big centre of employment. By the beginning of the 19th century, there were iron-furnaces in Shropshire each employing 700 men, in South Staffordshire 200 or 300 men. Even so, these industries did not do much more than create the characteristic mining villages or small industrial townships of those parts of the country. They pitted the countryside with works and mines, and round them sprang up small industrial communities. They contributed only indirectly to the formation of the large industrial towns of modern times with their characteristic problems.

The 17th and 18th centuries saw, therefore, the emergence of the West Midlands as an industrial region, although not yet as a region of very large towns. About the year 1600 the West Midland counties compared closely in density of population with other English counties; but in the 18th century the West Midland counties became much more densely populated than most parts of the country. This fact was established beyond all guesswork by the results, imperfect as they were, of the first Census of England and Wales, taken in 1801. By then, the old comparative uniformity of distribution of population between English counties had been decisively disturbed by the rise of a number of industrial regions of which the West Midland counties formed one.

Within the Region, one town—Birmingham—although not yet a town in its form of government, had taken the lead over the rest. In the Middle Ages, Coventry had been the great town of this part of the country. The effect of a long course of industrial development was to make Birmingham, which in the 17th century had been for long little more than a small market town, much the larger and the more important of the two towns. Thus the centre of the social geography of the West Midlands was changed. Other towns in the area, such as Wolverhampton and Walsall, also attained a relative importance, but they remained small towns until the 19th century.

GENERAL CONDITIONS OF THE RISE OF INDUSTRY IN THE CONURBATION

The growth of the Midland Industrial region in the 17th and 18th centuries was achieved in the face of considerable indifference and ignorance in ruling circles concerning things industrial. From time to time Parliament attempted to take cognizance of the interests of particular trades, usually in connection with the tariff; but such action was far more often the result than the cause of Midland industrial development. The State in those days, at any rate from the Civil War on, exercised no economic policy as distinct from a commercial policy; and its commercial policy was not intended to control anything so complicated as the localization of industry. Yet State action had, from time to time, important effects. The Severn, the great outlet for Midland goods to the West, was a free river under English law, and the freedom of its navigation was important to Birmingham and Black Country manufacturers. War contracts placed by Government with the Midland trades, as during the Napoleonic wars, did much to stimulate industry. But such action was never part of a considered policy. The Midland industries were free from intervention of any kind either by the central or by local government, except perhaps in an old town such as Coventry. This freedom from control was not wholly bad, nor was it part of a well-laid plan. It was rather the result of the limited powers of the State, both for good and ill. In the economic and social conditions of those centuries this freedom from control was an indispensable condition of the industrial growth of the Region.

It has seemed worth while to insist upon the steady evolution of modern industrial and social life in the Midlands, as there is a tendency to over-rate the importance of the

The Gin (from an etching by R. S. Chaddock, 1872). A horse-driven machine used for shallow pits.

Timber Tree Colliery, Cradley (from an etching by R. S. Chaddock, 1872). Typical of the hundreds of pits working the Thirty Foot Coal of the South Staffordshire Coalfield during the middle of the nineteenth century.

The Buffery (from an etching by R. S. Chaddock, 1872). An old pumping engine house.

Straightening Needles. A century ago manufactured needles were "soft straightened" by women. An expert could straighten 3,000 needles in an hour.

Cutting Steel for Saws. The man on the left is operating the mechanical shears while the craftsman holds the sheet still.

Rolling Bar Iron.

Soldering
Button Shanks.

Forging Files.

Making
Cut Brads.

Cutting the
Thread of Screws.

Making the
Heads of Screws.

*Stamping Press
for Buttons.*

Types of factory engaged in Metal Industries during the nineteenth century. The nineteenth century saw the replacement of the small metal workshops by big industrial plants, following the application of steam power to factory work. Throughout the century, moreover, the Black Country was one of the chief iron-producing centres in Britain. The illustrations show clearly how all-important the canal network was for heavy industries in an inland area. The picture in the lower left hand corner is an interesting illustration of early factory layout.

Boulton and Watt's Soho Factory, 1800.

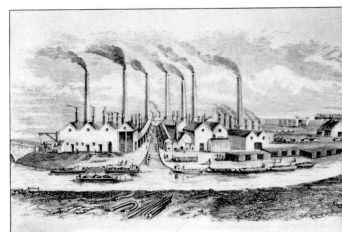

Bloomfield Iron Works, Tipton.

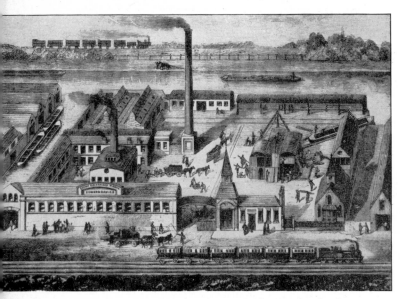

Edward Davies's Crown Galvanising Works, Wolverhampton.

The view of the Crown Galvanising Works.

Early growth of a great Midland firm. The first workshops of Messrs. Tangye Brothers a century ago.

" Our First Workshop—
4s. a week rent."

" Our Second Workshop—
10s. a week rent."

" Our First Smithy."

last hundred years in Midland history. From 1801 onwards, Midlanders lived in the light of official statistics and this has led to the under-rating of earlier periods when statistics were not kept. Yet the hundred years between the two great European wars, from 1815 to 1914, was a period of widespread, peaceful development. The further development of the industrial region of the West Midlands went on rapidly. Towns expanded, urban concentration went on apace, and across the industrialized countryside there grew up a conurbation, a cluster or a constellation of industrial towns.

Strictly speaking, this quick urban development had begun slightly earlier, for reasons closely connected with industry and its forms of organization. The period 1780 to 1820 was a time of rapid town growth for England as a whole. This was the result of many factors, of which one of the most important was the application of steam power to factory work and the growth of big industrial plants which followed. The process was slow in the Midlands—the number of steam-engines working in the town of Birmingham in the year 1836 was reckoned to be no more than 169, with an average of 16 horse power each—but it had a notable effect on the size of works, and on the growth of Birmingham, both before and after the town began to return Members to Parliament and to administer its own affairs as a borough.

The late eighteen-thirties, and still more the 'forties, saw the development of the main line railway system which was to have at least as much influence as steam upon the localization of trades. The railways were peculiarly important for the British industrial regions inland, which did much business both with London and countries abroad. The railways in the Midland districts, like the canals before them, did much to determine the siting of works in the heavier trades.

The industrial structure of the Midlands as it appeared in mid-Victorian times, say about 1860 or 1870, was therefore the result of the seventy or eighty years of vigorous development which had followed the introduction of steam-force into manufacturing industry.

THE RANGE OF PRODUCTS

The range of products had been widely extended and technical methods much improved, but the main industrial features of the Birmingham and district of the mid-19th century were still recognizably those of an earlier time. The region tended to fall into two parts. In the Black Country, the coal and iron industries were still of major importance. Notwithstanding the dwindling of its natural resources, this district was still one of the chief iron-producing centres of the country, and the temporary iron boom of the Franco-Prussian war was accompanied by a similar advance in coal and iron-ore mining. The Black Country also possessed hardware and other trades peculiar to itself, many of them very old. These included heavy manufactures, such as tube-making at Wednesbury, heavy springs and axles at West Bromwich, structural iron work at Tipton, Wolverhampton and Smethwick, heavy forgings at Brierley Hill, Tipton and Bilston, galvanized sheets at Wolverhampton, chains and anchors at Cradley and Netherton. Others were light trades, or what passed for such; spades and shovels at Halesowen, scythes at Belbroughton, flint glass tableware at Stourbridge, harness and saddlers' ironmongery at Walsall, locks and keys at Willenhall, tinplate, japan-ware and papier mâché at Wolverhampton, hollow-ware at West Bromwich, nails at Dudley and Stourbridge. High specialization was the rule in the Black Country. Birmingham, on the other hand, possessed a great variety of trades, many of which had been established for a long time. Outstanding Birmingham trades were brass and copper manufactures, jewellery of great variety, military and

36

sporting guns, buttons, pens, and bedsteads, flint-glass, screws, wire, and edge tools. The accumulation of the Birmingham trades in such wide variety was a natural development when we consider the needs and tastes of Victorian society and the ability of the Birmingham firms to supply them.

The years before the depression which followed the Franco-Prussian war, in 1875 and 1876, consequently represented the peak period of a type of industrialism which was already old in the Midlands. It had its origin in the natural resources of the Region, and in the ability of the inhabitants to turn them to account. The coal and iron of the Black Country were less important than they had been in the first half of the 19th century, but they were still fundamental to the industrial activity of the West Midlands. The link which connected these original heavy trades of the Region with the skill of the lighter industries was still obvious.

CHANGES AND RENEWAL IN INDUSTRY

The industrial depression of the late 'seventies was not confined to any part of the country. It was felt and suffered generally, but in the West Midlands it hastened a process of industrial transition. Industries, some of which were as old as the industrial region, died out or lost much of their importance within a few years. They included the coal-mining and the iron-smelting of the Black Country, which had done so much to give that part of the Region its name in earlier days. New industrial groups arose, including some which were foreign to Midland industrial tradition. The link between the coal and iron resources of the district and its industrial superstructure was cut, as the exploitation of these resources became of little importance. During the 'seventies, the 'eighties and especially during the 'nineties and onwards, the new economic structure of the Region may be said to have been founded.

The heavy industries of South Staffordshire had declined in the forty years before 1914. The decline was started by the exhaustion of much of the Black Country coal and iron-ore, the flooding of coal remaining underground, the development of coal-mining at much lower cost elsewhere, and the introduction of cheap steel; other factors contributed, but these were the main causes. However natural the change appears now, it was completely masked at the time by the active trade boom induced by the Franco-German war and by the high prices of the early 'seventies. It gradually became apparent, especially in the years of depressed trade between 1876 and 1886, that South Staffordshire was facing the most important change in its fortunes since its coal and iron resources first began to be vigorously exploited, nearly two centuries before. Yet the complexity of modern industrial life is such that few people realized the full significance of the change, even when it had run its course.

The decline in the Black Country of coal-mining, of iron-smelting and wrought-iron manufacture, and of many branches of hardware connected with them, persisted throughout the whole period from the 'seventies to the first World War. Despite the temporary stimulus given to the heavy industries by that war, the decline continued to be one of the permanent trends in the life of the Region down to the year 1939.

South Staffordshire ceased to be an important coalfield and a big national centre of iron- and steel-making. So far from the Conurbation of Birmingham and the Black Country providing its own industrial raw materials, it became increasingly dependent upon other centres at home and abroad. Meanwhile, the heavy engineering trades which generally flourish in coal and iron districts showed an increasing tendency to avoid the area, although in point of fact they had never been strong here. They developed their strength in the

37

northern counties and elsewhere. One effect of these changes was that, with the removal of the smoke and glare of the blast furnaces, the Black Country became less black. A less fortunate result was the derelict sites and equipment which remain as ugly blots on the landscape.

Accompanying this decline came a vigorous expansion of light and medium engineering. This had played a modest part in the Victorian economy of the district, but between 1890 and 1914 its development was most marked. It made wide use of steel as a raw material, in strong contrast to the old hardware trades of Birmingham and South Staffordshire which had been based upon the Black Country's supremacy as a centre of wrought-iron making. Many of the old industries of the region survived, and took on new life in the generation before the 1914 war; among them were the jewellery, brass, nut and bolt, screw, chain and anchor trades; while others, including some of the oldest industries of the Region, such as the making of the hand-wrought nail, disappeared or seriously declined.

This change was associated with the introduction of trades wholly new, some of which have since become the most important of the district. The cycle and automobile engineering trades, the electricity and artificial silk industries, and a number of food and drink industries, all had their origins in this period. They brought to the industrial structure of the West Midlands a character quite different from anything it possessed in the time of mid-Victorian prosperity. Changes in methods of production and marketing accompanied this period of decline and growth. Craftsmanship and manual skill, although they remained important in certain trades, gave ground increasingly to the engineer, the machine operator, and the semi-skilled labourer. Scientific knowledge was also enlisted in many fields. On the marketing side, the factor, who for many generations had played an important role in Midland business, especially in the Birmingham area, lost his old supremacy as modern methods of direct marketing came in.

THE INTER-WAR YEARS

Thus, the industrial outlook of the Conurbation was changed. The two great wars of the last thirty years have hastened rather than slowed down the transformation. In 1914, Birmingham and district, as the foremost centre of light engineering in the country, became one of the most important munition-making centres. Yet, although the period following the 1914-18 war was not without difficulties, the Region was, on the whole, fortunate in its inter-war history. It suffered little in comparison with other industrial areas. Since it was no longer wholly dependent upon the heavy industries, it did not share the long depression of the national coal and the steel industries, which suffered so heavily during the cyclical depression of 1929-1933.

The industrial and social growth which had marked the area before the First World War continued between the wars. The West Midlands were prosperous before 1929, and after a temporary setback they became active again in the 'thirties. From 1936 onwards, with the rearmament programme following on the general trade revival, this activity was most noticeable. Employers had a slight foretaste of the extreme labour shortage which was to follow the outbreak of war in 1939. Much new house-building accompanied this industrial activity. In the Birmingham city area alone, which had been rapidly expanding since the beginning of the century, private and municipal enterprise together put up over 113,000 houses between 1918 and 1939. Yet this building programme, generous as it was, by no means covered all needs, as the housing chapter of this Report shows, but it was a manifestation of the social vitality of the Conurbation in the years between the wars.

Municipal house-building is the indication of a significant trend in recent history, the growing intervention of public authority in social and economic affairs. As has been pointed out, the beginning of the industrialization of the West Midlands took place in the face of an almost complete indifference on the part of the State. It is difficult to say whether State intervention in those days would have helped or hindered; it was seldom attempted. This indifference only slowly disappeared throughout the great age of industrial expansion from 1815 to 1914. The town planning legislation of the present century, and the powers which government has recently taken to control the distribution of industry, show that the age of official indifference has passed. The enhanced power of the State over the distribution of industry and population is an indication of the need for a wider view of social and economic problems. The complex structure of modern life calls for planning on a national as well as on a local basis.

The industrial history of the Birmingham and Black Country Conurbation reveals that many of the present problems, such as bad housing and the haphazard location of works, are the result either of limited private planning in the past or of no planning at all. Yet the brief historical outline given here is not a mere catalogue of failure. It is also a record of industrial achievement, but an achievement in which many things that should have been preserved were sacrificed to the manufacturing demands of the moment. The industrial pattern of the Conurbation was woven piecemeal with no comprehensive eye to the general pattern; yet, if the present design is disorderly, it is at least drawn round strong and prosperous centres of industry founded and served by many generations of workers and craftsmen. These centres of industry must, of necessity, remain the pivots on which life in the Birmingham and Black Country Conurbation revolves: but that is no reason why order, seemliness and even beauty should not be imposed upon our inheritance from the past.

FIGURE I

GEOLOGY OF THE CONURBATION AND THE SURROUNDING AREA

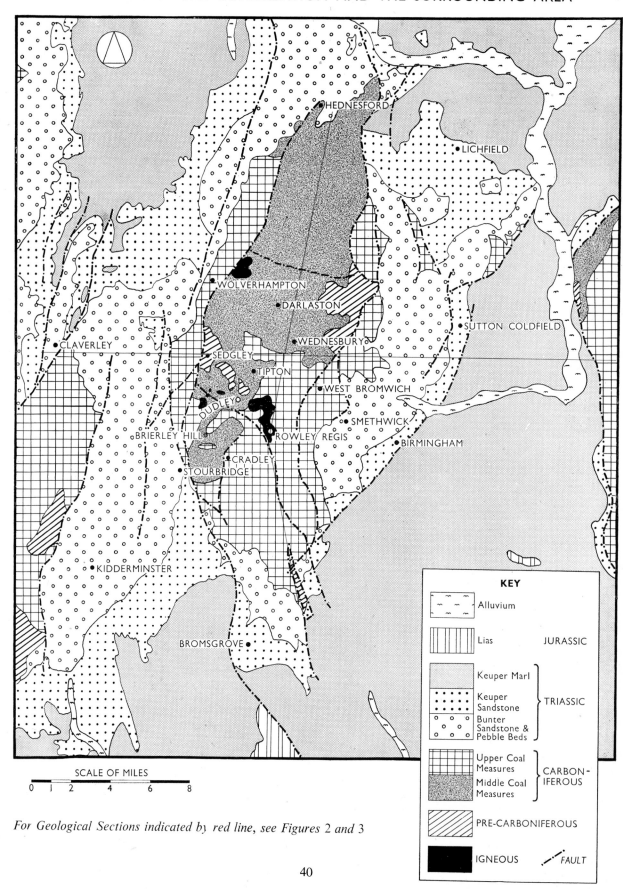

SCALE OF MILES

0   1   2   4   6   8

KEY

	Alluvium	
	Lias	JURASSIC
	Keuper Marl	
	Keuper Sandstone	TRIASSIC
	Bunter Sandstone & Pebble Beds	
	Upper Coal Measures	CARBON-IFEROUS
	Middle Coal Measures	
	PRE-CARBONIFEROUS	
	IGNEOUS	FAULT

For Geological Sections indicated by red line, see Figures 2 and 3

CHAPTER III

Physical Background

POSITION AND COMMUNICATIONS

THE CONURBATION forms the economic heart of the West Midland Region. It extends across parts of three counties, Staffordshire, Worcestershire and Warwickshire, and occupies a central position in relation to England and Wales. Its situation astride a major watershed ensures drainage to the west *via* the Stour and its tributaries to the Severn, while eastward the Tame carries away surface water to the Trent and the North Sea. This upland location has disadvantages in the matter of transport, especially water transport, yet the river valleys form clearly defined lines of communication.

Ease of communication with other parts of the country is hampered somewhat by the topography of the Midland Plateau on which the Conurbation stands, and by the situation of highland masses about its borders. The Pennines to the north and the uplands of the Welsh border to the west form obstacles that cause some deviation of main routes.

The major links of the district are summarized below :—

(1) North-westwards, between the south-west corner of the Pennines and the uplands of South Shropshire, there is a route followed by main road, canal, and railway lines, communicating with North Wales and North-west England. Often known as the " Midland Gate," this route affords easy access to the low-lying plain of Cheshire.

(2) To the north-east an easy route follows the Trent Valley and skirts the south-east reaches of the Pennines. In the early days of industrial development in South Staffordshire, river transport from Burton to Gainsborough and the Humber ports was of especial importance. Today main canals, railways, and roads follow the Tame and Trent Valleys to the South Yorkshire industrial region and the north-east generally.

(3) South-eastwards a number of fairly easy routes cross the intervening ridges to the Thames Valley. The descent from the Midland Plateau to the Avon Valley, however, involves steep gradients for both railway and canal, such as that at Hatton in Warwickshire.

(4) The Severn Valley is, on the whole, difficult of access from the Conurbation ; the steep westerly and south-westerly edges of the Midland Plateau entail the negotiation of difficult gradients, whether by road or by rail. Noteworthy examples are to be found on Mucklows Hill between Halesowen and Quinton, on the Lickey-Blackwell Incline on the L.M.S. Birmingham-Bristol main line, and the steep gradient at Old Hill on the G.W.R.

41

FIGURE 2

GEOLOGICAL SECTION FROM WEST TO EAST THROUGH THE CONURBATION

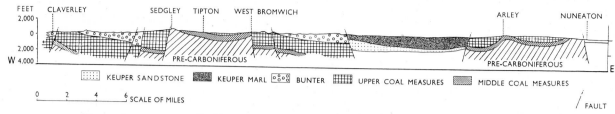

The coal measures and older rocks are up-faulted to form the South Staffordshire and East Warwickshire plateaux, separated by the shallow basin of the lower Tame.

RELIEF

The Conurbation includes much of the south-western section of the elliptically-shaped Midland Plateau, a region of relative upland. Almost the whole of this plateau lies above the 300-foot contour line and stretches from Stafford in the north to Stratford-on-Avon in the south, and from Nuneaton in the east to Kinver Edge in the west.[1] Within the plateau two separate upland areas may be distinguished, in South Staffordshire and East Warwickshire, both of which rise above the 650-foot contour and are separated by the shallow valley of the lower Tame. The Conurbation itself occupies almost the whole of the South Staffordshire Plateau ; only the heathland of Cannock Chase to the north and the Clent Hills to the south-west lie outside the boundaries of the built-up area.

Within the Conurbation, the South Staffordshire upland is sub-divided by the open basin of the upper Tame. The Tame flows gently south-eastwards from between Walsall and Wednesbury to Perry Barr, where an eastward swing carries it through the northern suburbs of Birmingham and past Castle Bromwich. Its wide upper valley, always subject to floods, has from earliest times been uninviting to settlement and is today marked by stretches of relatively open country projecting into the heart of the Conurbation. (See Figure 35).

To the west of the Tame a line of hills, the most conspicuous relief feature of the Conurbation area, extends from Penn Fields, a mile to the south of Wolverhampton in a south-south-easterly direction through Sedgley Beacon, the Wren's Nest, and Dudley Castle Hill, to Rowley in the south. The line is continued from Rowley, though in narrower and less well-marked form, through Quinton to Frankley Beeches (823 feet), and finally joins the well-known Clent-Lickey ridges which form a partially breached barrier to urban extension in a southerly and south-westerly direction.

The three hills of Sedgley, the Wren's Nest, and Dudley Castle, had considerable economic importance during the late 18th and 19th centuries, as sources of limestones for use in the blast furnaces of the industrial region. Quarrying has left its mark on the surface of the hills, particularly at the Wren's Nest and Dudley. All three hills are still partially wooded and are valuable assets to the Black Country on account of the scenic relief they bring to a monotonous landscape. Rowley Hills to the south are quarried for road metal, and here again the quarrying has altered the landscape of the district. Between Dudley Castle and Rowley Hills a low pass or *col* has provided an easy east-west route across the ridge upon which arose the medieval stronghold and town of Dudley.

---

[1] An account of the relief, structure and human geography of the Midland Plateau as a whole is given in R. H. Kinvig's *The North-West Midlands* in *Essays in Regional Geography*, ed. A. G. Ogilvie, Cambridge (1937).

FIGURE 3
GEOLOGICAL SECTION FROM NORTH TO SOUTH THROUGH THE CONURBATION

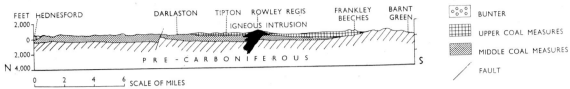

The Middle Coal Measures of the Cannock Chase and South Staffordshire coalfields are overlain south of Wednesbury by Upper Coal Measures, and thin out finally south of Halesowen.

The Sedgley-Rowley-Lickey ridge is part of the main watershed of England. Drainage to the west passes to the Severn *via* the Smestow-Stour system. To the east, surface water is carried away to the Trent and the North Sea by the Tame and its tributaries. A marked landscape contrast exists between the two drainage areas, a contrast which should be borne in mind when considering land utilisation. Great changes in the drainage of what is now the Severn valley took place during and immediately following the Ice Age. These changes resulted in the cutting of the gorge through which the river flows from Ironbridge southwards, and consequently the Stour and its tributaries have become " rejuvenated " and now flow in deeply incised channels. Slopes throughout the area are generally steep ; and this steepness has been increased in some localities as a result of the cutting down of the stream-beds. The swift streams provided abundant water power for use by the mills and forges during the period of early development of the area as an industrial district. The landscape as a whole presents greater variety and bolder relief than that of the Tame valley, where the streams flow more slowly in broader open valleys. The steep slopes from the Severn valley up to the plateau from the west and south-west offer difficult tasks to the railways. The Great Western Railway from Stour-bridge has some gradients of 1 in 50 in its eastward climb, and the Lickey-Blackwell Incline is the steepest gradient in England (1 in 37).

In the Tame Valley, in contrast, a monotonous landscape is broken only by low hills such as form the sites of Darlaston, Wednesbury, and Bilston. These hills were in many cases formed by glacial drift uneroded by the streams. The landscape is also marked by wasteheaps and pit banks, and relics of the industrial expansion of a hundred-and-fifty years ago.

To the east of the rather dreary valley of the upper Tame the land rises again, and in the north of the Conurbation a long narrow ridge extends southwards from Brownhills, through Aldridge, and culminates in Barr Beacon, a well-known local landmark. The high heathlands of Sutton and Streetly have little agricultural value, but have been largely developed as residential areas. A wide stretch of moor and heath, now totally surrounded by urban development, still exists as Sutton Park.

In the south-east of the Conurbation the main topographical feature is a long and narrow ridge, broken here and there, but persisting from Northfield at its south-western end, through Edgbaston and the heart of Birmingham, to Erdington and Sutton Coldfield. This ridge has undoubtedly had a considerable influence in determining original sites of settlement. It is well-drained and has the advantage of an elevated position relative to the valley and plain to the east; it has also a good and easily-accessible water supply.

Eastwards again, particularly in the valleys of the Rea, Cole, and Blythe (all tributaries of the middle Tame), extensions of the City of Birmingham have carried the Conurbation

43

over part of the gently undulating featureless clay plain of North Central Warwickshire. This is an area of slight relief. The location of its older settlements, such as Yardley, Coleshill, and Solihull, has been largely determined by the presence of patches of glacial drift or by outcrops of harder rock bands, which form hills and hummocks, and which originally yielded adequate water supply in a district where conditions are generally poor. The importance of topography in this respect has been largely masked and hidden by the urban spread of the last fifty years.

GEOLOGY

The distribution of rocks outcropping within the Conurbation and their great significance are shown in Figure 1, and are summarized in Table I below:—

GEOLOGICAL FORMATIONS IN THE CONURBATION

TABLE I

System	Formation	Lithology	Ecomonic Significance
Pleistocene	River terraces and glacial deposits	Sands, gravels and boulder clay	Building sand and gravel. Formerly some production of moulding sand, and brickmaking from the boulder clay.
Trias	Keuper Marl	Red Marls with the Arden sandstone	Brickmaking. Salt. Building stone formerly obtained from Arden sandstone.
	Keuper Sandstone	Fairly compact red sandstones	Formerly used as building stone. Good water supply.
	Upper Bunter Sandstone	Soft red sandstones	Moulding sand.
	Bunter Pebble beds	Pebble beds and red sandstones	Building sand and gravel.
	Lower Bunter Sandstone	Red sandstone	Of very limited distribution.
Carboniferous	Upper Coal Measures	Sandstones, marls and conglomerates	Brick- and tile-making. Sandstones have been used locally as building stone.
	Middle Coal Measures	Sandstones, shales and coal seams	Coal. Fireclay. Production of ironstones formerly of importance.
Silurian	Chiefly Ludlow and Wenlock	Limestone and Shales	Limestone for use as a flux in the production of pig iron.
Cambrian		Quartzite	Has been used as road metal and locally for walling and decorative garden stones.
Pre-Cambrian			Of very limited outcrop.
Igneous	Doubtful	Dolerite	Road metal.

It will be seen from the Geological Map (Figure 1) that the Conurbation straddles an outcrop of relatively older rocks, which form the heart of the South Staffordshire Plateau, and extends to east and west on to the younger (Triassic) rocks which bound and border the plateau.

The greater part of the Conurbation is floored by carboniferous rocks of the Upper and Middle Coal Measure series, though in some areas older rocks protrude through the carboniferous cover. To the east, the Middle Coal Measures are cut off by faults, which bring them against the sandstones and marls of the Upper Coal Measures. In the west, the Middle Coal Measures are faulted down and give place to clays and sandstones of the Keele and Enville Beds and to rocks of the Bunter series. In the south, the Middle Coal Measures thin out and pass beneath marls and sandstones of the barren Upper Coal Measures. In the north, though no apparent break in the surface outcrop of the Middle Coal Measures occurs, the series of fractures known as the Bentley Faults, which run approximately east-west along a line to the north of Walsall-Wolverhampton, have the effect of separating the coalfield of South Staffordshire from that of Cannock Chase. To the north of this fault zone, the famous Thick (30-foot) Coal, the exploitation of which contributed so largely to the value of the district as a mining and industrial area, is no longer present, being represented by 13 or 14 distinct thin seams. (See Appendix, *The South Staffordshire and Cannock Chase Coalfields and Future Planning in the Conurbation*, for a more detailed account of the geology of these coalfields).

Of the other formations within the Coal Measures, the Etruria Marls are still extensively worked for the manufacture of bricks, including the celebrated Staffordshire hard blue brick, widely used during the 19th century in the construction of the bridges and viaducts of the English railway system. The red marls of the Keele group have also been used for brick-making.

TABLE II   CARBONIFEROUS ROCKS PRESENT WITHIN THE CONURBATION

FORMATION	SUB-DIVISION	LITHOLOGY	ECONOMIC IMPORTANCE
Upper Coal Measures	Enville Beds	Red sandstones and marls	Sandstones formerly used locally for building purposes
	Keele Group	Red marls and sandstones	Brickmaking. Sandstones formerly used locally for building purposes
	Halesowen Group	Grey marls with clays and sandstones	Brickmaking. Sandstones formerly used locally for building purposes
	Etruria Marl	Red and purple marls	Brickmaking
Middle Coal (Productive) Measures		Shales, clays and sandstones with coal seams	Mining of coal, fireclay and (formerly) ironstone

Rocks older than carboniferous appear at the surface in two main areas. To the east of Walsall occurs an extensive outcrop of Silurian rocks which consists largely of shale with some limestone. This gives rise to no marked relief feature. Between Dudley and Sedgley, the three hills of Dudley Castle, the Wren's Nest, and Sedgley Beacon are formed by outcrops of Silurian rocks which in this case consist mainly of limestone. In the Lickey Hills rocks, even older than Silurian—of Cambrian and pre-Cambrian age—are exposed at the surface over limited areas. Resistant Cambrian rocks bounded to east and west by faults form the approximately north-south line of the Lickey Hills themselves.

The Rowley Hills, consisting of igneous dolerite (highly valued as road metal), are of uncertain age.

To the east and south-east of the South Staffordshire Coalfield geological conditions are different. Clays and sandstones of the Upper Coal Measures finally disappear beneath younger red sandstones and marls laid down during Triassic times. As one passes east-wards, successive outcrops of Bunter Pebble Beds, Upper Mottled Sandstone and Keuper Sandstone are crossed. The Bunter Pebble Beds, which consist of a mass of well-rounded pebbles alternating with coarse sandstones, give rise to the high heathland of Sutton Park and extend in a south-westerly direction through Handsworth to the Harborne district of Birmingham. The Upper Mottled Sandstone, of economic importance as a source of moulding sands for the metal industries of the area, is in turn overlain by the Keuper Sandstone which forms the narrow and discontinuous ridge from Northfield to Sutton Coldfield. Popularly known under the name " Keuper Waterstone," this for-mation yielded adequate and easily accessible water supply to Birmingham when the town was developing, though supplies from this source and from the sandstones and pebble beds lying beneath have, of course, long proved inadequate to supply the whole of the city's needs.

The Birmingham Fault bounds the sandstone to the east, bringing it against the impervious Keuper Marl with its characteristic poor water conditions, undulating and rather featureless landscape, and heavy clay soil.

Over extensive areas of the Conurbation the underlying rocks are masked by boulder clays, and by sands and gravels deposited during and immediately following the Ice Age. In the south-western sector of the Black Country, the glacial cover has been largely worn away by the swift-flowing Stour and its tributaries; but in the eastern sector, where the erosion of the Tame and its tributaries has been less powerful, the glacial cover is still mainly intact. In this sector the mantle of Boulder Clay masking the Middle Coal Measures was in some areas partly responsible for delaying the exploitation of the coal seams. This was particularly so in the neighbourhood of Darlaston. The hills formed by glacial drift provided sites for many of the original settlements. Wednesbury, Darlaston, and Bilston—to take but three examples—are all situated on hills of glacial drift standing out from the basin of the Upper Tame.

CHAPTER IV

Local Government

GROWTH

LOCAL GOVERNMENT within the Conurbation reflects the three factors which are typical of the present structure of local government in England generally.

There is, first, a survival of the forms which grew up during the Middle Ages and whose structure remained until the 19th century. The public health legislation of the 19th century

LOCAL GOVERNMENT AUTHORITIES AND RATEABLE VALUES IN THE CONURBATION

TABLE III

Name and Status	Date of Present Constitution	Rateable Value 1945-6	Population (Mid-year estimate, 1939).	Rateable Value per head		Area (National Register 1939).	Rateable Value per Acre	
				By Authorities	Average		By Authorities	Average
		£		£	£	acres	£	£
County Boroughs								
Birmingham	1838	7,517,517	1,052,900	7·140		51,147	146·978	
Dudley	1865	294,188	62,100	4·737		4,067	72·335	
Smethwick	1906	428,852	78,290	5·478		2,496	171·816	
Walsall	1835	555,511	107,600	5·163		8,780	63·270	
West Bromwich	1882	390,118	83,150	4·692		7,180	54·334	
Wolverhampton	1889	998,280	147,200	6·782		9,126	109·389	
Non-County Boroughs								
Bilston	1933	133,403	31,600	4·222		1,869	71·377	
Halesowen	1936	154,594	36,800	4·201		5,247	29·463	
Oldbury	1935	227,668	47,000	4·844		3,304	68·907	
Rowley Regis	1933	176,013	44,780	3·931		3,828	45·980	
Stourbridge	1914	183,492	35,310	5·197	6·255	4,214	43·543	75·599
Sutton Coldfield	1882	415,629	38,260	10·863		13,978	29·735	
Tipton	1938	147,700	37,390	3·950		2,167	68·159	
Wednesbury	1886	144,032	33,650	4·280		2,025	71·127	
Urban Districts								
Aldridge	1934	116,387	20,420	5·700		9,275	12·548	
Amblecote	1898	19,242	2,836	6·785		666	28·892	
Brierley Hill...	1894	175,048	47,040	3·721		5,927	29·534	
Coseley	1888	104,279	29,640	3·518		3,294	31·657	
Darlaston	1894	79,539	20,220	3·934		1,530	51·986	
Sedgley	1894	83,535	20,700	4·035		3,848	21·709	
Solihull	1932	430,373	52,260	8·235		20,189	21·317	
Tettenhall	1894	50,471	6,727	7·503		2,503	20·164	
Wednesfield...	1894	61,155	14,540	4·206		2,515	24·316	
Willenhall	1894	116,616	28,320	4·118		2,834	41·149	

FIGURE 4

LOCAL AUTHORITY BOUNDARIES—1947

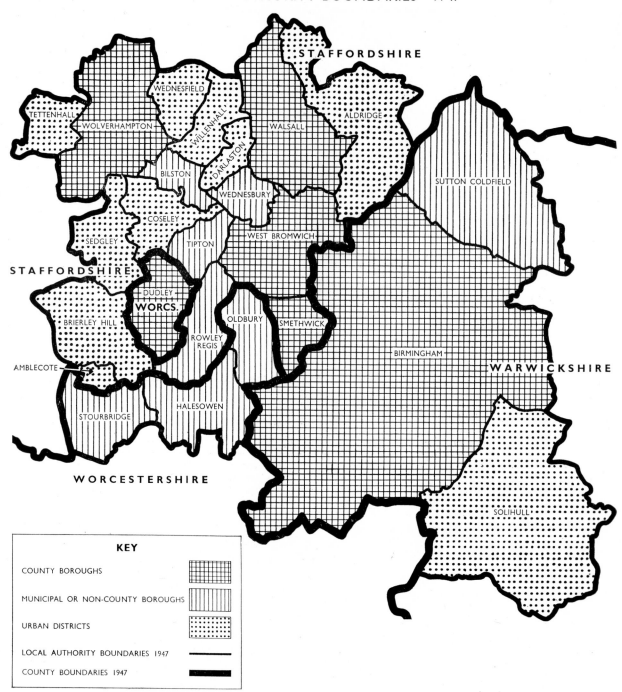

KEY

COUNTY BOROUGHS	
MUNICIPAL OR NON-COUNTY BOROUGHS	
URBAN DISTRICTS	
LOCAL AUTHORITY BOUNDARIES 1947	
COUNTY BOUNDARIES 1947	

introduced a fresh structure with its organization of the whole country into urban and rural areas for dealing with public services, such as sewage disposal and the repair and lighting of roads. Thirdly, there have accrued the enormous increase of powers, duties, and responsibilities brought to local government by the social legislation of the last sixty years. During this period urban development and boundary adjustment have increased the size of urban authorities.

Birmingham and Walsall can trace some measure of autonomy back to the Middle Ages. Birmingham received its Charter of Incorporation in 1838 and became a County Borough in 1888. Dudley, an urban centre of comparable age, had no status as a borough

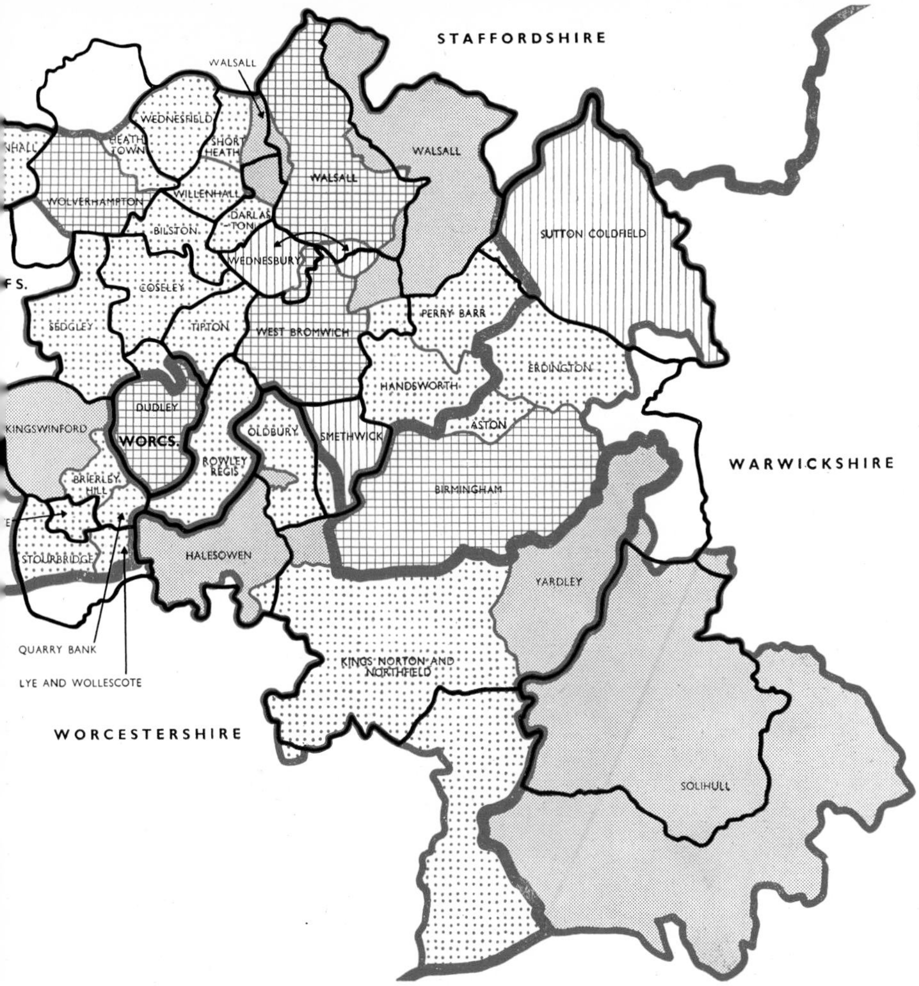

FIGURE 5

LOCAL AUTHORITY BOUNDARIES, 1898

There is surprisingly little difference between the boundaries of most Black Country areas in 1898 and 1947. Birmingham has absorbed five urban and rural districts and most of a sixth, and has grown in area from 12,365 acres to 51,147 acres. The expansion of Wolverhampton has not, for the most part, affected the adjoining urban areas.

KEY	
COUNTY BOROUGHS	
MUNICIPAL OR NON-COUNTY BOROUGHS	
URBAN DISTRICTS	
RURAL DISTRICTS	
LOCAL AUTHORITY BOUNDARIES 1898	
LOCAL AUTHORITY BOUNDARIES 1947	
COUNTY BOUNDARIES 1898	

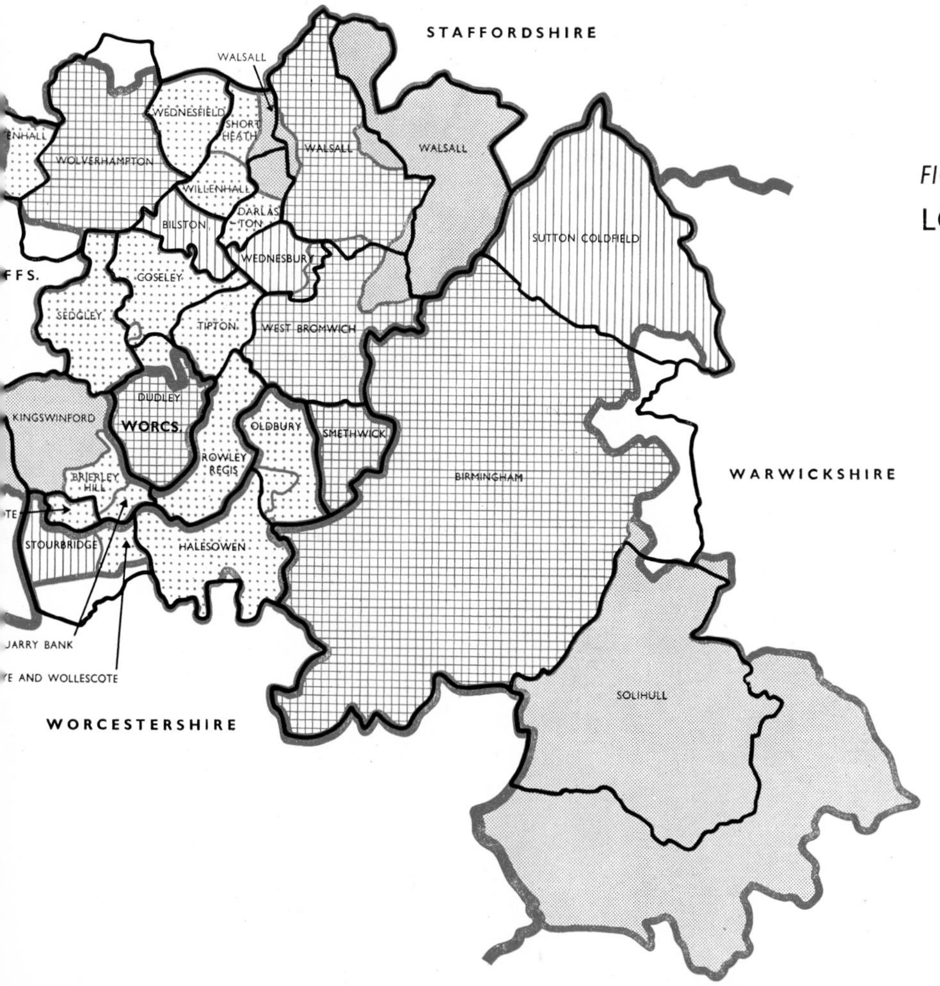

FIGURE 6

LOCAL AUTHORITY BOUNDARIES, 1931

Most of the changes in local authorities which have taken place in the Black Country side of the Conurbation during the last fifty years were effected during the 1930's, some time after Birmingham had expanded to a size almost equal to that existing now.

KEY	
COUNTY BOROUGHS	
MUNICIPAL OR NON-COUNTY BOROUGHS	
URBAN DISTRICTS	
RURAL DISTRICTS	
LOCAL AUTHORITY BOUNDARIES 1931	
LOCAL AUTHORITY BOUNDARIES 1947	
COUNTY BOUNDARIES 1931	

49

until the end of the 19th century, when, together with the new towns of Wolverhampton and West Bromwich, it qualified for recognition as a County Borough under the 1894 Act. Smethwick obtained recognition in 1906.

Municipal or non-County Boroughs were created at Stourbridge, Sutton Coldfield, and Wednesbury in the 1880's. All other authorities in the Conurbation were Urban or Rural Districts until the 1930's when Rowley Regis, Bilston, Oldbury and Tipton obtained recognition as Boroughs, Aldridge, Halesowen, Amblecote, and Solihull as Urban Districts.

FUNCTIONS

Since 1933, the only Councils to exercise the full range of powers normally accorded to Local Government Authorities have been those of the County Boroughs. Elsewhere these powers are divided between the Municipal Boroughs, Urban Districts or Rural Districts on the one hand, and the Counties on the other.

All the authorities of the types we are considering, that is, County Boroughs, Municipal Boroughs, and Urban Districts, have in common certain activities which they normally discharge; and fundamental to all is their ability to levy rates and to spend them. This is, in fact, the distinguishing function of a local government authority. The law, too, prescribes a minimum number of officers, whose departments discharge separate duties; these are the Clerk, Treasurer, Medical Officer of Health, Sanitary Inspector and Surveyor. All these Councils may engage in municipal trading. Within the Conurbation, gas and water are often supplied by local authority departments, and some supply electricity.

Table IV shows how closely parallel are the powers and duties of the Councils of Urban Districts and Municipal Boroughs.

Councils of County Boroughs exercise all the powers, relevant to their circumstances, which legislation has put into the hands of local authorities. The principal differences between them and other urban authorities lie in their right to receive Government grants direct from the Exchequer and in their existence as separate Local Education Authorities under the 1944 Education Act. Councils of County Boroughs are also entirely responsible for public assistance, other than the services provided by the Assistance Board, and for comprehensive services in connection with tuberculosis, maternity and child welfare, and venereal disease.

The 19th century legislation which brought into being the present system of local government was directed almost entirely to the improvement of sanitary conditions. Control over the production and sale of foods, the provision of sewage and refuse disposal services, and the supply of pure water, are still the central functions of local government; but legislation formulated by the Local Government Board and the Ministry of Health over the past fifty years has extended local control to hospitals, welfare and medical services. Housing, now a principal department of local government became the responsibility of local government by the Public Health Act of 1875.

It is outside this core of public health services that the differences between the large and the small authority are most apparent. For instance, in highway provision and maintenance and in public assistance, there is an uncomfortable division between Municipal Boroughs and district authorities, on the one hand, and the County Councils on the other. Since 1929 the General Exchequer Contribution, which amounts to almost half the revenue of local government, has been made in the first place to Counties and County Boroughs. A more marked division is that brought about by municipal trading, although this division was not created by Parliamentary Act. Large Corporations, such as Birmingham, operate extensive public utilities, but smaller Authorities cannot operate on

DISTRIBUTION OF THE FUNCTIONS OF LOCAL GOVERNMENT

TABLE IV

COUNTY BOROUGHS

MUNICIPAL BOROUGHS

URBAN DISTRICTS

RURAL DISTRICTS

COUNTY COUNCILS

COUNTY COUNCILS

COUNTY COUNCILS

COUNTY COUNCILS

PROVISION OF SUPPLIES AND SERVICES	REGULATION BY INSPECTION OR BY CONTROL
Cemeteries.	Building Bye-laws.
Housing.	Food Sampling.
Ambulance.	Slum Clearance.
Sewerage.	Lodging Houses.
Refuse Collection and Disposal.	Infectious Diseases.
Street Lighting and Cleaning.	Suppression of Nuisances.
Mortuaries.	Smoke Abatement.
Water Supply.	Watercourses, Sanitary Control.
Parks and Open Spaces.	Slaughterhouses.
	Land Charges Registration.

Allotments.	Offensive Trades.
Baths, Swimming Baths and Wash-houses.	Dairies, Workshops and Bakehouses.
Gas.	Petroleum Storage.
Electricity.	Petrol Stations.
Unclassified Roads and Streets.	
Libraries and Museums.	
Electors, Registration.	

Child Welfare	Bye-laws, various.
Borough Magistrates.	Shops.
	Weights and Measures.

Blind Welfare .	Registration of Births, Deaths and Marriages.
Children, Adoption, Boarding-out, and Control of Employment.	Cinemas and Theatres.
	Race-courses.
Education: Nursery, Primary, Secondary and Technical.	Fertilisers and Feeding Stuffs Analysis.
School Medical Services.	Food and Drugs, Milk Sampling and Analysis.
School Meals.	Nursing Homes Registration.
Service of Youth.	Wild Birds Protection.
Hospitals, Maternity and Child Welfare.	Motor Vehicles and Drivers' Licensing.
Midwives and Home Helps.	Bye-laws for Good Government.
Mental Health.	Town & Country Planning.
Housing (Assistance in Rural Areas).	
Classified Roads.	
Bridges.	
Police.	
Public Assistance.	
Remand Homes.	
Tuberculosis.	
Venereal Diseases.	
Smallholdings.	

a sufficiently large scale. Another complicating factor has been the marked increase in the duties of local government introduced by the social legislation of the past few decades.

Before the adoption of the 1944 Education Act, elementary education was the responsibility of Counties and of Municipal and County Boroughs with a population of over 10,000 and Urban District Authorities with a population of over 20,000, but higher education was in the hands of County Boroughs and Counties. While co-ordination of educational administration over a wide area is less vital to its effectiveness than is the case with town and country planning, the system revealed more clearly other drawbacks of administrative fragmentation. Both in financial support and administrative efficiency there was clear and inevitable disparity between the educational system of large and small Authorities. By reducing the number of Local Education Authorities so as to include Counties, and County Boroughs only, such discrepancies in the quality of school education have been reduced. The large population unit has the opportunity of creating a flexible system of schools, with curricula for special, advanced or older groups of pupils. Parallel considerations have given rise to a similar raising of the standard size of police area in the new Police Bill.

Early legislation for town planning was concerned with provisions for residential areas, and appeared as clauses of Acts mainly concerned with housing. This is possibly responsible for the association of these two functions of local government, an association which, up to the passing of the Town and Country Planning Act, 1947, gave full town planning powers to the smallest Local Authority, despite the weight of argument and public opinion in favour of a measure for leaving some control with planning authorities covering several Local Authorities or a whole region.

The need for the study of planning problems at the regional level was appreciated in the West Midlands as long ago as 1923, when the Midland Joint Town Planning Advisory Council was set up. This organization, a voluntary association of representatives of Local Authorities within the Conurbation, later extended the area under its review to the whole of Worcestershire and Warwickshire, and became the Warwickshire, Worcestershire and South Staffordshire Advisory Planning Council. It represents one of the earliest efforts in the country to formulate planning policy over a large but homogeneous area.

Opportunities for planning for a wider area given by both the 1932 and the 1944 Acts in provisions for Joint Planning Committees through which Local Authorities might pool either their planning ideas for advisory purposes, or their planning powers for carrying out a wide-scale plan.

Local Authorities in the Conurbation have grouped themselves into the following Joint Planning Committees, all of which have executive powers (see Figure 15) :—

South-East Staffordshire	Walsall, Wednesbury, Aldridge, Darlaston, and others outside the Conurbation.
West Bromwich, Smethwick & Oldbury	
Dudley & District.	Dudley, Bilston, Rowley Regis, Tipton, Amblecote, Brierley Hill, Coseley, Sedgley, Seisdon R.D. (part).
Solihull & District.	Solihull, Sutton Coldfield, Meriden.
North Worcestershire	Halesowen, Stourbridge, Bromsgrove U.D., Redditch U.D., Bromsgrove R.D.
Wolverhampton & District.	Wolverhampton, Wednesfield, Willenhall, Tettenhall, Cannock R.D., Seisdon R.D. (part).

FIGURE 7   LOCAL AUTHORITY BOUNDARIES   FIGURE 8

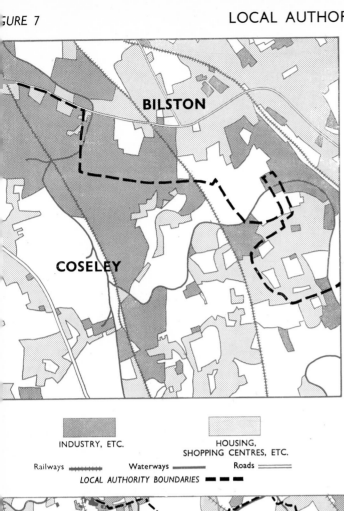

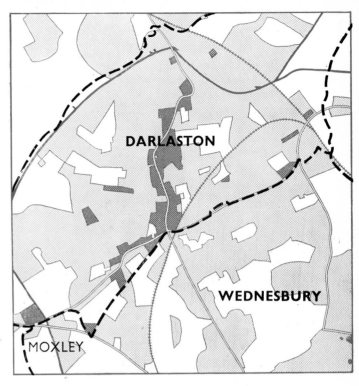

INDUSTRY, ETC.   HOUSING,
                    SHOPPING CENTRES, ETC.

Railways ⊢⊢⊢⊢⊢   Waterways ▬▬▬   Roads ═══

LOCAL AUTHORITY BOUNDARIES ▬ ▬ ▬ ▬

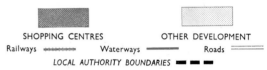

SHOPPING CENTRES   OTHER DEVELOPMENT

Railways ⊢⊢⊢⊢⊢   Waterways ▬▬▬   Roads ═══

LOCAL AUTHORITY BOUNDARIES ▬ ▬ ▬ ▬

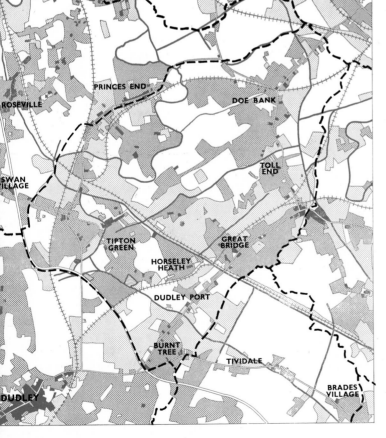

Figure 7. A large agglomeration of industry in the Black Country. Its growth has not been affected by the local government boundary which runs through it, but workers employed in the zone live in different administrative areas.

Figure 8. The people living in the part of Wednesbury shown on the map use the shops and cinemas of Darlaston, but their health and administrative services lie to the south-east.

Figure 9. Scattered small towns and villages collected into one borough. Residential areas and shopping centres lie along the boundaries; there is no clearly-defined centre. Major "natural" barriers, such as main line railways and canals, have prevented the growth of homogeneity.

FIGURE 9

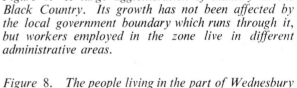

SHOPS   HOUSING, ETC.   INDUSTRY

Railways ⊢⊢⊢⊢⊢   Waterways ▬▬▬   Roads ═══

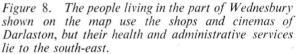

LOCAL AUTHORITY BOUNDARIES ▬ ▬ ▬ ▬

FIGURE 10   LOCAL AUTHORITY BOUNDARIES   FIGURE 11

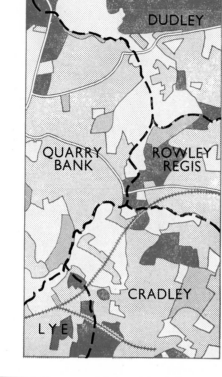

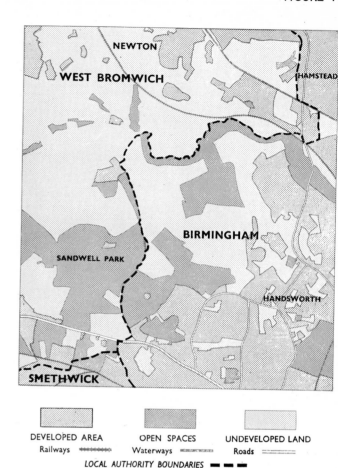

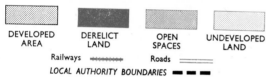

Figure 10. An effective siting of boundaries in the south-west of the Conurbation. Derelict land, undeveloped land, and open spaces (all shown in red) here mark the obvious administrative, social, and economic " watersheds ".

Figure 11. A " Green Setting " boundary where the preservation of open space on each side of the boundary line is the active concern of neighbouring Authorities. Most of the land here has been purchased jointly by Birmingham and West Bromwich for preservation as open space.

Local Authorities' plans are now submitted for approval to the Ministry of Town and Country Planning through the Regional Officer of the Ministry. His powers are confined to a veto on plans submitted ; no plans are initiated by the Ministry or by Regional Offices. Most Regional Offices perform an informative function and try to act as a clearing house for plans affecting the Region. It is doubtful, however, whether they yet provide an adequate medium for conveying information between authorities at the times when such information is most needed, *i.e.*, while plans are in the process of formulation and before they are submitted for approval.

It thus becomes apparent that, outside the services closely associated with public health there are certain well-defined trends towards larger and more uniform administrative units, and towards the grouping of Local Authorities for specific purposes.

PRESENT DIFFICULTIES

In the years before 1939 the chief difficulty which faced those concerned with provisions for social betterment was the poverty of many of the Local Authorities where improvement was most necessary. Poverty such as was rife in the Special Areas has only existed in isolated cases among the smaller Local Authorities of the Conurbation; but sufficiently striking differences in the rateable value per head are shown in Table III, the largest being 73.6 per cent. above the average for the whole Conurbation, and the lowest, 43.8 per cent. below the average. The lack of adequate financial resources has always been one of the biggest hindrances to the execution of planning schemes, and to the provision of improved amenities and services among a great number of smaller Authorities.

The shapes and boundaries of Local Government areas introduce many anomalies and obstacles in the way of effective administration.

It is inevitable that, for some functions of local government, boundary divisions between Authorities should appear to be arbitrary and illogical. For example, drainage is determined by factors of relief and geology, and will be planned to serve districts which may be quite unsuitable for police or public library services. Nevertheless, in the interests of good government, areas which have a geographical, social, economic or historical integrity should not be artificially divided for the purposes of administration and the supply of services and amenities. Local Government areas should coincide as far as possible with natural communities of people and the grouping of their work and interests, if all sections of the community are to be induced to participate in local affairs.

Study of the maps of Local Authority boundaries (Figures 7, 8 and 9) reveals how little these conditions obtain in the Conurbation. The townships of the Black Country, many of them reflecting the make-up and pattern of the villages from which they grew, are organic communities. Yet a municipal boundary line runs through the main street of Darlaston (Figure 8). Great Bridge, Bradley, Tipton, Blackheath, Princes End (Figure 9), Cradley, and Brownhills are other townships which have been divided between Local Authorities. S. H. Beaver, in his *Report on Derelict Land in the Black Country*[1], mentions the boundary which runs through the middle of Spring Vale Iron and Steel Works, so that one group of blast furnaces is in Coseley, and the other, a few yards away, is in Bilston; he continues : " Perhaps the strangest boundary of all is that of Coseley, with repeated staggerings on the west, against Sedgley, and two ' pan-handles ' on the east " (see Figure 4), "a large and almost completely derelict area sticking out for a mile between Bilston and Tipton, and a smaller one through the north of Bradley." (see also Figure 7).

Table XXXIV in Chapter XI (Surface Utilisation) shows clearly the acute problems facing certain Authorities which look within their own boundaries for land for housing and other developments. Bilston, for example, with a population of over 31,000 and 48.7 per cent. of its houses needing replacement (Table XIV), has only 90 acres of undeveloped land on which to build. Smethwick has already been driven to site housing estates outside its boundaries in the neighbouring Borough of Oldbury, and its Municipal Hospital in Birmingham.

The rapid growth, during the war, of regional administration by departments of the central government has thrown into relief a third major problem in the present constitution of local government, a difficulty which is less specific than others, and which reveals itself in a number of apparently dissociated forms. This problem lies in the formal isolation of each Authority from its neighbours. There is no permanent machinery by which questions affecting a large defined area, such as the Black Country, can be submitted

---

[1] Ministry of Town and Country Planning (January, 1946).

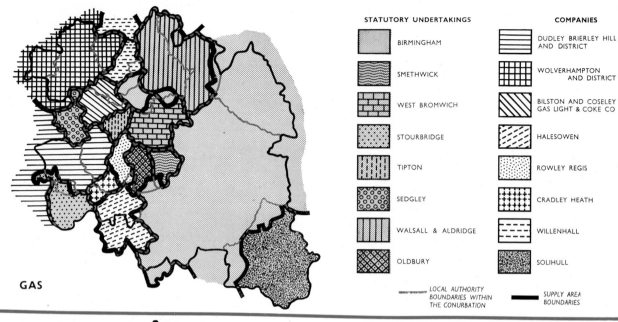

FIGURE 12

STATUTORY UNDERTAKINGS

BIRMINGHAM
SMETHWICK
WEST BROMWICH
STOURBRIDGE
TIPTON
SEDGLEY
WALSALL & ALDRIDGE
OLDBURY

COMPANIES

DUDLEY BRIERLEY HILL AND DISTRICT
WOLVERHAMPTON AND DISTRICT
BILSTON AND COSELEY GAS LIGHT & COKE CO
HALESOWEN
ROWLEY REGIS
CRADLEY HEATH
WILLENHALL
SOLIHULL

LOCAL AUTHORITY BOUNDARIES WITHIN THE CONURBATION

SUPPLY AREA BOUNDARIES

GAS

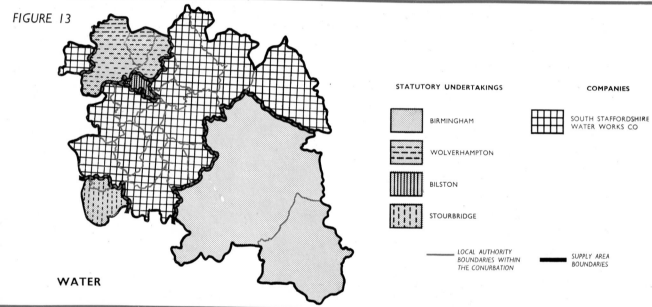

FIGURE 13

STATUTORY UNDERTAKINGS

BIRMINGHAM
WOLVERHAMPTON
BILSTON
STOURBRIDGE

COMPANIES

SOUTH STAFFORDSHIRE WATER WORKS CO

LOCAL AUTHORITY BOUNDARIES WITHIN THE CONURBATION

SUPPLY AREA BOUNDARIES

WATER

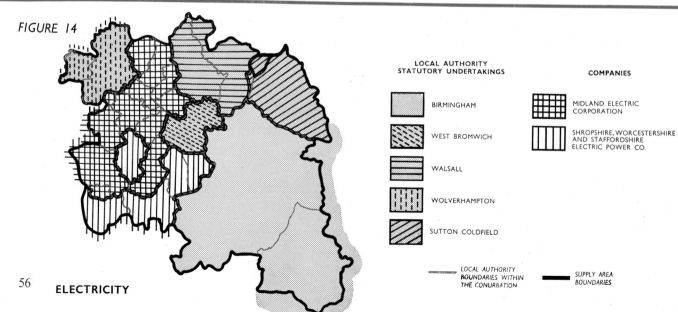

FIGURE 14

LOCAL AUTHORITY STATUTORY UNDERTAKINGS

BIRMINGHAM
WEST BROMWICH
WALSALL
WOLVERHAMPTON
SUTTON COLDFIELD

COMPANIES

MIDLAND ELECTRIC CORPORATION
SHROPSHIRE, WORCESTERSHIRE AND STAFFORDSHIRE ELECTRIC POWER CO.

LOCAL AUTHORITY BOUNDARIES WITHIN THE CONURBATION

SUPPLY AREA BOUNDARIES

56 ELECTRICITY

to a body representing the whole area and with power to act, or, except in a few instances, even to advise on action.

At present there are three ways in which such questions can be handled: firstly, by the individual Local Authorities in the area acting according to their own interests and view of the situation; secondly, by reference to, or intervention by, the central government; thirdly, by the voluntary co-operation of the Local Authorities in the formation of a joint *ad hoc* committee with power either to advise on or to carry out the measures necessary to deal with the question. In the matter nearest to hand, town planning, in which expert opinion is agreed that regional considerations should exert a dominant influence, Local Authorities in England have for the most part preferred to act independently. In the case of the 143 Authorities included in Greater London, the Ministry of Town and Country Planning itself sponsored and financed a survey and plan, and has now assumed special powers in order to secure the adherence of the Local Authorities to the plan. In the rest of the country, numbers of Local Authorities have combined with one, two or more neighbouring Authorities to form Joint Planning Advisory Committees. Some have formed Joint Planning Executive Committees. In the case of the Conurbation, twenty-three out of the twenty-four Authorities have formed themselves into the six Joint Planning Executive Committees, mentioned earlier in this Chapter.

A third manifestation of isolationist local government is in what might be termed the foreign relationships of Authorities. The storm of controversy between Counties and County Boroughs which began in 1926 and lasted many years, was a notable instance of this permanently disturbing element in local government. The subject of most disputes is territory, although the division of rates and administrative functions also contributes. When the population of a large town gradually spreads over the existing boundaries, the Council petitions for the inclusion of these new built-up areas within a newly-defined boundary line. These built-up areas clearly form part of the social and economic structure of the town whence they sprang, but their inclusion within its official boundary involves the surrender by neighbouring Authorities of thickly populated areas which have been expensive to develop and which now contribute to the rates. This constant raiding of the richer districts within the poorer Authorities has now produced a situation in which the value of rural districts as units of local government has been called in question with ominous frequency. It is not to be wondered at that the process is one which has been resisted at every step by County Councils and smaller Authorities.

This aspect of local government affairs has another side, especially in extensive built-up areas like the Black Country. Since the status of a Local Authority is generally proportionate to the size of its population, and since its efficiency is, for good and bad reasons alike, held to be similarly proportionate, there has been a more or less amicable competition between the larger or more rapidly growing Authorities for the partition of the smaller, more static, areas. This competitive process, an inevitable result of the separatism that has prevailed in the local government system, has produced the anomalous boundaries

---

Figures 12, 13 *and* 14 (*opposite*)

This series of diagrammatic maps shows the variations in the supply areas of public utility companies and local authority undertakings. There is a marked lack of uniformity in administration. Gas supply is in the hands of sixteen different undertakings and companies. The City of Birmingham Gas Department supplies sections of West Bromwich, Walsall, Wednesbury, and Darlaston, which are detached from its main area of supply. The map of Electricity supply areas shows a more rational system of local distribution. The larger authorities are supplied by their own statutory undertakings and two large public utility companies serve the remainder of the Conurbation. A still more uniform arrangement is apparent in the map of Water supply areas.

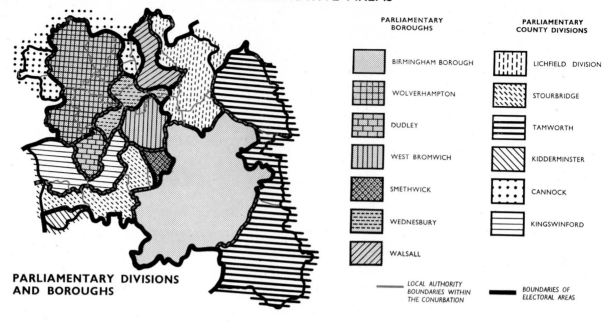

FIGURE 15

ADMINISTRATIVE AREAS

PARLIAMENTARY BOROUGHS

- BIRMINGHAM BOROUGH
- WOLVERHAMPTON
- DUDLEY
- WEST BROMWICH
- SMETHWICK
- WEDNESBURY
- WALSALL

PARLIAMENTARY COUNTY DIVISIONS

- LICHFIELD DIVISION
- STOURBRIDGE
- TAMWORTH
- KIDDERMINSTER
- CANNOCK
- KINGSWINFORD

LOCAL AUTHORITY BOUNDARIES WITHIN THE CONURBATION

BOUNDARIES OF ELECTORAL AREAS

PARLIAMENTARY DIVISIONS AND BOROUGHS

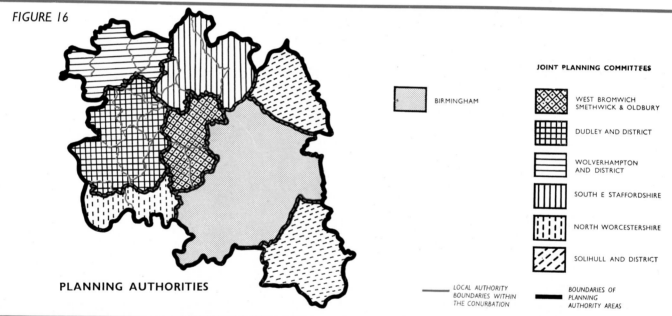

FIGURE 16

BIRMINGHAM

JOINT PLANNING COMMITTEES

- WEST BROMWICH SMETHWICK & OLDBURY
- DUDLEY AND DISTRICT
- WOLVERHAMPTON AND DISTRICT
- SOUTH E STAFFORDSHIRE
- NORTH WORCESTERSHIRE
- SOLIHULL AND DISTRICT

LOCAL AUTHORITY BOUNDARIES WITHIN THE CONURBATION

BOUNDARIES OF PLANNING AUTHORITY AREAS

PLANNING AUTHORITIES

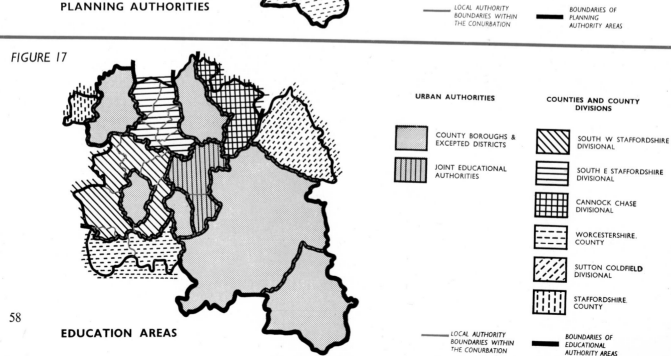

FIGURE 17

URBAN AUTHORITIES

- COUNTY BOROUGHS & EXCEPTED DISTRICTS
- JOINT EDUCATIONAL AUTHORITIES

COUNTIES AND COUNTY DIVISIONS

- SOUTH W STAFFORDSHIRE DIVISIONAL
- SOUTH E STAFFORDSHIRE DIVISIONAL
- CANNOCK CHASE DIVISIONAL
- WORCESTERSHIRE. COUNTY
- SUTTON COLDFIELD DIVISIONAL
- STAFFORDSHIRE. COUNTY

LOCAL AUTHORITY BOUNDARIES WITHIN THE CONURBATION

BOUNDARIES OF EDUCATIONAL AUTHORITY AREAS

58

EDUCATION AREAS

referred to previously. It has also produced local government areas in which main centres of population are spread around the borders and which have little inner cohesion or unity (see Figure 9).

RECENT MOVES

Most of the criticisms which have so far been brought forward are familiar to councillors and officials who have to work the existing machinery. There seems to be but one answer to the present administrative complications, and that is the creation of larger, and fewer, Authorities. In the creation of such larger Authorities, however, local considerations should be carefully weighed. These are set out in the following Section—" The Reconstruction of Local Government." The creation of fewer Authorities is part of the established procedure for the adjustment of Local Authority administration. By the Local Government Act of 1929, decennial reviews of the areas and status of Local Authorities are to be held by the Boundary Commission. The present Commission, appointed in 1945, is to make " such alterations in the status or boundaries of local government areas as will ensure individually and collectively effective and convenient units of local government administration ".

The Local Administration and Finance Committee of the West Midland Group, in its *Report on the Size and Function of Local Government Units*, published in 1944, recommended that all Local Government Authorities should possess at least the powers and duties of existing County Boroughs, and that councils of Boroughs, Urban Districts and Rural Districts with a population of less than 70,000 should, except in certain special cases, cease to operate as Local Authorities.

It was clear to the West Midland Group that the complex, variable, and often anomalous position of local government in the Conurbation demanded as a first step the setting up of four or five large Authorities which would incorporate at least all the present built-up area. The immediate advantages of this process are obvious. Financially, such Authorities would be able to plan on a much larger scale than is possible at present. Many services, especially municipal supply undertakings, may normally be expected to gain in efficiency when they are operated on a bigger scale. Many of the anomalies of boundary and area (although not necessarily all of them) would be eliminated. Many of the present difficulties arising from diversity of status, function and size would be greatly reduced. Not the least among these difficulties are those which result from the different standards of pay and the consequent differences in the qualifications required among principal officials carrying out similar duties in adjacent areas. The chances of redeveloping the Conurbation according to one overall plan would be greatly improved, since there would be fewer negotiations and, in practice, a few equals can agree on matters

---

Figures 15, 16 *and* 17 (*opposite*)

This second series of diagrammatic maps shows various groupings of areas in the Conurbation for different administrative purposes. In all three cases Birmingham is the largest unit and is always a separate one.

The degree to which the smaller authorities inside the Conurbation are treated as sub-divisions of the counties to which they belong varies considerably. The groupings for different purposes also vary.

Parliamentary electoral areas, especially in the Black Country, are often inconsistent with local authority areas. The confusion which the two different electoral areas produces helps to weaken the social integrity of communities.

All six county boroughs, together with Oldbury and Solihull, emerge clearly as separate and independent units in the map of education areas as they are laid down under the Education Act, 1944. The map illustrates the tendency of recent legislation to emphasise the independence and self-sufficiency of the county boroughs and to group all smaller authorities into ad hoc *divisions of counties.*

FOR LOCAL GOVERNMENT AND OTHER ADMINISTRA

TABLE V

Local Government Areas	SERVICES		
	Gas supplied by	Water supplied by	Electricity supplied b
County Boroughs			
Birmingham	Birmingham Gas Dept.	Birmingham Water Dept.	Birmingham Elec. Dep
Dudley	Dudley, Brierley Hill and District Gas Co.	S.Staffs. Water Works Co.	Shropshire, Worcs. Staffs. Electric Power
Smethwick	Smethwick Gas Dept.	,, ,, ,,	,, ,, ,, ,,
Walsall	Walsall Gas Dept.	,, ,, ,,	Walsall Electricity De
West Bromwich	West Bromwich Gas Dept.	,, ,, ,,	W. Bromwich Elec.
Wolverhampton	Wolverhampton and District Gas Co.	Wolverhampton Water Dept.	Wolverhampton Elec.
Municipal Boroughs			
Bilston	Bilston Gas, Light and Coke Co.	Bilston Water Dept.	Midland Electric Co
Halesowen	Halesowen Gas Co.	S.Staffs. Water Works Co.	Shropshire, Worcs. Staffs. Electric Power
Oldbury	Oldbury Gas Dept. and Birmingham Gas Dept.	,, ,, ,,	Shropshire, Worcs. Staffs. Electric Power and Birmingham Elec. [
Rowley Regis	Rowley Regis and Blackheath Gas Co. and Cradley Heath Gas Co.	,, ,, ,,	Midland Electric Co
Stourbridge	Stourbridge Gas Dept.	Stourbridge and District Water Board	Shropshire, Worcs. Staffs. Electric Power
Sutton Coldfield	Birmingham Gas Dept.	S.Staffs. Water Works Co.	Sutton Coldfield Elec. [
Tipton	Tipton Gas Dept.	,, ,, ,,	Midland Electric Cor
Wednesbury	Birmingham Gas Dept.	,, ,, ,,	,, ,, ,,
Urban Districts			
Aldridge	Walsall Gas Dept.	S.Staffs. Water Works Co.	Walsall Electricity Dep
Amblecote	Stourbridge Gas Dept. and Dudley, Brierley Hill and District Gas Co.	Stourbridge and District	Midland Electric Cor
Brierley Hill	Dudley, Brierley Hill and District Gas Co.	S.Staffs. Water Works Co.	,, ,, ,,
Coseley	Bilston Gas, Light and Coke Co.	,, ,, ,,	,, ,, ,,
Darlaston	Birmingham Gas Dept.	,, ,, ,,	,, ,, ,,
Sedgley	Sedgley Gas Dept.	,, ,, ,,	,, ,, ,,
Solihull	Birmingham Gas Dept.	Birmingham	Birmingham Elec. Dept
Tettenhall	Wolverhampton and District Gas Co.	S.Staffs. Water Works Co.	Wolverhampton Elec. D
Wednesfield	,, ,,	Wolverhampton Water Dept.	Midland Electric Corp
Willenhall	Willenhall Gas Co.	,, ,, ,,	,, ,, ,,

Parliamentary Representation	Education Authority	Planning Authority
Birmingham Borough	Birmingham	Birmingham
Dudley Borough	Dudley	Dudley and District
Smethwick	West Bromwich and Smethwick Joint Education Authority	West Bromwich, Smethwick and Oldbury
Walsall Borough	Walsall	S.E. Staffordshire
West Bromwich Borough	West Bromwich and Smethwick Joint Education Authority	West Bromwich, Smethwick and Oldbury
Wolverhampton	Wolverhampton	Wolverhampton
Wolverhampton Borough	S.E. Staffs. Division Education Authority	Dudley and District
Stourbridge Division	Worcestershire County	North Worcestershire
Stourbridge Division	Oldbury (Excepted District)	West Bromwich, Smethwick and Oldbury
Kingswinford Division	S.W. Staffs. Division Education Authority	Dudley and District
Stourbridge Division	Worcestershire County Education Authority	North Worcestershire
Tamworth Division	Sutton Coldfield	Solihull and District
Wednesbury Borough and Wolverhampton Borough	S.W. Staffs. Division Education Authority	Dudley and District
Wednesbury Borough	S.E. Staffs. Division Education Authority	S.E. Staffordshire
Lichfield Division	Cannock Chase Div. Education Authority	S.E. Staffordshire
Kingswinford Division	S.W. Staffs. Division Education Authority	Dudley and District
Kingswinford Division	S.W. Staffs. Division Education Authority	Dudley and District
Wolverhampton Borough	S.W. Staffs. Division Education Authority	Dudley and District
Wednesbury Borough	S.E. Staffs. Division Education Authority	S.E. Staffordshire
Wolverhampton Borough	S.W. Staffs. Division Education Authority	Dudley and District
Tamworth Division	Solihull (Excepted District)	Solihull and District
Cannock Division	Staffs. County Education Authority	Wolverhampton and District
Wolverhampton Borough	S.E. Staffs. Division Education Authority	Wolverhampton and District
Wolverhampton Borough	S.E. Staffs. Division Education Authority	Wolverhampton and District

This Table should be read in conjunction with Figures 12 to 17

of common interest where a score of different Authorities of varying magnitude would encounter a multitude of difficulties. The simple fact that areas were contiguous would remove one of the biggest obstacles to coherent planning in the Conurbation, namely, the present isolation of the major Authorities of Walsall, Dudley, and Wolverhampton from the large and compact group of Birmingham, Smethwick, and West Bromwich.

In 1945, a conference of the Association of Municipal Corporations passed a resolution which favoured the same procedure, calling for a uniform system of local government throughout the country, exercised by " all-purpose " Authorities similar to those specified in the West Midland Group's Report.

None of the major political parties, in the programmes prepared and published before the 1945 General Election, adopted similar proposals as part of their policy on local government, but the Labour Party acknowledged the need for revision of the system in its projected reduction of the types of Authority from six to two.

The appointment of the Boundary Commission in 1945 initiated a further series of moves, all over the Conurbation, designed to conclude the process of partition, absorption and growth.

The urgency of the problem and the difficulty of its solution are both demonstrated by the number of widely differing proposals put forward. In general, four possible major changes are variously suggested.

Birmingham, it should be noted, has apparently put forward no proposal and has made no move in the present negotiations.

Smethwick and West Bromwich have decided on amalgamation. The other County Boroughs of the Black Country have proposed that their areas should be substantially increased so as to include the whole of the Conurbation area and some parts of the adjoining rural districts.

Other proposals envisage the creation of seven, or, again, of six, County Boroughs which will amalgamate Local Authorities within the Conurbation into large urban aggregates.

Staffordshire County Council has advanced proposals for adjusting the boundary between Staffordshire and Worcestershire, an adjustment which would involve the inclusion of Dudley in Staffordshire and the transference of a corresponding area from Staffordshire to Worcestershire ; under this proposal the number of Local Authorities in the Conurbation would remain virtually unchanged.

A third major proposal has been for the creation of a single County Borough embracing an area with a population comparable with that of Birmingham.

The Boundary Commission itself has discussed the possibility of the formation of a county of South Staffordshire, on the model of the scheme put forward by Local Authorities in and around Manchester. This would involve the relinquishment by the five existing County Boroughs in the Black Country of their status, and its effect would be to create a County with about 1,000,000 persons and an area of 100,000 acres. The administration would be on a two-tier system such as that adopted for the administration of the County of London with its metropolitan boroughs.

The Commission has remarked that this possibility could not be considered without reference to the position of Birmingham, and stated, in an Interim Report published in May, 1947, that if a new county were contemplated one obvious possibility would be to make Birmingham the administrative centre, and to include a population of some two to two-and-a-half million persons.

Since the preliminary draft of this chapter was written, the Minister of Town and Country Planning has announced the appointment of a team, under the direction of Sir Patrick Abercrombie and Mr. Herbert Jackson, to prepare a plan for the Conurbation and West Midlands. The West Midland Group wholeheartedly welcomes the decision which, it feels, will go far to implement the ideas evolved from its programme of research. It hopes that the formulation of a plan will encourage co-operative organization in the Region, and that the plan will be carried out on a Regional level.

In view of the trend of expert and governmental opinion, it seems likely that the move in the Conurbation towards the amalgamation of Authorities will be approved. While the West Midland Group has declared itself in favour of the " all-purpose " Authority of the county borough type, it is to be hoped that any radical change in the local government system will take place only after full discussion on the widest possible basis of all the circumstances involved, and that there will be no piecemeal findings as the result of independent proposals put forward to meet individual cases. The County Boroughs' proposals, and the counter-suggestions put forward by the Boundary Commission have gone far to ensure that local government boundaries in the Conurbation will be treated as a single problem.

In considering that problem, there are certain factors which should be carefully weighed before a decision is reached.

The most serious difficulties under which planning and many other local government functions are carried on in the Conurbation are those arising from the number, variety and ill-adjusted sizes and boundaries of the Local Government Authorities. Efficient and co-ordinated local government is the first aim, and increased administrative efficiency should result from amalgamation. It is generally conceded, however, that there is a real loss in that the large unit tends to become impersonal, more remote and authoritarian in its dealings with people, reflecting less of the desires and attitudes of the population of the area.

It is further suggested that, except within certain strictly defined limits, control of the affairs of such large Authorities is so specialized and technical a matter that democratic control by an elected council of voluntary part-time members is a polite fiction. Almost all control is in the hands of permanent officials.

Throughout the country, smaller units afford an opportunity for a large number of people to take part in local government, especially as the small scale of operations does not entail a large expenditure of time by councillors and there is consequently opportunity for persons of a wide range of occupations and income levels to take part in the business of government. The small unit also encourages and preserves neighbourliness and local patriotism, civic assets which are of considerable importance to the morale, the way of life and the psychological stability of the people.

It is desirable, therefore, that due regard should be paid to the maintenance of coherent social, economic and political relationships in communities. There is no virtue in size if it means the sacrifice of the communal spirit. On the other hand, towns such as Birmingham, Norwich and Bristol reveal the characteristics of organic community more clearly than many towns of far smaller size ; there is a clear distinction between the processes of agglomeration and of growth.

The danger that the townships of the Black Country, in becoming suburbs of the larger urban centres, may lose individuality and social coherence is a real one. There is a possible solution of the dilemma, however. While the administrative amalgamation of existing Authorities will be beneficial, the physical amalgamation of the existing urban areas by building development would be a disaster. Planning schemes for the area, however it is administered, should aim at preserving that close neighbourliness and individualism which so many Black Country townships still retain. Existing social and urban groupings should be used as nuclei for neighbourhoods and districts. Geographical barriers some-times give indications of the natural boundaries between large communities, and we often find that natural groupings of urban areas are those within which movement and inter-course are most easy and usual. There are such natural barriers in the Conurbatino, principally the ridge 600 to 800 feet high, which runs north-west from the southern part of Oldbury, across Rowley Regis, and on through Dudley to Sedgley (see endpaper map). More effective barriers, moreover, are the principal transport systems, especially canals and railways, and spoilbanks and derelict land are perhaps the most effective of all.

If the recommendations made in this Report, together with those regarding the use of derelict land, can be carried into effect, the townships of the Black Country may emerge, when redeveloped, as corporate identities, separated by a " Green Setting." Towns and townships would be grouped together into County Boroughs for the purposes of adminis-tration. A centre such as Wolverhampton or Dudley, with its more clearly defined focal position, might serve the enlarged County Borough as a focus for weekly shopping and for principal services and amenities. The surrounding townships would be developed with the eventual aim of making each a complete Neighbourhood Unit—with its own industry, its own commercial and administrative services, and its own entertainments and amenities. In between, and forming a continuous pattern of countryside, and parkway throughout the Conurbation, green strips would be developed (see Chapter XIII and Figure 41). If this plan could be realized, some measure of local autonomy for the Neighbourhood Unit would be inevitable, as well as desirable.

An integral part of such a plan (which is more fully described in Chapter XIII) is control by the major Urban Authorities of the rural areas surrounding the Conurbation; not in order to facilitate urban spread into the countryside but that the wealth and influence of the County Borough may be used to preserve the rural margin, together with the green wedges and strips, as a permanent reservation of countryside. The present situation sometimes encourages the opposite result, since the Rural Authorities, in whose areas the projected rural reservation lies, have much to gain from the urban development of their areas, chiefly higher status and an increased rateable value.

Ideally, planning for the whole country should regard rural land as a foundation or backcloth upon which are set clearly-defined areas of urban development, the boundaries of which are maintained inviolable. Once this pattern is established, the danger of urban sprawl will have disappeared, but in the interim period, which may extend over many years, there is serious danger of sprawling development on all marginal land round existing towns. This is unsound from many aspects ; it occupies an undue proportion of space and creates uneconomic communications; it renders a large area of land " untidy " and unsuitable for agriculture; and it robs the urban areas of the cohesion and high rateable value which arise from a proper density of building. Such haphazard growth often leads to the formation of new urban districts whose main source of revenue is derived indirectly from the adjoining towns, the activities of which have created the land values and the population.

The marginal lands, extending to anything from one to five miles beyond the built-up areas of existing towns, are important areas in any compact and economic planning scheme, and it is urgent that they should be brought under control. Obviously, only the greater resources of the larger towns or the central government would be adequate to stand the strain of preserving these marginal areas, because of their high land value; but their proper preservation is important to any comprehensive plan; and the legislation necessary to such preservation should be passed as soon as possible[1].

---

[1]The Group is unanimous in recommending strict control, for planning purposes, of rural areas around towns. Some members, however, do not agree with the proposals outlined in the concluding paragraphs of the chapter for placing responsibility for such control in the hands of urban authorities.

FIGURE 18

RAILWAYS AND WATERWAYS

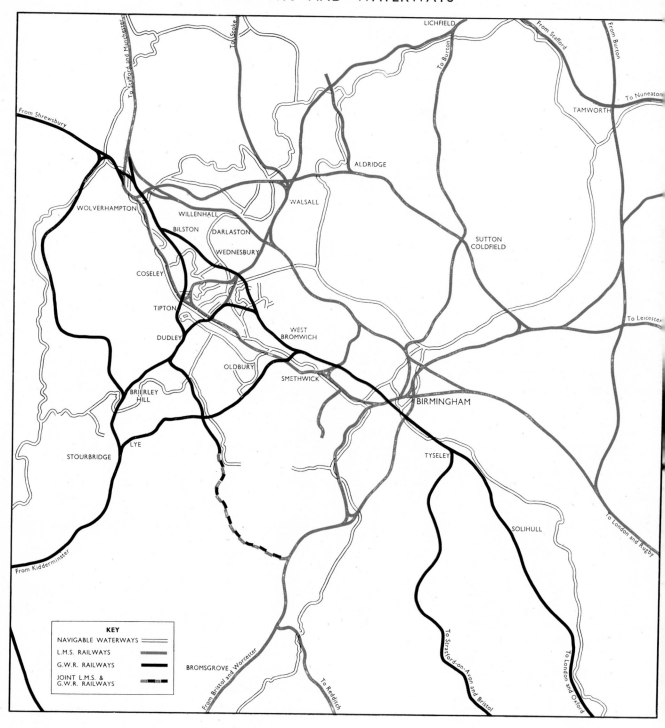

KEY

NAVIGABLE WATERWAYS

L.M.S. RAILWAYS

G.W.R. RAILWAYS

JOINT L.M.S. & G.W.R. RAILWAYS

CHAPTER V

Communications

As IN MOST thickly populated industrial districts, the problems of transport in the Conurbation area are ever present. During the rapid industrial expansion which took place in the 18th and 19th centuries, canals and railways were developed to carry the increasing traffic in raw materials and manufactured goods. The existing road system carried its share of traffic which increased to heavy proportions with the advent of motor transport. In the War period, 1939-1945, all forms of transport were heavily engaged, and the strenuous conditions of these busy years have disclosed several weaknesses. Just before the war, developments in air transport were promising, but these were halted by the outbreak of hostilities, although the emergency was responsible for the establishment of several airfields for military purposes within the area.

RAIL

The Midlands are well served in normal times by two of the railway groups, the L.M.S. and G.W., (see Figure 18) both of which are in a position to give efficient passenger and goods services to London, and to the western seaports. The most convenient outlets for overseas traffic from the Midlands are London, the Mersey, the Humber, and the Bristol Channel ports. At present, London and the Mersey handle the larger share of exports and imports. These two centres offer better shipping facilities than the others.

The Humber is next in importance from the shipping point of view, but the distance from the Midlands is much greater, and the railway facilities much inferior to those available to the three other shipping centres.

The Bristol Channel ports are the natural outlet for the Midlands. Railway connections are good, but shipping services are inferior to those at the three other ports. Fuller development of these services would enable the western ports to take their proper share of the import and export traffic from the Midlands. The docks themselves are well equipped: it is the services and organization which stand in need of expansion.

Rail services to the north and east of the Conurbation area are not nearly so good as those to the south and west. The routes to the Eastern Counties are long and circuitous. Passengers often find it more convenient to travel to London to reach the East Coast, than to proceed across country. Services to the east and to the north must be considerably developed and speeded up before communications with these parts of the country can be considered adequate.

Within the Conurbation itself the railway network is extensive and connections are good. Facilities for handling goods at the various goods yards are up-to-date and adequate. The use of the railways for local passenger transport, however, has declined in

FIGURE 19

PROPOSALS FOR NEW TRUNK ROADS

These suggestions for a trunk road system to link the Conurbation with the principal ports and to keep through traffic away from the built-up areas are based upon proposals outlined by the County Surveyors' Society.

Existing roads are shown in red, proposed new roads in black.

face of the challenge of road services. In Birmingham, for instance, three suburban lines have fallen into disuse for passenger traffic within the past twenty years. The stations have been dismantled and on one such line grass grows on the track. Yet the development of the outer districts of the city has gone on and these disused railways might now usefully supplement the heavily strained road services. Electrification of these suburban tracks and the rehabilitation of stations on modern lines appear to offer the only chances of reviving these derelict services. There is little need to build new lines or to change the positions of stations, which, in most instances are suitably placed, but swift and comfortable services must be instituted in order to attract passengers back to the habit of thirty years ago when the city train was the most popular and convenient method of travel to business.

Interesting figures have been collected to show the method of travel to work adopted by employees at the Austin Motor Works, Longbridge (on the south-western outskirts of Birmingham) and by the employees at Castle Bromwich Aero Factory (to the north-east of Birmingham); a census taken in 1937 gave the following analysis:

 8.5% travelled by Train
27.0%   ,,   ,, Tram
25.0%   ,,   ,, 'Bus or Coach
14.0%   ,,   ,, Private Car
 2.0%   ,,   ,, Motor Cycle
13.5%   ,,   ,, Pedal Cycle
10.0%   ,,   ,, Walking

Each of these factories is situated on a railway line: yet 91.5 per cent. of the employees get to and from work by using the roads in one way or another.

ROADS

The present road system from the Midlands to the ports is inadequate to meet the increasing traffic demands. (For existing systems of roads see Figure 19, in which they are shown in red). The construction of new trunk roads is an urgent necessity on grounds of speed, convenience, and safety.

A new main road to London is the first requirement. Census figures show that traffic on the existing road is heavier than on any other route leading out of the Midlands. Next in importance is the road leading to the Mersey and Lancashire. The third is the route to Bristol, South Wales and the west.

A new direct traffic route to Leicester and the Eastern Counties, and another to Yorkshire and the north-east are also needed. Such roads, while not so important as those to the ports, will need to be planned on different lines from the existing routes if traffic is to flow rapidly and economically.

The needs of the area for main road communications with the rest of the country appear to be met in the plans for new trunk roads prepared for the whole country by the County Surveyors' Society (see Figure 19). A trunk road from London to the Midlands has been designed to pass on the south side of the Conurbation area and to continue past Wolverhampton to the Mersey. Another trunk road to the west, to be linked with Birmingham, is planned to pass near Bromsgrove, continuing on to the east of Worcester and thence to Bristol, with a fork-off at Worcester continuing past Ross to South Wales. On the north a road is to pass near Derby and on towards Doncaster, thereby giving easy access to Leicester, Nottingham and the Humber.

If the roads leading to the Mersey and the Humber were joined together by a new link north of the Conurbation, there could in fact be a ring road completely surrounding

FIGURE 20

WATERWAYS
PROPOSALS FOR INCREASED CAPACITY

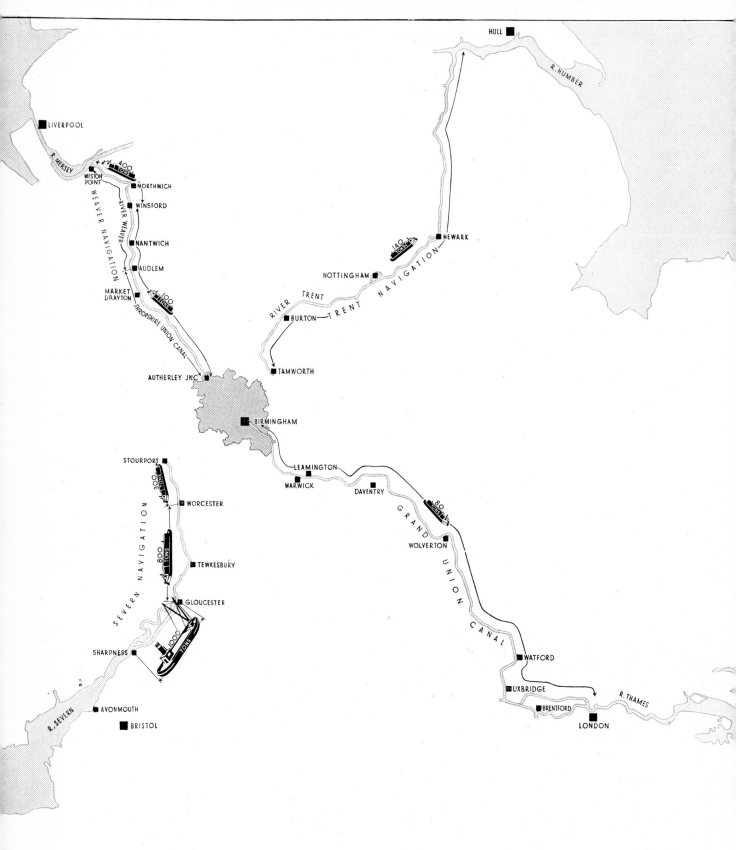

These suggestions for increasing the width and capacity of the rivers and canals connecting the Conurbation with the Mersey, Humber and Bristol Channel Ports are based upon proposals put forward by the Severn, the Trent and the Weaver Navigation Boards.

the built-up area, offering easy connections to the Mersey, the Humber, the Thames, and the Bristol Channel. The actual lines and levels of the suggested motor roads of the County Surveyors' scheme have been surveyed in some detail, and would be available for use in any plan to put the scheme into execution.

These proposals have been widely debated and have been considered by the Ministry of Transport, which has carried out extensive research into the problem. The whole scheme of co-ordinated road construction involves national policy of high importance. Whether single-purpose roads or motor roads are to be built between the major centres of population has not yet been decided, but the recent Trunk Roads Act, extending the control of the Ministry of Transport to more than 3,000 miles of additional highways, seems to indicate a policy of improving existing roads rather than building new ones.

The network of communicating roads within the built-up area is dependent upon the planning and redevelopment of the urban centres. The long-term plan for the road system of Birmingham, which constitutes about half the Conurbation, was settled as long ago as 1917, and involves over 100 miles of radial and ring roads of double carriageway standard, more than 100-ft. in width. More than 25 miles have been completed and considerable progress has been made towards the completion of the remainder.

An important improvement in the road communications of the Conurbation was made by the construction of the Birmingham to Wolverhampton road which was completed in 1927. This highway is some ten miles in length and traverses the western half of the area. It provides swift and direct communication between the two largest industrial centres in the area, and its extensive use has proved the wisdom of bold and energetic planning. New roads of a similar character are desirable in other parts of the Conurbation, but precise plans for these can only be drawn up when the new urban centres have been determined on a plan of redevelopment.

An increasing weight of local passenger traffic is being carried on the roads by 'bus services. Goods services and express passenger trains are more and more occupying the railways at the expense of local passenger trains. In addition to this mounting load of passenger traffic on the roads, the war years have also seen an enormous increase in the number of goods lorries crowding the highways. With the ultimate freeing of petrol from rationing and the removal of restrictions on private cars an even further increase in road traffic is to be expected, and it is certain that in some areas this combined traffic will reach almost unmanageable proportions. This delay and confusion may have the effect of forcing some of the goods traffic back on to the already burdened railway system and on to the extensive, but old-fashioned waterways. If commerce is to flow freely to and from the Midlands, the road and rail channels must be improved both inside and outside the area.

WATERWAYS

The construction of the first canal in the Conurbation area was begun in 1767, when a waterway was cut between Birmingham and the colliery district near Wolverhampton. By the end of the century the whole district was linked up by canals, and this extensive system of narrow waterways was important in two respects: it provided transport, slow but cheap, for heavy industries, and it determined the sites of hundreds of factories. Along the canal banks industrial buildings sprang up to take advantage of the waterways that ran to their very gates (see Figure 36). While this easy access to the waterfront was a convenience to industry, it also provided an early example of " ribbon development."

The more leisured industrial organization of a century-and-a-half ago was well served by its canals, but the geographical position of the Midlands on a high table-land makes it

71

unlikely that first-class waterways can ever be built to carry more than a small proportion of the urgent traffic of this busier age. The difficulties of contour are considerable; the level of the main Birmingham waterway is over 400-feet above sea level, and at this height there is always the likelihood of a shortage of water.

The waterways of the area were constructed for narrow boats, involving trans-shipment to barges before goods could go alongside steamers at the ports. This double handling could be overcome by bringing the larger barges into the Conurbation or to points conveniently situated to link up with road or rail transport.

The widening of canals necessary to bring the larger barges into the Conurbation would involve very great expense, except in a few instances such as that afforded by the main Birmingham and Wolverhampton canal. The present narrow canals, however, would function more effectively by the elimination of certain locks, and by the electrification of the remainder. Handling facilities along the canal routes could be made more efficient, and bottlenecks, caused by low bridges and inadequate tunnels, could be cleared away. Were these improvements effected, the existing system of canals could handle more efficiently the coal and quarried materials traffic carried on between Cannock, Warwickshire and the industrial areas.

Improvements on these lines are indicated in the proposals now being advanced by the Severn, Trent and Weaver Navigation Boards, and are illustrated in Figure 20. The development of efficient rail and road connections to the respective waterheads would open up the Midlands to good water routes to the ports and expedite the incoming flow of raw materials and the despatch of goods for export.

The Severn navigation scheme, at present under discussion, proposes the improvement of the Severn to accommodate sea-going vessels of 800 to 900 tons as far as Worcester, which is thirty miles from the centre of the Conurbation, and to improve the river as far as Stourport for the passage of 300-ton barges. Stourport is within twenty miles of the centre of the Conurbation. Similarly, the Trent Navigation Board is considering the improvement of the Trent and the Tame to allow 140-ton barges to pass from the port of Hull and the Yorkshire rivers to a waterhead near Tamworth, some 15 to 20 miles from the centre of the Conurbation. The Weaver Navigation Board proposes to improve the present Shropshire Union Canal to Autherley, near Wolverhampton, for the passage of 100-ton barges capable of navigation to the Mersey ports.

AIR

Before the war considerable developments in air transport had taken place within the Conurbation. Civil aerodromes had been set up at Birmingham, Walsall, and Wolverhampton. Those at Walsall and Wolverhampton were unsuitable to the operation of liner traffic, but provided facilities for aircraft-testing and private flying, with the prospect of later feeder-traffic. The Birmingham airport, however, functioned on a considerable scale. Restoration of some of its services may be looked for shortly. It provided direct access to Manchester, Liverpool, Belfast, Glasgow, Croydon, Brighton, the South Coast, Bristol, Weston-super-Mare, and South Wales.

At these points, or at intermediate ports of call, air transport was available to the North of Scotland, Eire, Isle of Man, Cornwall, Isle of Wight, Southampton, the Channel Islands, and the Scillies, and via Croydon to Amsterdam, Paris, and the great Continental junctions. All these air lines were suspended on the outbreak of war.

A number of service aerodromes now exist within the Conurbation. Upon the development of the national air plan, such of these as possess the necessary facilities may be released for civil traffic. It is not likely that intercommunication by air in the Conurbation area itself will develop to any extent, except in the provision of air-taxi and feeder-line traffic between the main centres of population and the principal airfield from which the main home and continental air lines will start.

The airport of Birmingham, at Elmdon, has terminal facilities and is capable of extension. The airport is gradually returning to its former functions and, although not yet fully restored, services are available. In the near future new routes will probably be added, especially to those places in the British Isles at present served inadequately by surface transport. Direct contact between the Midlands and the Continent is necessary, and could be achieved by the extension northward of services hitherto terminating in London, or by the extension to Amsterdam of the service to East Anglia. Services from the Midlands to the Baltic area could be achieved *via* the Scottish terminal.

Freight-carrying as well as passenger aircraft may be expected to ply between the Midlands and the Continent as well as to centres in this country. Precision engineering products, jewellery and the like, as well as more perishable commodities such as fruit and flowers, may be conveniently transported in specially designed aircraft.

The intensive development of air transport to places in this country which are already well served by fast surface transport is not to be looked for at present; but direct services from the Midlands to the British terminals of the trans-Atlantic and Imperial services, and to the less accessible parts of this country, should be economically practicable and capable of development immediately aircraft become available.

SUMMARY

This review of communications in the Conurbation area may be summarized briefly as follows: Railways within the area are adequate and connections good, but improvements are desirable in services to the North and to the Eastern counties. There is need for considerable development of main trunk roads to the coast in four directions from the Midlands if they are fully to serve their purpose for passenger and goods traffic. The waterways function usefully within the area in the transport of coal and other materials from the local collieries and quarries, but are not suitable for other transport to the coast. The development of the three main rivers, however, will bring barges of an economical size from all the four ports to within 15 to 20 miles of the centre of the Conurbation area for distribution by road or rail. Pre-war air communications were promising. The restoration of these, and their expansion to join with Continental and Overseas services, should be encouraged.

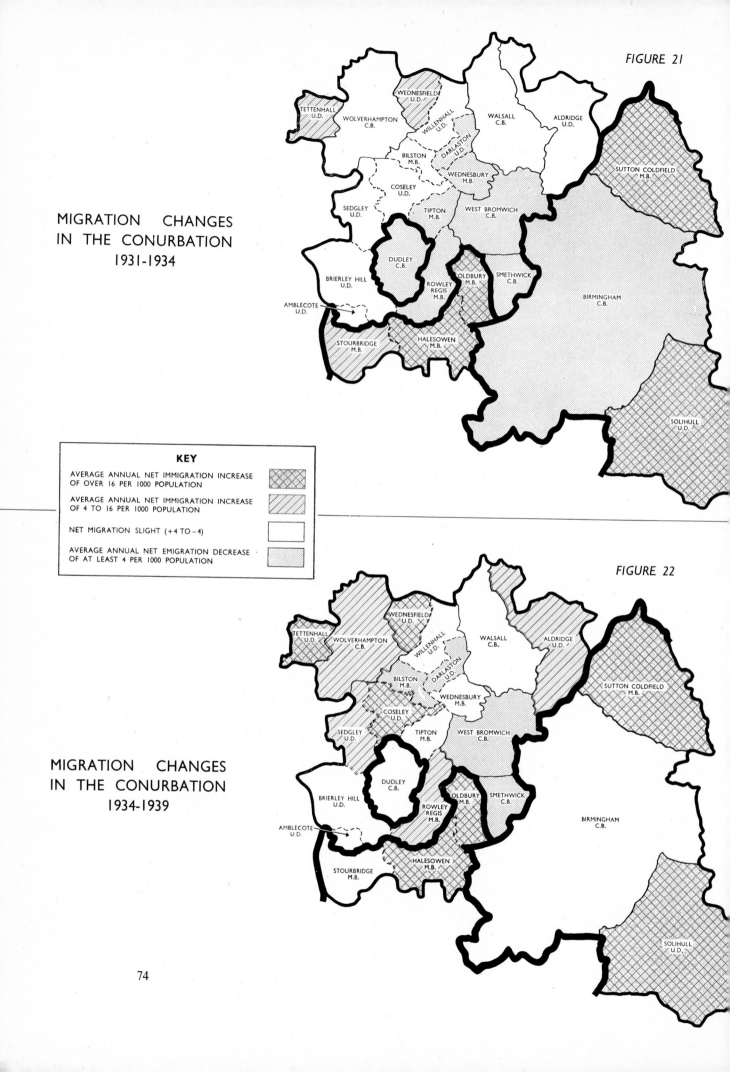

FIGURE 21

MIGRATION CHANGES
IN THE CONURBATION
1931-1934

KEY

AVERAGE ANNUAL NET IMMIGRATION INCREASE
OF OVER 16 PER 1000 POPULATION

AVERAGE ANNUAL NET IMMIGRATION INCREASE
OF 4 TO 16 PER 1000 POPULATION

NET MIGRATION SLIGHT (+4 TO –4)

AVERAGE ANNUAL NET EMIGRATION DECREASE
OF AT LEAST 4 PER 1000 POPULATION

FIGURE 22

MIGRATION CHANGES
IN THE CONURBATION
1934-1939

74

CHAPTER VI

Population[1]

THE TOTAL population of the Conurbation had passed the two million mark by mid-year 1939. The distribution and density of the population at that date within the 24 Local Authority areas of the Conurbation (see Figure 4) is given in Table VI.

ACREAGE AND POPULATION IN 1939 OF THE 24 ADMINISTRATIVE AREAS FORMING THE CONURBATION

TABLE VI

Administrative Area	Acres*	Population†	Persons per Acre
County Boroughs :			
Birmingham	51,147	1,052,900	20·6
Dudley	4,067	62,100	15·3
Smethwick	2,496	78,290	31·4
Walsall	8,780	107,600	12·3
West Bromwich	7,180	83,150	11·6
Wolverhampton	9,126	147,200	16·1
Total	82,796	1,531,240	18·5
Municipal Boroughs and Urban Districts :			
Aldridge	9,275	20,420	2·2
Amblecote	666	2,836	4·3
Bilston	1,869	31,600	16·9
Brierley Hill	5,927	47,040	7·9
Coseley	3,294	29,640	9·0
Darlaston	1,530	20,220	13·2
Halesowen	5,247	36,800	7·0
Oldbury	3,304	47,000	14·2
Rowley Regis...	3,828	44,780	11·7
Sedgley	3,848	20,700	5·4
Solihull	20,189	52,260	2·6
Stourbridge	4,214	35,310	8·4
Sutton Coldfield	13,978	38,260	2·7
Tettenhall	2,503	6,727	2·7
Tipton	2,167	37,390	17·3
Wednesbury	2,025	33,650	16·6
Wednesfield	2,515	14,540	5·8
Willenhall	2,834	28,320	10·0
Total	89,213	547,493	6·1
Total Conurbation	172,009	2,078,733	12·1

*As given in the National Register, 1939.
†Registrar-General's Mid-year Estimate.

[1] Acknowledgment is made to Dr. G. J. Walker, Professor of Economics, University of Birmingham, for the use made of his original studies in natural population increase and immigration in the area of the Conurbation.

The most outstanding increase during this century occurred in the five years before the 1939 war, when the rate of increase was as high as 21,000 persons per annum. The rates of increase for 1911-21, for 1921-31, and for the three years 1931-34, were about 14,000, 13,000, and 6,000 per annum respectively. The population trends since 1911 are

POPULATION CHANGES BY NATURAL INCREASE AND MIGRATION :
THE CONURBATION AND SURROUNDING DISTRICTS 1911-39

TABLE VII

The increases given for each period are based on the acreage of the later date. Owing to numerous boundary changes it is not possible to obtain a total increase 1921-39 on the existing acreage by adding together Cols. 1-4.)

District	POPULATION CHANGES 1911 - 1939								
	1		2		3		4		5
	Average per annum 1911–21*		Average per annum 1921–31†		Average per annum 1931–34‡		Average per annum 1934–39‡		‡Population
	Numbers	Rate per Thousand	Numbers	Rate per Thousand	Numbers	Rate per Thousand	Numbers	Rate per Thousand	1939 (Mid-year)
Conurbation Total increase ... ... Natural increase ...	13,972 18,743	8·6 11·5	12,831 15,129	7·1 8·4	6,511 9,744	3·3 5·0	21,622 11,670	11·0 6·0	2,078,733
Loss or gain by migration	−4,771	−2·9	−2,298	−1·3	−3,233	−1·7	+9,952	+5·0	
Meriden R.D., Bromsgrove U.D. and R.D.: Seisdon R.D. Total increase ... ... Natural increase ...	579 410	10·6 7·5	1,272 331	24·1 6·3	1,050 328	13·6 4·2	2,509 510	31·3 6·4	92,750
Loss or gain by migration ...	+169	+3·1	+941	+17·8	+722	+9·4	+1,999	+24·9	
Cannock U.D. and R.D. Lichfield R.D.: Tamworth R.D. Brownhills U.D. Total increase ... ... Natural increase ...	958 1,716	8·3 14·9	398 1,382	3·2 11·2	631 873	5·3 7·3	1,127 801	9·2 6·6	127,690
Loss or gain by migration	−758	−6·6	−984	−8·0	−242	−2·0	+326	+2·6	
Greater Conurbation (i.e., total of above figures) Total increase ... ... Natural increase ...	15,509 20,869	8·6 11·6	14,501 16,842	7·3 8·5	8,192 10,945	3·8 5·1	25,258 12,981	11·6 5·9	2,299,173
Loss or gain by migration	−5,360	−3·0	−2,341	−1·2	−2,753	−1·3	+12,277	+5·7	

*1921 Census : enumerated population. (The figures for this decade take no account of war casualties which appear as emigration. They amounted to 3.1 per thousand p.a. of the total adult male population.)
†1931 Census : est. mid-year resident population.
‡Registrar-General's Statistical Review : est. mid-year resident population.

analysed in Table VII to show that this population increase was neither uniform over the whole Conurbation, nor due to the same causes throughout the whole period. The two causes of change are the migration movements into and out of the area, and the rate of natural increase, *i.e.*, excess of births over deaths. The Registrar-General's Statistical Review shows that the annual net increases up to about 1934 were due to a high rate of natural increase and that this was only partially offset by a net loss by emigration which amounted to approximately 80,000 persons between 1911 and 1934. (War casualties amounting to 3.1 per cent. of adult male population for the period 1911-21 have been included as emigration, so that the actual emigration was slightly less than appears from the figures of Table VII). The fall that occurred in the rates of net increase over the period thus reflect the declining trend—both national and local—in the rates of natural increase. From 1934-39 the position was changed. The Conurbation as a whole was increasing, not only through natural increase but also by a net immigration. Since the change in migration trends more than offset the decline in the annual rates of natural increase, the average rate of total increase for the five years preceding the war rose to 11.0 persons per thousand.

The effects of both migration and natural increase trends will have to be considered in detail, as they are important in estimating future population tendencies. Upon these figures depend calculations of overall densities, housing, employment, school and amenity requirements.

Migration Changes

The change in migration movements which occurred around 1934 is clear from the figures given in Table VII. From 1911 to 1934 the area was losing steadily by migration, and even during the 1931-34 period the average annual net emigration was as much as 3,233 persons. After 1934, however, immigration figures show an annual average of 9,952 persons up to the middle of 1939. Over this period the total net gain by immigration was almost 50,000 persons.

The estimated migration changes inside the Conurbation for the periods 1931-34 and 1934-39 are shown in Figures 21 and 22, but these do not illustrate the movement from the centre to the outer suburbs within Birmingham, Wolverhampton, and Walsall, as changes can only be calculated by considering Local Authority areas as a whole. A general movement from the central areas of the Black Country is evident. Seven administrative Black Country areas, including the County Boroughs of Smethwick, West Bromwich, and Dudley, were losing by emigration in 1931-34 at a rate higher than four per thousand.

This emigration was partially offset by the immigration increases in the outer areas of the Conurbation, especially in Sutton Coldfield and Solihull, and in the rural areas lying outside the Conurbation to the east and south. It is evident, however, from Table VII, which gives figures for the "Greater Conurbation," that only a small part of the exodus from the centre could have been absorbed by the Conurbation's outlying areas. It was only in the southerly areas, namely Meriden R.D., Bromsgrove U.D. and R.D., and Seisdon R.D., that immigration increase occurred over the periods 1911-21 and 1921-31. This was more than offset by the emigration from the northerly mining district of Cannock U.D. and R.D., Lichfield R.D., Tamworth R.D. and Brownhills U.D. These northern areas showed an immigration increase only after 1934, as did the conurbation generally.

Migration movement shows a net increase for the period 1934-39, and the only areas which showed a substantial loss by emigration were the County Boroughs of West Bromwich and Smethwick and the smaller districts of Bilston and Darlaston (see Figure 22).

NATURAL INCREASE

The rates of natural increase have been declining both nationally and locally over the present century. Comparative figures of average annual increase by excess of births over deaths are given in Table IX for the Conurbation, England and Wales and other districts.

Forecasts of the future population of the country, based on this slowing down in the rate of natural increase, suggest that the national population is approaching a temporary stability which will be followed by a decline. The maximum population, it is said, will probably be reached about 1950, after which it will start to decline. This decline will be slow at first but will become more rapid. The total population in 1970 is not likely to be very much less than the present population, though its composition will have changed; the numbers of children under 15 will have decreased while the number of old people over 65 will have increased[1].

THE REGISTRAR-GENERAL'S FORECAST OF THE TOTAL FUTURE POPULATION OF GREAT BRITAIN

(From the Report of the Royal Commission on the Distribution of the Industrial Population, 1940.)

TABLE VIII

Actual Population	Forecast population			
1937	1941	1951	1961	1971
46,008,000	46,565,000	47,501,000	47,192,000	45,980,000
Deviation*	$\pm$ 25,000	$\pm$ 280,000	$\pm$ 805,000	$\pm$ 1,579,000
Rise or fall on 1937	+ 1·2%	+ 3·2%	+ 2·6%	— 0·6%

*Adjustments to be made, *plus* or *minus*, to allow for the most favourable or least favourable situations respectively.

The Barlow Report estimate of future population given in Table VIII is based on the probable trend as between the most favourable and least favourable estimates of the future trend. The least favourable estimate assumes a 10 per cent. fall in fertility rates and a 10 per cent. rise in mortality rates, over the period 1937-71. The most favourable estimate assumes a 10 per cent. rise in fertility rates and a 10 per cent. fall in mortality. The *plus* or *minus* deviations under each figure in the table represent these two possibilities. This forecast has been criticized by other experts, but there is general agreement that the maximum population will be reached about 1950, and that it will subsequently decline.

The rate of natural increase both influences and is affected by changes in the age-structure of the population. If the rate of natural increase is declining, and the younger age-groups are forming a smaller proportion of the population, the future population will have a smaller proportion in the reproductive age-groups; consequently, the rate of natural increase will fall still lower. Unless, therefore, there is a rise in fertility rates or in marriage rates, the downward trend will continue, and the age-structure of the population will become increasingly older.

---

[1] An estimate of the number of families living in Birmingham in 1939 and of the number of families which will be found in Birmingham in 1971 has been made by Dr. M. Abrams, and is printed as an Appendix to this Chapter.

FIGURE 23

THE CHANGING AGE-STRUCTURE OF THE POPULATION
ENGLAND AND WALES

1921 —— 1931 —— 1939

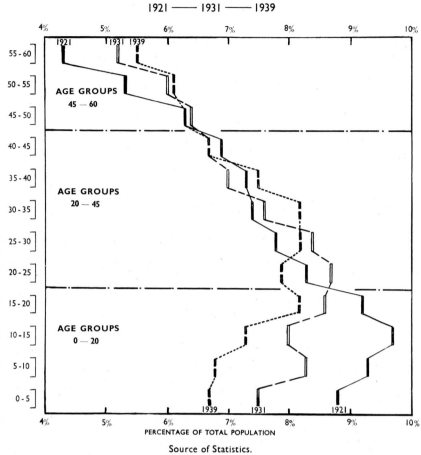

The decline in the rate of increase is reflected in the decreasing proportion of the population included in the lower age groups. As these decreasing proportions enter the reproductive age groups, the decline in the birth-rate may be expected to become steeper.

Source of Statistics.

1921—Census of Population.

1931— Census of Population.

1939—Estimate :   Based on National Register (September 29th, 1939) and adjusted to include all persons in H.M. Forces.

The changing age-structure of the population of England and Wales 1921-39 is illustrated diagrammatically in Figure 23. The three curves show that the proportion in the 0-5 age-group has formed a declining proportion of the total population since 1921, indicating the decline in the birth-rate. The change in the proportion in this age-group would have been even more noticeable if population trends had not been upset by the first World War 1914-18. The birth-rate over that period fell temporarily and then rose again with the return of the men from the Forces. This disturbance in the trends can be seen in the curve for 1931 : the 0-5 age-group had by that time become the 10-15 group, and the higher birth-rate following the war is indicated by a higher proportion in the 5-10 group. The figures for 1921 and 1931 have been taken direct from the Census of Population for these years ; those for 1939 have been estimated from the figures given in the National Register, September 29th 1939, and adjustment has been made to allow for persons in the Forces who were not included in the Register.

The national trends in the future population will not become evident simultaneously in all parts of the country, nor with the same degree of rise and fall, as differential fertility rates and migration movements both affect the age-structure of any particular district.

Comparison of Tables IX and X shows a correlation of trends in natural increase and migration with age-structure of the population in different districts. For example, the high fertility of the mining districts is indicated by the comparatively high proportion of the 0-20 group in the Durham-Northumberland district and in the Black Country in 1921. From the Durham-Northumberland district, however, there has been large emigration of people seeking employment, and this is reflected in the relatively low proportion of its population in the 20-45 age-group. On the other hand, the large numbers of people of working age who have been crowding in to the Greater London area have given it a higher proportion in the 20-45 groups (*i.e.*, in the reproductive age-groups) than in any other of the districts instanced. Consequently, the rate of natural increase for that area has been maintained above the average for England and Wales. In the south-west counties the trend towards an older population has been brought about by low rates of natural increase and a low proportion of the population in the younger and reproductive age-groups; and this trend has not been disturbed by migration.

RATES OF NET INCREASE BY BIRTHS OVER DEATHS AND BY IMMIGRATION
IN SELECTED DISTRICTS 1921-31-39

TABLE IX

| DISTRICT | Average net increase p.a. per thousand population | | | | | |
| | 1921–31 | | | 1931–39 | | |
	By births over deaths	By net immigration*	Total net increase	By births over deaths	By net immigration*	Total net increase
England and Wales	6·0	−0·4	5·6	2·8	1·8	4·6
†Greater London	6·1	3·2	9·3	3·4	4·6	8·0
Conurbation	8·4	−1·3	7·1	5·7	3·8	9·5
‡Black Country	10·6	−6·1	4·5	7·0	−2·0	5·0
Durham and Northumberland	9·7	−9·2	0·5	4·8	−7·4	−2·6
S. West Counties	3·4	1·0	4·4	0·5	1·7	2·2

*Net decrease through migration shown as a minus increase.
†Area of 15 miles radius round the centre of London.
‡For statistical purposes, the administrative areas included in Area II in Figure 27. These figures are also incorporated in those for the total Conurbation shown on the line above.

Figures 24 and 25 show diagrammatically the differences in age-structure of the populations of the Conurbation, the Black Country, the London district, and England and Wales in 1921 and 1931. Figure 26 estimates the age-structure for 1939, but, unlike Figure 23, makes no allowance for the Forces personnel excluded from the National Register. This exclusion of persons in the Forces gives an abnormally low proportion in the 20-25 age-group, and for the Conurbation the proportions are distorted by the evacuation of young children. However, Figure 26 serves to show that in 1939 the population of the Conurbation, and especially of the Black Country, was still younger than average for the country.

The fact that the Conurbation shows a higher proportion in the younger age-groups than the average for England and Wales is indeed due to the inclusion of the Black Country. In the Birmingham area the population, age-structure, and rates of natural increase have been very similar to the country as a whole. But in the Black Country, as in the Durham-Northumberland district, higher fertility rates and larger families maintained the comparatively high rates of natural increase between 1931-1939, in spite of emigration. The actual difference in the average size of family, an important factor in estimating housing requirements, is calculated in the next chapter.

Table IX shows how the total net increase figures are made up of the net increases by births over deaths, and by immigration (or emigration). For example, the total net increase in England and Wales during 1931-9 was 4.6 per thousand per annum, while the population of the Conurbation increased by the balance of births over deaths alone by 5.7 per thousand per annum. In addition to this greater rate of natural increase, the Conurbation had a net immigration rate of 3.8 per thousand per annum. Though it is unlikely that national rates of change will prove to be the same after 1945 as they were before 1939, it is probable that the Conurbation will maintain its relatively higher rate of natural increase, because apart from general changes in fertility, marriage and death rates, which affect both the nation and the Conurbation, the population in the Conurbation in 1939 was younger than average. We shall, therefore, continue to see the Conurbation growing relatively to the rest of the country. This consequence of the higher rate of increase can only be offset by relative changes in fertility (which are unlikely to reverse their present relation, or to be big enough to make much difference), or by emigration from the Conurbation, or by immigration from abroad to the country as a whole but not to the Conurbation.

THE PROPORTION OF THE POPULATION IN THE YOUNGER AGE-GROUPS
IN SELECTED DISTRICTS 1921 & 1931

TABLE X

DISTRICT	Percentage of the total population in specified age groups					
	1921			1931		
	0–20	20–45	Total 0–45	0–20	20–45	Total 0–45
England and Wales	37·0	37·7	74·7	32·4	38·4	70·8
London and 5 surrounding Counties (1921)	35·9	38·3	74·2	31·0	39·9	70·9
†Greater London (1931)	**	**	**	30·9	40·7	71·6
Conurbation	39·4	37·9	77·3	34·9	39·0	73·9
‡Black Country	42·7	36·3	79·0	38·0	38·0	76·3
Durham and Northumberland	42·2	36·4	78·9	37·6	36·8	74·4
S. West Counties	33·7	36·4	70·1	29·9	36·8	66·7

**Statistics not available for age-structure in 1921.
†Area of 15 miles radius round the centre of London.
‡For statistical purposes, the administrative areas included in Area II in Figure 27. These figures are also incorporated in those for the total Conurbation shown on the line above.

DISTRIBUTION OF THE POPULATION

The geographical distribution of the population is seen most clearly in Figure 37 showing the housing areas. For statistical calculations of increases and distribution both in population and housing, the Conurbation has been divided into the three areas shown in Figure 27. Area I comprises Birmingham and Smethwick—between which it is difficult to draw any dividing line. Area II includes the main part of the Black Country. Area III incorporates the outer

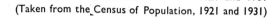

THE POPULATION AGE-STRUCTURE OF THE BLACK COUNTRY AND THE
WHOLE CONURBATION COMPARED WITH ENGLAND AND WALES AND
THE LONDON DISTRICT   1921 and 1931
(Taken from the Census of Population, 1921 and 1931)

FIGURE 24

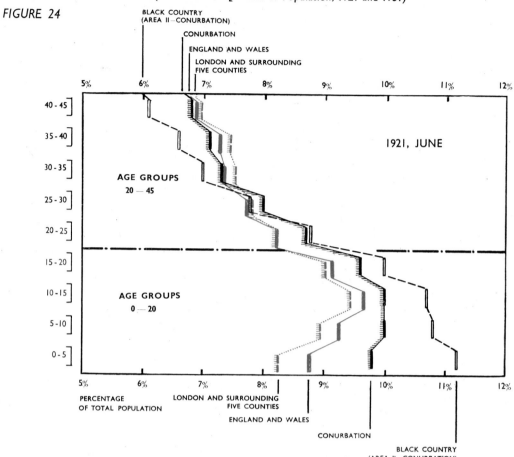

FIGURE 25

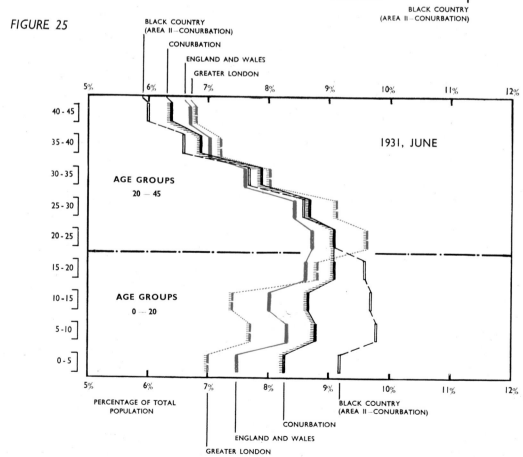

FIGURE 26

THE ESTIMATED POPULATION AGE-STRUCTURE OF THE BLACK COUNTRY
AND THE WHOLE CONURBATION COMPARED WITH
ENGLAND AND WALES—1939

Based on the National Register, September 29th, 1939.   The census included only
persons in H.M. Forces if they were home on leave at that date.   The Percentage fall in
the 5 - 10 age group in the Conurbation indicates the evacuation of children.

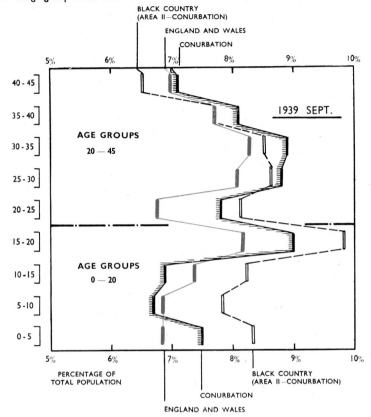

districts of the Conurbation, which are shown in Figures 21 and 22 as having absorbed, almost entirely, the immigration increase between 1931 and 1939.   Area III is also the only one of the three areas which appears definitely to have had a further net immigration increase over the war years 1939-45 (see Table XVII, Chapter VII).   At the same time, this area incorporates a relatively large part of the land which should be left free from urban development and retained as part of the Green Setting of the Conurbation (see Chapter XIII and Figures 40 and 41).

As already stated, the population of the Conurbation in 1939 was just over two million, according to the Registrar-General's mid-year estimate.   About 54 per cent. was concentrated in Area I (Birmingham and Smethwick), where the density was 21.1 persons per acre.   The density of the main Black Country was much lower, being only 12.1 persons per acre.   Table XI gives figures in detail.

The Black Country (Area II), however, has had a lower proportion of the between-war housing than the Outer Districts (see Table XIV, Chapter VII), which reflects the tendency for new development to move outwards.   The main responsibility for this outward spread may be traced to the scattered unplanned development of the central areas in the past, to the large areas of land left derelict by industry, and to the general lack of amenities.   Unless there is a planned scheme for redevelopment of these older areas, there will be a further spread of the population that will encroach on those surrounding areas of green land, the reservation of which is so important for agricultural and recreational purposes.

A comprehensive plan for the whole Conurbation could provide accommodation within its present overall area for such population increase as is likely to occur through natural increase, and, at the same time, provide sufficient space for the Green Setting proposed in Chapter XIII. But any population increase greater than this would imply the relative growth of an area which is already large enough, together with the industrial decay of developed areas in other parts of the country and the subsequent decline of morale, the waste of capital and skill, and all the ills that spring up in a depressed area.

FIGURE 27   THREE AREAS OF THE CONURBATION

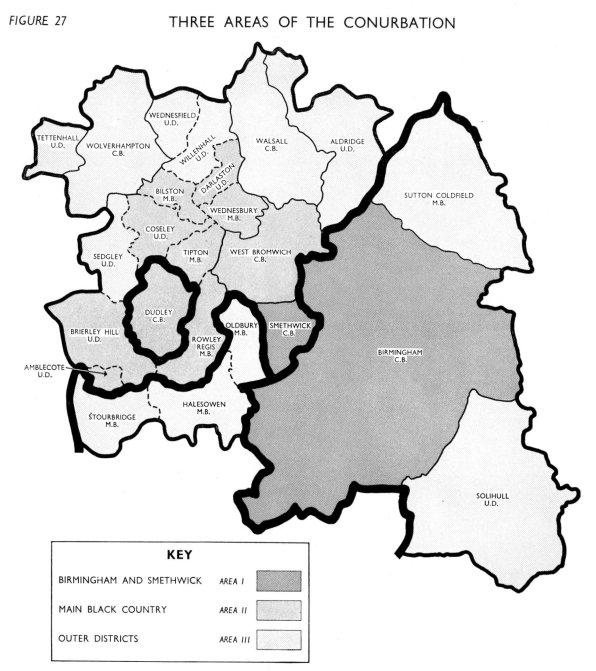

This division of the total area of the Conurbation into three has been made so as to elucidate tendencies in growth of population and distribution of housing. The Areas I, II and III in this map are referred to in Tables XI, XIV, XV, XVI and XVII.

The West Midland Group therefore advocates that the population of the Conurbation should be allowed to grow only to the extent that will arise through the natural balance of births over deaths. As has already been pointed out, this is somewhat greater than the national rate on account of the higher fertility rates. In the opinion of the Group, efforts should be made through control of industry (see Chapter VIII) to prevent a net immigration increase such as occurred over the pre-war period 1934-39.

THE POPULATION (1939) AND AREA IN SQUARE MILES OF AREAS I, II AND III

TABLE XI

THE THREE AREAS OF THE CONURBATION	Population (Mid-year estimate 1939)		Area in Sq. Miles	Persons per acre
	Nos.	Percentage of Conurbation Total		
Area I (Birmingham & Smethwick)	1,131,190	54	84	21·1
Area II (Main Black Country)	392,406	19	51	12·1
Area III (Outer Districts)	555,137	27	134	6·5
Total Conurbation	2,078,733	100	269	12·7

SUMMARY

The population of the Conurbation was increasing over the first forty years of this century at a rate far higher than occurred over the country as a whole. Up to about 1934, this expansion was caused by high fertility rates rather than by the influx of people from other places. It was only over the few years prior to the 1939 war that immigration into the area was also responsible for substantial increases.

It seems likely that the Conurbation will continue to have a rate of growth higher than the national rate, though both national and local rates of increase are slowing down. It is expected that the national population will soon reach a peak and then decline. The population of the Conurbation will continue for a time to increase by natural causes, but this increase will sooner or later cease. Just before the war, immigration accounted for nearly as many additional people as came by natural increase, and this factor may continue, diminish, or increase, quite independently of the birthrate. Conservatively, it may be said that over the period 1940-1970 an average addition of 5 per thousand per annum is a possible contingency. In other words, by 1970 the population of the Conurbation may have increased by 300,000 unless some measure of control over immigration is exercised.

Within the present area of the Conurbation two million people can be housed at reasonable density, and a good measure of open space and undeveloped land retained. If the population rises much higher than this, the future Conurbation will be spoilt by encroachment on the surrounding agricultural areas and other open land, in order to meet temporary and local needs, which may not be valid in fifty years time—when the downward trend may have been well established, or when the national population has been stabilised at a lower figure than now. National arguments are even stronger than local arguments for preventing further substantial increase in the population of the Conurbation.

As a result of analysis of past trends and the present position, the West Midland Group recommends that the population of the Conurbation should be allowed to continue to grow, but only to the extent that will arise through the natural balance of births over deaths. There will, of course, be immigration and emigration, but these should as far as possible balance each other. In other words, no pressure should be brought to bear on Local Authorities and industrialists to cause a net emigration from the Conurbation, but every effort should be made in the other direction to prevent any increase occurring through net immigration.

Appendix to Chapter VI

ESTIMATED NUMBER OF FAMILIES, BIRMINGHAM. 1939 & 1971.

At mid-1939 the estimated population of Birmingham was, in round figures, 1,050,000 (including temporary absentees). Its composition was as follows :—

				Per Cent. of Total.
Children 0–14	..	..	195,000	18.6
Males 15–29	..	..	140,000	13.3
„ 30–44	..	..	130,000	12.4
„ 45–64	..	..	105,000	10.0
Females 15–29	..	..	140,000	13.3
„ 30–44	..	..	135,000	12.9
„ 45–64	..	..	125,000	11.9
Persons, 65 and over	..	80,000	7.6
			1,050,000	100.0

Approximately 50,000 of these were living in institutions, hotels, schools, etc., and the remaining 1,000,000 constituted 285,000 families.

On the assumption that the present population within the city boundaries is not affected by either emigration or immigration and that the trends in fertility rates and mortality rates of the past ten years are maintained, then by 1971 their numbers will have fallen slightly—to 1,000,000. Their composition will be :—

				Per Cent. of Total.
Children 0–14	..	..	160,000	16.0
Males 15–29	..	..	100,000	10.0
„ 30–44	..	..	90,000	9.0
„ 45–64	..	..	140,000	14.0
Females 15–29	..	..	100,000	10.0
„ 30–44	..	..	95,000	9.5
„ 45–64	..	..	160,000	16.0
Persons, 65 and over	..	155,000	15.5
			1,000,000	100.0

Again, some 5 per cent. of these will presumably be living in institutions, etc., and the balance, assuming marriage rates are the same as today, will be living in 305,000 family units—an increase of 25,000 as compared with 1939.

CHAPTER VII

Housing

THE RELATION between the growth and distribution of population and housing is so close that the two cannot be considered separately. This chapter is, therefore, the complement of Chapter VI.

The distribution of settlement in Birmingham and the Black Country is shown in the Distribution Map of housing and social centres (Figure 37). The sample maps from the Housing Survey (Plates 1 and 2) reveal in detail how different types of housing are distributed in Birmingham on the one hand, and in the Black Country on the other. The old slum and near-slum areas are represented on the sample maps by the red and purple sections, while the areas of better houses, including housing estates of the post-1918 development schemes, are shown in blue and yellow. The two maps bring out the striking difference in the pattern of housing development in Birmingham and the Black Country. Plate 1 shows the consistent outward spread of Birmingham from its central core, now devoted to commerce and industry. Plate 2, on the other hand, illustrates the comparatively scattered development of the Black Country, where numerous small centres, based originally on local supplies of coal and iron ore, have grown individually. All the coloured areas—red, purple, blue and yellow—shown on the sample Housing Maps correspond to the yellow areas on the Surface Utilisation Map. (See for example Plates 10 and 11).

The extent of the areas coloured red and purple in the sample sheets of the Housing Survey is witness to the outstanding need for slum clearance, a need made more urgent by the cessation of building during the war.

Yet any future housing programme must not only take into account the number of houses necessary to replace unfit dwellings, but also calculate the additional number required to meet population growth and the gradual increase in the number of families. This chapter makes an assessment of such replacements and additions.

REPLACEMENT OF UNFIT DWELLINGS

In assessing the immediate and future replacement of existing bad houses, the Group carried out a visual survey of the Conurbation. This was undertaken in its entirety by one investigator so that the standard of assessment should be uniform over the whole area. The same method and standards were used as in the Group's survey of Herefordshire.* The houses were classified as follows:—

Category I—Houses classified for replacement

Type 1   Property which should be condemned as insanitary under the Housing Acts
(*Red*)   and is, therefore, ripe for demolition.

---

* *English County*, Faber and Faber, 1946.

A

B

C

D

HOUSING

E 1 HOUSING (A)

e sub-standard houses are usually structurally
ctive and all are 70 or more years old.
he larger towns the density may be sixty
ore to the net acre (excluding roads and other
ic spaces). Bomb damage has cleared sufficient
nd for the layout of the block of back-to-backs
n to be appreciated. The one block contains
separate houses, four facing the street on the
and four facing the court. All eight use the
t with its communal lavatory and stand-pipe.

E 2 HOUSING (B)

Structurally rather better than those of Type 1
without major sanitary defects. They are,
ever, usually crowded together and are below
ern standards. Sheer badness of siting and
ut are often the worst defects in houses of this
Type 2 houses are identified as those which
ld be replaced immediately after the completion
lum clearance programmes.

E 3 HOUSING (C)

Type 3 includes houses which are reasonably
fortable dwellings and are structurally sound.
ertheless, when shortages are made good and
e urgent replacement programmes completed,
is, in perhaps 30 to 50 years' time, they will be
lete and should be cleared and replaced.

USES BUILT BETWEEN THE WARS (D)

Not classified for replacement. Those shown
he left-hand photograph are part of a municipal
te of 2,600 houses. The houses in the other
tograph are typical of those built by private
rprise. The appeal of the privately-built, low-
house often lies in the ornamented brickwork
ront of the garden, and a more popular arrange-
t of interior space.

PROBLEM HOUSING

The four photographs on this page reveal some
special problems of the Black Country which face
those responsible for housing.

(E) These cottages at Bilston are representative of
slum conditions of a degree of insanitary squalor
now rarely met in the Conurbation. Some of the
living rooms had earth floors. The new dwellings of
the borough's rehousing programme are close by.

(F) The effect of mining subsidence. Hundreds of
acres of land in the Black Country are undermined
by disused colliery workings. Precautions against
damage by subsidence raise the cost of building.

(G) Factories—terrace housing—undeveloped land—
derelict land.

(H) Smethwick. The Conurbation has 40 per cent.
of its area undeveloped. Smethwick has only 1.2
per cent. The site of this temporary housing scheme
is on a narrow strip of land between two canal
cuttings, one of which is shown here.

Type 2　Similar houses, but of a somewhat better standard than those of Type 1, which
(*Purple*)　would not normally be condemned, but which should be replaced immediately
　　　　the slum clearance is complete.

Type 3　Reasonably comfortable houses, which would not normally be taken down as
(*Blue*)　part of any immediate re-planning scheme, but which in thirty to fifty years'
　　　　time will be ripe for demolition because of the age of the structures and the
　　　　monotony of the street layout.

Category II—Houses not classified for replacement
Type A　Old houses of historical or other interest sufficient to justify their repair and
　　　　preservation.　(The number of these is negligible in the Conurbation and
　　　　where any exist, they have, for purposes of the Tables, been included in Type
　　　　B).

Type B　Houses built before 1918 which are in good or reasonably good condition
(*Yellow*)　and are of a satisfactory type.

Type C　Houses built between 1918 and 1945.
(*Yellow*)

Examples of these types as they occur in the Conurbation are shown in the photographs
on the two previous pages.

The findings of the survey have been mapped on 6-in. scale Ordnance Survey sheets
covering the whole area—in all 64 sheets.　Red, purple and blue have been used to dis-
tinguish houses of Types 1, 2 and 3 respectively.　Samples of four of these ordnance
sheets have been reproduced on a small scale in Plates 10 and 11, showing central areas
both in Birmingham and in the Black Country.

These detailed maps are intended to provide each Local Authority with a standard
basis which will be of assistance in formulating its redevelopment programme.　Not only
can the worst housing areas be seen immediately, but a long-term programme can best
be prepared when the sequence in which neighbouring areas should be redeveloped is
known.

In most of the older centres, factories and other premises, as well as houses, are in a
poor condition.　The maps illustrating the Factory Survey, Chapter IX, show that the
areas of poor factories and poor houses often coincide (see also Plates 5 and 15).　To
decide the order in which areas should be re-developed, it is necessary to take into account
the condition of both houses and factory premises, as in many areas factories and houses
have been erected haphazard, without plan for either in view.　The areas generally covered
by housing and by industry are shown by Figures 36 and 37, but the scale of these maps
is too small to show the numerous small factories which occur on sites where housing
predominates.

The problem of bad houses has been so acute in some areas that Local Authorities,
notably Smethwick and Oldbury, have undertaken extensive reconditioning in some of
their worst districts.　As a temporary and speedy remedy this has been successful.　But
where Type 1 houses have been reconditioned, and supplied with damp courses, bathroom
and separate W.C., they are still classified as Type 2 by the West Midland Group, since
they are usually poor in design and layout, and are not fit to remain in use for more than
fifteen to twenty years.

A properly planned urban centre may well have a high density of dwellings; for example, a proportion of well-planned flats is an advantage. In the Conurbation, twenty to thirty dwellings per acre is a common standard even for the smaller urban centres, but the high density of these old types of houses was achieved by crowding them together on the ground. Many were built back-to-back and around courts, and were usually provided with only communal W.C. and washing facilities. It was disclosed in the Birmingham Survey of 1946 that out of 300,000 houses in Birmingham there were still about 29,000 back-to-back houses, built during the latter half of the 19th century. (See *Public Health Committee: Report on the Housing Survey, 1946*, City of Birmingham).

The statistical results of the Group's Housing survey are given in Tables XII and XIII.

ESTIMATED NUMBER OF HOUSES CLASSIFIED* AS TYPES 1, 2 & 3 AND THEIR DENSITY PER ACRE IN EACH ADMINISTRATIVE AREA : 1945

TABLE XII

ADMINISTRATIVE AREA	TYPE 1*			TYPE 2*			TYPE 3*			Total types 1, 2, & 3	
	Acres †	Houses	Av. density per acre	Acres †	Houses	Av. density per acre	Acres †	Houses	Av. density per acre	Acres	Houses
County Boroughs :											
Birmingham **	1,600	63,400	40	1,600	45,400	28	2,400	46,200	19	5,600	155,000
Dudley	140	4,600	33	84	2,000	24	82	1,500	18	306	8,100
Smethwick	27	650	24	197	5,350	27	505	9,600	19	729	15,600
Walsall	147	4,100	28	382	7,700	20	244	3,800	16	773	15,600
West Bromwich ...	180	5,200	29	169	3,600	21	146	2,500	17	495	11,300
Wolverhampton ...	83	2,600	31	479	11,100	23	113	1,800	16	675	15,500
TOTALS	2,177	80,550	37	2,911	75,150	26	3,490	65,400	19	8,578	221,100
Municipal Boroughs and Urban Districts:											
Aldridge	37	600	16	36	500	14	29	350	12	102	1,450
Amblecote	5	130	26	10	160	16	11	180	17	26	470
Bilston	80	2,100	26	37	850	23	52	850	16	169	3,800
Brierley Hill	92	1,500	16	225	3,400	15	158	1,500	10	475	6,400
Coseley	114	2,900	25	39	800	21	48	700	15	201	4,400
Darlaston	74	1,700	23	26	550	21	27	450	17	127	2,700
Halesowen	45	1,200	27	104	2,300	22	98	1,550	16	247	5,050
Oldbury	61	2,000	33	59	1,700	29	92	1,600	17	212	5,300
Rowley Regis	118	2,450	21	135	2,150	16	78	1,000	13	331	5,600
Sedgley	64	1,350	21	61	900	15	31	400	13	156	2,650
Solihull	–‡	10	25	32	420	13	46	580	13	78	1,010
Stourbridge	61	1,500	25	66	1,400	21	79	1,100	14	206	4,000
Sutton Coldfield ...	1	20	20	57	580	10	118	1,500	13	176	2,100
Tettenhall	7	100	14	23	300	13	37	400	11	67	800
Tipton	87	2,000	23	73	1,100	15	49	650	13	209	3,750
Wednesbury	25	700	28	104	2,100	20	39	700	18	168	3,500
Wednesfield	30	570	19	13	230	18	31	450	14	74	1,250
Willenhall	55	2,000	36	33	750	23	40	770	19	128	3,520
TOTALS	956	22,830	24	1,133	20,190	18	1,063	14,730	14	3,152	57,750
GRAND TOTALS ...	3,133	103,380	33	4,044	95,340	24	4,553	80,130	18	11,730	278,850

*Explanation of classification is given on pages 87 and 90.
†Acres calculated by taking plot on which the houses stand plus half the area of adjacent roads.
**For calculation of housing densities no deduction has been made for houses destroyed beyond repair through enemy action. This number has been estimated as 12,000 in Birmingham of which at least 75 per cent. were either of Types 1 or 2. In the other areas the numbers are too small to affect the estimates.
‡Actually 0·4 acres.

The numbers of houses classified into Types 1, 2 and 3, and their density per acre for each Local Authority area, are given in Table XII. It will be seen that as many as a third of all the houses in the Conurbation are of Types 1 and 2.

The County Boroughs have, on the whole, a higher density in each type—as would be expected of the more closely-packed centres where land is scarce. There is a preponderance of Type 1 houses, at an average of 24 houses per acre, and the density of these is fairly consistent among the Municipal Boroughs and Urban Districts, though it is exceptionally high in the old parts of Oldbury and Willenhall. In the County Boroughs the lowest density is 29 houses per acre and the highest 40 per acre. In both Smethwick and Oldbury, where there has been a considerable amount of reconditioning, many houses which would

OLDER HOUSES AND POST-1918 HOUSES IN EACH ADMINISTRATIVE AREA, 1945

TABLE XIII

ADMINISTRATIVE AREA	OLDER HOUSES*		POST-1918 HOUSES*	Total (All Houses) ‡
	Types 1, 2 & 3 (Last col. Table XII) †	Type B †	Type C ‡	
County Boroughs : ...				
Birmingham	155,000	29,000	113,600	297,600
Dudley	8,100	800	7,600	16,500
Smethwick	15,600	1,200	4,600	21,400
Walsall	15,600	2,100	11,200	28,900
West Bromwich ...	11,300	1,500	9,000	21,800
Wolverhampton ...	15,500	5,500	20,300	41,300
TOTALS	221,100	40,100	166,300	427,500
Municipal Boroughs and Urban Districts :				
Aldridge	1,450	650	5,000	7,100
Amblecote	470	180	200	850
Bilston	3,800	350	3,650	7,800
Brierley Hill	6,400	1,100	5,500	13,000
Coseley	4,400	250	3,850	8,500
Darlaston	2,700	250	2,250	5,200
Halesowen	5,050	800	5,150	11,000
Oldbury	5,300	400	8,200	13,900
Rowley Regis	5,600	500	6,600	12,700
Sedgley	2,650	450	2,900	6,000
Solihull	1,010	2,440	14,950	18,400
Stourbridge	4,000	2,400	4,000	10,400
Sutton Coldfield ...	2,100	2,900	7,900	12,900
Tettenhall	800	550	850	2,200
Tipton	3,750	400	5,100	9,250
Wednesbury	3,500	650	4,300	8,450
Wednesfield	1,250	200	2,800	4,250
Willenhall	3,520	180	4,600	8,300
TOTALS	57,750	14,650	87,800	160,200
	278,850	54,750		
GRAND TOTALS ...	333,600		254,100	587,700

* Explanation of classification is given on pages 87 and 90.
† West Midland Group estimates.
‡ As supplied by the Local Rating Officers (figures taken to the nearest 50).

otherwise have been classified as Type 1 are included under Type 2, which consequently shows a comparatively high density.

The proportion of the total houses which the different types form within each Local Authority area is shown in Table XIV. The different areas have been grouped into Areas I, II and III (shown in Figure 27) for closer correlation with the statistics of the population movements described in Chapter VI.

The redistribution of the population caused by the overall increase in the Conurbation and by dispersion from the congested central areas, is reflected in the number of houses built within the different parts of the Conurbation since 1918 (see Table XIII). For example, it can be seen that Area III (see Figure 27) contains a more than proportionate share of the new houses. This is mainly attributable to the large building expansion in Solihull, Sutton Coldfield, Aldridge, Wednesfield, and Oldbury; and, as a natural consequence, population in these areas, with the exception of Aldridge, has increased by immigration since 1931, as is shown by Figures 21 and 22. In the central Black Country areas there has long been a shortage of land available for building. Of the whole Conurbation area, about 50 per cent is potential building land. But the distribution is uneven, and it is evident that several Local Authorities, such as Smethwick, Bilston, Darlaston, Tipton, and Wednesbury, cannot develop new housing in their area unless existing houses are pulled down, or derelict land is reclaimed. The shortage of building land has been particularly acute in Smethwick; it is not surprising, therefore, that Smethwick shows a lower percentage of post-1918 (Type C) houses than any other area. In fact nearly 1,000 houses were recently built by the Smethwick Corporation within the area of the Borough of Oldbury.

The central Black Country areas contain the highest proportion of slum houses. A quarter of the total number of houses in Dudley, Darlaston, Bilston, and Coseley are of Type 1, the worst slum type. Within Area III however, there are only two Local Authority areas—Sedgley and Willenhall—with more than 15 per cent slum houses. These two areas are partly rural and partly urban.

Birmingham, with Smethwick, contains 319,000 out of the Conurbation total of 587,700 houses (i.e., 54.2 per cent). In general, Types 1 and 2 houses are concentrated within the city centre, but there are groups of such houses forming the centre of most of the older suburbs. Type 3 houses form a " middle ring," stretching westwards to include Smethwick. The " outer ring," in which the newer housing estates have been sited, stretches north, south and east to the city boundary[1].

It can be seen from Table XIV that, in spite of the slum clearance achieved before the war, the Conurbation area as a whole still contained in 1945 as many as 103,380 slum (Type 1) houses, and a further 95,350 borderline slum (Type 2) houses. In other words, over one-third of all the houses in the Conurbation require replacement as soon as possible.

During the war, more than 12,000 houses were destroyed or seriously damaged by bombing. These were nearly all in the Birmingham area. They were mostly in the category of Type 1, and are included in the 103,380 given above.

NEW DEMAND DUE TO POPULATION GROWTH AND INCREASE IN THE NUMBER OF FAMILIES

Apart from replacement of houses demolished in slum clearance or for other reasons, the main demand for new houses arises from increase in the population and in the number of families. In any particular area, this growth is affected by population changes due to

---

[1] A description and illustrations of types of housing in Birmingham are given in *When We Build Again* (Allen and Unwin, 1941).

migration and natural causes, and by national trends bringing about changes in family structure.

Population growth. It has been shown in Chapter VI that the migration trend from

THE PROPORTION OF HOUSES OF EACH TYPE SHOWN AS A PERCENTAGE OF THE TOTAL NUMBER OF HOUSES IN EACH LOCAL AUTHORITY AREA, 1945

TABLE XIV

AREA*	Total No. of Houses †	Percentage of each Type				
		Type 1 Houses **	Type 2 Houses **	Type 3 Houses **	Type B **	Type C (Post-1918) Houses†
Area I :		%	%	%	%	%
Birmingham	297,600	21·3	15·2	15·5	9·8	38·2
Smethwick	21,400	3·0	25·0	44·9	5·6	21·5
TOTAL (%)	100·0	20·1	15·9	17·5	9·5	37·0
Nos.	319,000	64,050	50,750	55,800	30,200	118,200
Area II :		%	%	%	%	%
Dudley	16,500	27·9	12·1	9·1	4·8	46·1
West Bromwich ...	21,800	23·8	16·5	11·5	6·9	41·3
Amblecote	850	15·3	18·8	21·2	21·2	23·5
Bilston	7,800	26·9	10·9	10·9	4·5	46·8
Brierley Hill	13,000	11·5	26·2	11·5	8·5	42·3
Coseley	8,500	34·1	9·4	8·2	3·0	45·3
Darlaston	5,200	32·7	10·6	8·6	4·8	43·3
Rowley Regis... ...	12,700	19·3	16·9	7·9	3·9	52·0
Tipton	9,250	21·6	11·9	7·0	4·3	55·2
Wednesbury	8,450	8·3	24·8	8·3	7·7	50·9
TOTAL (%)	100·0	22·4	16·1	9·6	5·7	46·2
Nos.	104,050	23,280	16,710	10,030	5,980	48,050
Area III :		%	%	%	%	%
Walsall	28,900	14·2	26·6	13·1	7·3	38·8
Wolverhampton ...	41,300	6·3	26·9	4·3	13·3	49·2
Aldridge...	7,100	8·5	7·0	4·9	9·2	70·4
Halesowen	11,000	10·9	20·9	14·1	7·3	46·8
Oldbury	13,900	14·4	12·2	11·5	2·9	59·0
Sedgley	6,000	22·5	15·0	6·7	7·5	48·3
Solihull	18,400	‡	2·3	3·1	13·3	81·3
Stourbridge	10,400	14·4	13·4	10·6	23·1	38·5
Sutton Coldfield ...	12,900	‡	4·5	11·6	27·9	76·0
Tettenhall	2,200	4·5	13·6	18·2	25·0	38·7
Wednesfield	4,250	13·4	5·4	10·6	4·7	65·9
Willenhall	8,300	24·1	9·0	9·3	2·2	55·4
TOTAL (%)	100·0	9·7	16·9	8·7	11·3	53·4
Nos.	164,650	16,050	27,880	14,300	18,570	87,850
Total Conurbation % ...	100·0	17·6	16·2	13·6	9·3	43·3
Nos.	587,700	103,380	95,340	80,130	54,750	254,100

* For boundary of Areas I, II, II see Fig. 27 (Chap. VI).
† As supplied by the Local Rating Officers (figures taken to the nearest 50).
** West Midland Group estimates. Explanation of classification is given on pages 87 and 90.
‡ Negligible.

1934 to 1939 was effecting a net immigration into the Conurbation. Up to 1934, however, the net balance had been outward from the Conurbation; and, if it is to be taken as a basic assumption that the Conurbation shall not be allowed to increase in the future to an extent greater than its natural increase, there should not be any increase due to more immigration than emigration.

In estimating a first post-war housing programme, a small allowance is made for a net immigration which occurred in parts of the Conurbation over the war years (see Table XVII), but the programme is drawn up mainly on estimates of the natural increase of the population and on the average number of persons per family and per dwelling. No separate estimate is made of houses needed to relieve overcrowding.

The minimum increase which has probably taken place from 1939 to 1945 in Areas I, II and III of the Conurbation is estimated in Table XVII as 40,000 through natural increase and 25,700 through net immigration[1].

Influence of increasing number of families. There are no statistics of the number of families in the area. The number of separate families is growing at a rate not directly related to population trends. There are more family groups, but fewer persons in each family. Yet, from such figures as are available, an estimate may be made of the number of persons per dwelling-house (see Table XV). At any given moment about 2.5 per cent of all dwelling-houses are unoccupied as a result of the movement of families in and out. If, therefore, 2.5 per cent be deducted from the number of available dwelling-houses, totals of occupied houses may be arrived at as follows :—

Area I	..	..	..	311,000)
Area II	..	..	..	101,500 } Total for Conurbation, 573,000
Area III	..	..	..	160,500)

The 1931 Census shows that 97 per cent. of all persons lived in private families. Assuming that this is true for 1939 also, we obtain directly the figures given in columns 2 and 3 of Table XV (Population in Private Families, and Persons per Occupied Dwelling-house). In all areas less people lived in each house in 1939 than in 1931. The average for the whole Conurbation was 3.5 persons per house in 1939, against 4.17 persons per house in 1931. In the Census year 1931, the Conurbation average was exactly the same as the average for the whole country.

These changes reflect the improvement in the housing position between 1931 and 1939—and imply a considerable reduction of overcrowding. They reflect also the national trend towards smaller families, and, in fact, show a decline far steeper than was predicted for

---

[1]The estimate is based on the following argument:—Figures are available for England and Wales for the years 1939-45, but are not available for estimating the natural increase within the Conurbation during the war years. A calculation was, therefore, made of the average rate of natural increase per thousand population per year for England and Wales for these five years. This rate was 3.31 per thousand of the mid-1939 population. By applying 3.31 to the mid-1939 estimate for the Conurbation and multiplying by 6, we obtain a figure which may be taken as the *minimum* increase for the Conurbation in the six years up to mid-1945. Actually, the average annual rate of natural increase for the Conurbation has been consistently higher than for the country as a whole throughout this century—right up to 1939. There is also reason to suppose that the higher rate of natural increase in the Conurbation persisted throughout the war, since an analysis of comparative age-structures in 1939 (see Figure 26, Chapter VI) seemed to show that the Conurbation, and particularly the Black Country, still contained a higher proportion of its population both in the younger and in the reproductive age-groups.

The mid-1945 population estimates supplied by the Registrar-General show a decline in Areas I and II on the 1939 figure of 5.7 per cent. and 3.4 per cent. respectively; this is consistent with the number of persons estimated as being in the Forces at that date. In Area III, however, the 1945 estimate shows an increase of 1.7 per cent. on the 1939 figure. This indicates that the immigration that was taking place into these areas prior to the war persisted—though to a lesser degree—during 1939-45. Therefore, in estimating the number of persons in private families in 1945 (see Table XVII) an allowance has been made for an immigration increase into Area III. This allows for withdrawal to the Forces, which for Great Britain was 11 per cent; but for the Conurbation, with its high proportion of people in reserved occupations and other temporary war workers, is taken as 5 per cent. If the only factors at work had been a withdrawal to the Forces by mid-1945 equivalent to this 5 per cent. of the total mid-1939 population, and a rate of natural increase averaging 3.31 per thousand per year of the 1939 population, then the 1945 mid-year population would have been 16,250 lower than the 1939 figure; in fact, it was 9,416 higher. The minimum immigration increase has therefore been calculated in Table XVII as 16,250 + 9,416, or about 25,700 persons.

the country as a whole over the decade 1931-1941 in the Housing Report of the 1931 Population Census[1].

The forward estimate of the Registrar-General in 1931 was that by 1941 there would be an increase of 2.6 per cent. of the whole population, and an increase of 9 per cent. in the number of families. These changes would reduce the national average of 3.72 persons per family to 3.5. The estimate for population increase was, in fact, realised by 1939.

ESTIMATED CHANGES 1931-39 IN NUMBER OF PERSONS PER DWELLING
AND IN AVERAGE SIZE OF FAMILY

TABLE XV. (The 1931 figures are derived from the Census of Population)

AREA	1 No. of Occupied Private Dwellings *		2 Population in Private Families ¶		3 Persons per occupied Private Dwelling		4 Families per occupied Private Dwelling	5 Persons per Family	
	1931	1939†	1931	1939**	1931	1939	1931	1931	1939‡
Area I: Birmingham (incl. Smethwick) ..	256,600	311,000	1,045,900	1,088,000	4·08	3·50	1·06	3·85	3·33
Area II: Main Black Country	82,400	101,500	367,592	386,000	4·46	3·80	1·06	4·22	3·62
Area III: Outer Conurbation Districts	110,600	160,500	459,217	539,000	4·15	3·36	1·05	3·95	3·20
TOTAL CONURBATION ...	449,500	573,000	1,872,600	2,013,000	4·17	3·51	1·05	3·95	3·34
ENGLAND and WALES	9,123,300	11,302,000 ††	38,042,500	40,216,200	4·17	3·56	1·12	3·72	3·39

* See page 95. ¶ Definition given in footnote to Table XVI.
† The totals shown in Table XIV less 2.5 per cent. for vacant dwellings.
** Calculated by applying the 1931 per cent. of total population in private families (97 per cent.) to the 1939 mid-year estimate.
‡ Estimated by allowing 1.05 families per occupied private dwelling.
†† Based on the estimate of M. J. Elsas, *Housing and the Family*, 1947.

Even in 1931, however, the Conurbation had a larger family unit than the average of the country as a whole. The Birmingham and Smethwick area (Area I) stood at 3.85; the main Black Country (Area II) stood at 4.22; and the other districts (Area III) at 3.95.

[1] The Housing Report of the 1931 Population Census explains the decline in the average size of family in the following way. The main upward force is the birthrate—which has declined considerably—whereas the downward force of mortality has changed only slowly in the opposite direction, and the marriage rate has kept pace with an increasing population of increasingly adult character. Thus "on balance the movement presses increasingly downwards in the scale of family sizes; the larger families are reduced and broken up and there is less replacement from the families of the next smaller sizes." In addition, there has over recent years been a great increase in the lodger type, and probably in part due to social changes, *e.g.*, Old Age Pensions—an encouragement to greater independence among the old people. The net result of these changes has been a re-distribution of the population into families of smaller sizes, and an increase in the number of families proportionately greater than the increase in the total population.

The whole Conurbation average was 3.95 against the national average of 3.72 (see Table XVI).

As has been pointed out in Chapter VI, the relatively lower age composition of the population of the Conurbation gives grounds for expecting a higher rate of natural increase to persist, and that such figures as we have confirm this trend up to 1939.

Let us assume then that the changes in the size of family for the Conurbation were roughly parallel to those for the country as a whole at a slightly higher level. The Table shows both the National and the Conurbation figures for 1921 and 1931.

CHANGES IN THE AVERAGE SIZE OF FAMILY 1921-31
THE CONURBATION AND ENGLAND AND WALES

TABLE XVI

	Average Size of Family*	
	1921	1931
Conurbation	4·50	3·95
Birmingham and Smethwick (Area I)	4·43	3·85
Main Black Country (Area II)	4·71	4·22
Outer Districts (Area III)	4·47	3·95
England and Wales...	4·14	3·72

* The definition of private family adopted throughout is the same as that used in the 1931 Census. In broad outline, the term " applies ordinarily to the private domestic household inclusive of resident indoor servants.
  It also applies to a resident caretaker of a house to let or other premises.
  A lodger occupying part of a house or flat and not boarding with the family is treated as a separate private family, and where two or more lodgers in similar circumstances share a part of a house in common they are treated as one private family.
  A lodger boarding with a family is not treated as a separate unit but is included with the family with which he boards." (1931 Census. Housing Report and Tables, p. viii.)

The National averages for persons per private family were 4.14 for 1921, 3.72 for 1931, and 3.5 for 1939 (estimated in Census). For the Conurbation the averages were 4.50 for 1921, and 3.95 for 1931. From these figures an estimate for the Conurbation family unit in 1939 may be made in two different ways; either by continuing the Conurbation trend by itself, or by relating the Conurbation figures to the National figures. Both methods give a 1939 Conurbation family of 3.7 approximately. Probably the family dropped even below this size. The number of dwellings needed on this basis can be calculated by dividing the estimated population in private families of 2,013,000 (see Table XV, col. 2) by 3.7. This gives a requirement of 542,000 dwellings, against an available supply, which, even allowing for 2.5 per cent. vacant, stands in Table XV at 573,000. This large apparent excess of about 30,000 dwellings over needs was, however, not borne out by experience. It was generally held in 1939 that the supply and demand for houses were fairly balanced in the Conurbation as a whole; and, in fact, there was no easy situation such as a surplus of 30,000 houses would produce.

The probable explanation is that slum clearance, the improvement of housing supply from 1931 to 1939, and the consequent alleviation of overcrowding, revealed the existence of a large number of additional families, and that a plentiful supply of houses gives encouragement to further division of families into more and smaller independent units.

On the average, there will always be more than one family per house. Families share a house, but a single family does not usually live in two different houses. As we have seen, the average number of persons per occupied dwelling for the Conurbation has fallen from 4.17 in 1931 to 3.51 in 1939 (Table XV, col. 3). The average size of family must therefore be less than 3.51.

Figures are available on the question of the number of families per house. The national figure for 1931 was 1.12; the comparable figure for the Conurbation was 1.05. It is by dividing this figure of 1.05 into the number of persons per occupied private dwelling, quoted earlier as 3.51, that we obtain the estimate which we accept of approximately 3.34 persons per family.

ESTIMATED CHANGE IN THE NUMBER OF PERSONS IN PRIVATE FAMILIES 1939-45

TABLE XVII

Area	Population in private families mid-1939*	Estimated Natural increase 1939-1945 (Six years)†	Estimated Minimum immigration increase 1939-45	Total estimated minimum net increase 1939-45
Area I : (Birmingham & Smethwick) ...	1,088,000	21,600	—	21,600
Area II : (Main Black Country)	386,000	7,700	—	7,700
Area III : (Outer Districts)	539,000	10,700	25,700	36,400
Total Conurbation	2,013,000	40,000	25,700	65,700

* Totals as given in Table XV. Col. 2.
† Calculated at average rate of 3·31 persons per thousand per annum (the average annual rate for England and Wales 1939-44. See text and footnote, page 95).

In Table XVII we see the estimated change in the number of persons living in private families in the period 1939-45. The total is 65,700. At 3.5 persons per occupied dwelling this gives a needed increase in houses of 18,800 (Table XVIII).

CALCULATION OF IMMEDIATE MINIMUM HOUSING NEEDS
(AS AT MID-YEAR 1945)

TABLE XVIII

A.	Number of houses required to meet population increase of 65,700 (see Table XVII) at rate of 3·51* persons per occupied dwelling	18,720
B.	Number of houses required to replace those destroyed by enemy action	12,000
C.	Houses of Type 1, due for replacement (less 6,000, estimated number destroyed by enemy action)	97,380
	Total requirements for first programme	128,100

*The average estimated for the Conurbation 1939 (Table XV. Col. 3).

It is estimated that bombing has destroyed or irreparably damaged 12,000 houses. Under Slum Clearance Acts, 103,380 houses of Type 1 were due for replacement.   6,000 of these having been destroyed by bombing, the figure for this type of house now stands at 97,380.   The total for a first housing programme (1945) therefore stands at 128,100.

Starting from Birmingham's New Street Station, the train runs between the old central factory quarter and streets of

a break, begins the Smethwick industrial zone, with its jumble of roads, railways and canals. Running alongside the canal

Canal junction and old spoilbanks lie north of the line, and to the south lies Oldbury, the first Black Country town. A stee

and pitmounds. Open land stretches towards Rowley Regis. Houses advance across land evacuated by industry. Across the canal the ca

gs, past a vista of Middle Ring industrial buildings, by Monument Lane and on to the edge of Birmingham.   Here, without

n enters the Black Country leaving the congested industry of Smethwick for the waste lands left derelict by earlier industries.

the persistence of heavy industry in the middle of the Conurbation.   The River Tame winds through a landscape of slagheaps

still looks on to tracts of derelict land, with a brickworks marking the midway point.   Close by, this desolation . . . .

.... *forms the setting of a new housing estate.   The train halts at Dudley Port Station, a Black Country railway centre.   I*

streets and new municipal housing as far as Tipton Station.   Just beyond, new industry is using old derelict land across

the backyards of houses and factories, and a stretch of loosely knit development before reaching the extensive steel pl

line is Rough Hills, a slum built on and among slag heaps.   As the chimneys of Bilston recede, the train enters the fringe of Wolverh

s stand among heaps of ash, spoil and scrap. Roads, railway and canals overlap at Tipton and straighten to cut through terrace

the township of Tipton Green, and tips are filling the open space between three embankments. Through Coseley the train passes

mills at Spring Vale, Bilston, a centre of the heavy industry formerly characteristic of this part of the Conurbation. Across the

hich the zone of increasingly older and denser industrial building reaches into the heart of the town, 14 miles from New Street.

FIGURE 28

THE INDUSTRIAL STRUCTURE OF THE CONURBATION AND ITS 6 COUNTY BOROUGHS COMPARED WITH THAT OF ENGLAND & WALES

BASED ON EMPLOYED PERSONS — 1931 CENSUS OF POPULATION

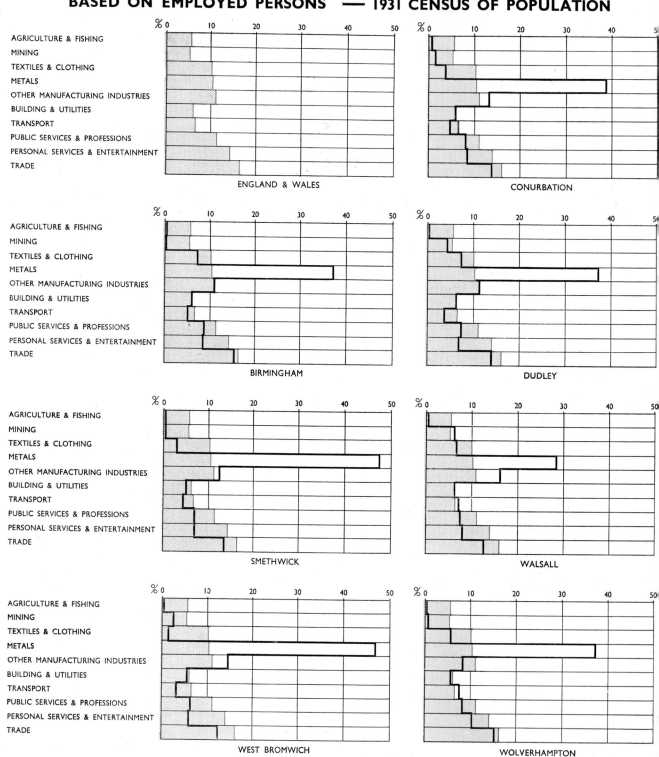

CHAPTER VIII

A Survey of Industry within the Conurbation

1. The Industrial Structure of the Conurbation as a Whole

PRACTICAL PLANNING for the future of industry in any region demands a knowledge of the present structure of industry within that region. This structure can be measured conveniently by expressing the number of workers in different industries or groupings of industries as percentages of the total of workers[1]. In Figure 28 the industrial structure of the Conurbation as a whole, and of parts of the Conurbation, is measured in this way, on a broad grouping of industries, and is compared with a similar grouping for England and Wales. The " profile " charts used in Figure 28 graphically present the chief features of industry and have been adopted as standard procedure[2] to demonstrate the " balance " of industries.

In the case of the Conurbation and all the six County Boroughs it includes, the group of metal industries in the " nose " of the profile is vastly more prominent, and the service industries in the " chin " of the profile are somewhat less prominent than the national proportions. In textiles and clothing all the six towns fall short of the national proportions. Dudley, with its clothing industry, has the highest proportion (7.4 per cent.) so employed; Birmingham comes next (3.5 per cent.). In the group of other manufacturing industries the six towns vary round the national average of 11.3 per cent., but Walsall, because of its leather industry, comes first with 16.2 per cent. employed.

In any industry local prominence or shortcoming can be compared with national importance by what is called the Location Quotient. For instance, Figure 28 and Table XIX show that 38.9 per cent. of all workers in the Conurbation are in the metal manufacturing group; for England and Wales the figure is 10.6 per cent. The Location Quotient is the figure which states the relation between these two percentages and is arrived at by dividing the local by the national percentage. Thus, the Location Quotient of the metal manufacturing group in the Conurbation is $38 \cdot 9$ per cent. $\div$ 10.6 per cent $= 3.7$. Similarly, the Location Quotient of the professions in the Conurbation given in Table XIX is 2.31 per cent. $\div$ 3.41 per cent. $= 0.7$. In general terms the *Location Quotient of a particular industry in a particular place is calculated by dividing the proportion which that industry contains of all workers in that place by the proportion which that industry contains of all workers for the country as a whole.*

---

[1] " Workers " will be used as a general term to refer to persons actually employed or persons insured or normally occupied (whether employed or unemployed at the time) according to the source of information.

[2] See Paper by Professor P. Sargant Florence, *The Town and Country Planning Summer School 1943*, pp. 41-42, published by the Town Planning Institute. The main industries comprised in the groupings are listed in Table XIX with the precise percentages for England and Wales, the Conurbation, and Birmingham.

TABLE XIX   CENSUS OF POPULATION, 1931.

Grouped Industries (Comparative structure of Groups, marked in bold type, is illustrated in Figure 28)	England and Wales % of all employed in industry	Conurbation % of all employed in industry	Conurbation Location Quotient	Birmingham C.B. % of all employed in industry	Birmingham C.B. Location Quotient	Reference numbers (see next column) of particular industries within grouped industries (see first column) important and distinctive within the Conurbation	List of particul[ar] industries im-portant and distinctive with[in] the Conurbatio[n] (See Table XX[V])
	(a)	(b)	(b)÷(a)*	(c)	(c)÷(a)*		1. Smelting and Rolling Iron and Steel
Agriculture and Fishing	6·0	0·6	**0·1**	0·3	**0·0**		
Mining	5·9	1·5	**0·2**	0·2	**0·0**		2. Extracting a[nd] Refining (No[n]-ferrous)
Textiles and Clothing							
Textiles	5·8	0·8	**0·1**	0·6	**0·1**		
Clothing	4·7	3·1	**0·7**	2·9	**0·6**		3. Later Pro-cesses (Non-ferrous)
Total Textiles and Clothing	10·5	3·9		3·5			
Metals							
Metal Processes and Industries	3·5	21·6	**6·1**	15·9	**4·5**	1, 2, 3, 4, 5, 6	4. Tubes—Iron and Steel
General Engineering†	2·4	3·2	**1·3**	3·2	**1·3**	7	
Vehicles†	2·0	8·2	**4·2**	10·2	**5·2**	8, 9	5. Bolts, Nuts, Screws, etc.
Shipbuilding†	0·7	0·05	**0·0**	0·0	**0·0**		
Elec. Eng. and Apparatus†	1·4	3·1	**2·2**	3·7	**2·7**	10	6. (a) Other Foundry and Secondary Processes
Tools, Jewellery, etc.†	0·5	2·8	**5·4**	4·1	**7·7**	11, 12	
Total Metals	10·5	38·9		37·1			(b) Other Metal
Other Manufacturing Industries							
Bricks, Pottery, Glass	1·1	1·6	**1·4**	0·6	**0·5**	16, 17	7. Construction Engineering
Chemicals	1·1	1·0	**0·8**	0·9	**0·8**		
Food, Drink, Tobacco	3·3	3·6	**1·1**	4·3	**1·3**	13	8. Motor Cars, Cycles, and Aircraft
Woodwork	1·5	1·7	**1·1**	2·3	**1·6**		
Paper and Printing	2·5	2·1	**0·8**	2·6	**1·0**		9. Railway Car-riages, Trams, etc.
Miscellaneous Manufacturing	1·8	3·2	**2·1**	3·8	**2·5**	14, 15	
Total Other Manufacturing	11·3	13·2		14·5			10. Electrical Engineering
Building and Utilities							
Building	5·1	4·6	**0·9**	4·7	**0·9**		11. Cutlery and Small Tools
Gas, Water, Electricity	1·2	1·3	**1·1**	1·3	**1·0**		
Total Building and Utilities	6·3	5·9		6·0			12. Jewellery, etc
All Transport							
Railways	2·8	2·4	**0·8**	2·4	**0·8**		13. Cocoa, etc.
Road	2·5	2·3	**0·9**	2·4	**1·0**		
Other Transport (sea, etc.)	1·5	0·2	**0·1**	0·2	**0·1**		14. Leather Good[s]
Total Transport	6·8	4·9		5·0			15. Rubber Good[s]
Public Services and Professions							
Defence	1·4	0·1	**0·1**	0·1	**0·1**		16. Glass
Central Government	1·9	1·4	**0·7**	1·8	**0·9**		
Local Government	5·0	4·4	**0·9**	4·5	**0·0**		17. Bricks
Professions	3·4	2·3	**0·7**	2·6	**0·8**		
Total Public Services and Pro-fessions	11·7	8·2		9·0			
Personal Services and Entertain-ment							
Entertainment and Sport	0·9	0·7	**0·8**	0·9	**0·9**		
Personal Service	13·5	7·9	**0·6**	8·0	**0·6**		
Total Personal Services and Enter-tainment	14·4	8·6		8·9			
Trade							
Distribution	14·4	12·4	**0·8**	13·4	**0·9**		
Finance	2·2	1·7	**0·8**	1·9	**0·9**		
Total Trade	16·6	14·1		15·3			
Other Industries	0·2	0·2		0·2			
All Industries	100·0	100·0		100·0			
Actual Numbers	(16,686,570)	(822,997)		(444,981)			

* Figures in this column are based on those in (a), (b) and (c) taken to two places of decimals.
† Sub-divisions of standard groups. See first footnote, page 107.

Table XIX adopts within the framework of Figure 28 more detailed standard groupings of industries to show and compare the industrial structure of Birmingham and the whole Conurbation with that of England and Wales[1]. The broad groupings of Figure 28, printed in bold type, are broken down into finer groups. The predominance in the Conurbation of the broad metal grouping of the Profile Chart is shown by the location quotients of these finer groups to be due to a concentration of the Conurbation on metal processes, vehicles, tools and jewellery rather than on general engineering, or on shipbuilding.

In the last two columns of Table XIX, particular industries are listed opposite whichever of the fourteen manufacturing groups they form part. These industries are selected as important and " distinctive " in the Conurbation. Their importance is measured by the total number employed. their distinctiveness by the high location quotient for the Conurbation. According to the Ministry of Labour count for 1931, they all employed over 5,000 workers within the Conurbation, and had a location quotient for the Conurbation of over 1.5. Twelve of them are metal industries[2], five are not. The twelve metal industries taken together account for 85 per cent. of all persons in the metal industry of the Conurbation. The seventeen industries taken together account for 72 per cent. of persons in the total of the Conurbation's manufacturing industries. Except for these seventeen, no other manufacturing industry (or any industry) that can be distinguished as an entity from the official statistics satisfies these minimum tests for qualifying as important or distinctive in the Conurbation.

These seventeen[3] industries will be analysed in Section 4 from the standpoint of providing employment locally and of fulfilling certain national requirements.

The main obstacle to any attempt to proceed further with the analysis and to obtain a " close-up " of the structure of the metal industries lies in the arbitrary lines of classification that are drawn between different metal industries.

Widely different classifications are adopted by different government departments and even by sections of one department, such as the Board of Trade. So widely do these classifications differ that for all main purposes we must discard the data of the Census of Production as not being comparable with the data of the two main sources which are used :—The *Census of Population Industry Tables*, and the Ministry of Labour's *Statistics of the Insured Population*.

The Census of Population does not analyse the population of areas below the rank of County Boroughs in sufficient detail by industries, so that for the Conurbation *as a whole* the Ministry of Labour statistics must normally be used. Unfortunately, the classification of industries adopted by the Ministry of Labour lumps many industries that are usually distinguished into a single somewhat mixed bag. The worst examples of this occur in the metal group; and many industries well known to be localized in the Conurbation, such as gun-making, sheet-metal working, drop-forging, lock and key, needles and pins, pens, chain and anchor, springs, bedsteads, hearth furniture, appear under the title " Metal Industries not Separately Specified " (symbol GW)[4]. For Great Britain as a

[1] This grouping is adopted as a standard by the West Midland Group for analysing Census of Population or Ministry of Labour data. It is used in the Worcester Civic Survey (see *County Town*, pp. 43-58). Mining forms one group and manufactures are divided into eleven groups. In Table XIX two of these eleven groups are further sub-divided into (a) general engineering; vehicles; shipbuilding; and (b) electrical engineering; tools, jewellery, etc.

[2] Some sources permit one of these metal industries to be divided up into (a) Foundry and Other Secondary Processes and (b) Other Metal Industries.

[3] Eighteen, wherever the sub-division mentioned in the previous footnote is possible.

[4] Hereinafter called " Other Metal Industries."

whole this miscellaneous group included in 1931 as many as 206,330 insured workers.

The questions which this section of the present Chapter should answer about the Conurbation as a whole are:—What industries can be said to be localized in the Conurbation to various degrees? What industries are definitely localized elsewhere? What industries are fairly evenly spread inside and outside the Conurbation?

On the Ministry of Labour classification, the industries distinguished can be assigned to four categories significant to planning by the application of objective tests such as the location quotient described above and the co-efficient of localization[1].

(A.) *Localized Industries mainly localized in the Conurbation (as measured by a location quotient of 1.5 or over)*

This test produces the seventeen industries with over 5,000 workers in the Conurbation listed in the last column of Table XIX, whose characteristics are measured in Table XXVI, (pages 122 and 123).

(B.) *Moderately Localized Industries present to some extent in the Conurbation*

Five such industries had, in the Conurbation in 1931, over 5,000 insured workers according to the Ministry of Labour; their location quotient in the Conurbation may be given:—

General Engineering	35,062 workers.	Quotient 1.1
Coal Mining	12,835 ,,	,, 0.2
Tailoring	8,074 ,,	,, 0.7
Furniture	7,730 ,,	,, 1.1
Electrical Apparatus	7,693 ,,	,, 1.3

Industries in this category with less than 5,000 workers in the conurbation in 1931 were (roughly in order of workers insured) Shirts, Underclothing, etc.; Miscellaneous Foods; Chemicals; Explosives; Wire; Carriages; Dressmaking; Artificial Silk Yarn; Cardboard Boxes, etc.; Heating and Ventilation Apparatus; Boots and Shoes; Brushes and Brooms; Scientific Instruments.

(C.) *Localized Industries virtually absent from the Conurbation*

The chief examples are given below with the total insured in Great Britain in 1931— larger industries in the first column, less large in the second.

(1) *Over 60,000 workers.*	(2) *30,000 to 60,000 workers*
Cotton	Marine Engineering
Woollen and Worsted	Tobacco
Shipbuilding	Stone Quarrying
Textile Bleaching, etc.	Jute
Hosiery	Hats and Caps
Pottery	Tinplate
Linen	
Soaps, Oil	

---

[1] The *coefficient* of *localization* measures in one figure the general pattern of the distribution of a particular industry over a whole country compared with the distribution of the working population as a whole. When workers are divided up, region by region, as percentages of their total over the country, the coefficient is the sum (divided by 100) of the plus deviations of the regional percentages in the particular industry from the corresponding regional percentages of workers in all industry. For examples of calculation see Florence, *Investment, Location and Size of Plant.*

Complete coincidence region by region of the particular industry with all industry gives a coefficient of 0; extreme localization gives a figure approaching 1. Coefficients of localization have here been calculated on the basis of the 1931 Census of Population as summarized on a regional distribution in the Appendix to the P.E.P. *Report on the Location of Industry*, 1939.

Industries are assigned to category A if they have a location quotient (based on the Ministry of Labour's Count, 1931) of 1.5 or over in the Conurbation. Industries with a medium or high coefficient of localization (generally over 0.20) but a quotient in the Conurbation between 0.2 and 1.5 are assigned to category B. Industries with a high or fairly high coefficient of localization, at least over 0.33, but a quotient in the Conurbation of less than 0.2 are assigned to category C. Dispersed industries have a co-efficient of less than 0.20 and location quotients in every Census region of 0.3 or over.

No industry in column 1 employed as many as 2,000 in the Conurbation, and no industry in column 2 more more than 500.

(D.) The Dispersed Industries found in all Regions

The Conurbation will have a share of each of these, more or less proportionate to its population.

These dispersed industries consist largely of services some of which were not insurable in 1931, (*e.g.*, domestic services) and others that had a high proportion of employers and non-manual workers not insurable. Census data must therefore be used instead of the Ministry of Labour count of insured workers. Table XIX gives in considerable detail the proportion of all workers that are employed in the several service industries in England and Wales, in the Conurbation, and in Birmingham. The location quotients in the Conurbation are all fairly near unity, indicating full dispersion, except in the cases that might be expected of Other Transport (mainly by sea), Central Government (centred in London) and Defence. But the quotients are unexpectedly low in Professions (0.7) and Personal Service (0.6). These two groups are worth analysing in greater detail for the Conurbation, and Table XX gives the location quotients of the constituent service industries in the six County Boroughs. The data is not available for the smaller areas of the Conurbation. The location of industry in different parts of the Conurbation will be discussed in the next section; but a certain similarity is observable in the proportions in which each of these dispersed types of services occur in Birmingham and in the Conurbation generally. Both have low proportions compared with the country as a whole.

Besides services, there are some productive industries which are widely dispersed. Building and Gas-Water-Electricity (*i.e.*, " Utilities ") are seen in Table XIX to have location quotients near unity. Some of the constituent industries within the manufacturing groups, notably Bread, Drink, Electric-wiring and Printing, are also widely dispersed. Location quotients are not available for the Conurbation as a whole, but for Birmingham they were 0.9, 1.1, 1.0 and 1.0 respectively for these four productive industries.

This parallel development of certain industries and services with the population is not difficult of explanation. They are industries whose products would spoil if transported far, and services which are demanded on the spot by the community. These industries and services must reside where the population is, and, on the analogy of Residentiary Canons, may be called residentiary.

The significance of these categories is that before discussing practical plans for the re-location of industry, the limits to the mobility of certain industries must be realized. The dispersed residentiary industries and services of category D are obviously not free to choose location. Figure 28 and Table XIX show that, for the country as a whole, transport and other services alone accounted for 49.6 per cent of the employed population, and extractive industries a further 11.9 per cent. Added to these immobile industries are the manufactures generally rooted by raw materials costly to transport, such as brickmaking or primary metal processes, and residentiary manufactures such as baking.

Immobile industries and services, in short, employ from two-thirds to three-quarters of the country's total workers. In the Conurbation the immobile industries employ a somewhat smaller proportion, though hardly less than a half. But in considering possibilities of reconstruction, it must be realized that many of these technically mobile industries, such as some of category A, are localized in the Conurbation for substantial economic reasons which will be discussed later. Since there are by definition virtually no industries within the Conurbation of category C, the selection of industries to be moved away from or kept out of the Conurbation must come either from this category A, or from category B—the industries partially localized in the Conurbation.

2. Localization of Industries within the Conurbation

Where a region consists of a regular pattern of country and town, certain industries, mainly service, will be localized in the towns. Thus the Herefordshire Survey[1] showed that in each of the six market towns of the county between 20 per cent. and 23 per cent of all employed persons were consistently employed in distributive trades, compared to a proportion of 14.4 per cent nationally. This localization of services in the larger concentrations of populations is not nearly so clear in the Conurbation. The six towns of highest and most dense population, recognised as County Boroughs, have not a particularly

LOCATION QUOTIENT OF *SERVICE INDUSTRIES

TABLE XX
(1.0=Proportionate to Distribution of Total Working Population)

Service	Birmingham	Wolverhampton	Walsall	Smethwick	West Bromwich	Dudley
Private Domestic	0·5	0·6	0·5	0·3	0·3	0·4
Laundries	0·7	0·8	0·7	1·4	0·3	0·2
Hotels, Inns, etc.	0·7	0·8	0·6	0·5	0·6	0·6
Restaurants, etc.	0·8	0·6	0·4	0·6	0·4	0·4
Hairdressing ...	1·0	1·0	1·0	0·9	0·6	1·0
Undertaking ..	1·2	0·8	1·0	1·0	0·8	0·4
Other	1·2	1·2	1·0	1·0	0·6	1·1
All Personal Service	*0·6*	*0·7*	*0·5*	*0·5*	*0·4*	*0·5*
Medicine	0·8	1·2	0·6	0·3	0·5	0·6
Dentistry	1·0	1·2	1·0	0·6	0·5	0·8
Education	0·7	0·6	0·4	0·3	0·2	0·4
Other —	0·7	0·7	0·5	0·5	0·4	0·6
All Professions ...	*0·8*	*0·8*	*0·5*	*0·4*	*0·4*	*0·6*

* This Table is based on the Census of Population and location quotients are, therefore, related to the resident population.

high proportion of workers—as the Profile Chart (Figure 28) shows—in Trade (mainly Distribution), in Public Services and Professions, or in Personal Service and Entertainment In none of the three types of service does any of the six largest towns extend beyond the national proportions, nor have these larger towns on the average a higher proportion in those services than the whole Conurbation consisting of large towns, small towns and scattered houses. Birmingham and Wolverhampton have the highest proportion, totalling for the three service groups (excluding transport) 33.1 per cent and 33.8 per cent of all employed workers, but this is not markedly higher than the corresponding 30.8 per cent. for the Conurbation as a whole, and considerably lower than the proportion of 42.6 per cent for the country as a whole (shown in red in Figure 28).

In Table XX the comparative lack of services in the six main centres of the Conurbation

---

[1] *English County* (Faber and Faber, 1946).

is seen in greater detail. Few location quotients rise above unity, indicating that the service industry has a proportion of all workers equal to the national proportion; and this in spite of the fact that the six towns are more or less centres for services rendered to the rest of the population of the Conurbation. The only specific services in which half the towns show a quotient of not less than unity is Undertaking. It is true that these towns do not pretend to be health resorts, but there is no question that the lack of services and amenities indicated by these quotients considerably below unity keeps many managers and salaried staff from working in the Conurbation, and explains the drift to London. It is also a serious matter when firms in the Conurbation try to entertain possible foreign customers. Many an order must have been lost because of dreary evenings spent by potential buyers.

When attention is turned from service to productive industries, the facts are very different. Within the whole Conurbation there are many mining and manufacturing industries highly localized in small areas. The intensity of this localization can be conveniently measured by the location quotient already explained. Since the Census of Population classification of industries is extremely detailed for several of the administrative areas within the Conurbation, quotients in this section are based on the Census returns, unless otherwise stated. Excluding all freak quotients due to small numbers (*i.e.*, less than 1,500), classification based on the Census of Population disclosed six quotients of over 30 in local government areas, indicating that there were at least thirty times as many workers in the industry in these areas as would be expected from the random distribution of industries among the population of England and Wales.

Industry	Administrative Area	No. of Workers	Location Quotient
Saddlery and Leather Goods ..	Walsall	3,257	44.1
Iron and Steel Tubes	West Bromwich ..	1,506	43.2
" Other Metal Industries " ..	Darlaston* ..	3,990	38.4
Bolts, Nuts, Rivets, Screws ..	Smethwick ..	1,736	37.9
" Other Metal Industries " ..	Willenhall* ..	3,812	34.1
Founding and Other Secondary Processes	Halesowen* ..	3,800	31.9

* In areas not County Boroughs, Bolts, etc., are included in " Other Metal Industries " and Tubes in Founding and Other Secondary Processes.

High localization of one industry or group of industries is often accompanied by high localization of another industry or group of industries in the same area. The outstanding case of this " co-location " within the Conurbation is that between Founding and Other Secondary Processes on the one hand and Other Metal Industries on the other. This is distinguishable in the Census of Population for all 28 Local Government Areas. Taking a location quotient of 10 or over as " very high," a quotient between 5 and 10 as " high," between 1 and 5 as a " fair " concentration, and below 1 as no concentration, the location quotients of the two industrial groups are *both* " very high " in twelve of the 28 areas[1], *both* " fair " in five others. There is thus agreement on degree of concentration between both groups of industries in seventeen out of the 28 areas. In the remaining eleven areas the two groups of industries are (among the four grades) only one grade of concentration apart. In no area is there any wider difference, *i.e.*, one group very highly concentrated, the other only fairly concentrated or not concentrated at all.

[1] These can be seen in Figure 30 :—Wednesfield, Short Heath, Willenhall, Bilston, Darlaston, Wednesbury, Coseley, Tipton, West Bromwich, Rowley Regis, Quarry Bank and Halesowen.

FIGURE 29

INDUSTRIAL LOCALIZATION
IN BIRMINGHAM AND SMETHWICK 1931

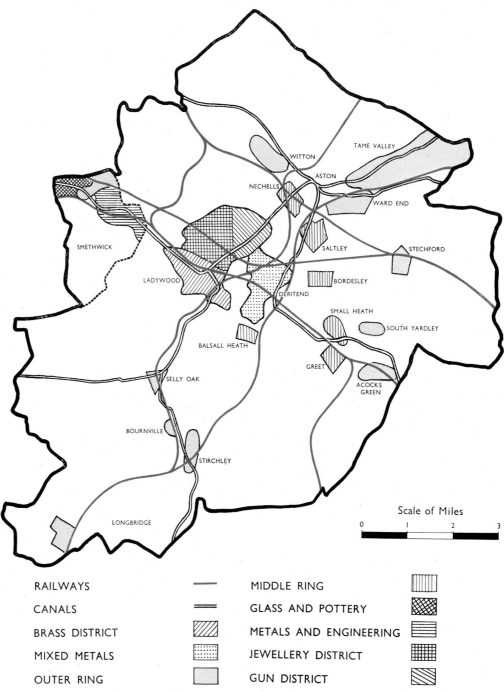

RAILWAYS	—	MIDDLE RING	
CANALS	=	GLASS AND POTTERY	
BRASS DISTRICT		METALS AND ENGINEERING	
MIXED METALS		JEWELLERY DISTRICT	
OUTER RING		GUN DISTRICT	

This map is a diagrammatic sketch to show the approximate areas (printed in black) in which certain industries are localized in Birmingham and Smethwick, and the location of the larger groups of factories in the middle ring (hatched red) and outer ring (stippled red) of Birmingham.   The shapes outlined are not intended to represent the exact areas of industrial zones (see Figure 36).

This " co-location " suggests a certain linkage between the two groups of industries. Generally, industries in the " Other Metal Industries " group make finished goods, *e.g.*, hardware, locks and keys, and are engaged at a tertiary stage later than foundry and the secondary processes. The linkage between the two can thus be called " vertical," and the economy of their " co-location " is much the same as the economics of vertical integration within a factory, involving a saving of transport costs.

Some of the administrative areas, in particular Birmingham, have such a large population that intense localizations of industries are lost in the general total and can, as in Figure 29[1], only be discovered by direct survey. This map shows within the boundaries of Birmingham and Smethwick, the famous jewellery quarter, the gun quarter, and other districts where particular industries were concentrated in 1931, such as those devoted to brass, glass and mixed metals. The map also shows a general industrial zoning by middle and outer rings in the south, east and north-east areas of Birmingham. Since Birmingham forms a single area for Census purposes, the degree of localization in these areas cannot be shown by any statistical quotient. But it is evident from the map that if the jewellery quarter, for instance, were a separate administrative area with its own statistics separated off by the Census, jewellery would show there a prodigiously high location quotient. Some statistical evidence of this is obtainable from the classified telephone directory. Three-quarters of silversmiths, jewellers, needle-, and lock-making firms are confined to two telephone exchange areas[2]. Here, however, we must be content with the more exact official statistics available.

Many of these highly concentrated localizations of industries within the Conurbation cannot be brought into the scope of any generalization. But seven observable tendencies may be noted. These are here set out, and all except the first refer to the mining and metal trades and are enumerated in order of the actual technical process—extractive, primary, secondary, and so on—through later stages of production.

(1) Industries employing the vast majority of workers localized in the Conurbation are not dependent on proximity to any natural advantage. Of the seventeen distinctive industries distinguished in Section I, only brick-making can claim to be rooted to its raw material today. In the past, others of these seventeen industries, such as blast furnaces and iron and steel smelting and rolling, were rooted near coal and iron mining. This past rooting continues as a historical factor in location today.

(2) The pre-manufacturing process of coal-mining is found localized, as shown in Figure 30, only in a few of the administrative areas of the Conurbation and even in those it is not highly localized. For the whole Conurbation the Location Quotient for coal-mining (see Table XIX) is as low as 0.2: therefore, all areas that have a quotient of 1.0 or over are marked. In 1931 only two areas, Walsall R.D. and Short Heath, had Location quotients over 3 (3.7 and 3.1 respectively), and only two other areas, Sedgley, with 2.6, and Kingswinford, with 1.3, had a quotient over 1.1. In Walsall the quotient is 1.1.

(3) The primary manufacturing process of iron and steel smelting and rolling tends to be found, largely for historical reasons, nearest to the coal-mining areas. It is localized more widely and intensely than coal-mining—though in a well-defined territory. For the whole Conurbation, the Location Quotient for iron and steel smelting and rolling, based on the Census of Population, was 2.0. Seven administrative areas shown in Figure 30 had Location Quotients over 6, extending as an arc inside the coal-mining areas in the

[1] Sketch map prepared from original data by the Geography Dept., University of Birmingham, for Nuffield College Social Survey.
[2] P. Sargant Florence. *Investment, Location and Size of Plant*, Chapter IV.

FIGURE 30

THE LOCALIZATION
OF MINERS AND WORKERS IN EARLIER METAL PROCESSES
WITHIN THE CONURBATION — 1931

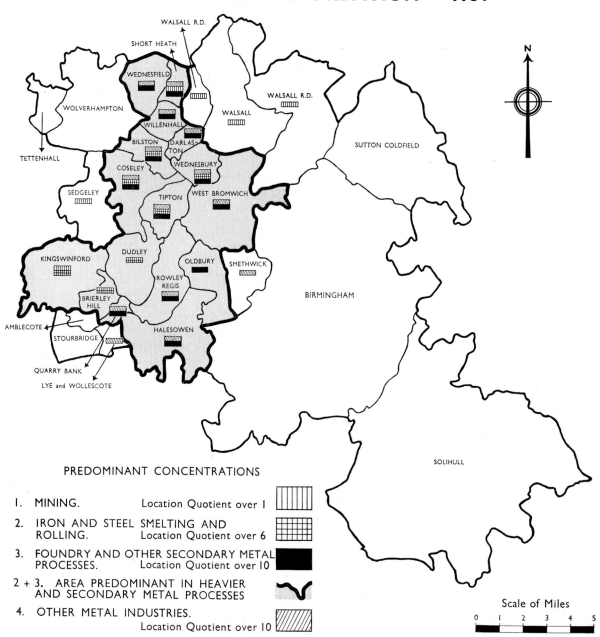

PREDOMINANT CONCENTRATIONS

1. MINING.   Location Quotient over 1

2. IRON AND STEEL SMELTING AND
    ROLLING.   Location Quotient over 6

3. FOUNDRY AND OTHER SECONDARY METAL
    PROCESSES.   Location Quotient over 10

2 + 3. AREA PREDOMINANT IN HEAVIER
        AND SECONDARY METAL PROCESSES

4. OTHER METAL INDUSTRIES.
        Location Quotient over 10

Scale of Miles
0   1   2   3   4   5

Coal-mining was localized in 1931 only in a few areas of the Conurbation, and nowhere was the location quotient higher than 3.7 (Walsall). Primary processes, such as iron and steel smelting and rolling, were located near the mining areas, but were localized more intensely and widely. Secondary metal processes were localized even more widely and more intensely; the location quotient in thirteen areas was over 10.

Note the grouping of earlier metal processes in the centre, north and west of the Black Country.

western section of the Conurbation, from Kingswinford (quotient 12.8) and Brierley Hill (quotient 21.7), through Dudley (quotient 7.6), Coseley (quotient 15.2), and Tipton (quotient 6.3), to Bilston (quotient 12.8) and Wednesbury (quotient 13.6).

(4) In the secondary metal manufacturing process such as Founding[1] localization within the Conurbation was yet wider and more intense, but still was clearly defined in territory. The Location Quotient for the whole Conurbation, based on the Census, was 8.9; so that a higher test may be used than the quotient of 6 used for marking local concentration of the primary process. Thirteen administrative areas had a Location Quotient over 10. They all lie, as Figure 30 shows, in the western half of the Conurbation on or round the primary process belt.

(5) In the territory where either mining or the primary or secondary metal processes are relatively localized, as measured in paragraphs 2, 3 and 4 above (roughly speaking a west-central block), the proportion of women employed is relatively low. This can be seen clearly in Figure 34. In none of the areas involved is the percentage of employed women over 30.37 of the total employed residing there, except in Walsall, where mining has a Location Quotient only just over 1.0. On the other hand, in the areas outside this west-central arc or belt where the earlier processes are important, employed women form a high proportion of the resident total employed. To the east, Birmingham has a percentage of 35.13, Sutton Coldfield of 34.56 and Smethwick of 32.05; to the west, Tettenhall has a percentage of 35.15 and Wolverhampton 31.1; while to the south of the belt, at Lye and Wollescote, 31.8 per cent of the total employed are women.

(6) While the heavy-material, earlier-process metal industries tend to localize in the west centre of the Conurbation, many of light-material later-process metal industries tend to localize in the south and east of the Conurbation. Available statistical classifications of the Census permit the tracing in each of the 28 administrative areas of two such industries, cutlery and small tools, and jewellery and plate[2]. For the Conurbation as a whole, cutlery and small tools had a Location Quotient based on the Census data of 4.0; jewellery and plate a Location Quotient of 6.7. Local areas are, therefore, marked in Figure 31 when their quotients exceed 4 and 7 respectively in these two industries. By these tests both industries have peculiarly high concentrations in Birmingham. The high concentration of the small tool industry extends westwards to Halesowen, Oldbury, Rowley Regis, Dudley, Lye and Wollescote, Stourbridge, and Amblecote, thus covering a continuous area in the south-centre of the Conurbation, and there is also high concentration in Wolverhampton. The high concentration of the jewellery industry, on the other hand, is confined to Birmingham and Smethwick.

(7) The main assembly industry of the conurbation, the making of motor vehicles, follows much the same pattern as the later-processes metal industries. The census only permits data for all vehicles, including carriages, etc., to be presented for all administrative areas. Table XIX shows that for the conurbation as a whole the Location Quotient for all vehicles is 4.2. All areas are accordingly marked in Figure 31 if they have a quotient over 4. A peculiarly high concentration is shown in the south-central area of the Conurbation and in Wolverhampton—all areas where either the small tool or the jewellery industry is concentrated.

If Figures 30 and 31 are considered together, it will be seen that all the local government areas of the Conurbation have either some concentration in the coal industry

---

[1] Covering Census Code Numbers 130, 133-41, 149 and including Tube and Wire Making.
[2] Census of Population, Industry Tables VI 8 and VI 10.

or a high concentration in some branch of the metal industry, with the exception of three fringe areas of Tettenhall, Sutton Coldfield and Solihull. In 1931 these fringe areas were largely residential and dormitory. The essential industrial unity of the Conurbation round a core of mining and metal industries is thus clearly brought out. But the metal industries branch out, and the several branches have intense localizations of their own in different parts of the Conurbation.

3. RECENT INDUSTRIAL CHANGES

The total population of the Conurbation was found to have increased over the periods 1921-31 and 1931-39 faster than that of England and Wales (see Table IX, Chapter VI).

COMPARISON IN GROWTH IN POPULATION, 1911-1939

TABLE XXI

Period	England and Wales	Conurbation
	Rate of increase per thousand : Average per annum	Rate of increase per thousand : Average per annum
1911-21	5·6	8·0
1921-31	5·6	7·1
1931-34	4·0	3·3
1934-39	4·9	11·0
Total population, 1939 ...	41,460,000 *	2,078,733 *

* Registrar's mid-year estimate.

Table XXI indicates that this faster rate of growth, generally speaking, has been fairly constant since 1911. Within the period of the 'thirties, however, there is evident a relative set-back to the population of the Conurbation from 1931 to 1934, followed from 1934 to 1939 by a faster than average growth relative to the country as a whole. The relative set-back is possibly attributable to the high unemployment rates in the western part of the Conurbation in 1931 to which attention is drawn in Section 4[1]; the rapid outpacing of the country as a whole in 1935-39 was probably the result of the remarkable industrial recovery of the Conurbation after 1931. This recovery can be measured for the three counties containing the Conurbation and compared to the trend in other industrial regions by means of data from the Census of Production. Table XXII shows that the persons employed in establishments covered by the Census[2] increased 7.43 per cent. between 1930 and 1935 in the three counties containing the Conurbation as against a slight decrease for the United Kingdom and heavy decreases in Scotland and South Wales. In the value of net output, there was an increase in these three counties during the same period even larger than in the Greater London region.

The recent increase in population of the Conurbation relative to the country as a whole is thus associated since 1931 with a relative increase in its industrial activity in general. In attempting to determine in what sort of industrial activity the relative increase occurred, a paradox appears. The Conurbation did not, generally speaking, increase the number of its workers much faster than the country as a whole in any particular industrial activity.

---

[1] Mainly by failing to retain the relatively high natural increase in these areas.
[2] Only establishments employing over ten persons are included and only manfacturing, mining and building industries.

FIGURE 31

THE LOCALIZATION OF FINAL METAL PRODUCT INDUSTRIES WITHIN THE CONURBATION 1931

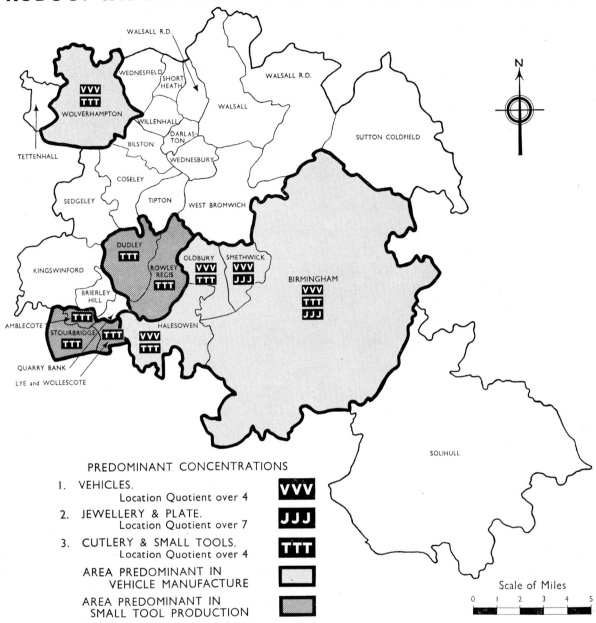

PREDOMINANT CONCENTRATIONS

1. VEHICLES.
   Location Quotient over 4   **VVV**

2. JEWELLERY & PLATE.
   Location Quotient over 7   **JJJ**

3. CUTLERY & SMALL TOOLS.
   Location Quotient over 4   **TTT**

AREA PREDOMINANT IN
VEHICLE MANUFACTURE

AREA PREDOMINANT IN
SMALL TOOL PRODUCTION

Scale of Miles

0   1   2   3   4   5

Later process metal industries tended, in 1931, to be localized in the south and east of the Conurbation. The main assembly industry of the Conurbation—motor vehicles—was localized in much the same areas.

Note the way in which the areas on this map complement those in Figure 30.

COMPARISON IN GROWTH OF INDUSTRIAL PRODUCTION, 1930-35
Changes in Numbers of Establishments and their Employment and Net Output in the U.K. and Main Areas
(Source—Census of Production)

TABLE XXII

| Area | Persons Employed | | | | Establishments | | Net Output |
	1930 (Thousands)	1935 (Thousands)	Change 1930-35 (Thousands)	%	Number 1930	Change in Number 1930-35 %	Change 1930-35 %
United Kingdom	7,143	7,077	— 66	— 0·92	58,038	+ 2·85	+ 4·79
Greater London	1,218	1,411	+193	+15·85	11,858	+10·54	+13·82
Warwickshire Worcestershire Staffordshire ...	808	868	+ 60	+ 7·43	5,752	+ 7·63	+15·46
South Wales	292	241	— 51	—17·46	1,292	+ 9·44	—10·06
Scotland	717	646	— 71	— 9·90	6,235	— 6·16	— 3·33

This is clear from Table XXIII. Between 1931 and 1937 the insured workers in the Ministry of Labour counts grew more slowly in the Conurbation than in the country as a whole in the case of nine out of its seventeen distinctive industries and sub-industries. The

LOCAL AND NATIONAL DEVELOPMENT OF INDUSTRIES LOCALIZED* IN THE CONURBATION 1931-37
(Source : Ministry of Labour Count of Insured Workers)

TABLE XXIII

Industries, important and distinctive, within the Conurbation	Conurbation Changes		National Changes	
	Insured Workers in 1931	Index of Growth 1931/37 (1931=100)	Insured Workers in 1931	Index of Growth 1931/37 (1931=100)
1 Iron and Steel—Blast Furnaces, Smelting and Rolling Mills	15,367	97·1	188,830	105·4
2 Non-ferrous Metals—Extracting and Refining ...	14,846	114·5	38,190	131·6
3 Non-ferrous Metals—later Processes & Wares	19,486	123·6	27,600	109·3
4 Tubes—Iron and Steel	16,141	125·8	29,820	109·7
5 Bolts, Nuts, Rivets, Screws, Nails, etc.	18,609	114·5	26,250	107·4
6 (A) Foundry and Secondary Processes	21,372	138·2	92,440	113·1
(B) Other Metal Industries	97,246	124·3	206,330	128·8
7 Constructional Engineering	6,732	141·5	29,580	135·4
8 Motor Vehicles, Cycles and Aircraft	48,915	121·4	251,320	139·9
9 Railway Carriage, Trams, etc.	8,582	118·5	51,550	98·2
10 Electrical Engineering (Generators, etc.)	14,331	166·4	92,470	123·9
11 Hand Tools, Cutlery, etc.	5,269	98·0	34,580	98·5
12 Jewellery, Plate, etc.	18,668	91·1	42,100	92·5
13 Cocoa, Chocolate and Sugar Confectionery ...	9,122	141·0	71,290	108·9
14 Saddlery, Harness and other Leather Goods ...	6,930	106·6	24,820	108·3
15 Rubber Manufactures	10,380	101·0	67,330	96·2
16 Glass (not Bottles)	6,448	108·5	27,470	113·7
17 Bricks, Unglazed Tiles, Fireclay Goods, etc. ...	7,675	118·9	87,620	121·6
Total Insured in all Industries	686,594	123·3	12,770,000	107·0

* *i.e.,* with Location Quotients over 1.5

industries that grew substantially faster in the Conurbation were " Foundry and Secondary Processes " (a very large employer of labour), Electrical Engineering (generators, etc.), Cocoa and Sugar Confectionery, Later Processes and Wares in Non-Ferrous Metals, Iron and Steel Tubes, and Railway Carriages and Trams. On the other hand, the Conurbation fell substantially behind the national increase in insured workers in Iron and Steel (Blast Furnaces, Smelting and Rolling), Extracting and Refining Non-Ferrous Metals, and the important industry of Motor Vehicles.

On the whole the *Conurbation held its growth of population not so much because its industries grew faster there than elsewhere, but because it happened to contain industries that were growing relatively fast everywhere and to exclude industries that were diminishing everywhere.*

This fact was pointed out in 1940 by Wensley and Florence[1] and is clearly brought

GROWTH AND DECLINE OF LOCALIZED MANUFACTURES, 1923-1937

Industries listed in order of National Growth, 1923-1937

Sources :—Ministry of Labour Gazette for Indexes ; Population Census (1931) for Location Quotients

TABLE XXIV

Industries Localized in Conurbation i.e. with Location Quotients (given in brackets) over 1·5	National Growth 1923—1937 1923=100		Industries Localized in Areas other than the Conurbation and with Location Quotients* under 0·2 in Conurbation. (Figures in brackets give highest Location Quotient in any Region)	National Growth 1923—1937 1923=100	
Electrical Engineering (Generators, etc.) (2·9) ...	199·6				
Motor Vehicles, Cycles and Aircraft (3·6)	196·4				
Bricks, Unglazed Tiles, Fireclay Goods (1·6) ...	185·5	G			G
Constructional Engineering (4·3)	184·0				
Other Metal Industries (4·3)	175·6	R			R
Foundry and Secondary Processes (9·0)	148·4				
Tubes—Iron and Steel (10·0)	146·2	O			O
Non-Ferrous Metals—Extracting and Refining (7·3)	142·5		Hosiery (11·8)	136·2	
Hand Tools and Cutlery (2·8)...	128·6	W			W
Glass (not bottles) (4·4)	126·9				
Rubber Manufactures (2·9)	122·1	I			I
Non-Ferrous Metals—Later Wares and Processes (13·1)	116·6	N			N
Cocoa, Chocolate and Sugar Confectionery (2·4)	111·1				
Bolts, Nuts, Rivets, Screws, Nails, etc. (13·1) ...	110·8	G			G
Railway Carriage, Trams, etc. (3·1)	104·7		Pottery, Earthenware, etc. (7·7)...	104·8	
Sadlery, Harness and other Leather Goods (5·2)	101·8		Oil, Soap (3·3)	102·6	
	100·0				
Iron and Steel : Blast Furnaces, Smelting and Rolling (1·5)	96·5	D E C L I N I N G	Tobacco, Cigars, Cigarettes (2·3)	99·3	D E C L I N I N G
			Marine Engineering (6·0)†	97·7	
			Linen (14·6)	94·4	
			Shipbuilding and Ship Repairing (6·0)†	91·6	
			Tinplate (25·6)	90·6	
			Textile, Bleaching, Printing, Dyeing (3·4)	89·0	
Jewellery, Plate, etc. (8·3)	88·8		Hat and Cap (3·3)	88·7	
			Wool (10·2)	84·5	
			Cotton (5·9)	83·4	
			Jute (29·9)	67·7	

* See Appendix Table I, P.E.P. *Report on Location of Industry*—based on Census of Population, occupied persons in Great Britain.
† Marine Engineering and Shipbuilding not distinguished.

[1]A. J. Wensley and P. Sargant Florence, *Recent Industrial Concentration especially in the Midlands.* (Review of Economic Studies, June 1940. pp. 149-154).

to view in Table XXIV giving rates of growth nationally for manufacturing industries localized in the Conurbation (category A in Section 1), and localized elsewhere (mainly category C in Section 1). Of the seventeen industries picked out as localized in and distinctive of the conurbation, only two fell in the numbers employed nationally between 1923 and 1937 : Jewellery, and Iron and Steel (Blast Furnaces Smelting and Rolling[1]). Of thirteen manufacturing industries localized in other regions but almost absent in the Conurbation ten fell in numbers employed nationally. Table XXIV proclaims this remarkable dichotomy vividly by the blank spaces in its left bottom and right top quarters compared with the crowding in its other diagonally opposed quarters.

SUBSTANTIAL CHANGES IN THE INDUSTRIAL STRUCTURE OF THE CONURBATION—1931-1937
TABLE XXV

Industries (in order of total additions to workers)	Addition to workers	% of all insured workers	
		1931	1937
Other Metal Products	37,072	14·16	15·87
Distribution	17,065	9·59	9·52
Motor Vehicles	10,513	7·12	7·02
Electrical Engineering (Generators), etc.	9,525	2·09	2·82
Founding and Secondary Processes	5,213	3·11	3·14
General Engineering	5,163	5·11	4·75
Electrical Cables and Apparatus	4,846	1·12	1·48

As a result of these differing rates of growth, the industrial structure of the Conurbation in 1937 might be expected to differ somewhat from that in 1931. The differences can be measured in the Ministry of Labour's count of insured persons. The more substantial additions to the numbers in any industry (*i.e.*, about 5,000 or more) are given in Table XXV. There was in those years a rise in the total of insured workers in the Conurbation from 686,594 to 846,437[2] so that these increases do not mean any great change in the proportion which the different industries form of the total. Though specialization in " Other " Metal Trades is increased and the Electrical trades press forward, the industrial structure of the Conurbation remains substantially the same.

4.   CHARACTERISTICS OF THE INDUSTRIES DISTINCTIVE OF THE CONURBATION
    An attempt is made in Table XXVI to measure certain characteristics that are significant in planning the future of the Conurbation. The word " attempt " is used since the measures available from published statistics are usually only a somewhat arbitrary index of the characteristic actually significant. Nevertheless, the attempt is worth making as an objective guide to policy. Table XXVI presents standard indices for all the industries which have been established as important and distinctive of the Conurbation by reason

---

[1] If smelting and rolling is separated off from blast-furnaces no decrease appears.
[2] The rise in numbers is partly accounted for by the inclusion in the later figure of two categories of workers who were not insurable in 1931—boys and girls under 16 years of age, and agricultural workers. The number of boys and girls in the area in 1938 was 52,962, and of agricultural workers 6,500. The real increase in insured workers between 1931 and 1937 is, therefore, about 100,000 (14.5 per cent). About 70 per cent. of this increase occurred in Birmingham.

of the numbers employed (shown in column 2), and the high location quotient (shown in column 3. A further column (No. 10) in this table indicates any other regions of localization with a quotient of 2 or over for the industry, from information drawn from the Census of Population[1]. This multi-focal location will prove important in our conclusions about the possible mobility of industries. Clearly, if any industry localized in the Conurbation should leave it, another localization, if there is one, is likely to be a magnet.

(A) Liability to Unemployment

Measures significant for coping with the danger of unemployment are given in columns 4, 5 and 6. It is customary to attribute unemployment to seasonal and cyclical fluctuations in trade, and to decline in certain industries, among other immediate causes.

Seasonal fluctuation in unemployment was not found to be heavy in the areas of the Conurbation—not so heavy as say in Coventry[2] or Worcester[3]. The wide fluctuations at Coventry were determined by the predominance of the motor-car industry, and this may serve as a warning to the Conurbation. The comparative stability of industry seasonally in the Conurbation during 1931-39 was no doubt due to the characteristics of the distinctive industries of the Conurbation taken severally and jointly. Severally (as indicated in column 4 of Table XXVI), only five of the distinctive industries have any " appreciable " seasonal fluctuation. Saunders[4] lists 63 industries (Ministry of Labour classification) according to the amplitude of their seasonal fluctuation. Not one of the seventeen industries distinctive of the Conurbation appears among the first eighteen, and only four in the first half of the list—Jewellery, 19th, Cocoa, etc., 23rd, Bricks, 25th, and Motor Vehicles, 28th. It can be seen from column 4 that the seasonal fluctuations where they exist, tend to cancel out, as the months of peak employment are different. This joint cancelling out is presented graphically in Figure 32, where the monthly fluctuations in employment over the country as a whole are given for the five distinctive industries, together with those for the highly fluctuating dispersed industry of building. The curves for the several industries are almost like a rhythmical series of waves, one coming up as the other subsides. The only period without waves at or near their crest is January and February.

Cyclical employment involves the comparison of years rather than months. The rates of unemployment suffered in each of the eight years before the War, that is from 1931-38, are given in Table XXVII for all employment exchange areas in the Conurbation. The wide differences between areas shown in the years 1931-2 are illustrated in Figure 33, and Table XXVII places the areas in order of their rate of unemployment in the period. Among the six County Boroughs, Birmingham experienced, on the average, only half the unemployed rate of Walsall and less than half that of Dudley. In Dudley, unemployment in 1931 was considerably heavier than in South Wales. In the months of January, August and October of that year, Dudley unemployment rates were actually 42.4 per cent, 41.4 per cent and 41.6 per cent of the total insured population. The Dudley average for the year 1931 was 38.8 per cent. The average unemployment rate for the same year in Wales was 33.5 per cent and in Scotland 27.4 per cent. Wales was also exceeded in unemployment that year by Cradley Heath, with 36.3 per cent, and by Wednesbury with 35.7 per cent.; Scotland was exceeded in unemployment by Brierley Hill with 33.2

---

[1] See P.E.P. *Report on Location of Industry*, Table 1 in Appendix 1.
[2] See Shenfield and Florence, *War-time Experience of Coventry*, (" Review of Economic Studies," pp. 144-5, 1946).
[3] See Glaisyer, Brennan, Ritchie and Florence, *County Town*, Chapter IV.
[4] *Seasonal Variations in Employment.*

TABLE XXVI

Serial No.	INDUSTRY (Brief description)	1 Ministry of Labour Symbol	2 Total Employed in Conurbation	3 Location Quotient in Conurbation	4 Seasonal Fluctuation if Appreciable Peak Months	Cyclical Fluct.
	SOURCE					MINISTRY OF
1	Iron and Steel Blast Furnaces, Smelting and Rolling Mills	(GA) (GC)	15,367	1·5		6
2	Non-Ferrous Metals — Extracting and Refining	(GF)	14,846	7·3		7
3	Non-Ferrous Metals—Later Processes and Wares	(GX)	19,486	13·1		7.
4	Tubes—Iron and Steel	(GP)	16,141	10·1		6
5	Bolts, Nuts, Rivets, Screws, Nails, etc. ...	(GS)	18,609	13·2		7
6a	Foundry and Secondary Processes	(CE)	21,372	8·8		8
6b	Other Metal Industries	(GW)	97,246	4·3	December	82
7	Constructional Engineering	(CZ)	6,732	4·3		72
8	Motor Vehicles, Cycles and Aircraft... ...	(DA)	48,915	3·6	Mar.-May	80
9	Railway Carriage, Trams, etc.	(DE)	8,582	3·1		78
10	Electrical Engineering (Generators, etc.) ...	(CN)	14,331	2·9		94
11	Hand Tools, Cutlery, etc.	(GM)	5,269	2·8		78
12	Jewellery, Plate, etc.	(HA)	18,668	8·3	Oct.-Dec.	87
13	Cocoa, Chocolate and Sugar Confectionery	(XE)	9,122	2·4	Aug.-Nov.	92
14	Saddlery, Harness and other Leather Goods	(KF)	6,930	5·2		88
15	Rubber Manufactures	(KA)	10,380	2·9		91
16	Glass (not Bottles)	(MP)	6,448	4·4		84
17	Bricks, Unglazed Tiles, Fireclay Goods, etc.	(MF)	7,765	1·6	May-Aug.	83

* Should be higher in Ministry of Labour industrial classification
** Census of Production separates into several industries

† By grades : 5=over 50% in plants employing over 1,000
3= ,, ,, ,, ,, ,, 100–1,000
1= ,, ,, ,, ,, ,, under 100
2 and 4=intermediate

per cent, by Bilston with 31.8 per cent, by Darlaston with 28.6 per cent, by West Bromwich with 28.6 per cent, and by Walsall with 28.4 per cent. After 1931, unemployment in the Conurbation area fell off more rapidly than in Wales and Scotland. While Wales still had in 1937 an unemployment rate of 22.4 per cent and Scotland a rate of 16.0 per cent, Walsall's rate had fallen to 9.4 per cent, Dudley's to 9.3 per cent, and Birmingham's to 4.3 per cent. Smethwick had an unemployment rate in that year of 3.7 per cent, and

6 growth .3-37 orkers loyed	7 Women: % of Total Insured 1936	8 Juveniles 14-16: % of Total Insured 1936	POPULATION CENSUS		PRODUCTION CENSUS		Serial No.
			9 Persons Independent and in Management as Percentage of Total Workers	10 Other Regions with Localization Quotients of 2 or over	11 Prevailing Size of Plant (if any) †	12 Horse Power per Worker	
-3·5	2·5	2·1	1·7	North II Wales II Scot. III	5	14·0	1
42·5	9·1	3·4	3·8*	Wales I	3‡ All sizes§	3·9‡ 5·5§	2
16·6	38·7	8·4	5·0	None	**	**	3
46·2	5·9	4·6	2·2	Wales II Scot. III	4	4·4	4
10·8	45·1	7·7	2·6	None	3	2·0	5
30·2	10·0	6·7	8·8	None	All sizes	1·7	6a
65·7	38·1	10·1		None	**	**	6b
84·0	4·3	5·4	2·6	Scot. III	3	2·9	7
96·4	10·2	5·8	8·6	None	5	1·4	8
04·7	3·0	4·2	0·9	Mid. II	4	4·4	9
99·6	22·2	10·0	2·3	None	5	1·9	10
28·6	32·0	12·6	7·9	North III	3	2·7	11
-11·2	46·9	10·2	23·4	North III	2	0·8	12
-11·1	66·8	14·9	3·5	North III	4	1·3	13
-01·8	55·9	15·3	17·7	London	2	0·2	14
-22·1	41·8	7·1	3·7	Scot. II	5	3·7	15
-26·9	23·6	7·3	4·2	North IV	5	2·8	16
-85·5	8·4	5·8	2·9	None	2	3·1	17

‡ Aluminium   § Copper and Brass

actually achieved a rate as low as 3.2 per cent in April and in June of 1937, and 3.1 per cent in December, 1935—equivalent to "Full Employment" as defined by Sir William Beveridge[1].

The relative unemployment suffered locally in any one year is largely the result of two measurable factors: first, the nature of the distinctive industries—that is the industrial

[1] *Full Employment in a Free Society*, page 128.

FIGURE 32

VARIATION OF EMPLOYMENT IN BUILDING AND FIVE SEASONAL TRADES DISTINCTIVE OF THE CONURBATION

Source.—C. Saunders "Seasonal Variations in Employment"

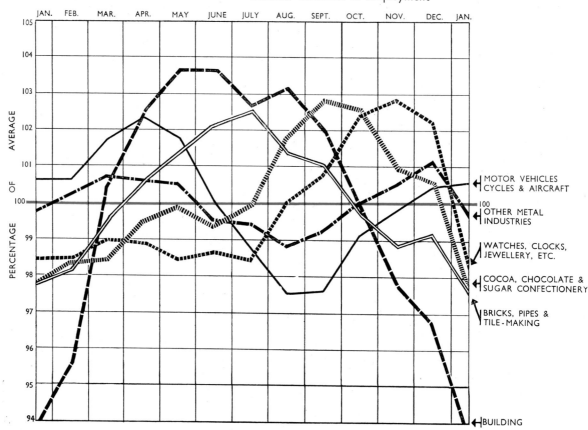

Only five of the seventeen industries distinctive of the Conurbation have any appreciable seasonal fluctuation, and the crests and troughs of the fluctuations in these five industries tend to cancel out.

structure of the locality as analysed in Sections 1 and 2; second, the unemployment experienced nationally by those distinctive industries[1]. Nationally, the main cause of unemployment was the cyclical depressions, such as that of 1930-33 ; the depth of this depression is given for each of the distinctive industries of the Conurbation in column 5 of Table XXVI[2]. For all manufacturing industries, employment nationally for 1932 was 86.4 per cent, compared to the average of 1929 and 1935. For the country as a whole— thirteen of the eighteen[3] industries distinctive of the Conurbation dropped lower than this average in their employment. Only electrical engineering, jewellery and plate, cocoa and sugar confectionery, saddlery and leather goods, and rubber showed less than the

---

[1] This explanation cannot account completely for relative local unemployment rates, since, quite apart from the different business of local firms, the precise sub-type of industry within each broad category of industry may vary locally.

[2] An index is here chosen that measures the amplitude of the depression in one figure. 1932 was the year of lowest employment for all industry in the country as a whole, 1929 was the previous peak year and by 1935 trade was again fairly normal for the inter-war period. The percentage employed in 1932 compared to the average of 1929 and 1935 is therefore at least a rough indication of the depth of the dip.

[3] See footnote 2, page 107.

average depression for manufactures. All the metal industries[1] were more depressed than average ; tubes, iron and steel, and constructional engineering particularly so. On the whole, earlier processes suffered more cyclical unemployment than the later processes, including motor-car assembly.

The joint effect of industrial structure and the unemployment experience of the industries concerned may be illustrated from various areas in the Conurbation and else-where. Table XXVII shows that unemployment is relatively high in Dudley and South

UNEMPLOYMENT RATES 1931 to 1938 FOR EXCHANGE AREAS WITHIN THE CONURBATION
COMPARED WITH GREAT BRITAIN, ENGLAND, WALES AND SCOTLAND

Ministry of Labour Local Unemployment Index

TABLE XXVII

Area	Average of Monthly Percentage Rates								Average for Eight Years
	1931	1932	1933	1934	1935	1936	1937	1938	
Great Britain	22·0	22·2	20·3	17·3	16·2	13·9	10·7	12·7	16·9
England	20·7	20·6	18·6	15·4	14·3	12·0	9·6	11·8	15·4
Wales	33·5	37·5	35·4	33·5	33·1	31·4	22·4	24·8	31·5
Scotland	27·4	27·8	27·4	24·6	23·2	20·5	16·0	16·4	22·9
Exchange Areas in order of Unemployment 1931									
Dudley	38·8	34·6	21·7	21·2	18·2	13·8	9·3	14·8	21·6
Cradley Heath	36·3	31·8	25·0	18·4*	14·1*	10·4*	8·6*	17·9*	20·3*
Wednesbury	35·7	36·8	31·1	20·8	18·2	11·7	7·1	12·7	21·8
Brierley Hill	33·2	29·5	24·7	17·9	14·6	10·2	8·1	13·4	19·0
Bilston	31·8	29·0	24·5	16·4	14·0	10·1	8·4	14·5	18·5
Darlaston	28·6	27·9	22·8	13·7	10·4	6·4	6·7	8·5	15·6
West Bromwich ...	28·6	27·1	21·6	12·3	11·3	7·9	5·2	9·4	15·4
Walsall	28·4	26·6	24·6	18·1	14·4	11·5	9·4	16·3	18·6
Sutton Coldfield ...	27·7	23·3	22·9	12·3	10·4	7·3	6·2	7·1	14·6
Tipton	27·2	27·6	23·6	14·7	12·3	8·3	6·8	11·1	16·5
Stourbridge	27·2	26·5	24·3	17·4	15·4	12·4	11·0	14·7	18·6
Wolverhampton ...	27·0	25·0	21·8	16·1	14·8	11·2	7·2	10·6	16·7
Willenhall	26·3	25·6	20·7	14·9	11·5	8·1	5·6	11·2	15·5
Oldbury	23·6	26·6	20·2	11·1	7·0	5·2	3·8	9·2	13·4
Smethwick	18·9	17·5	14·5	9·5	7·5	5·0	3·7	7·2	10·5
Birmingham	17·7	15·3	12·1	8·1	6·6	5·2	4·3	7·7	9·6

*Halesowen Employment Exchange began in 1934. Previously, it is believed, the bulk of workers exchanged their books at Cradley Heath.

Wales, and Figure 30 that Dudley (like South Wales) specialized in the earlier iron and steel processes (smelting, rolling, etc), which suffered severe unemployment generally throughout England and Wales. On the other hand, unemployment was below average in Birmingham, and Birmingham specialized in motor vehicles and the later metal processes and wares, industries in which unemployment throughout England and Wales was relatively moderate.

The comparatively low unemployment rates for areas in the Conurbation, particularly after 1934, can also be attributed to the paucity of declining industries in its industrial

---

[1] Except electrical engineering. Here the steep upward general trend of the industry probably flattened out the drop.

FIGURE 33

UNEMPLOYMENT RATES IN EXCHANGE AREAS

AVERAGE 1931 and 1932

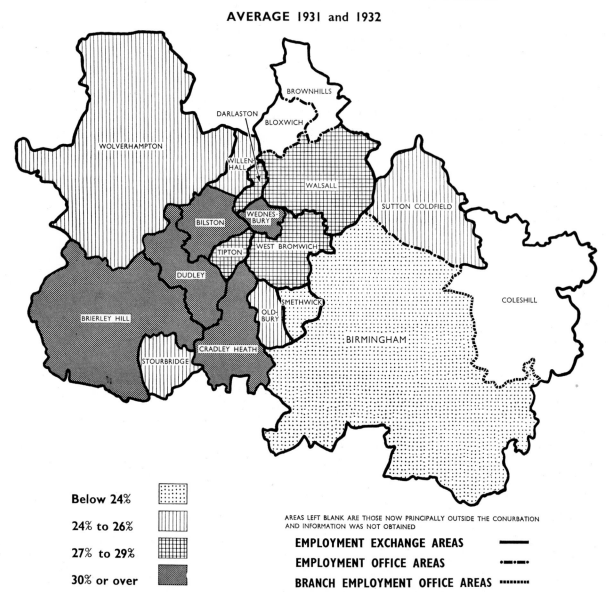

Below 24%

24% to 26%

27% to 29%

30% or over

AREAS LEFT BLANK ARE THOSE NOW PRINCIPALLY OUTSIDE THE CONURBATION AND INFORMATION WAS NOT OBTAINED

EMPLOYMENT EXCHANGE AREAS ———

EMPLOYMENT OFFICE AREAS ▪—▪—▪

BRANCH EMPLOYMENT OFFICE AREAS ▪▪▪▪▪▪▪▪▪

structure compared to the structure of other areas of industrial localization. Table XXIV, page 119 is clear on this point, and column 6 of Table XXVI shows the change, + or −, based on the index numbers of growth from 1923 to 1937 given there. These index numbers measuring the growth of the eighteen industries distinctive of the Conurbation, ranged from 88.8 to 199.6. Corresponding index numbers in the main localized manufactures virtually absent from the Conurbation (given on the right hand side in Table XXIV) ranged from as low as 67.7 to 136.2, with only two over 100. This clearly reinforces the argument that an area's unemployment is largely dependent on its industrial structure. The argument applies equally to unemployment due to the decline of industries and to cyclical depressions.

The risk of unemployment in the Conurbation which planning should guard against, is thus on the whole not the risk of its industries declining, but the risk of cyclical depression present in most metal industries. Metal industries make durable goods whose

FIGURE 34

PROPORTION OF EMPLOYED WOMEN TO ALL EMPLOYED WORKERS LIVING IN THE CONURBATION—1931

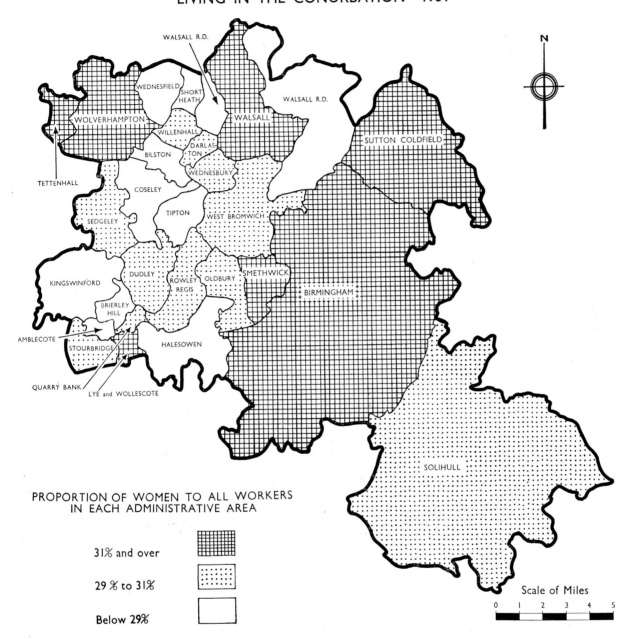

PROPORTION OF WOMEN TO ALL WORKERS
IN EACH ADMINISTRATIVE AREA

31% and over

29 % to 31%

Below 29%

Scale of Miles

Where a low proportion of women is employed there tend to be lower family incomes. The number of women employed in any area is closely related to the nature of the distinctive industries in it.

purchase can be postponed, and for which the demand is often as capital equipment for other industries; this means that a general industrial depression will hit these industries particularly hard. To meet the risk, metal industries—particularly those making capital goods—should be diversified with more stable industries in those areas which specialize somewhat exclusively in metal industries, as in the western parts of the Conurbation.

(B) The Proportion of Women in Industry

The significance to planning of the percentage of women among the total insured, is that areas where the percentage is low will thereby tend to have lower family incomes and lower standards of living than they would otherwise have. South Wales, for instance, has been hard hit financially, not only because of unemployment among the men during the depressions, but because there were never many women bringing in additional income. The variations in the proportions of women employed from one part of the country to another are remarkable[1]. The differences are mainly due to the industrial structure of the different areas, that is to the nature of their distinctive industries. Hence column 7 of Table XXVI should be a valuable guide in correcting industrial structure by selecting industries that do or do not employ many women according to the needs of the area.

In 1931 the Conurbation employed women in a proportion of 32.9 per cent of the total employed. This compares with 30.7 per cent. for England and Wales, and is higher than might be expected from a region without industries such as Cotton, Wool, Hosiery or Pottery, employing women in skilled trades[2].

The conclusions from the indices in Table XXVI is that the Conurbation as a whole has a high proportion of women employed in several of its distinctive industries, particularly Cocoa and Sugar Confectionery, Saddlery and Leather wares, Jewellery, Bolts, Screws, etc., " Non-Ferrous " wares, and the large group of " Other Metal Industries." These industries " balance " several other distinctive industries employing practically no women, such as Iron and Steel, Railway Carriage and Tram, Constructional Engineering, and Iron and Steel Tubes. But the balance is not evenly distributed over the whole area, and, in the western belt, industries employing higher proportions of women should be developed.

Figure 34 maps the differences in the percentage of women employed among the total employed in the various administrative areas of the Conurbation. In Section 2 it was pointed out that the areas with a lower percentage, requiring more women's industries to be added, are the areas specializing in the early (and usually heavier) metal processes. The lowest percentages were found at Kingswinford, 26.97 per cent, Tipton, 27.29 per cent, Coseley, 27.6 per cent, and Wednesfield, 27.73 per cent—all in the mining and early metal process " belt." These proportions contrast significantly with Sutton Coldfield, 34.56 per cent, Birmingham, 35.13 per cent, and Tettenhall, 35.15 per cent.

(C) *The Proportion of Juveniles* 14-16 *in Industry*

While the employment of juveniles, like that of women, may help materially in raising the family standard of living, and while their lack of occupation after leaving school presents social problems, the main significance of this measure is to act as a warning of under-supply. If too many industries employing many juveniles settle in one area, the supply of juveniles may well run out. With falling birth-rates and a rising school-leaving age, this is likely to be a serious consideration in those areas, like Walsall and the south-west fringe of the Conurbation, which specialize in Saddlery and Leather goods and Hand Tools respectively, two industries which—together with Cocoa—stand out among Conurbation industries as employers of juveniles. In 1936, the proportion aged 14-16 among the total insured was 6.6 per cent. The Saddlery and Leather goods trade, with its 15.3 per cent, had the highest percentage recorded for any industry in that year.

The general upshot of the indices in column 8 of Table XXVII is that there is sufficient variety among the distinctive industries of the Conurbation to balance out the employment

---

[1] Among English and Welsh counties in 1931 the percentage gainfully occupied among women over 14 varied from 44.5 per cent. for London and 43.7 per cent for Leicestershire, to 19.8 per cent for Glamorgan and 17.9 per cent, for Monmouthshire.

[2] In 1921 it appeared that in the larger industrial towns of the Conurbation and of the region few unmarried women were unoccupied or idle. See Florence, *A Statistical Contribution to the Theory of Women and Wages* (" Economic Journal," March, 1931).

of juveniles and to have full employment, but not scarcity, in any one area. Though Saddlery and Leather goods, and Cocoa and Sugar Confectionery employ a high proportion of juveniles, distinctive industries like Iron and Steel, Non-Ferrous earlier processes, Railway Carriage and Tram, and Iron and Steel Tubes employ only a very small proportion.

It will be noticed that those industries which employ few juveniles are often industries employing few women. This is partly, but not entirely, accounted for by girls 14-16 being both juveniles and women. The Iron and Steel, the Tube and the Railway Carriage and Tram industries, to name only a few, must be recognized from their employing capacity as poor " family investments," and must be supplemented in any area by industries employing members of the family other than adult men.

(D) The Proportion of Employers, Managers, and Workers on Own Account in Industry

In planning the industries of an area, attention must not be exclusively devoted to the more obvious objectives, such as full employment and higher family incomes. There is also the quality of employment to be considered in relation to the type and quality of the persons to be employed. The proportion of women and of juveniles employed by an industry has already been discussed, but sex and age are not the only distinctions between persons to be taken into account. Scope should be given, for instance, for inherent capacity and skill and for inherent enterprise and managing ability. Reliable statistics of skilled jobs available in any area are not obtainable, mainly because of the difficulty of defining skill. But it is possible to calculate for separate industries the proportion of employers, managers, and " workers on own account," from the Census of Population's tabulations on Industrial Status. This proportion is, of course, only a rough guide to the opportunities of responsible or independent status offered by the industries of an area[1], but it is worth making some attempt at such a " responsible job " index, particularly for the area of the Conurbation, which has always prided itself as the home of the " small man." The small man is important not only because he is trying to maintain economic independence, and is at least willing to take responsibility, but also because a certain number of his fellows (if not he himself) are getting valuable experience for greater responsibilities to come. An area or an industry without small men has lost one of its sources of recruitment and training for the controlling positions. In manufacturing industries as a whole, the West Midland Region had in 1931:—

Employers and Managers	29,917
Workers on Own Account	22,071
	51,988 (6.2 per cent.)
Total in Industry	836,275 (100 per cent.)

The percentage of employers, managers and independents was thus 6.2 ; the corresponding percentage for England and Wales as a whole was 5.8. Thus the Conurbation was slightly over average in this index of enterprise in manufacturing.

An analysis into separate manufacturing industries explains this position. The five Census industries (corresponding roughly with five among the seventeen[2] industries

---

[1] It is unfortunate, for instance, that the Census does not separate independent employers from managers.
[2] See footnotes, page 107.

distinctive of the Conurbation) with largest numbers of workers have the following percentages of employers, managers and independents among all workers :—

1. Founding.. .. .. 12.5
2. Motor Vehicles 8.6
3. Other Metal Industries 6.0
4. Non-Ferrous Later Processes and Wares .. 3.8
5. Jewellery and Plate 23.4

Four out of the five have a larger index than the national proportion or average of 5.8, and it is probable that if the Ministry of Labour classification could have been used, non-ferrous wares would also have shown a larger percentage.

(E) Equipment and Size of Plant in Industry

A " small man ratio " is significant also in considering the mobility of an industry. But more significant perhaps is the size and capital equipment of its plant. Though the source is the Census of Production with rather a different classification of industries, it is worth adding, in column 10 of Table XXVI, the grade (numbered 1 to 5) of size of plant prevailing in the industry, and, in Column 11, the average horse power in use per worker.

Heavy fixed equipment which consumes much power is obviously the less likely to be abandoned, though high power consumption is no argument against building additional plant outside the existing area of localization of the industry. The small man and the small plant are usually dependent on other small men and plants in the locality and could only operate efficiently if the whole inter-dependent complex of industries were moved in a body[1]. This argument applies both to physical movement out of the area of localization and to the starting of additional factories and firms outside.

" Mobility " conveys too narrowly the notion of actually moving a factory out of an area. The adjective " footloose " is perhaps more appropriate. It conveys ability to move *or* ability to start additional plant anywhere. The last three columns of Table XXVI may thus be said to indicate some of the conditions for making an industry economically less or more footloose; other important conditions such as linkage of industries are discussed in Section 5, Full Employment, Mobility and Efficiency (page 133). Points may be given for a low proportion of small men, for a large or medium size of plant, and for a light equipment using little power. Tested in this way, Electrical Engineering is, on points, the most footloose of the seventeen or eighteen industries, and is followed at some distance by Bolts and Screws, Cocoa and Confectionery, Railway Carriage and Tram. At the opposite extreme, fixed and far from footloose, appear Non-Ferrous processes, Jewellery, Hand Tools, Bricks and Fireclay, and Saddlery and Leather goods.

(F) Economic Characteristics Significant to Location

In measuring the existing situation of an industry, it must not be assumed that the present location, determined mainly by business considerations, is necessarily the most desirable. There are social costs which should be taken into consideration, such as liability to unemployment of a single-industry undiversified area, or the spoiling of fine landscape, which might even, in certain cases, over-ride economic factors. Nor, in spite of the determining business considerations, is the existing location necessarily the most efficient. Business considerations must be given weight only if based on a sound calculation of returns and costs.

It must be recognized in the first place that the existing location of the majority of

---

[1] See Florence, *Investment, Location and Size of Plant*, Chapter IV.

factories in the Conurbation was decided a considerable time ago. What was an economically sound decision at the time may now be out-of-date. Secondly, even if time has not changed the factors involved, the original decision may not have been economically sound. Small firms in particular did not in the past, and do not at present, make any elaborate enquiry when deciding to settle in one place or another. In many cases, existing premises were, no doubt, found fairly convenient for manufacturing purposes, and, to save capital costs of building, these premises were secured[1] without considering very deeply the costs of the particular location. In the third place, the person actually making the decision may not in the last resort have been moved by strictly economic reasons. The evidence is substantial for concluding that the London area has often drawn businesses to itself by reason not of advantages to the firm but because of its amenities to individual persons (and their families) making the decisions.

Factories located for sound economic reasons now out-of-date, or for economic reasons never sound, or not primarily for economic reasons at all, are likely, it is true, to go out of commission. Most existing factories are no doubt survivals of a competitive struggle and may be the fittest to survive. But such trial and error is in itself a costly process, and before the struggle is abandoned many a factory has produced at a loss over a considerable period, and many a factory will do so in future. Indeed many factory owners today realize that their business would be more successful if it were in another place. This is particularly evident where the present site is cramped and extensions impossible. But unless the owners have sufficient capital to make the move, they are unable to alter the original decision on location. It would seem better, therefore, to consider beforehand the economic costs and returns before making decisions about locations.

No statistics exist that can give an automatic answer to the question whether a factory organization should stay where it is or move elsewhere. Statistical investigation has therefore been supplemented for the purposes of this Report by interviews with over a hundred key business men representing specific industries or branches of industry in the Conurbation. As a result of these interviews it is possible to indicate certain of the less mobile industries of the Conurbation and to classify them according to the reasons for their immobility. The more mobile industries, left over after this analysis, are indicated in the next Section, which deals largely with conclusions on mobility. Section 5 also discusses the important practical question of what particular industries could have factories moved out of the Conurbation without substantial loss of economic efficiency (*i.e.*, old factories abandoned and replaced by new factories elsewhere), or at least could have further growth inside the Conurbation checked. Such radical policy requires, first, a restatement of ultimate objectives.

Lack of mobility was attributed in the interviews mainly to two causes, linkage with other industries and the use of skilled labour in the Conurbation. Four types of linkage could be distinguished, and the branches of industries represented by the key person interviewed may first be classified according to type of linkage. All these branches are included in the eighteen industries taken as distinctive of the Conurbation.

(i) *Industries performing a series of successive processes* (Vertical relation or linkage) :
   The non-ferrous series.
       Brass and copper plate, sheet, strip, rod.
       Brass and copper tube.

---

[1] See Board of Trade Survey of Industrial Development, 1933, and following years.

131

Brass wire.

Nickel silver.

Iron and steel processes : (These are often linked to metal industries under iv) :

Ironfounding.

Wrought iron.

Drop forging.

High duty castings.

(ii) *Industries serving a number of industries and having to be in continual contact with them* (Diagonal relation or linkage) :

Die-sinking, stamping, piercing.

Platers and gilders (*e.g.,* for jewellery).

Galvanizing.

Machine tools.

Hand or " small " tools.

Constructional engineering.

(iii) *Industries producing parts and accessories for an assembly industry, to the needs of which the design of the part has often to be adjusted experimentally.* (The relation here is lateral—each part of the industry converging on its market, the assembly industry).

For the assembly of motor cars :

Radiators.

Carburettors (esp. high precision).

Body hardware.

Steel pressings.

Electrical accessories and fittings.

Fine gear cutting.

For the assembly of saddlery and harness, etc. :

Leatherwork.

Malleable iron castings.

Other industries linked as making and assembling parts :

Perambulators.

Coffin furniture.

Cycles and motor cycles.

Weighing and testing machines.

Railway carriage and trams.

Springs (esp. for carriages and weighing machines).

(iv) *Industries using in common or diverging from certain processes, services or skills, provided locally and not elsewhere to any extent.* (In the Conurbation several industries diverge from the secondary metal-working processes and are thus laterally related to one another. Most of them depend not only on common processes but on a common pool of labour specially skilled):

Bolts and nuts.

Buckle and metal fittings.

Chain, cable and anchor.

Gun-making.

Locks.

Pens.

Pins.

Tubes.

(v) *Distinctive industries, not specially linked to other industries in the Conurbation, but immobile mainly for other reasons :*

Glass (on account of skilled labour).

Brick and Fireclay (on account of materials of low transportability).

5. Conclusions, with Special Reference to Full Employment, Mobility, and Efficiency

The objectives of any regional plan for industrial reconstruction are taken to be: (a) stable and high employment regionally in work using the various capacities of the population, and resulting in a high standard of living and amenities; and (b) participation in any national policy, such as dispersion. Recommendations should, therefore, be made under the headings of :—

(A) Stable employment.
(B) High employment.
(C) Use of the capacities of the population.
(D) The standard of living, and
(E) Participation in National policies.

(A) Stable Employment

A review of fluctuations in employment in the past has been coupled with an analysis of the Region's industrial structure. Thanks to diversity of industry, seasonal fluctuations were found not to be severe, but part of the Conurbation suffered high "cyclical" unemployment during the 1931-33 depression. Sections particularly affected were the Dudley, Bilston, Cradley Heath, Wednesbury, and Brierley Hill Labour Exchange Areas, in all of which the average level of unemployment was over 30 per cent. during 1931. This extreme unemployment can be associated with the high specialization of those areas in the earlier (primary and secondary) iron and steel processes, and in constructional engineering, which are subject to cyclical fluctuation.

The first conclusion is, therefore, that these areas of unstable employment should be diversified by extending their more stable industries (such as Clothing, in Dudley), and by bringing in industries from the more stable areas (such as Birmingham and Smethwick).

(B) High Employment

To ensure a general high level of employment, care must be taken to replace declining industries. The industrial population of the Conurbation increased between the wars relatively to the country as a whole, mainly by reason of having specialized in industries which grew generally throughout the country at that period. Of the eighteen industries picked out as localized in and distinctive of the Conurbation, only two—Jewellery, and Iron and Steel smelting and rolling—fell in the numbers employed nationally between 1923 and 1937. Of eleven industries localized in other regions but almost absent in the Conurbation, nine fell in numbers employed nationally. These industries localized in the Conurbation often grew less quickly in the Conurbation than in the country as a whole, but they grew fast enough in the Conurbation to permit its population to increase in relation to that of the country as a whole.

Analysing these industries localized in the Conurbation, such as Motor-cars and Metal goods, and forecasting the probable demand for their main products, there is no reason to suppose that their growth will be checked. It may be assumed that their trend in the near future will not depart radically from the upward 1923-37 trend. The Conurbation may, therefore, be expected to continue to grow relatively to the country as a whole. If our objective is to keep the growth or the decline of the population of the Conurbation consistent with forecast trends in the rate of natural increase, and not to allow immigration to exceed emigration, a second conclusion can be stated. *There is no need to introduce completely new industries into the Conurbation.*

This recommendation does not exclude re-distribution or decentralization of industries already within the conurbation for the sake of replacing industries declining locally. Indeed, our third conclusion is that *industries should be re-distributed within the Conurbation to make up for the relative decline of Coal-mining and the primary processes of Iron and Steel smelting and rolling in the northern and western areas of the Conurbation.* Decentralization will normally not entail much extra loss of efficiency in matters of transport, packing, etc., since the area of the Conurbation is small and the extra distance involved, if covered by lorry from door-to-door, would be negligible. Key men may not even have to change their homes.

Nor does the (second) conclusion, adverse to the introduction of completely new industries, exclude new branches of existing industries. The two distinctive basic industries of the Conurbation are metal assembly industries, particularly Motor cars; and a related group of Metal processes, (*e.g.*, founding) and products. Some of these processes and products, unlike general engineering, may recede in importance—in fact, the jewellery industry has shown signs of doing so. Our fourth conclusion is, therefore, that *within the established group of Metal Industries, conditions favourable to re-juvenation and re-development should be encouraged, i.e. the continual opening up and development of new branches within a given industry.* Many of the conditions favourable to this are discussed below. They include the maintenance of a supply of enterprising small employers with powers of adaptation, fuller provision of technical and market research locally, and the high localization of linked industries each in contact with one another.

(C) Use of Capacity of the Population

The employable population of any area possesses varying capacities and it is important to provide a variety of employment to fit those capacities. Though there is some deficiency in opportunities for women in the central north-west belt and the coal-mining areas, the Conurbation (thanks to its many localized industries) provides on the whole a wide range of employment for men, women, and young persons, and offers opportunities for the skilled craftsmen and for small employers or workers on their own account. Given equal efficiency, small firms are important as offering independent status and often opportunities for real enterprise; they also form a recruiting and training ground for larger scale management.

Our fifth conclusion is that *this diversity of occupation and of status should be preserved, and the opportunities met halfway, by the provision of wider technical education, including training in management. The small man might possibly be helped (especially in the export trades) by the provision of pooled technical and market (including design) research facilities and by the building of Trading Estates or (in more densely populated areas) "flatted" factories.*

(D) The Standard of Living

As standards of living rise, it is found that a higher proportion of income is spent on certain services. Services (unlike goods) must be produced in the place where they are "consumed" which gives us a chance of comparing in some measure the standards of different regions.

The Conurbation has been found to have a comparatively low proportion of workers rendering the services that mark a higher standard of living. In distribution, in professional services, in hotels, restaurants, inns, etc., in entertainment and sport, and in laundry work, the proportion of workers is lower than the national average by 15 per cent. to 50 per cent.

The comparatively low proportions indicate a deficiency in amenity and in opportunities for enjoyment within the area, and substantiate common observation. The deficiency applies to Birmingham as well as the Black Country areas. Since lack of services, amenities and cultural life keeps or drives away possible customers for goods, as well as the technical and managerial staff on which modern production methods so much depend, a sixth conclusion is that *Shopping centres, Hotels, Restaurants, Theatres, Concert Halls, and Assembly Rooms should be developed throughout the Conurbation.*

(E) Participation in National Policies

A regional plan, such as that for the Conurbation, should fit in with, and be part of, a national plan for industry. If the recommendations of the Barlow Commission and the Scott Committee are to be implemented, policies of redevelopment, decentralization, dispersion, and diversification will be applied. As far as the Conurbation is concerned, re-development and decentralization have already been recommended *within the Conurbation*, and, for parts of the Conurbation, greater diversification. The Conurbation as a whole is relatively congested and likely to grow further in population. The Group suggests that it is desirable that further growth in total population should be no faster than the natural increase. This may imply the deliberate dispersal of certain industries to prevent net immigration. Before making positive recommendations, a detailed analysis has been undertaken into the economic dependence of the industries of the Conurbation upon their present location, and the possible loss of efficiency entailed by moving them or checking their development.

(i) ECONOMIC REASONS FOR PRESENT LOCATION

With the exception of Coal-mining, Brick-making and possibly a few other branches of heavy industries (probably not accounting altogether for more than 5 per cent. of the industrial population of the Conurbation) there are now no industries absolutely dependent upon proximity to the natural resources of the area. The outstanding present reasons on the score of efficiency of the Conurbation's large localization of factories and industries is their *inter*dependence, and the existence of a *pool of skilled labour and technicians* in various trades.

(a) Interdependence of Industries

The danger to efficiency in the limitation or removal of any one manufacturing industry or factory is that of a break in the economic link with other manufacturing industries or factories. These economic links are of various types. Factories in the Conurbation are connected by performing consecutive processes, by performing similar processes involving similar materials or similar markets, or by serving one another. Or, they may be linked by using complementary material or labour (*e.g.*, men and women) available locally. Such linkage has been measured statistically by the very high localization within the same narrow areas of factories in various industries. The removal or check in the expansion of one factory might in these cases upset the balance of efficient production. There is a particular danger of upsetting efficiency where each of a number of small factories is specializing in part of a whole process or product, and the production of some of the factories is in small lots. Transport costs *per unit of output* and personal contacts are then important factors. There is less danger of upsetting the efficient balance of production where that balance is achieved within a large factory or within the several factories of a large firm; or where small manufacturers (by producing in large, possibly standardized, lots) do not have to get into contact so often.

Following upon this analysis our seventh conclusion is that *the further entry into the Conurbation of large self-contained factories, or of factories owned by large self-contained firms, is undesirable, and that in scrutinizing the claims of small firms to settle in the Conurbation the efficiency of large-lot production in reducing the need for constant personal contacts, should be kept in mind.*

Our eighth conclusion is that *local expansion is not desirable for industries shown to be less closely linked with other industries in the Conurbation, and that factories shown to be less closely linked with factories in the same industry in the Conurbation should be discouraged.*

The seventh recommendation is particularly difficult to apply in actual practice. However, localized industries and factories whose close linkage appears necessary from economic argument, from the statistical evidence, or from the answers of industrialists can be sieved out as immobile.

Obvious cases include:—

(1) Localized industries performing one or a few processes in the middle of a succession of processes performed locally. If placed elsewhere, a double journey of the material would be involved.

(2) Localized industries serving a number of local industries (*e.g.*, die-sinking, plating), and having to be in continual contact with the industry served.

(3) Localized industries producing parts or accessories for a local assembly industry (and for no other), where the design of the part has continually to be adjusted by experiment to the needs of the assembly industry.

(4) Localized industries or factories each using in common certain processes, services, or skills, mainly provided locally and not elsewhere.

After such a sieving, several industries localized in the Conurbation yet appear as mobile and controllable. Among the distinctive industries (or branches of them) the rubber industry is linked with motor assembly in its supply of tyres. Yet the tyre is not such a part of the car as under (3) requires continual adjustment to needs, and more than half the tyres are for replacement and not for original assembly. In fact, the American rubber industry is localized at Akron, Ohio, some considerable distance from the centre of the motor car trade in Detroit and surrounding parts of Michigan. Again, such factories as perform almost all the consecutive processes in producing aircraft frames, or engines, or hollow-ware, escape through the mesh of (1). Nor does electrical engineering (*e.g.*, electric motors), or screw manufacture, or edge tools, or cocoa and sugar confectionery, appear to be so exclusively linked to the main Conurbation industries as to preclude some measure of control such as the prohibition of the entry of large new factories.

Among the industries only moderately localized in the Conurbation (Category B; see page 108), some others may be found that could be discouraged from further localization there—for instance, brushes and brooms, furniture, electrical apparatus, and scientific apparatus. The last three are growing fast for the country as a whole, and their settlement in the Conurbation might add considerably to the congestion.

(b) Location near Pool of Skilled Labour

This reason for the efficiency of the present location and for lack of mobility was given in interviews more often than any other. Skilled labour is particularly important in the process of founding as carried on at present. But it must not be forgotten that methods are changing and that with mechanization, standardization, and larger-lot production the proportion of skilled men may be reduced and diluted.

Our ninth conclusion is that, *in judging the mobility of existing industries, the alleged need for a large pool of skilled labour should be reviewed in the light of modern production methods. It may always be possible to move the small staff of technicians, foremen, mechanics, toolmakers, etc., required under the newer methods and find the " dilutees " in the new area. It should be borne in mind that removal will involve a certain standard of services in the new area, and that the existence of adequate amenities will be a factor of some importance.*

(ii) LIKELY ALTERNATIVE LOCATION

Since dispersion implies a place *to* which as well as *from* which industries are to shift, it is important to make sure that the industries, branches of industries, or factories that are controlled or even prevented from settling in the West Midland Conurbation do not settle in some equally congested area. This is by no means a theoretical objection. Many of the industries localized primarily in the Conurbation have a secondary location to which they would most naturally resort if denied the Conurbation. For several of the industries surveyed this secondary location is London, or else Sheffield and the South Yorkshire Conurbation. But several other industries that might be restricted in the West Midland Conurbation could probably settle either in some hitherto industrially undiversified area, such as the Potteries or Kidderminster; or in some recognized " depressed " area (depressed probably because of lack of diversity), or else in some country town. The tenth and final conclusion is *that, in considering what industries or factories should be restricted, attention should be paid to the likely area to which they would resort if checked in the West Midland Conurbation, and to favour the restriction of only such cases as would result in true dispersion or diversification.*

(iii) A QUANTITATIVE ESTIMATE OF DISPERSION

If there is to be no population increase due to net immigration into the Conurbation, the size of the conurbation is unlikely to grow faster than the rate of 5 per thousand per annum (see Chapter VI) over the first few years, and at a slower rate as time goes on. Five per thousand of 2,078,733 (the population of the Conurbation in 1939) is 10,400.

Immigration will depend upon the technical success of national measures of control, upon the local housing position, and upon the availability of sites for industry. This last, however, is not a severely limiting factor, as re-development would probably effect economies in space. At present there is a heavy demand for labour in Birmingham, and immigration is restricted partly by control and partly by shortage of houses. If the forward estimates of all Birmingham manufacturers were totalled, they would show an expectation of a greatly increased industrial population in the Conurbation within the next year or two. It can be expected that the magnet influences will continue, unless national policy intervenes and can be made effective.

As a guide to policy, it may be estimated that, for every hundred persons occupied in a non-residentiary industry which could possibly be controlled, one further hundred are occupied in non-mobile or residentiary industries or services, and a further 250— mostly women and children—are unoccupied. To limit the population expansion of the

Conurbation to a maximum of 10,400 per annum over the first few years, and subsequently to a less amount, will require an initial limitation to $10,400 \times \frac{100}{450}$ or 2,300 per annum in the increased number of workers in non-residentiary industries, and more severe limitation later on.

CHAPTER IX

Survey of Factory Buildings

PURPOSE AND SURVEY

ON THE Surface Utilisation Map of the Conurbation the areas occupied by Industry are shown in relation to the Housing and other areas. This relationship reveals the lack of plan in the siting of factories, many of which, particularly in the congested areas, are mingled with houses in haphazard fashion. Factories are closely packed together, they are often obnoxious or noisy, and many thousands of them were, at some period in the last hundred years or so, converted from dwelling houses to the purposes of manufacture. Without further enquiry, this knowledge raises the question whether it is desirable or practicable, in the interest of the inhabitants of a particular neighbourhood, to separate factories and houses as part of a planned scheme of development. It is now generally recognized that, with some minor exceptions (such as bakehouses), factories and dwelling houses should not normally be contiguous, although they may be sited to advantage in adjoining areas. Under good planning, newly-developed areas and re-developed areas alike should provide for the accommodation of all noisy or noxious factories in zones separated from residential neighbourhoods.

Redevelopment is, however, a two-fold process. Besides laying down the zones in which new or re-built factories must be located, one must determine which existing areas are in need of clearing. To do this, it is as necessary to know the condition of the factory buildings in it as it is to know the condition of the houses. Further, a long-term programme of redevelopment will require an assessment of the degrees of urgency in the need for redevelopment in different areas. In deciding such priority there are two questions to be considered. The first is concerned with the relative density of the actual buildings within any area. Closely packed factory buildings impede both light and air and so reduce the physical amenities of all factories in the group. No detailed enquiry into the factor of congestion has been possible during the present survey, although in the central sectors of Birmingham and of other towns in the Conurbation the degree of congestion of factory buildings is usually much higher than is desirable. The second question relates to the condition of the individual factory buildings. To deal adequately with this factor would have required a thorough external and internal inspection of the many thousands of buildings in the Conurbation. Though it was not in the Group's power to undertake such a survey, it was thought that it would be worth while to carry out a survey of factory buildings in as many areas as possible in the time available. The results of such a survey can only be regarded as tentative. They are presented to show the need of, and to point the way to, a more thorough investigation by the appropriate authorities. Such an investigation is an essential part of the research upon which a sound planning scheme should be based.

METHOD OF SURVEY

Considerable thought was given to the working out of the best method of conducting an external survey of factory buildings. A pointing system was first devised. This took into account such factors as siting, structure, lighting, sanitation, etc. On application to particular factories, to which, of course, there was no right of entry, this method was found to be unduly elaborate. After this experiment, it was decided to proceed with a visual survey carried out by one investigator in order to maintain a constant standard. The buildings were classified and mapped on 6-inch Ordnance Survey sheets, and the survey took into account the three factors of age, structure, and general appearance of the buildings. (For examples of the Survey Maps see Plates 13, 14 and 15.)

Buildings were classified into three broad categories, as follows:—

Class 1 (*Bad*)

Buildings suffering from age or bad structural conditions to such an extent as to justify their immediate replacement under a replanning scheme. Included in this class are houses converted into workshops and offices, and the old narrow workshops erected in the 19th century, with low ceilings, timber floors and inadequate natural lighting.

Class 2 (*Moderate*)

Buildings appearing to be reasonably satisfactory premises in " fair-to-good " structural condition. They possess one or more of the characteristics of Class 1 buildings to such an extent that their replacement will, in the opinion of the Group, be required within the next 30 years.

Class 3 (*Good*)

Buildings which are good industrial premises, structurally sound and not likely to fall below the standard of Class 3 within the next 30 years. Included in this class are most of the factories built since 1914.

Besides these main classes, two other descriptions were used to designate areas of factories of intermingled and intermediate characteristics: " Bad-to-moderate " (Class 1-2), " Moderate-to-good " (Class 2-3). Buildings which from an external survey appeared to be temporary, *e.g.*, corrugated iron structures, have been placed in Class 2 if in good condition, and in Class I if in poor or bad condition. It should be mentioned that unoccupied land which was classed as " industrial " in the Surface Utilisation Survey has not been included in the Survey of Factory Buildings.

Some of the problems arising from a survey of this kind should be mentioned. Large factories, covering in some cases an area of up to a square mile, presented great difficulties, although canal banks, elevated view points, and the previous acquaintance of the investigator with the inside of some of these factories, made it possible to reduce the volume of guesswork more than might at first appear. Most of the factories seemed to fall readily into one of the three main categories, but there were many border-line cases. To these it was difficult to apply a fair standard, partly because of the great variety in the appearance and structure of the buildings, and partly because of the difficulty of keeping a constant standard in mind throughout the period of the survey. This difficulty could be overcome in any detailed survey by including a written description of each building.

e Jewellery Quarter, Birmingham. Many streets which 100
ago formed a quiet residential neighbourhood have been
over, house by house, to light industries.

Factories of this sort occupy a large proportion of the industrial
area of every urban centre in the Conurbation.

Over one-third of the population of the Conurbation lives in slum houses. Possibly
one-fifth of the factory workers are employed in such buildings as those shown on this page.

Factory buildings dating from the end of the nineteenth century. Most of the buildings are structurally sound and working conditions may be fairly good, although buildings may not be up-to-date from the point of view of industrial efficiency.

Typical of factories in central urban areas. A congested assortment of structures, built at different times and filling all available ground space.

The layout and accessibility to transport of even quite well-built factories were made to conform with ideas based on ordinary residential streets.

142

Temporary buildings of the sort shown here were classified with permanent buildings having a similar length of useful life.

A modern factory in the middle ring of Birmingham. Its design is aimed at working efficiency.

Rear view of a modern factory. A varied collection of buildings behind an impressive "modernist" front.

...rmingham outer ring factory. Some attempt has been
...to improve the environment of the factory by preserving
...al features. Compare this with the more impressive
...more expensive building in the right-hand photograph.

*A new factory on a main road, typical of many built
just before 1939. The rapid growth of industrial ribbon
development side by side with the increase of road transport has produced a major planning problem.*

Factories and houses packed together around a narrow alley.

Larger factories dominate the surrounding streets of small houses.

A few yards from the main street of Walsall. Factories and houses face each other across an alley.

In most of the older centres, factories in bad condition and sub-standard houses are usually found side by side.

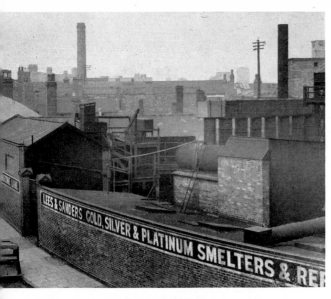

ongestion in the central areas of the larger towns.

verted houses, old multi-storeyed factories and modern
·ial plant tightly packed in a strange confusion.

There is often no room for proper access or for traffic ; no room
for amenities, and no room for individual factories to expand.

The photographs on these two pages illustrate some of the major
complications in the task of planning and redeveloping industrialized central
areas. Besides the unfitness of individual structure, sheer lack of space is
the most serious of the adverse conditions affecting health, amenity,
efficiency and economic vitality. The intermixture of uses, especially of
housing and industry, is usually undesirable, and certainly so in the
instances shown here, which are common throughout the Conurbation.

145

The principal industrial area of Wolverhampton—south-west of the town.

Duddeston and Nechells—a Birmingham problem area.

iecemeal redevelopment without planning—a cliff face of k and glass confronts the houses that remain.

The former thoroughfares survive, dissecting the new factory, but the social character of the neighbourhood has gone.

w from the multi-storeyed factory shown above. Thousands kers add a new congestion to the streets and courts of the l areas.

View of a redevelopment area. The industrial character of this part of the replanned central area is already established.

The obvious solution for the congested areas of obsolete houses and bad factory buildings in urban centres lies in comprehensive schemes of redevelopment. But many complications arise from the presence in those areas of large modern factory buildings. The factory shown in the two upper photographs is situated near the centre of Birmingham in the same ward as the Jewellery Quarter and dominates a large area of slum streets due for redevelopment (lower photographs).

AREA COVERED

The survey of factory buildings extended over nearly half the total area of the Conurbation, and covered the following towns:—Birmingham, Wolverhampton, Wednesfield, Bilston, Oldbury, West Bromwich, Smethwick, Halesowen, Lye, and Wollescote, and parts of Sutton Coldfield, Brierley Hill, Rowley Regis, and Cradley. The area surveyed includes congested districts, such as the centres of most of the towns; new industrial development districts which are found on the outskirts of such towns as Birmingham and Wolverhampton; and centres of long-established industries, such as the jewellery trade in the St. Paul's Ward of Birmingham, and the chain and nail trades in the Cradley district. Altogether, though individual differences would undoubtedly be found in the towns and districts which have not been covered by the survey, it is believed that the survey includes a sufficient total area and variety of types of area to give a representative picture of the situation in the Conurbation as a whole.

RESULTS OF SURVEY

Tables XXVIII, XXIX, and XXX show some of the results of the survey:—

CLASSIFICATION OF FACTORY BUILDINGS :

(a) FOR AREA SURVEYED

TABLE XXVIII

Class of Building		Area (Acres)	Area as percentage of Total of Area Surveyed
I	Bad	369·8	7·3
I–2	Bad-to-Moderate	105·2	2·1
2	Moderate	1,287·2	25·4
2–3	Moderate-to-Good	402·4	7·9
3	Good	2,911·4	57·3
	Total	5,076·0	100·0

The analysis of the classification of factory buildings in the whole area surveyed (Table XXVIII) shows that between 7 per cent. and 10 per cent. of the factory buildings, when measured by the area of ground occupied, are out of date, and need reconstruction or replacement. Between 25 per cent and 33 per cent of the buildings are in moderate condition and should have a life of twenty to thirty years. The balance of about 57 per cent is new or in good condition. These proportions do not show the number of individual buildings in the different categories ; nor do they indicate the number of people who work in the different classes of factory building. In general, the number of people employed in a given area is higher in the older factories, many of which are multi-storey buildings. The proportion of those employed in bad factory buildings may therefore be considerably higher than the ground area classification indicates. It is quite probable that as many as 20 per cent. of the factory workers of the Conurbation are employed in factories which should be rebuilt or reconditioned.

Table XXIX shows the classification of factory buildings in the boroughs or urban districts which were surveyed.

148

Table XXX shows the classification of selected areas in Birmingham and Wolverhampton, and throws into relief the condition of factory buildings in the central areas of the two towns. The Survey Maps of the two areas are reproduced in Plates 13 and 14. In both, about 25 per cent of the buildings in the central areas are " Bad " or " Bad-to-Moderate ", compared with 8 per cent (Birmingham) and 12 per cent (Wolverhampton) for the whole of the respective boroughs.

CLASSIFICATION OF FACTORY BUILDINGS :
TABLE XXIX (b) BY TOWNS

Part of Conurbation		Class I	Class I-2	Class 2	Class 2-3	Class 3	Total
Birmingham	Acres	185·0	13·2	455·4	175·9	1612·0	2441·5
	%	7·6	0·6	18·6	7·2	66·0	100·0
Wolverhampton	Acres	53·6	18·9	122·1	12·5	393·2	600·3
	%	8·9	3·1	20·4	2·1	65·5	100·0
Oldbury	Acres	19·0	—	126·2	—	228·6	373·8
	%	5·1	—	33·7	—	61·2	100·0
Smethwick	Acres	14·9	66·4	86·8	13·0	198·7	379·8
	%	3·9	17·5	22·9	3·4	52·3	100·0
Halesowen (part)	Acres	30·2	—	132·1	9·3	55·2	226·8
	%	13·3	—	58·3	4·1	24·3	100·0
West Bromwich (part)	Acres	18·7	—	113·7	61·4	127·0	320·8
	%	5·8	—	35·5	19·1	39·6	100·0
Wednesfield (part)	Acres	9·3	—	38·4	9·8	52·2	109·7
	%	8·5	—	35·0	8·9	47·6	100·0
Coseley (part)	Acres	4·7	3·7	60·5	58·4	5·7	133·0
	%	3·5	2·8	45·5	43·9	4·3	100·0
Bilston (part)	Acres	12·9	3·0	58·3	50·1	57·4	181·7
	%	7·1	1·6	32·1	27·6	31·6	100·0
Willenhall (part)	Acres	—	—	0·9	—	0·2	1·1
	%	—	—	—	—	—	—
Sutton Coldfield (part)	Acres	0·4	—	15·6	—	17·9	33·9
	%	1·2	—	46·0	52·8	52·8	100·0
Aldridge (part)	Acres	0·2	—	0·2	—	—	0·4
	%	—	—	—	—	—	—
Solihull (part)	Acres	—	—	3·6	—	73·6	77·2
	%	—	—	4·7	—	95·3	100·0
Rowley Regis (part)	Acres	16·6	—	37·9	12·0	65·2	131·7
	%	12·6	—	28·8	9·1	49·5	100·0
Brierley Hill (part)	Acres	0·7	—	13·5	—	—	14·2
	%	4·9	—	95·1	—	—	100·0
Stourbridge (part)	Acres	3·6	—	15·2	—	3·5	22·3
	%	16·1	—	68·2	—	15·7	100·0
Tipton (part)	Acres	—	—	6·8	—	21·0	27·8
	%	—	—	4·5	—	75·5	100·0
TOTALS	Acres	369·8	105·2	1287·2	402·4	2911·4	5076·0
	%	7·3	2·1	25·4	7·9	57·3	100·0

The survey, as a whole, gives an indication of the scale of the problem of " factory slums." These buildings are found most often in the congested central areas of towns and are usually converted houses, narrow small-windowed workshops with low ceilings and timber floors, or more modern buildings of a ramshackle construction and in a bad state of maintenance; motor repair works are often found in this class. On the outskirts of towns there are fewer " slum factories ", but many of those that do exist, such as old brick and tile works, are associated with long-established trades.

From the point of view of redevelopment, it is unfortunate that between the wars so many modern factory buildings were built in congested areas which should in many cases have been scheduled for housing only. This will be one of the most difficult problems which town planning authorities have to face, and the situation will be aggravated in the future if the powers of zoning which can now be exercised under Town Planning laws are not applied with knowledge and foresight. There are, of course, many factors to be considered in the siting of factories—the distance between place of residence of workers and the factory, the accessibility of transport facilities, and so on. But this survey points

CLASSIFICATION OF FACTORY BUILDINGS :
(c) BY SELECTED AREAS
(see maps, Plates 13 and 14)

TABLE XXX

Parts of Conurbation		Class 1	Class 1-2	Class 2	Class 2-3	Class 3	Total
BIRMINGHAM :							
Central Area* ...	...Acres	104·2	8·5	153·4	2·5	170·0	438·6
	%	23·7	1·9	35·0	0·6	38·8	100%
Outer District ...	...Acres	80·8	4·7	302·0	173·4	1442·0	2002·9
	%	4·0	0·2	15·1	8·7	72·0	100%
Whole City	...Acres	185·0	13·2	455·4	175·9	1612·0	2441·5
	%	7·6	0·6	18·6	7·2	66·0	100%
WOLVERHAMPTON :							
Central Area† ...	...Acres	29·2	11·2	43·8	11·6	62·2	158·0
	%	18·5	7·1	27·7	7·3	39·4	100%
Outer District ...	...Acres	24·5	7·7	78·3	0·9	331·0	442·3
	%	5·5	1·6	17·7	0·2	74·9	100%
Whole Town	...Acres	53·6	18·9	122·1	12·5	393·2	600·3
	%	8·9	3·1	20·4	2·1	65·5	100%

* *i.e.* area within a circle of one mile radius from Birmingham Cathedral.
† *i.e.* area within a circle of ⅔ of a mile radius from Queen Square, Wolverhampton.

clearly to the undesirable results of the largely uncontrolled factory building in the past; undesirable from the point of view both of neighbouring householders and of those working in the factories. It is dangerous to be dogmatic after a merely external survey, and it is true that some houses can be converted into suitable factories for some trades. It is also true that some old factory buildings can be modernized and made to provide decent working conditions according to contemporary standards. But if conditions are to be improved, it is essential that standards for factory buildings should be laid down, and that a definite " life " should be placed on those buildings which fall below a minimum standard. This is a complicated question which is discussed further in a later paragraph.

A new factory district, like the Tyseley area of Birmingham, is in striking contrast to the old central industrial districts. In Tyseley there are more buildings of a high standard, more north-light single storey buildings and larger areas of open space between most of the buildings. The factory grounds are often laid out with gardens. Although even in some of the newly developed areas a general plan could have prevented such overcrowding of buildings as there is, the line of progress is clearly apparent. Better results in the planning of future factory areas would be achieved if local area committees were set up and given powers to supervise the general lay-out of buildings, open spaces, and gardens throughout the area.

RECOMMENDATIONS

(1) The existence of "factory slums" points to the need for *factory slum clearance schemes*. These will require the establishment of recognized standards for factory buildings as regards spacing, structure, sanitary conditions, lighting, and ventilation. Some standards already exist in the Factories Act and Regulations, and for cotton cloth factories detailed legal standards are laid down for new buildings and are enforced by the Factory Inspector[1]. It should be possible to lay down minimum standards for all factory buildings. Various needs of different trades would call for some variation from the general standard; for example, the type of building needed for drop forging is different from that required for light metal work or for cotton weaving. Local authorities might be empowered to enforce such standards. To assist them it might be possible, for example, to make it obligatory for industrial concerns wishing to build new premises or to improve or convert old ones to obtain a certificate of approval by the government authorities responsible for conditions in factories. The special knowledge of such government authorities would supplement that of the local authority in the case of certain special industries, *e.g.*, industries involved in hot processes, where unsuitable structures will defy even the most determined efforts to affect real improvements in conditions by altering the ventilating system. The general standard for new buildings and conversions would then be enforced by local authorities whose byelaws should be strengthened to this end. The deviations from the general standard allowed to special industries would naturally demand reference to the government authorities responsible for conditions in factories. Although past experience shows the need of standards for factory buildings which can be enforced by law, every encouragement should be given to voluntary schemes such as that of the Birmingham Jewellers and Silversmiths Association for flatted factories. This scheme for the re-habilitation of an old Birmingham industry is both practical and far-seeing, and the possibility of similar schemes for other industries should be explored by those concerned with industrial welfare and with town planning, especially as such schemes offer new possibilities for increasing the open space in the centres of towns. When the standards have been defined it will be possible to apply them to factory buildings, to decide which of these are "unfit to be used as places of work" and require improvements within a given period, or, in the case of a clearance scheme, to schedule buildings for demolition after a certain date.

(2) Consideration should be given to working out more comprehensive *standards for new factory buildings*.

Under present Acts and Bye-laws, new buildings have to comply with certain standards relating, among other things, to structure and fire exits. But the provisions relating to daylight lighting, ventilation, and some of the sanitary arrangements can, as a rule, only be enforced *after* the factory has been built. Existing legislation naturally influences the work of architects and builders. The influence would be more effective if, as in the case of

---

[1] Section 63 of the Factories Act, 1937, reads as follows :—

" Certificates required before approval of building plans relating to Cotton Cloth Factories.—No plans or sections relating to the erection or conversion of a building proposed to be used as a cotton cloth factory shall be approved by any local authority to whom they have been submitted in pursuance of any Act or of any byelaw made under any Act unless they are accompanied by a certificate in writing, issued by the superintending inspector of factories for the division in which the building is proposed to be erected or converted, certifying that the building to which the plans and sections relate would not, if erected or converted in accordance therewith, contravene or fail to comply with the regulations made under the Factory and Workshop (Cotton Cloth Factories) Act, 1929 ".

cotton cloth factories, more comprehensive standards, ensuring adequate environmental conditions, were applied to all plans for the erection of new factories.

(3) *The conversion of existing buildings*, such as halls and private houses, *to manufacturing purposes, should be controlled.* Otherwise, new " slum factories " are likely to be created. It would seem that some authority should have the power to prevent or refuse all unsatisfactory schemes of conversion, and that this authority should be in a position to enforce the same minimum standards as would be applied to new buildings.

(4) Steps should be taken to *maintain sufficient open space in new industrial areas* to prevent the over-congestion of buildings, which reduces the access of daylight to work-rooms, and to provide for workers during mealtimes. This might be controlled by the establishment of area committees, representative of the industrialists and workers of the area, and with responsibility for the general planning and development of the amenities of the area, subject to the over-riding power of the local town-planning authority.

(5) *Areas made derelict* in the future by the operations of certain industries, such as brick-making and certain types of chemical works, *should always be rehabilitated by the industries responsible.*

(6) A detailed survey of factory buildings should be undertaken by Local Authorities, as a part of the duty of preparing comprehensive town planning schemes. The position and the quality of their places of work, whether in factories, warehouses, offices or shops, is almost as important to the inhabitants of towns as the position and quality of their homes.

CHAPTER X

Smoke Pollution

A HUNDRED YEARS AGO the area of the Conurbation was marked by "the dingy hue of every object visible, the murky atmosphere, and the volumes of dense smoke issuing heavily forth from high toppling chimneys, blackening and obscuring everything around[1]." Since then the consumption of coal has multiplied four-fold, and the smoke screen has increased accordingly. The Black Country has lived up to its name. Nine thousand acres of land have been scarred and pitted by quarries and mines, or smothered by spoilbanks and tips. Waste of land has been accompanied by waste of coal, and the two-fold extravagance is patent in the pall in the sky and in the grime on the littered ground.

Smoke pollution is harmful to humanity, to buildings and to vegetation. It is also evidence of industrial inefficiency and waste. The rise in the price of coal and difficulties of supply are imposing an economic urgency on the whole problem of smoke pollution. The reduction of smoke pollution is essential to increased efficiency in coal utilization. Removal of cause will not only abolish effect; it will also result in a saving of valuable raw material.

In 1750, some five million tons of coal were burned in Britain. By 1850, annual consumption had reached fifty million tons; and by 1938, one hundred and seventy-eight million tons. Of the 1938 total, 22 per cent, that is about forty million tons, was broken down in gas and coke ovens for more efficient use by carbonization. This provided solid smokeless fuels, gas, tar, motor spirit, fertilizers and chemical products. The remainder was burned for direct heating in industry, transport, electricity power stations, and dwellings. Table XXXI shows the figures for the consumption of coal in the United Kingdom during 1946.

There has been a marked increase during and since the war in the use of coal. Consumption at electricity power stations has risen to over twenty million tons a year, and modern extensions in the use of electricity will further increase consumption. Industrial undertakings consume a high proportion of coal, in addition to gas and electricity. Many industries still use coal to generate their own power from steam, and consume coal also for smelting and heating purposes.

The heavy consumption of coal for domestic purposes has aroused considerable attention during the past few years. To the direct burning, in 1938, of forty-seven million tons in household grates and stoves must be added a further fifteen million tons used in the provision of domestic gas and electricity. The ordinary house-chimney is a heavy

---

[1] *Pickwick Papers.*

contributor to smoke pollution ; 5.4 per cent of the weight of coal burnt in the ordinary open fire escapes into the air by way of the chimney. This proportion is made up of 2.7 per cent soot and tar, 0.3 per cent ash, and 2.4 per cent sulphur dioxide[1]. These polluting substances may be further analysed as follows :—

(*a*) *Solid*

Particles of carbon causing black smoke, and particles of mineral matter or ash carried forward with the gaseous products.

(*b*) *Liquid carbonaceous material*

Fine particles of tarry matter, causing yellowish or brown smoke.

(*c*) *Unburned and partially burned gases*

Gaseous hydrocarbons and carbon monoxide.

(*d*) *Sulphur oxides*

Sulphur dioxide and some sulphur trioxide, which with water give sulphuric acid.

MAIN USES OF COAL IN BRITAIN, 1946
(Source : Ministry of Fuel and Power).

TABLE XXXI

Purpose	Millions of Tons
Public utility undertakings *	
Gas	22·7
Electricity † ... ... †	26·2
Railways	15·0
Coke ovens	20·0
Industrial consumers ‡	
Iron and Steel	9·6
Engineering and other metal trades	3·7
Other industries	29·6
Domestic	
Miners' coal	4·8
House coal **	28·7
Anthracite and boiler fuel **	2·5
Collieries	10·6
Miscellaneous (including Service Departments and shipments to Northern Ireland)	11·0
TOTAL	184·4

* Excluding consumption of coal at waterworks, which amounts on an average to 8,000 tons per week.
† Authorised electricity undertakings and railway and transport authorities only.
‡ Undertakings with an annual consumption of 100 tons or more of coal and/or coke.
** Including disposals to shops, offices and other establishments, partly or entirely non-residential, with an annual consumption of less than 100 tons of coal and/or coke.

[1] *Atmospheric Pollution in Leicester.* H.M.S.O. 1945.

The open domestic grate, with its annual consumption, before 1939, of forty-seven million tons, is not the only contributor to atmospheric pollution. Railways and industry between them produce polluting substances almost equal to those rising from the domestic chimney. The Egerton Report on Heating and Ventilation[1] estimates the total weight of the polluting substances produced annually in Great Britain to be over eight million tons. Responsibility for this total may be divided as follows :—

TOTAL ATMOSPHERIC POLLUTION PRODUCED IN 1938*

TABLE XXXII

	Fuel used (million tons) per annum	Pollution produced (million tons) p.a.		
		Smoke	Ash	Sulphur dioxide
Bituminous coal used by " domestic " consumers	47·7	1·29	0·14	1·14
Electricity : (i) at stations	14·9	0·01	0·10	0·38
(ii) in use	—	—	—	—
Gas industry : (i) carbonized at works	19·1	0·01		0·12
(ii) in use of gas	314,000 million cu. ft.	—		0·01
(iii) in use of coke	(8·3)	—	0·02	0·21
Anthracite	2·7	—	0·01	0·04
Low Temperature Coke	0·5	—	—	0·01
Coke ovens	19·1	small	small	0·5 (incl. use of coke made)
Railways	12·5	0·4	0·1	0·45
Other industrial uses	61·3	0·7	0·2	2·20
Total	177·8	2·40	0·57	5·06

*Table reproduced by permission of the Ministry of Works, from *Heating and Ventilation of Dwellings*.

THE SMOKE PALL

Many of the effects of smoke pollution are evident to the casual observer, but the more insidious damage is not so apparent. A closer examination of the smoke pall reveals all sorts of disquieting facts.

In towns, the soot and tarry globules discharged from domestic chimneys, factory stacks, and railway engines form a smoke-charged atmosphere which hangs suspended over the area. The recent survey of smoke pollution in Leicester revealed that the highest concentration of smoke and sulphurous effluent was always within half-a-mile of the centre of the city. At times, changes in weather affected the degree of concentration, and more than once such a change produced a density six times the average.

The principal effect of the smoke pall is to reduce considerably the ultra-violet radiation reaching the ground from the sun. Winter clouds reduce this by half, and the Leicester

---

[1] *Heating and Ventilation of Dwellings*, by the Heating and Ventilation (Reconstruction) Committee of the Building Research Board, Dept. of Scientific and Industrial Research (H.M.S.O. 1945).

survey revealed that the smoke pall can rob life below it of a further third. The loss suffered in the Conurbation area is probably as high as the loss of 51 per cent experienced at Salford. Such reductions in ultra-violet radiation have a devitalizing effect on all life, human, animal and vegetable. Certain diseases, notably rickets, are specifically related to lack of sunshine, while respiratory diseases are undoubtedly aggravated by smoke-polluted air. Plant life suffers from the deposit of coal and tar on the leaves which prevents the absorption of carbon dioxide. According to the Egerton Report, highly polluted areas may suffer a loss of 50 per cent in hours of sunshine in winter and about 15 per cent in summer. This loss of sunshine results in decreased visibility, which in its turn has to be remedied by costly artificial lighting.

It is impossible to estimate the extra cost in laundry and house cleaning incurred by those living beneath the smoke pall, but this added expense is well known as a factor in the higher cost of living borne by urban populations. The smoke pall bears heavily on the housewife.

In addition to the damage by soot and tarry globules emitted by industrial and domestic fires, the accompanying sulphurous compounds and ash have a deleterious effect, especially upon vegetation. Experiments in Leeds revealed that the germination of seeds in the country outside amounted to 98 per cent; in the central area germination was only 17 per cent; and the weight of cabbages grown in the city was found to be one-seventh of those grown outside. The poison deposited by smoke affects the plant in every aspect of its environment, impregnating the air, the rain-water and the soil. In Canada it has been established that plant life is impaired by concentrations in the air of sulphur dioxide greater than one part in two million. In the heart of the Black Country the highest concentrations likely to occur are—of smoke, 2.5 milligrams per cubic metre in summer and winter, and of sulphur dioxide 0.5 parts per million by volume in summer and 1.0 parts per million in winter. It is not possible, except within very wide limits, to estimate the financial loss to the Conurbation caused by smoke damage, but it must be very considerable, both within the area itself and for a considerable distance round.

The damage wrought by smoke pollution on buildings within cities is extensive. Many English monuments and buildings of historical importance in industrial towns show the ravages of a century or more of intensive pollution of the atmosphere. Even protective paint on wood and metal is seriously affected by pollution. Atmospheric sulphur dioxide promotes the rusting of iron and steel and corrodes non-ferrous metals. It has been observed that in Birmingham non-ferrous metals corrode three times more quickly than at Cardington, in Bedfordshire.

Nor is damage confined to the immediate area in which the smoke is discharged. The distribution of the polluting agents is so wide that the problem can be effectively dealt with only on a regional or national basis. While ash and grit are deposited comparatively near to the chimney from which they are discharged, smoke and sulphurous fumes spread for many miles. In a test made at Leicester, it was calculated that 25 per cent of the smoke and sulphur dioxide found at ground level emanated from the Conurbation area forty miles away.

The rate and quantity of pollution varies from place to place. Table XXXIII gives annual figures recorded at centres inside the Conurbation and elsewhere:—

ANNUAL RATE OF DEPOSIT OF POLLUTION IN VARIOUS CENTRES*

TABLE XXXIII

Recording Station	Soluble matter (lime, chlorides, sulphates)	Insoluble matter (tar, carbonates, ash)	Total
	(Tons per square mile)		
Birmingham (Gt. Charles Street)	93·79	203·03	296·82
Birmingham (Bournville)	63·49	63·10	126·59
Bilston*	84·76	192·17	276·93
Walsall (Goscote Isolation Hospital)	80·32	75·31	155·63
Coventry	90·58	153·76	244·34
Loggerheads (Cheshire Joint Sanatorium)	43·91	16·68	60·59
London (Battersea Park)	84·23	198·44	282·67
London (Kew)	67·47	64·44	131·91
Manchester (Booth Hall)	85·83	90·15	175·98
Stoke-on-Trent (Leek Road)	78·18	123·79	201·97

*All figures, except in the case of Bilston, are yearly averages of the five-year period, 1939/1944. Figures for Bilston do not refer to an average, but are for one year.

It has already been pointed out that smoke pollution is caused in part by the inefficient use of coal. The efficiency of generation of steam in large modern boiler installations is often as high as 80 per cent; but this efficiency can be maintained only if equipment is kept in first-class condition and is operated under close scientific supervision. In the past, too little attention has been given to the efficient conservation and use of heat in boilers and furnaces. In most types of installation, heat is wasted in the discharge of hot gases and liquids, large quantities of steam are inefficiently used or directly wasted, and unnecessary losses of heat occur through inattention to the lagging and insulation of steam pipes and equipment. Many furnaces used to heat metals employ no more than five per cent of the heat value of the coal consumed. It is unlikely that the efficiency of use of the 52 million tons of coal, shown in Table XXXI as consumed for industrial purposes, is as high as 50 per cent. An even worse state of affairs obtains in the domestic grate, where under average household conditions efficiency is as low as 20 per cent; while railway undertakings, in spite of much research work, have not been able to raise the figure of overall efficiency higher than 5 per cent.

This widespread waste, and its concomitant evil of pollution, points directly to the need for improvement in the design of coal-burning appliances and in methods of using coal. A notable advance has been made in this direction as the result of work at the Fuel Research Station. Recognizing that much of the smoke produced in any large industrial area is caused by the careless operation of hand-fired boilers, the Fuel Research Station has evolved a modification of the door of the Lancashire type boiler. This improvement has made possible the almost complete elimination of smoke, even in the periods immediately following firing. The apparatus is inexpensive, easily fitted and very simple in operation. Even where no drastic changes in plant can be carried out, the intelligent use of existing plant can achieve substantial improvements. A wealth of practical information is readily available to those managers, engineers and stokers who are alert to economic improvements and to the necessity for dispelling the smoke screen.

Every user of coal is ultimately dependent upon the pits for his fuel supply. The practice of washing and hand-picking coal at the pit-head can effect enormous improvements in every area where coal is burned. At present 60 per cent of the total output of coal is washed, and 10 per cent is hand-picked. An extension of this useful process at the source would help to abolish dirt and waste in distant furnace or grate.

The household grate, as well as the industrial furnace, is coming more and more under the scrutiny of commercial concerns and research organizations, which are attempting more efficient designs in domestic coal-burning appliances. Already, fires that can be opened and closed at will have been devised to provide not only radiant heat but also convected heat from air which is heated by passage through ducts adjacent to the fire. It has been successfully demonstrated that this type of fire increases heating efficiency to 30-40 per cent. This increased efficiency is accompanied by a substantial reduction in the amount of smoke emitted in relation to the weight of bituminous coal consumed. There is still much to be accomplished in this field; even with improved types of grate the smoke produced is still not less than half of that from the ordinary fire. Further reduction of smoke and increase of heat would result from a wider use of efficient fires which close or open and from a fuller use of solid smokeless fuels.

Many large blocks of flats use central heating installations to burn bituminous coal. This communal heating greatly reduces the smoke emission per head of the population. There are also a few cases in which " district heating " is supplied from a central boiler installation. These are two encouraging examples of the way in which efficiency in heating increases with reduction in smoke.

The extended use of gas or electricity will obviously reduce the present amount of smoke pollution. The last twenty years have seen a great expansion in the use of electricity and more efficient methods of generation. In 1921 an average quantity of 3.4 lbs. of coal was consumed to produce one unit of electricity; in 1938 the quantity was 1.4 lbs per unit. Yet even at this improved figure, the efficiency of generation and distribution in 1938 was only about 18 per cent. of the heat potential of coal consumed. Though the efficiency of generation is low, the efficiency of utilization is often very high; electric fires, for instance, are practically 100 per cent. efficient in utilization of current.

The carbonization of coal in coke ovens and at gas works has reached the high average of approximately 75 per cent. in efficiency. Each ton of coal carbonized produces about 14 cwts. of coke, 60-80 therms of gas, 2.5-3.0 gallons of benzol, 10-15 gallons of tar, and ammonia equivalent to about 25 lbs. of ammonium sulphate. The efficiency of gas appliances in general is higher than that of similar apparatus using coal or coke. The modern gas fire has an efficiency of anything up to 50 per cent. under average conditions.

Gas-washing plant installed at large power stations has been successful in removing from the flue gases all soot, grit and dust, and 95 per cent. of the sulphur.

The problem of smoke pollution is as urgent in the Conurbation as anywhere in the country. Whatever adjustments in living and working conditions the future may bring, a large population and extensive industry will be constant factors in the area, and, unless active steps are taken to deal with smoke pollution, future planning schemes will be overshadowed by those arch-enemies of light, health and happiness, the domestic chimney and the factory stack.

CHAPTER XI

Surface Utilisation

NATURE AND PURPOSE

THE MAIN FUNCTION of town and country planning is the right use of land. This cannot be achieved without a full knowledge of how the land is already being used. The collection and presentation of this information about the Conurbation in an easily assimilable form was the chief purpose of the Surface Utilisation Survey undertaken by the Group.

The map which this Survey produced has two further functions. The first of these is probably the more important. The map presents a clear picture of the present pattern of the urban structure of the Conurbation in the form which it has assumed through evolution. Certain typical forms in the urban structure result from traditional and deeply ingrained social and economic trends. These forms should be recognized for what they are and not redesigned without good reason.

The second and more familiar function of the Surface Utilisation Map is to be found in its presentation of many of the evils and mistakes inherent in the present urban pattern.

METHOD AND DEFINITION

A scale of six inches to the mile was adopted for the Survey as the one which would permit the showing of the whole Conurbation on one map and in sufficient detail. It has not been found possible to publish the Surface Utilisation Map in any form which would reproduce the original and yet be of practical value. Two facsimiles of the sixty-four six-inch Ordnance Survey sheets on which the Surface Utilisation Map has been based are shown on Plates 8 and 9; the scale, of course, is reduced. The three Distribution Maps—Commerce and Industry, Housing and Social Centres, and Open Land—shown in Figures 35, 36 and 37, have been derived from the six-inch map.

In general, each Local Authority supplied the information relating to its own area. The final comprehensive map was checked in certain cases by a visual survey to ensure that areas were being classified according to standard definitions. The classification adopted for the comprehensive map was made as simple as possible in order to give the overall pictures of the distribution of housing and industry, and of the extent and distribution of derelict land, etc. To this end, instead of the classification recommended by the Ministry of Town and Country Planning, which involves some dozens of categories, eight divisions of use were distinguished (see Plates 8 and 9):—

(1) *Open Space* (Green)
    This includes—
        Existing public open spaces
        Private open spaces

Areas scheduled in approved Town Planning Schemes
Permanent allotments
Cemeteries
Sports grounds or other open spaces which, although not dedicated to the public, are considered to be sufficiently permanent to warrant inclusion.

(2) *" Undeveloped" Land* (White)
Land mainly agricultural which is not used or is not dedicated to the public for open spaces, nor used for building development, industrial purposes, roads, railways, canals, etc. (Derelict land is separately classified because of its extent and its significance in the re-planning of the Conurbation).

(3) *Derelict Land* (Brown)
Land spoiled by the workings, now ceased, of extractive industry, by old industrial waste or by abandoned buildings.
(Most of this land requires rehabilitation before use can be made of it).

(4) *Industrial* (Purple)
Land occupied by factories, workshops, etc., or being mined or quarried, or being used by industry.

(5) *Residential* (Yellow)
Land occupied by houses, flats, etc., and their adjoining gardens.

(6) *Commercial* (Blue)
Land occupied by shops, business and professional premises. It has not been found practicable to include every space devoted to this use. Normally, in the 6-inch map, areas containing less than three shops or similar small premises are not shown. (All such premises are shown in the Surface Use Map of Smethwick). (see Plates 1 and 4).

(7) *Administrative, Health and Educational Services, Public Resorts, etc.* (Red)
Land occupied by—
Local government and public buildings
Schools
Churches
Public halls
Hospitals
Cinemas
and other such institutions and resorts.

(8) *Transport* (Grey)
Railways, canals, and classified roads, including depots, goods yards, wharves, etc. Airports.
(Residential or subsidiary roads are included in the use areas adjacent to them).

These major categories are consistent with, although simpler than, the practice of the Ministry of Town and Country Planning. (See specimen sheets, Plates 8 and 9). The colour system adopted for marking the categories was worked out in consultation with the Ministry of Town and Country Planning at the beginning of the survey; it is not in accordance with the system recommended by the Ministry in Circular 29 (September, 1947) as a standard notation for surface utilisation maps.

SURFACE UTILISATION — SMETHWICK
MAJOR CATEGORIES

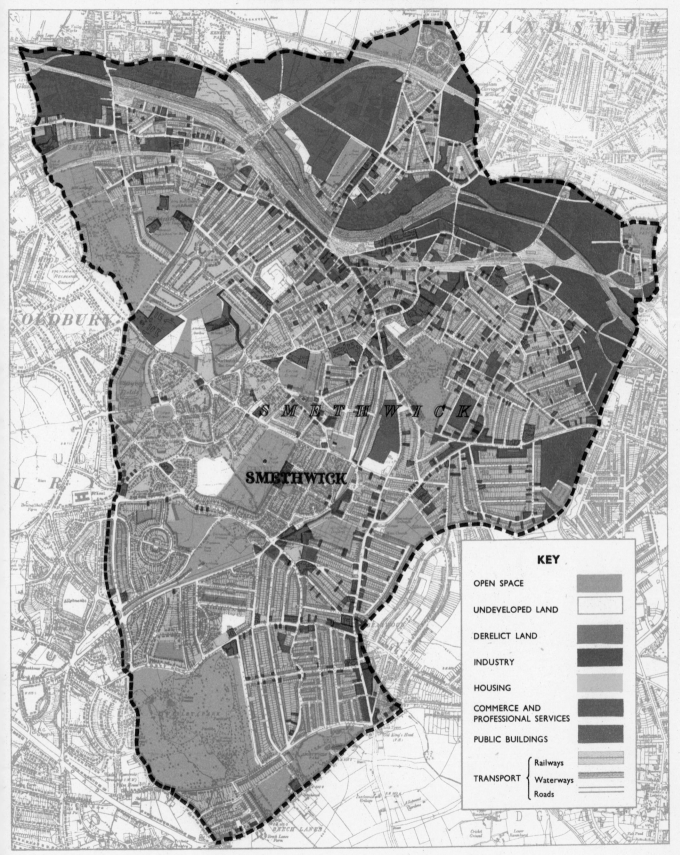

KEY

OPEN SPACE

UNDEVELOPED LAND

DERELICT LAND

INDUSTRY

HOUSING

COMMERCE AND
PROFESSIONAL SERVICES

PUBLIC BUILDINGS

TRANSPORT { Railways

Waterways

Roads

"Based on the Ordnance Survey Map, with the sanction of the Controller of H.M. Stationery Office."

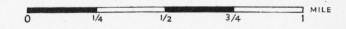

0   1/4   1/2   3/4   1   MILE

PLATE I

SURFACE UTILISATION — SMETHWICK
INDUSTRY

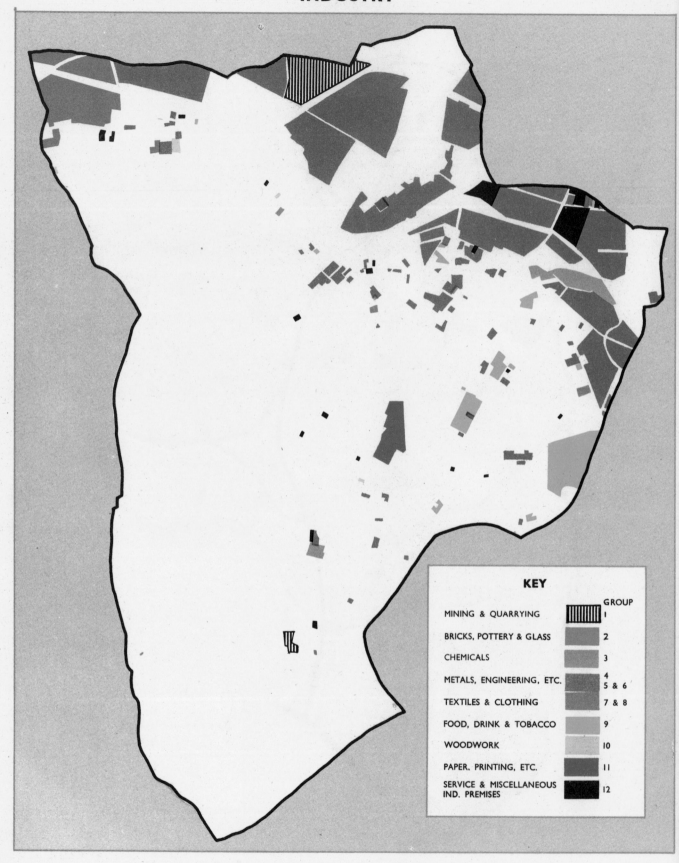

KEY

		GROUP
MINING & QUARRYING		I
BRICKS, POTTERY & GLASS		2
CHEMICALS		3
METALS, ENGINEERING, ETC.		4 5 & 6
TEXTILES & CLOTHING		7 & 8
FOOD, DRINK & TOBACCO		9
WOODWORK		10
PAPER, PRINTING, ETC.		11
SERVICE & MISCELLANEOUS IND. PREMISES		12

PLATE 2

SURFACE UTILISATION — SMETHWICK
TRANSPORT

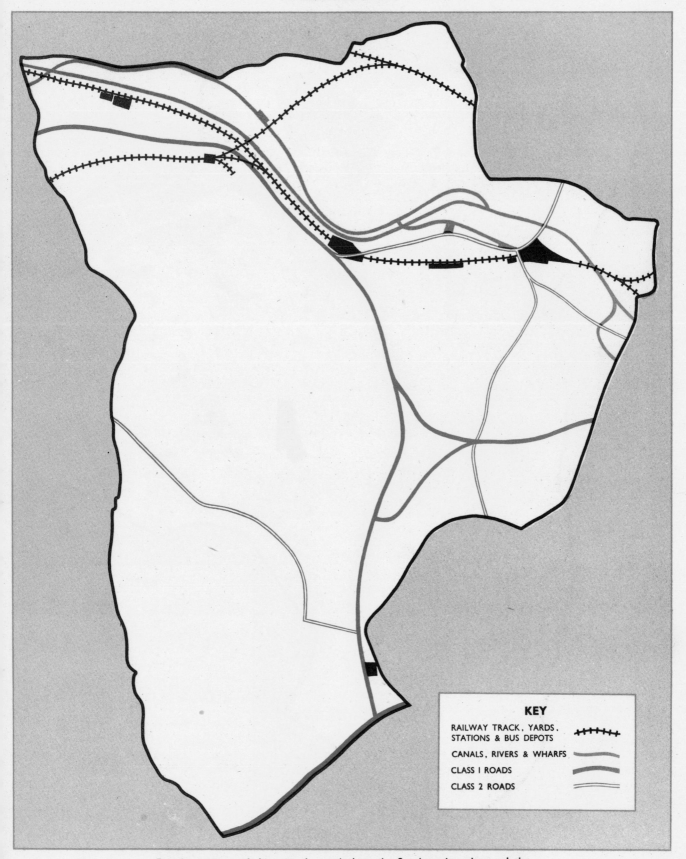

KEY

RAILWAY TRACK, YARDS, STATIONS & BUS DEPOTS	++++++++
CANALS, RIVERS & WHARFS	
CLASS 1 ROADS	
CLASS 2 ROADS	

For the purpose of this map the road along the Southern boundary and the canal along the northern boundary are shown inside the borough, whereas the boundary proper lies along the middle of the canal and the road.

PLATE 3

SURFACE UTILISATION — SMETHWICK
COMMERCE AND PROFESSIONAL SERVICES

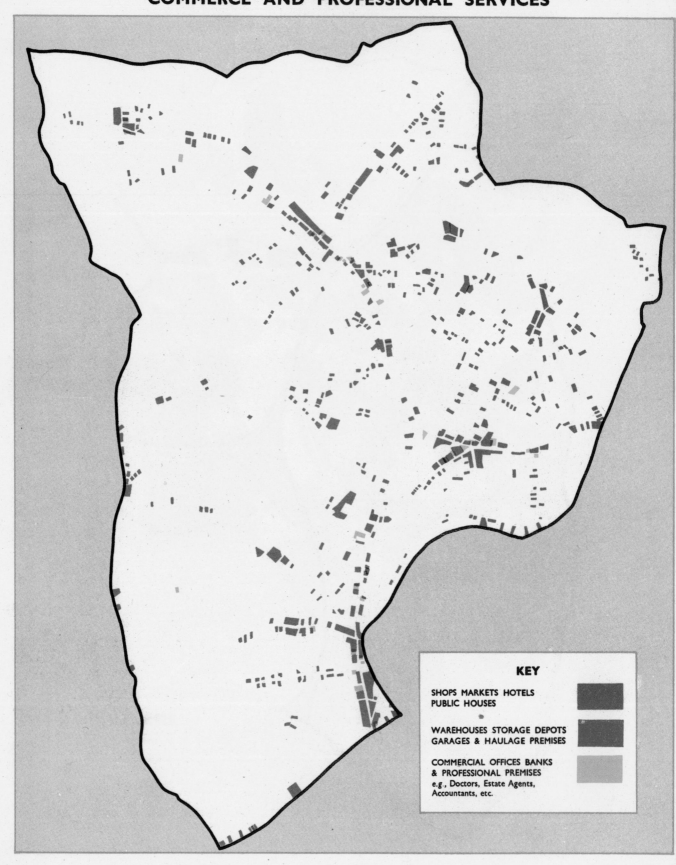

KEY

SHOPS MARKETS HOTELS
PUBLIC HOUSES

WAREHOUSES STORAGE DEPOTS
GARAGES & HAULAGE PREMISES

COMMERCIAL OFFICES BANKS
& PROFESSIONAL PREMISES
e.g., Doctors, Estate Agents,
Accountants, etc.

PLATE 4

SURFACE UTILISATION — SMETHWICK
HOUSING

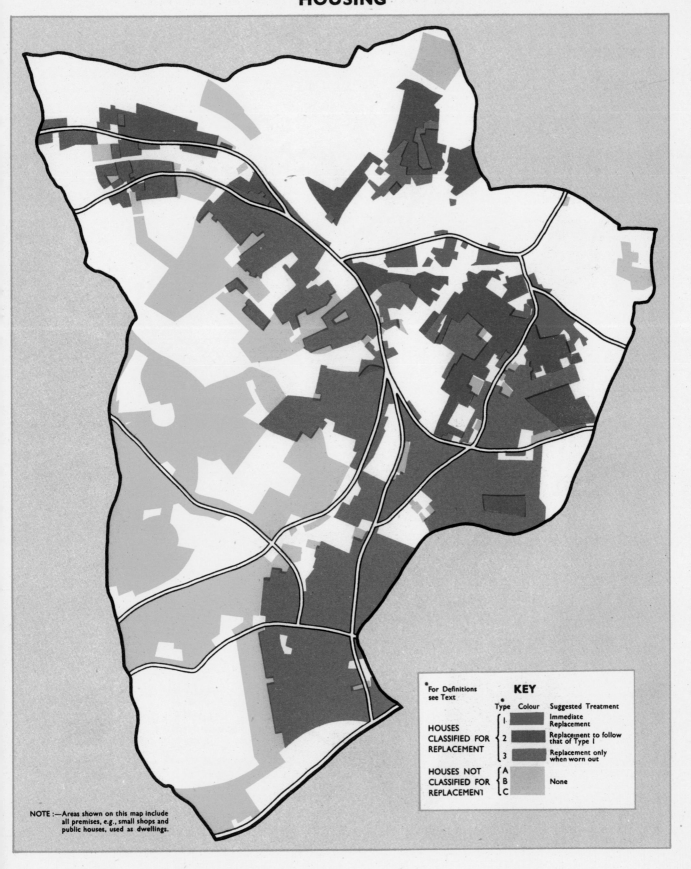

*For Definitions
see Text

KEY

Type	Colour	Suggested Treatment
HOUSES CLASSIFIED FOR REPLACEMENT { 1		Immediate Replacement
2		Replacement to follow that of Type 1
3		Replacement only when worn out
HOUSES NOT CLASSIFIED FOR REPLACEMENT { A		
B		None
C		

NOTE :—Areas shown on this map include
all premises, e.g., small shops and
public houses, used as dwellings.

PLATE 5

SURFACE UTILISATION — SMETHWICK

OPEN SPACE

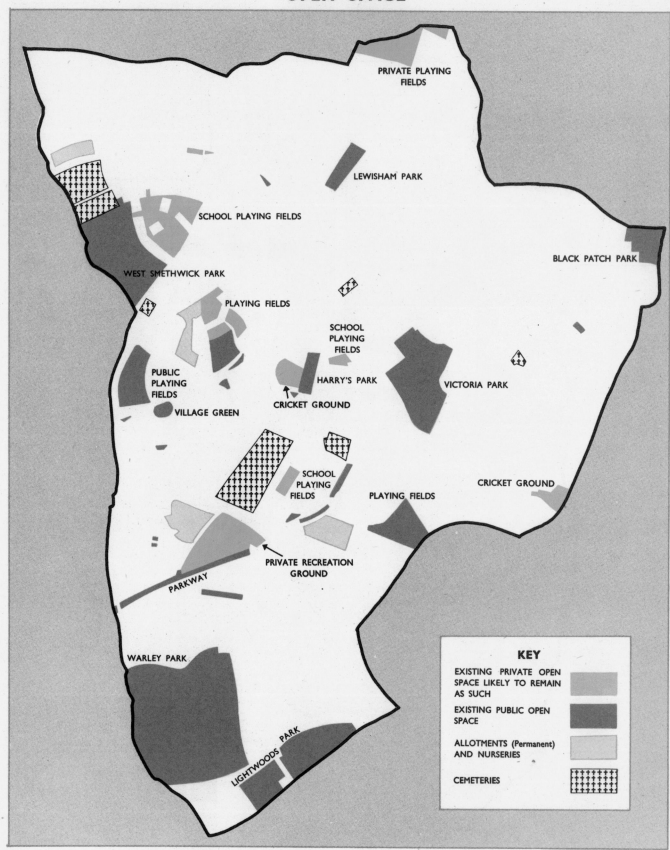

PRIVATE PLAYING FIELDS

LEWISHAM PARK

SCHOOL PLAYING FIELDS

BLACK PATCH PARK

WEST SMETHWICK PARK

PLAYING FIELDS

SCHOOL PLAYING FIELDS

HARRY'S PARK

VICTORIA PARK

PUBLIC PLAYING FIELDS

CRICKET GROUND

VILLAGE GREEN

SCHOOL PLAYING FIELDS

PLAYING FIELDS

CRICKET GROUND

PRIVATE RECREATION GROUND

PARKWAY

WARLEY PARK

LIGHTWOODS PARK

KEY

EXISTING PRIVATE OPEN SPACE LIKELY TO REMAIN AS SUCH

EXISTING PUBLIC OPEN SPACE

ALLOTMENTS (Permanent) AND NURSERIES

CEMETERIES

PLATE 6

SURFACE UTILISATION — SMETHWICK

UNDEVELOPED LAND

DERELICT LAND

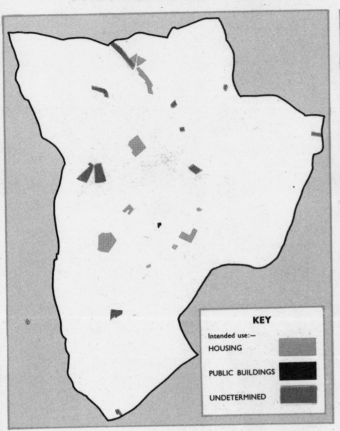

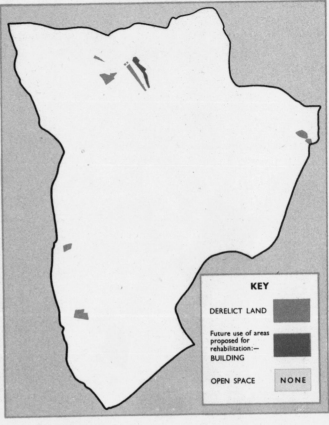

KEY

Intended use:—

HOUSING

PUBLIC BUILDINGS

UNDETERMINED

KEY

DERELICT LAND

Future use of areas
proposed for
rehabilitation:—
BUILDING

OPEN SPACE   NONE

PUBLIC BUILDINGS

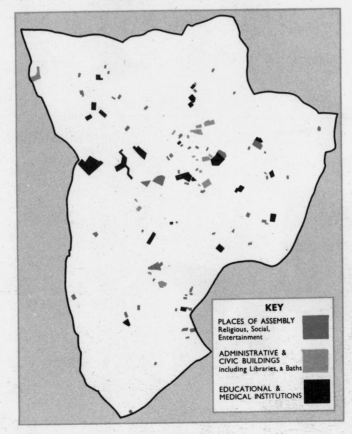

KEY

PLACES OF ASSEMBLY
Religious, Social,
Entertainment

ADMINISTRATIVE &
CIVIC BUILDINGS
including Libraries, & Baths

EDUCATIONAL &
MEDICAL INSTITUTIONS

PLATE 7

SURFACE UTILISATION

(These two sheets are reproduced as specimens of the sixty-four covering the whole Conurbation)

Based on the Ordnance Survey Map, with the sanction of the Controller of H.M. Stationery Office.

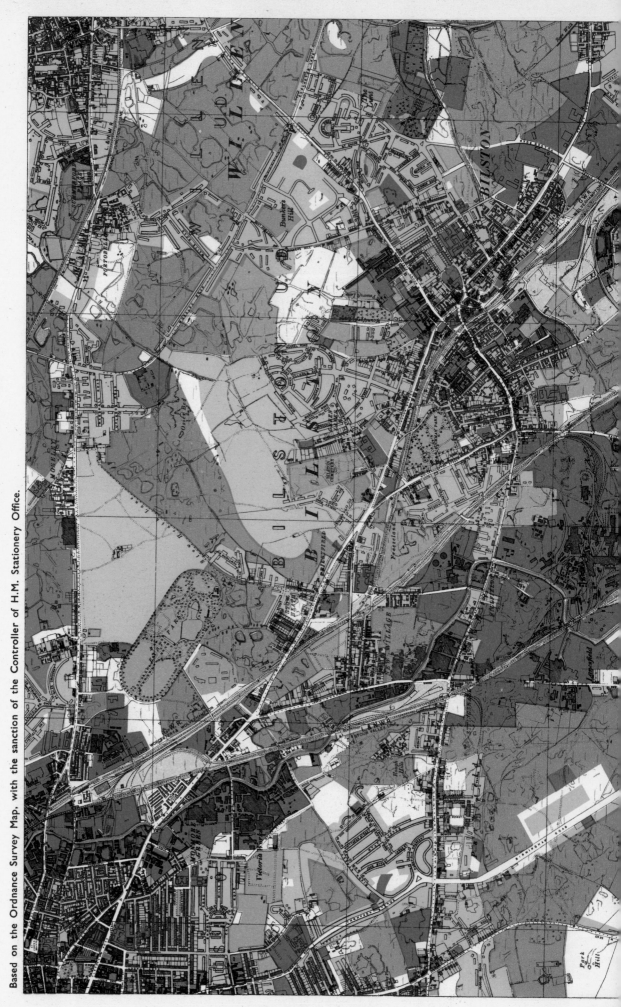

PLATE

NOTE: For definitions see Chapter XI

OPEN SPACE

"UNDEVELOPED" LAND

DERELICT LAND

INDUSTRIAL

RESIDENTIAL

COMMERCIAL

PUBLIC BUILDINGS

RAILWAYS, 'BUS DEPOTS, Etc.

WATERWAYS

MAIN ROADS

0   ¼   ½   ¾   1

HOUSING IN BIRMINGHAM

HOUSING IN THE BLACK COUNTRY

UPPER GORNAL

LOWER GORNAL

TIPTON GREEN

DUDLEY

NETHERTON

BRIERLEY HILL

OLD HILL

QUARRY BANK

*For Definitions
see Text

HOUSES CLASSIFIED FOR REPLACEMENT

HOUSES NOT CLASSIFIED FOR REPLACEMENT

*TYPE   1   2   3   A   B   C

SUGGESTED TREATMENT	Immediate Replacement	Replacement to follow that of Type 1	Replacement only when worn out

GREEN AREAS INDICATE OPEN SPACES

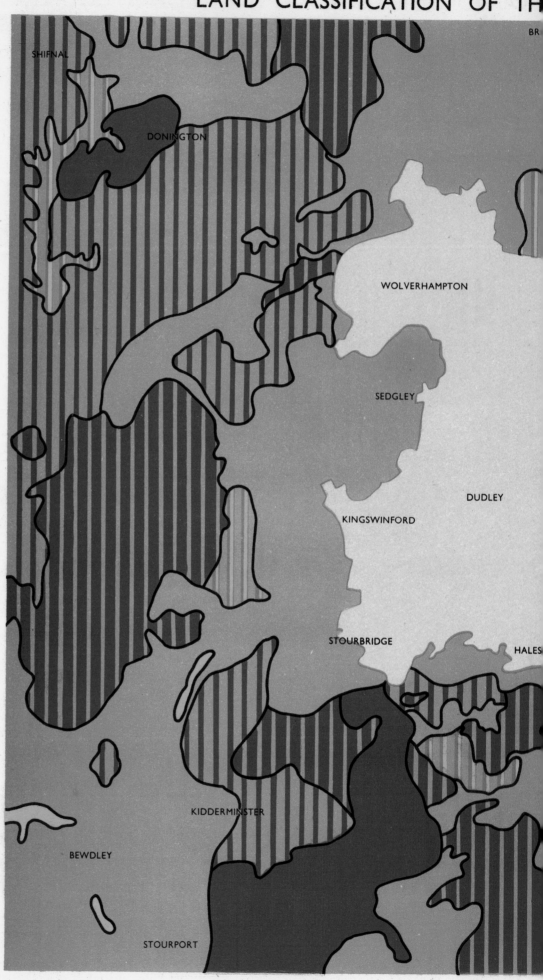

THE LAND CLASSES
SHOWN ON THIS
MAP ARE BASED
ON :—

1 THE SOIL CHARACTER
(Depth, Texture and Water
Conditions)

2 THE SITE CHARACTER
(Elevation, Relief, Climate
and Aspect)

Category 1 comprises the
highest grade land and as far
as possible should be retained
for agriculture

Category 2 comprises a wide
range of land, of which the
best should also be retained

ROUND THE CONURBATION

CATEGORY 1

CATEGORY 2

CATEGORY 3

Striping indicates complex intermixture of land categories; the wider stripe relates to the preponderance of one category over another

The approximate area already lost to agriculture is shaded grey

LICHFIELD

BROWNHILLS

TAMWORTH

ALDRIDGE

SUTTON PARK

CASTLE BROMWICH

COLESHILL

BIRMINGHAM

SOLIHULL

KNOWLE

DORRIDGE

SCALE OF MILES

0 1 2 3 4 5

FACTORY BUILDINGS IN BIRMINGHAM

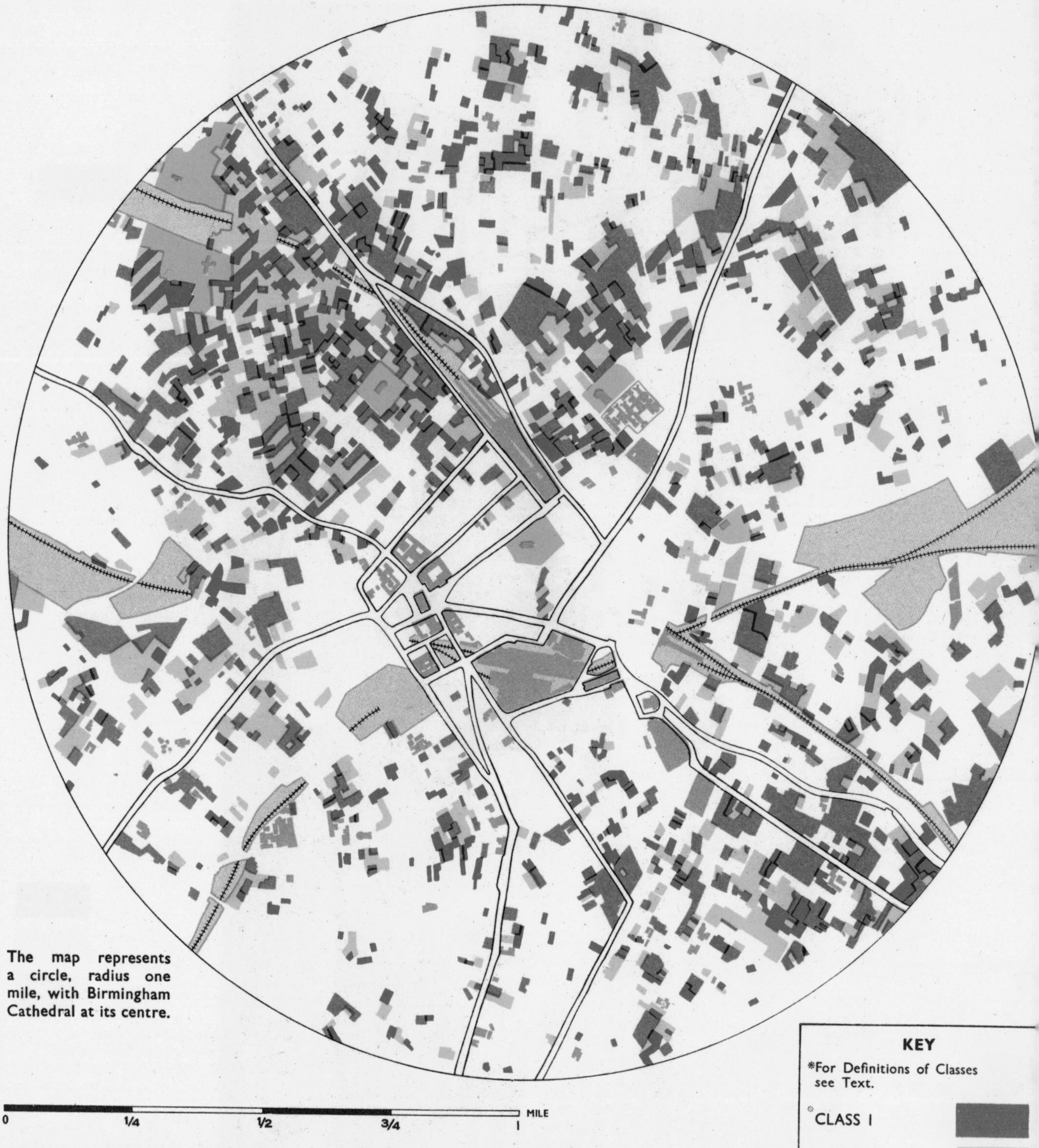

The map represents a circle, radius one mile, with Birmingham Cathedral at its centre.

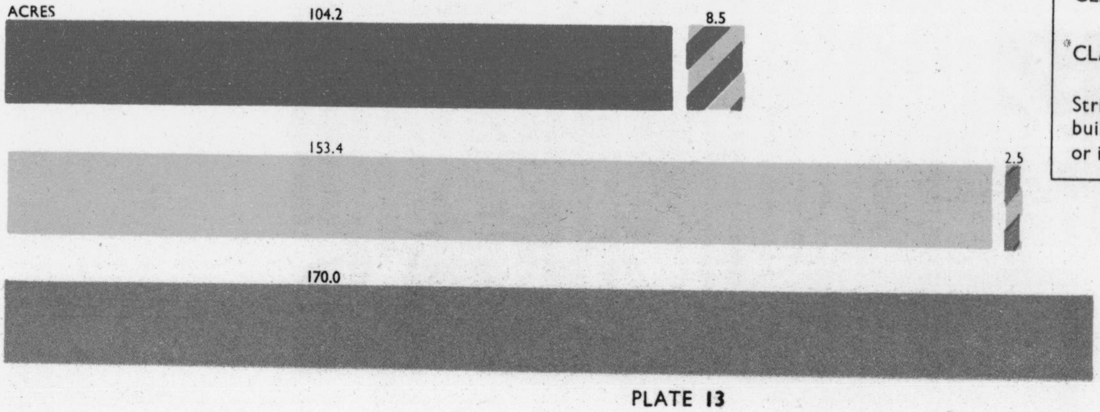

0   1/4   1/2   3/4   1   MILE

ACRES   104.2   8.5

153.4   2.5

170.0

PLATE 13

FACTORY BUILDINGS IN WOLVERHAMPTON

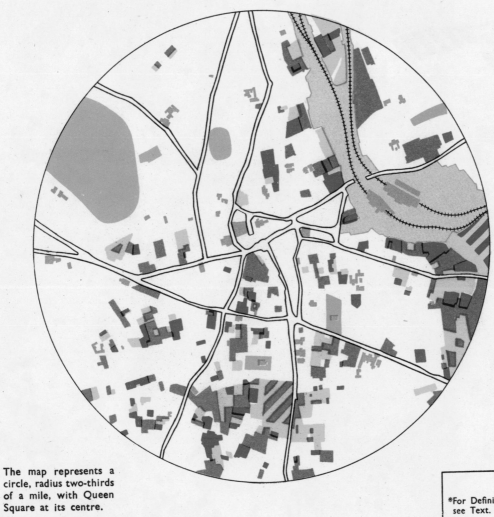

The map represents a
circle, radius two-thirds
of a mile, with Queen
Square at its centre.

0   1/4   1/2   3/4   1   MILE

KEY

*For Definitions of Classes
see Text.

*CLASS 1

*CLASS 2

*CLASS 3

Striped Areas indicate
buildings of intermediate
or intermingled classes

GREEN AREAS INDICATE
OPEN SPACES

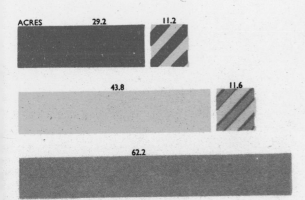

ACRES   29.2   11.2

43.8   11.6

62.2

The bar diagrams represent
the aggregate areas of the
classes of Factory Buildings
shown in the map, and are
drawn to the same scale.

PLATE 14

SURFACE UTILISATION — SMETHWICK
FACTORY BUILDINGS

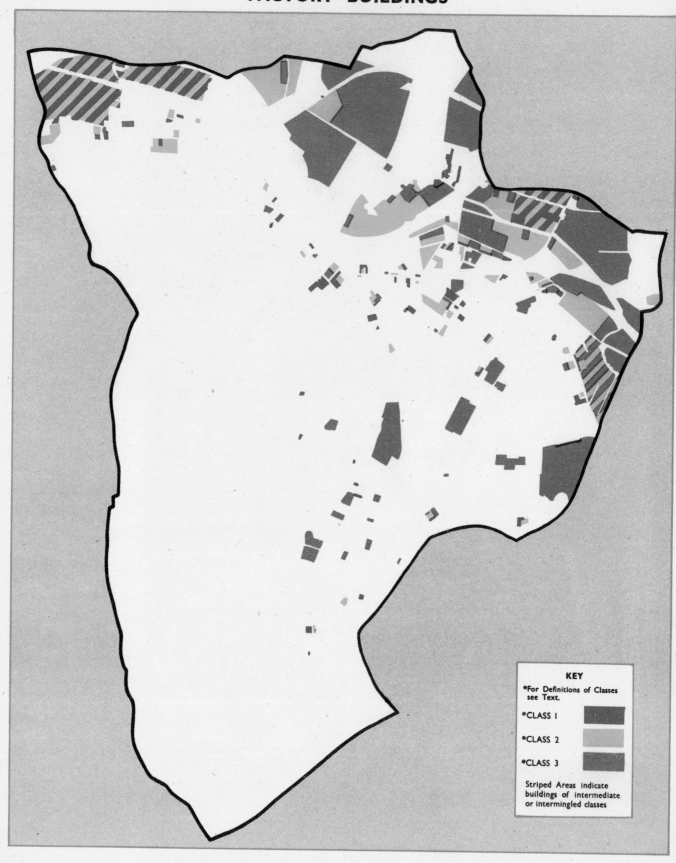

KEY

*For Definitions of Classes
 see Text.

*CLASS 1

*CLASS 2

*CLASS 3

Striped Areas indicate
buildings of intermediate
or intermingled classes

PLATE 15

The preparation of a General Surface Utilisation Map may be regarded as the essential first move in the planning of any area. It offers an invaluable overall view of the make-up of the areas concerned, and, what is at the outset of very great importance, of the areas around it. Before detailed schemes can be drawn up, however, more detailed information is required about each particular " use." This does not involve merely the mapping of the same areas on a larger scale ; information is needed about each use in far greater detail than the General Surface Utilisation map can present. The General Surface Utilisation map, therefore, should be supplemented by a series of maps analysing each use. The form of analysis of any use will be determined by particular considerations or purposes involved in the planning or replanning of an area. In general, however, the Group feels that the following considerations should apply to most analyses of major categories.

Open Space

Present-day standards in town and country planning require adequate provision of open space for a large variety of functions. The analysis of open space should, therefore, indicate the exact use of each existing open space, marking it as public park, playing fields, permanent allotment, school playing field, public or private golf course, private sports ground, private park, or woodland. (See Plate 6).

Undeveloped Land

It is important that the area and exact location of undeveloped land which might, if necessary, be used as building land or open space, should be known with some accuracy. The map of undeveloped land should, therefore, indicate all areas which are not suitable for building by reason of liability to flood, mining subsidence, or excessive slope. The map should also indicate the presence of woods or other major natural features which should, if possible, be preserved. (This method of analysis is not shown on Plate 7 because, in the case of Smethwick, the amount of land remaining undeveloped is very small and has been already reserved for different uses).

Derelict Land

Before derelict land can be brought back into use, some form of rehabilitation is, by definition, necessary. It is, of course, impossible to determine the cost and time necessary to do this without an expert and detailed survey or deciding its future use. At least, however, the analysis map should show the type of derelict land, whether spoil heap, pit mound, disused quarry, etc. From this, some preliminary judgment of the suitability of any particular area for housing development, industrial use, or open space may be made. (This is not shown in the analysis map of Smethwick, Plate 7 ; the amount of derelict land left in Smethwick is negligible).

Industry

The analysis map of land used by industry should show to which broad type of industry each industrial concern belongs. By condensing a schedule identifying all the industries in the area into broad categories it is possible to obtain a general picture of the geographical distribution and concentration of concerns engaged in the same type of work. In the map (Plate 2) twelve types of industrial concern have been distinguished. In closely built-up areas with wide varieties of trades crowded together, sometimes into the same building, it will, of course, be necessary to use the map in combination with a schedule. A map of this sort is almost essential to the solution of planning problems connected with the diversification of employment and zoning for industry.

Business quarter, principal shopping streets and administrative centre; provision for entertainment and kindred services is abnormally low. The area shown here is encircled by districts of small factories and slums.

The main roads and railways radiating from the central area cut through the regular pattern of uniform bye-law streets which stretch between the centre and the new housing estates on the edge of the city. Shops line the main roads for almost their whole length.

Birmingham :
Middle Ring.

Birmingham is linked with Wolverhampton by a complex and interwoven system of road, water and rail transport lines. Part of this system is shown here, as it passes through the factory district in Smethwick.

The flat-topped spoil banks (right) are made up of chemical waste. Between them and the cross-roads are flooded disused marl pits, with (left) marl pits still in use. The Birmingham-Wolverhampton Road runs across the foreground.

Oldbury :
Industrial
Development.

Oldbury

Around the loose knot formed by the junction, sidings, canal and roads, stand the factories and houses. A large patch of undeveloped land still remains.

Rood End a
Tat Bank.

Coseley.

Typical sprawl near the edge of the Conurbation.   The very high proportion of land left unused in an urbanized area reveals the fundamental problem of the Black Country and shows the need for planned tidying-up.

Closely interwoven strands of the Conurbation transport system separate out into the countryside.

North-west of Wolverhampton.

Since 1920, nearly 100,000 houses have been built for Birmingham's population.   Half of these are municipal.   90 per cent. were built on the outskirts of Birmingham.

Ribbon development and sprawl along the Redditch Road from King's Norton, Birmingham.

A line of urban development can be seen stretching out beyond the municipal housing estates to the factory and small housing estate in the distance.

Modern industrial plant on the edge of the Conurbation at Wolverhampton. The new housing across the canal and railway is outside the boundary of the Conurbation.

A second analysis of the area covered by industry should be made to show the age and fitness of factory buildings. This might be carried out according to the principles suggested in Chapter IX (see Plate 15).

Housing

Property which is or should be condemned under the Housing Acts should be marked, but it is also desirable to show other types of property according to their probable length of life. The system of classification recommended by the Group is that described in Chapter VII, and the analysis map of housing should follow these lines (see Plate 5).

Commerce

The analysis of commercial premises should have as its purpose the assessment of the nature and adequacy of the services provided, both as regards the numbers of population served and the location of the premises. The three divisions into which such services naturally fall are :—

1. Shops, markets, hotels and public houses.
2. Warehouses, storage depots, garages, haulage premises.
3. Commercial offices, banks and professional premises, such as doctors' surgeries and estate agents' offices.

After these different types of premises have been mapped, their relations with the residential areas (Plate 5) should be studied. This analysis is in some respects complementary to the information given in a statistical analysis of the number of persons employed in them compared with other occupations (see Table XX) (An " accessibility " map is sometimes useful in this connection, provided that the area marked out as being served by each shop or professional premises is determined by the length of time taken to reach the premises from the houses around, and is not represented simply as a circle). (see Plate 4).

Public Buildings

Similar considerations apply to public buildings as to commerce. The analysis should show at least a preliminary division into :—

1. Administrative and public buildings, such as town halls, libraries, fire stations, museums, public baths.
2. Churches, cinemas and other social and entertainment centres.
3. Schools, hospitals, clinics and similar buildings.

This map should be studied in conjunction with the map of housing (see Plate 7).

Transport (Railways, Canals, Airports)

The minimum requirements of the transport map are that it should show Class 1 and Class 2 roads, tram and omnibus depots; canals (used and unused), wharves and navigable rivers ; railway tracks, yards and sidings, passenger and goods stations ; aerodromes.

(An example of a General Surface Utilisation map and of analyses of each category of surface use is shown in Plates 1 to 7 and in 15, in which the County Borough of Smethwick is taken as a specimen area.)

GENERAL CONSIDERATIONS

Geographically, economically and socially there are strong connections between Birmingham and the rest of the Conurbation, and these links are sufficient to make it necessary in planning to treat the Conurbation as a whole. The General Surface Utilisation Map, however, reveals that the urban structure of Birmingham has many fundamental differences from that of the Black Country.

The urban structure of the city of Birmingham reflects the result of continuous growth outwards from a firmly established centre of settlement. The town pattern is reasonably coherent. Many Black Country towns and districts, on the other hand, are agglomerations resulting from the location of industries, housing areas, social centres, transport lines, and so on, according to separate and unrelated considerations. The different uses of land which make up urban development have spread and duplicated themselves and, in some cases, have merged together. The two sides of the Conurbation represent two extremes of urban structure—the industrial city, with its more or less regular pattern, and the area of the Black Country, which has been covered piecemeal by urban development.

There is another difference, equally significant. Large areas of the outer districts of Birmingham have been under statutory town planning schemes for periods of up to thirty-five years. The most striking results of this period of planning control are shown in the industrial zoning and in the related and carefully disposed series of open spaces which stretch from the Middle Ring area to the outer suburbs. In the Black Country, planned development is largely absent. Chapter IV indicates how far the multiplicity of Local Government and planning Authorities in the area has prevented coherent planning.

The picture presented by Birmingham[1] is one of an enormous spider's web, with the principal roads radiating from the centre of the city. The centre of this web is the closely-nucleated shopping and commercial centre. Around the centre, especially to the north-west and south-east, are areas which are heavily industrialized, but whose street pattern is still determined by the residential use the areas originally served. Most of the factories are small and many of them occupy converted houses. The city spreads around this commercial and industrial nucleus, with the Middle Ring of housing development, penetrated by later factory areas, located between the principal roads and stretching out to the new housing estates and suburbs. The extensive housing areas become increasingly broken by open spaces and parkways.

To the north-east, south-east, south-west and north-west, zones of industry spread along railway and canal routes. This spread is continuous north-east along the line of the River Rea, to Castle Bromwich, with a branch leading north-west along the Tame Valley ; south-east along the line of Bordesley, Greet and Tyseley; and north-west along the main railway and canal routes through Smethwick and West Bromwich towards Wolverhampton and the Black Country. In the south-west area the zone is more scattered, spreading from Selly Oak through Kings Norton to Longbridge along the railway and canal.

In contrast to Birmingham, the Black Country still consists in great part of old and scattered settlements, a network of canals and railways which have done much to determine the siting of works in the heavier trades, and numerous and extensive patches of derelict land. This last feature is a striking example of waste, the result largely of mining subsidence, pit mounds, spoilbanks and worked-out quarries, and of the removal after the end of the 19th century of some of the heavy engineering trades to more newly-developed mining districts. The whole area is an amorphous accumulation of industry, derelict land and housing, and takes the form of a rough cross stretching between Birmingham, Wolverhampton, Stourbridge and Walsall, with Great Bridge almost exactly in the centre. What might be called the axis of the Black Country stretches along the line Birmingham-Wolverhampton, with industry clearly following the main railways and canals. It has already been shown that, by the uncontrolled accumulation of factories in various districts, as well as by design, zones of industry have developed in Birmingham. One of

---

[1] This paragraph and the section which follows are illustrated by the Distribution Maps, Figures 35, 36 and 37.

these zones continues as a heavily-concentrated area of industry between Smethwick and West Bromwich up to the north of Oldbury. This area is flanked by commercial and administrative areas in Smethwick and West Bromwich and by housing development. No similar zone appears until the continuous belt of industry along the same line of communications between Roseville and Wolverhampton is reached; this is flanked by Bilston on the one side and by a continuous belt of derelict land on the other. Large settlements are strung along the old roads to the north and south of this central line— West Bromwich, Hill Top, Wednesbury, and Bilston to the north, and Smethwick, Oldbury, Dudley and Sedgley to the south.

The Development Map (Figure 40) reveals the much more extensive sprawling of the Black Country towards the north. Scattered housing, industry and mining to the west, north and east of Walsall have carried the landscape of the Black Country as far north as Cannock (see Appendix). The area north of the Black Country presents, if anything, a more difficult problem of town and country planning than that south of Birmingham, which is dealt with in Chapter XIV.

DETAILED CONSIDERATIONS

Open Space

The amount of land devoted to open space forms just over 10 per cent of the whole Conurbation area, but the exact figures of the acreage or proportion of open space in any particular local authority area have little significance without reference to the size of the population of the area and the amount of open space accessible in adjoining areas. For example, areas lying on the outer fringe of the Conurbation appear to have a low proportion of open space, but this may not be important since the open country is so readily accessible. Tables XXXIV and XXXV should therefore be considered in conjunction with Figure 35, which shows in generalized form the main patches and wedges of " open " land—open in the sense that they are not covered by building development. It is important that the population of each Local Authority should be adequately provided with playing fields, allotments, and small local recreation grounds for children. The adequacy of such provision is entirely lost sight of in overall figures of open space that may include a golf course, zoological garden or larger parks, or where there is considerable acreage of private open space sometimes of little value to the general public. The West Midland Group, however, is here less concerned with local plans for the provision of the smaller open

---

Figure 35.—Open Land. The map opposite shows the distribution of " undeveloped " land, derelict land and open spaces in the Conurbation. The very considerable proportion (40 per cent) of agricultural and other undeveloped land is perhaps the principal fact revealed by the Surface Utilisation Survey. The map also reveals, however, that considerable stretches of open land are present in the form of more or less continuous belts if " undeveloped " land, derelict land and open space are considered together.

There are four major belts of open land, one starting from the wide stretch of " undeveloped " land in the Conurbation boundary at Brierley Hill due west of Dudley, passing south of Dudley and connecting with the considerable stretch of open land in the centre of the Black Country. This belt also connects with the southern boundary of the Conurbation by an almost continuous series of derelict and undeveloped sites stretching south from Dudley.

The second almost continuous belt stretches from Himley Park, the large open space on the western boundary of the Conurbation, to the large patches of derelict land north of West Bromwich and so linking with the wedge of " undeveloped " land and open space extending into the Conurbation between Sutton Coldfield and Walsall.

There is almost complete encirclement of Walsall by derelict and " undeveloped " land and by open spaces.

The fourth belt of open land lies with its open end at the northern boundary of the Conurbation between Wolverhampton and Walsall, and stretches due south to connect with the second major belt. The extent to which these belts can form the basis for the Green Setting proposed in Chapter XIII is shown in Figure 41.

OPEN LAND

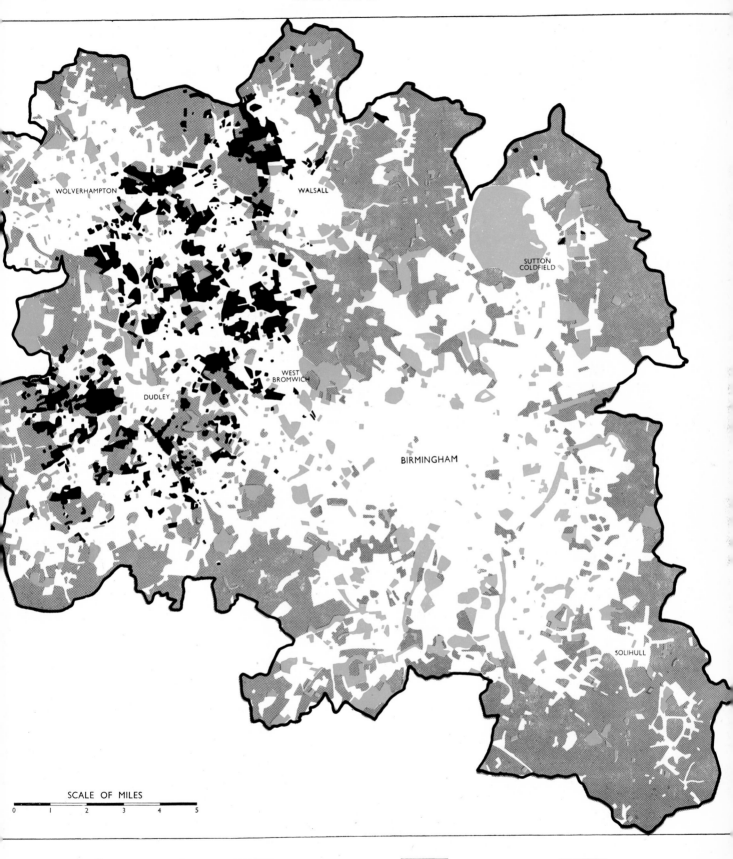

SCALE OF MILES

0   1   2   3   4   5

"UNDEVELOPED" LAND   DERELICT LAND   OPEN SPACE

spaces than with the broader proposals for ensuring sufficient and well-planned provision of the larger parks, with green areas separating the towns, and with the preservation of all sites that are an asset to the landscape.

Figure 35 thus gives existing distribution over the area, not only of the land laid out specifically as open space, but also of undeveloped land and of derelict land which might well be rehabilitated for the purpose of additional open space.

It is mentioned elsewhere in this Report (page 212) that the Conurbation is fortunate in having two wedges of open land, each of considerable extent, running in from open country to within two miles of each other—the Clent-Woodgate wedge between Birmingham and Halesowen as far as Harborne, and the Aldridge-Sandwell Park wedge between Birmingham on the east and Walsall and West Bromwich on the west. It is extremely unfortunate that the northern wedge should have been cut in the Great Barr area by housing development, and that it is in danger of being cut a second time further south, between Perry Barr

SURFACE UTILISATION

TABLE XXXIV

The total acreage of each Local Authority has been classified into six broad categories :—

1. Open space, private and public—including public open space in approved Town Planning Schemes, permanent allotments and nurseries, and cemeteries.
2. Undeveloped land, not used as an open space and not in derelict condition. (This mainly consists of rural and agricultural land. It is not necessarily suitable for building development).
3. Land formerly used by industry, now abandoned and unsuitable for development in its present condition.
4. Land used for industrial purposes and for public services, such as gas, electricity and sewerage.
5. Residential development, excluding commercial premises with living accommodation.
6. (i) Commercial, business and professional premises.
   (ii) Local government and public buildings. Social, religious, educational, health and entertainment centres.
   (iii) Road, rail and water transport : routes, stations, depots, wharves, etc. Airfields.

(Acreage figures are correct to nearest 10 acres.)

Local Authority		Not built up			Built up			
		1 Open space	2 Undeveloped (largely agricultural)	3 Derelict and not in use	4 Industry	5 Housing	6 Commerce, Public Buildings, and Transport	Total acreage
County Boroughs								
Birmingham	Acres	6,970	15,190	—	3,450	21,900	3,640	51,150
	%	13·7	29·7	—	6·7	42·8	7·1	100·0
Dudley	Acres	450	710	770	420	1,410	310	4,070
	%	11·1	17·4	18·9	10·3	34·7	7·6	100·0
Smethwick	Acres	480	30	20	420	1,260	290	2,500
	%	19·2	1·2	0·8	16·8	50·4	11·6	100·0
Walsall	Acres	900	3,110	780	500	2,900	590	8,780
	%	10·3	35·4	8·9	5·7	33·0	6·7	100·0
West Bromwich	Acres	660	2,860	650	760	1,860	390	7,180
	%	9·2	39·9	9·0	10·5	26·0	5·4	100·0
Wolverhampton	Acres	1,080	2,210	340	960	3,610	930	9,130
	%	11·8	24·2	3·7	10·6	39·5	10·2	100·0
Total :	Acres	**10,540**	**24,110**	**2,560**	**6,510**	**32,940**	**6,150**	**82,810**
	%	**12·7**	**29·1**	**3·1**	**7·9**	**39·8**	**7·4**	**100·0**

TABLE XXXIV—continued

Local Authority	Not built up			Built up			
	1 Open space	2 Undeveloped (largely agricultural)	3 Derelict and not in use	4 Industry	5 Housing	6 Commerce, Public Buildings and Transport	Total acreage
Municipal Boroughs and Urban Districts							
Aldridge ... Acres	810	6,580	10	340	1,150	390	9,280
%	8·7	70·9	0·1	3·7	12·4	4·2	100·0
Amblecote ... Acres	60	320	60	70	100	60	670
%	9·0	47·7	9·0	10·4	14·9	9·0	100·0
Bilston ... Acres	190	90	410	270	630	280	1,870
%	10·2	4·8	21·9	14·4	33·7	15·0	100·0
Brierley Hill ... Acres	180	2,450	1,020	520	1,370	390	5,930
%	3·0	41·3	17·2	8·8	23·1	6·6	100·0
Coseley ... Acres	180	740	1,090	350	760	170	3,290
%	5·5	22·5	33·1	10·6	23·1	5·2	100·0
Darlaston ... Acres	90	430	240	220	420	130	1,530
%	5·9	28·1	15·7	14·4	27·4	8·5	100·0
Halesowen ... Acres	290	3,070	120	460	1,060	250	5,250
%	5·5	58·5	2·3	8·8	20·2	4·7	100·0
Oldbury ... Acres	330	820	140	560	1,280	170	3,300
%	10·0	24·9	4·2	17·0	38·8	5·1	100·0
Rowley Regis ... Acres	320	1,110	710	400	1,090	200	3,830
%	8·4	29·0	18·5	10·4	28·5	5·2	100·0
Sedgley ... Acres	590	1,570	310	330	980	70	3,850
%	15·3	40·8	8·0	8·6	25·5	1·8	100·0
Solihull ... Acres	1,240	13,940	—	200	4,050	760	20,190
%	6·1	69·1	—	1·9	20·1	3·8	100·0
Stourbridge ... Acres	370	1,890	60	160	1,510	220	4,210
%	8·8	44·9	1·4	3·8	35·9	5·2	100·0
Sutton Coldfield Acres	3,260	6,980	30	520	2,710	480	13,980
%	23·3	50·0	0·2	3·7	19·4	3·4	100·0
Tettenhall... ... Acres	160	1,620	20	10	640	50	2,500
%	6·4	64·8	0·8	0·4	25·6	2·0	100·0
Tipton ... ... Acres	150	140	470	420	680	310	2,170
%	6·9	6·4	21·7	19·4	31·3	14·3	100·0
Wednesbury ... Acres	170	240	520	250	700	150	2,030
%	8·4	11·8	25·6	12·3	34·5	7·4	100·0
Wednesfield ... Acres	40	1,510	210	150	460	150	2,520
%	1·6	60·0	8·3	5·9	18·3	5·9	100·0
Willenhall ... Acres	50	1,360	620	100	550	150	2,830
%	1·8	48·1	21·9	3·5	19·4	5·3	100·0
Total : ... Acres	**8,480**	**44,860**	**6,040**	**5,330**	**20,140**	**4,380**	**89,230**
%	**9·5**	**50·2**	**6·8**	**6·0**	**22·6**	**4·9**	**100·0**
Summary							
County Boroughs ...	10,540	24,110	2,560	6,510	32,940	6,150	82,810
Municipal Boroughs and Urban Districts	8,480	44,860	6,040	5,330	20,140	4,380	89,230
Conurbation... Acres	**19,020**	**68,970**	**8,600**	**11,840**	**53,080**	**10,530**	**172,040**
%	**11·0**	**40·1**	**5·0**	**6·9**	**30·9**	**6·1**	**100·0**

and Wednesbury, and also that tentacles of development should have spread through the southern wedge at Bartley Green and Woodgate. The Group feel strongly that considerable efforts should be made to reinstate and maintain both wedges as open space.

Much could be done to extend wedges of open country into the Conurbation in the form either of agricultural land or of public open space. Other considerations may operate to render these suggestions impracticable, but it is desirable, and it seems possible, to develop as public open spaces those very considerable areas of derelict land which stretch from the new Wolverhampton Road, where it enters Wolverhampton, through Coseley, Tipton, and Wednesbury. There is also a notable concentration of "undeveloped" land in the north of Rowley Regis, extending also into West Bromwich and Oldbury. The development of this area as open space, together with the rehabilitation of the not un-picturesque derelict land nearby, would add considerably to the amenities of the Conurbation (pages 227-241).

"Undeveloped" Land

The "undeveloped" land (see definition, page 160) in the Conurbation totals 68,970 acres, practically 40 per cent of the area. "Undeveloped" land varies in quantity in different areas. Non-County Boroughs and Urban Districts on the edge of the Conurbation have from 40 to 70 per cent of their areas undeveloped, while Bilston has only 4.8 per cent, and Smethwick 1.2 per cent. The total figure of 68,970 acres, given for May, 1946, is declining rapidly in some districts.

A considerable proportion of the "undeveloped" land, though not described as derelict, is unsuitable for development because of its elevation, its liability to severe mining subsidence, or because of some other limiting factor.

The acreages of "undeveloped" land have been added to those of open space and derelict land in Table XXXV to show that as much as 56.1 per cent of the whole area is not built up. The location of these vacant sites has been mapped in Figure 35, which reveals how valuable an asset the "undeveloped" areas may prove in the carrying-out of redevelopment schemes. Temporary buildings for housing or other purposes can be accommodated on undeveloped sites while redevelopment is in progress in the adjacent areas. The wide dispersal of "undeveloped" land over most of the 260 square miles of the Conurbation means that redevelopment of the old congested centres of industry and population can proceed with much less disturbance to the life of the community than is usual. The "undeveloped" land will be extremely useful in the realisation of plans stage by stage, before its development eventually for housing, open space or other uses.

Derelict Land[1]

Many factors have contributed to the spoiling of hundreds of acres of land in the Conurbation. For years spoilbanks have been accumulating around the coal mines; quarries have been worked to exhaustion and remain derelict; slag heaps have been built up of the residues from the smelting and puddling furnaces; marl holes have been worked and abandoned; rubbish and industrial waste of all kinds has been strewn over wide areas; and extensive tracts liable to mining subsidence have been allowed to lie unused and untended. This gradual accumulation of derelict land has contributed almost as much as industrial sprawl to the desolate appearance of the Conurbation.

Reclamation of the land left derelict through industrial working has been proceeding rapidly since the close of the war. Since the beginning of 1945, when a survey of the derelict land of the area was undertaken by Mr. S. H. Beaver for the Ministry of Town

---

[1] This category of Surface Use includes no site which is still being used either wholly or partly for industrial purposes. While this strictness of definition is necessary for the purposes of the general Surface Utilisation Survey, it means that in the total acreage included in industrial land there are some areas which are to all appearances derelict land. The area of such land apparently derelict but still in use by industry is put by S. H. Beaver in his *Report on Derelict Land in the Black Country* at over 3,000 acres, compared with the 6,100 acres of derelict land in the strict sense which lay in the area of his survey.

DEGREE OF " BRICK-AND-MORTAR " DEVELOPMENT WITHIN THE CONURBATION

TABLE XXXV

Local Authority		Not built-up	Built-up	Total acreage
County Boroughs				
Birmingham	Acres	22,160	28,990	51,150
	%	43·4	56·6	100·0
Dudley	Acres	1,930	2,140	4,070
	%	47·4	52·6	100·0
Smethwick	Acres	530	1,970	2,500
	%	21·2	78·8	100·0
Walsall	Acres	4,790	3,990	8,780
	%	54·6	45·4	100·0
West Bromwich	Acres	4,170	3,010	7,180
	%	58·1	41·9	100·0
Wolverhampton	Acres	3,630	5,500	9,130
	%	39·7	60·3	100·0
Totals		**37,210**	**54,600**	**82,810**
		44·9	**55·1**	**100·0**
Municipal Boroughs and Urban Districts				
Aldridge	Acres	7,400	1,880	9,280
	%	79·7	20·3	100·0
Amblecote	Acres	440	230	670
	%	65·7	34·3	100·0
Bilston	Acres	690	1,180	1,870
	%	36·9	63·1	100·0
Brierley Hill	Acres	3,650	2,280	5,930
	%	61·5	38·5	100·0
Coseley	Acres	2,010	1,280	3,290
	%	61·1	38·9	100·0
Darlaston	Acres	760	770	1,530
	%	49·7	50·3	100·0
Halesowen	Acres	3,480	1,770	5,250
	%	66·3	33·7	100·0
Oldbury	Acres	1,290	2,010	3,300
	%	39·1	60·9	100·0
Rowley Regis	Acres	2,140	1,690	3,830
	%	55·9	44·1	100·0
Sedgley	Acres	2,470	1,380	3,850
	%	64·1	35·9	100·0
Solihull	Acres	15,180	5,010	20,190
	%	75·2	24·8	100·0
Stourbridge	Acres	2,320	1,890	4,210
	%	55·1	44·9	100·0
Sutton Coldfield	Acres	10,270	3,710	13,980
	%	73·5	26·5	100·0
Tettenhall	Acres	1,800	700	2,500
	%	72·0	28·0	100·0
Tipton	Acres	760	1,410	2,170
	%	35·0	65·0	100·0
Wednesbury	Acres	930	1,100	2,030
	%	45·8	54·2	100·0
Wednesfield	Acres	1,760	760	2,520
	%	69·9	30·1	100·0
Willenhall	Acres	2,030	800	2,830
	%	71·8	28·2	100·0
Total :	Acres	**59,380**	**29,850**	**89,230**
	%	**66·5**	**33·5**	**100·0**
Conurbation Total	Acres	**96,590**	**75,450**	**172,040**
	%	**56·1**	**43·9**	**100·0**

Darlaston Brook Valley, between Bilston (left) and the Walsall Canal. Apart from a few sites, such as the Bilston sewage works, all the open land shown in the centre of the photograph is derelict.

Derelict land (right) and allotment gardens forming the southern tip of a belt of agricultural land and derelict areas stretching for some miles into the Conurbation. (Willenhall top centre, Darlaston left).

Old slag heaps now covered with a litter of domestic rubbish.   The hummocks in the background are chemical waste.

Derelict tip at Sandwell Park Colliery.   This pit is no longer worked, but coal raised at the Jubilee Pit, a mile and a half to the north, is brought to the plant (left) for washing and screening.

Tipton. Flooded subsidence area being filled by ash from power station.

Willenhall. Spoil banks retained to support pylons. Around them all the ground has been cleared for housing.

Walsall.   Derelict site of an old foundry.

In the centre of an industrial area at Walsall.   Blast furnace slag.

TYPES OF
EXTRACTIVE
INDUSTRIES
STILL
CREATING
DERELICT
LAND

Marl pits for brickworks at Oldbury.

Dolerite for road metal, being quarried at Rowley Regis. These workings, which form a series of three large craters, one inside the other, are removing the top of a hill crest visible for miles around. The building (top right) is a farm house.

and Country Planning, more than 800 acres have been developed as housing sites. Further large stretches are in process of being levelled.

Areas in which derelict land still comprises more than 15 per cent. of the total acreage are Dudley—an area particularly badly affected by mining subsidence—and all the central districts of the Black Country. This high proportion of derelict land is indeed one of the features that distinguishes the Black Country area from the eastern, *i.e.*, the Birmingham half of the Conurbation. If the figures for the Birmingham district—in which the extent of derelict land is negligible—were subtracted from the total, the derelict land would be found to comprise more than a tenth of the Black Country area.

Derelict land inside the Conurbation is chiefly a legacy from the past. The historical sketch of the Conurbation (Chapter II) pointed out how the Black Country entered upon a new lease of life after the mining and quarrying, typical of the 19th century, was beginning to decline. Large industrial concerns were attracted to the heart of the Black Country by transport facilities, by the supply of skilled labour, and by the proximity of Birmingham with its wealth of small industrial concerns occupied with secondary metal processes and the production of consumer goods. Nevertheless, the area occupied by industrial plant is inconsiderable in comparison with that taken up by the earlier extractive industries. Today, land is not being spoiled to anything like the same extent as formerly. Nevertheless, it should be mentioned that, although less land is now being made derelict in the inner areas of the Conurbation, extractive industry on the fringe of the Conurbation and in the areas around it is affecting very considerable areas of open land. Sand and gravel workings have been developed on an increasing scale during the last few decades, keeping pace with the acceleration in the rate of building, The size and location of such pits affect the amenities of some of the countryside areas around the Conurbation (Chapter XIII).

Industry

The location of the main industrial centres is shown in the Distribution Map (Figure 36). It can be seen that in the Black Country the largest areas are those lying alongside the canal and railway lines. Smaller industrial centres are, however, scattered throughout the Black Country and there is no segregation of the " black " or heavily industrialized areas of noxious factories from the housing areas.

The old industries of the Black Country, such as mining, quarrying, and brickmaking, used and laid waste a considerable amount of land, while the manufacturing side of industry was mainly undertaken locally in small establishments. But more recently large industrial concerns have taken advantage of the Midland localization of engineering, chemical, and other industries, and have built extensive factories in the Black Country where they could find room for expansion and also be near urban centres at points conveniently accessible to lines of transport and communication.

The centre of Birmingham is still largely occupied by small factories. Larger undertakings are to be found in recently established zones at Tyseley, in the Tame Valley, and at Castle Bromwich, and these districts have now taken on the aspect of industrial zones reaching out from the centre along main railway lines. Lighter industries have tended to move outside even the most distant suburbs, and the Surface Utilisation Map shows a considerable sprinkling of large industrial concerns all around Birmingham, and indeed throughout the whole Conurbation fringe. This process is to some extent the product of the Government's war-time policy of dispersal, and there is no doubt that the ability to expand, and the relative cheapness of land have made the peripheral areas attractive to industrialists.

In the post-war period, industrialists have also to keep in mind the siting of their plants within easy distance of the labour now being housed in large suburban housing estates.

The difference in the acreage occupied by industry in the Black Country and in the Birmingham district is given in Table XXXVI. In the Black Country area it is 8.5 acres per thousand population, whereas in the Birmingham district the comparable figure is only 3.8. In planning the future industrial areas of the Black Country it must be realized that, in order to maintain the prosperity of the area, planning controls must take account of the needs of its existing industries, especially as regards space. Certain past evils, left as a legacy by industry, can be guarded against by measures such as controlled tipping and the encouragement of fuller use of industrial by-products.

THE ACREAGE USED FOR INDUSTRY AND HOUSING PER THOUSAND INHABITANTS
Birmingham and the Black Country compared

TABLE XXXVI

AREA	POPULATION (June 1939)	INDUSTRY		HOUSING	
		Total Acreage	Acres per 1000 Population	Total Acreage	Acres per 1000 Population
*Birmingham District	1,221,710	4,590	3.8	29,920	24.5
†Rest of Conurbation	857,023	7,250	8.5	24,160	28.2
Total Conurbation	2,078,733	11,840	5.7	53,080	25.5

    * Birmingham, Smethwick, Solihull and Sutton Coldfield.
    † Including the whole of the Black Country.

Housing

The considerable amount of house building carried on between 1920 and 1939 resulted in the establishment of large suburban housing estates, municipal and private. The rapid development of road transport between the wars produced, in addition, a new phenomenon—the sprawling " residential area " which spread out in ribbon development beyond the

---

Figure 36. Communications and the Distribution of Industry.

Communications and the Distribution of Industry. The map opposite shows areas occupied by industry, as marked in the General Surface Utilisation Map, and by canals, railways and classified roads.

Striking differences are revealed between the distribution of industry in Birmingham and in the western part of the Conurbation. The central areas of Birmingham are occupied by small factories. These small factories are heavily concentrated to the north-west and south-east of the commercial centre of the city; so much so that the areas have been coloured a uniform red as though no other uses were present in these areas. Outside the central areas of Birmingham, factory zones stretch along the road, canal and rail routes leading to the north-east, south-east, south-west, west and north-west.

There is no discernible pattern in the scatter of industries over the Black Country. In the central areas where the heavier industries are localized, most of the larger industrial areas are to be found along the sides of canals and railways. This is especially so in the case of the railways and waterways connecting Birmingham with Wolverhampton.

A noticeable feature is the large factory sites which have been developed in recent years on the fringe of the Conurbation, especially around Birmingham.

There is a considerable difference in the acreages occupied by industry in the Black Country and in the Birmingham district (see Table XXXVI). Industry in the Black Country occupies more than twice as much land in proportion to the population as in Birmingham. This difference in proportion is of major importance in planning industrial zones for the Conurbation.

The railway network serving the interior of the Conurbation is adequate to its needs, but there is a clear deficiency of through roads for motor traffic.

FIGURE 36

COMMUNICATIONS AND THE DISTRIBUTION OF INDUSTRY

LAND USED FOR INDUSTRIAL PURPOSES   SEWAGE DISPOSAL PLANT

CANALS – – – –   RAILWAYS ++++++++++   PRINCIPAL ROADS ——

suburbs for miles into the surrounding country. The most outstanding examples of this penetration of town into country are to the north and south of Birmingham, and along the western edge of the Conurbation (see also Development Map, Figure 40).

The new Birmingham housing areas are revealed as large masses of housing development, relieved by open space spreading between and beyond the industrial zones. Similar extensive zones stretch through the southern parts of Smethwick and Oldbury, and north of Walsall (see Figure 37).

Commerce

On the Surface Utilisation Maps (see specimen sheets, Plates 8 and 9) the centres of commerce are shown in blue, and are included in the acreage figures where three or more shops are grouped together. Public houses and garages are for the most part mapped in this category. These areas marked blue also indicate the social centres of the Conurbation townships and suburbs.

Major centres for shopping and commerce, and the activities that normally go with them, exist in West Bromwich, Wednesbury, Darlaston, Bilston, Old Hill, and Blackheath, in the interior of the Black Country, and what might be called an exterior ring takes in Halesowen, Stourbridge, Dudley, Wolverhampton, Walsall, and Birmingham (see Figure 37).

It is only in Birmingham and Wolverhampton, and in the older towns, such as Walsall, Dudley, and Wednesbury, that compact shopping areas appear. Elsewhere the shops tend to follow the line of the main road rather than to be grouped at focal points in residential areas. An example of this may be seen along the old Birmingham-Wolverhampton Road running through Handsworth, West Bromwich, Wednesbury, and Bilston. At the Birmingham end, the string of shops runs almost continuously for four miles, and there is a particularly heavy incidence through the whole length of West Bromwich. All the main traffic routes out of Birmingham are lined with shops for long distances. The Bilston and Darlaston shopping areas also stretch along main roads. In the south, Blackheath and Old Hill centres show the same characteristics. In view of the speed and congestion of modern traffic, this ribbon-spread is clearly dangerous and undesirable. It is interesting to note, however, that the long avenue characteristic of unplanned shopping centres is recognized in the new plan for Rotterdam, where main shopping centres are being planned along streets rather than in precincts. But, whatever pattern is adopted for them, the separation of shopping areas from main traffic roads should be a main objective in future planning, particularly in the central redevelopment areas in the large towns.

Figure 37. Housing and Social Centres.

Housing and Social Centres. This map is necessarily more generalized than the preceding distribution maps, especially in its presentation of the areas devoted to shops, commerce and centres of social activity generally.

The " shoe-string " development of shopping centres along the roads leading out from the main towns, especially Birmingham, and connecting the settlements of the Black Country is clearly revealed, noticeable examples outside Birmingham being at Old Hill, West Bromwich and Bilston. The existence of major shopping and social centres is clearly indicated at Birmingham, Wolverhampton, Walsall and Dudley.

The residential development which constitutes Birmingham's middle ring is clearly shown around the centre of the city, and it is noteworthy that housing development in Birmingham appears to be grouped in much larger masses than elsewhere in the Conurbation. Approximately two-fifths of the area occupied by housing in the whole Conurbation is located in Birmingham as against half the population. Ribbon development and sprawl on the fringe of the Conurbation are especially noticeable on the south-east, north-east, north and west. Ribbon development round the north of Walsall, it should be noted, dates from the end of the nineteenth century and usually indicates the presence of mining villages.

HOUSING AND SOCIAL CENTRES

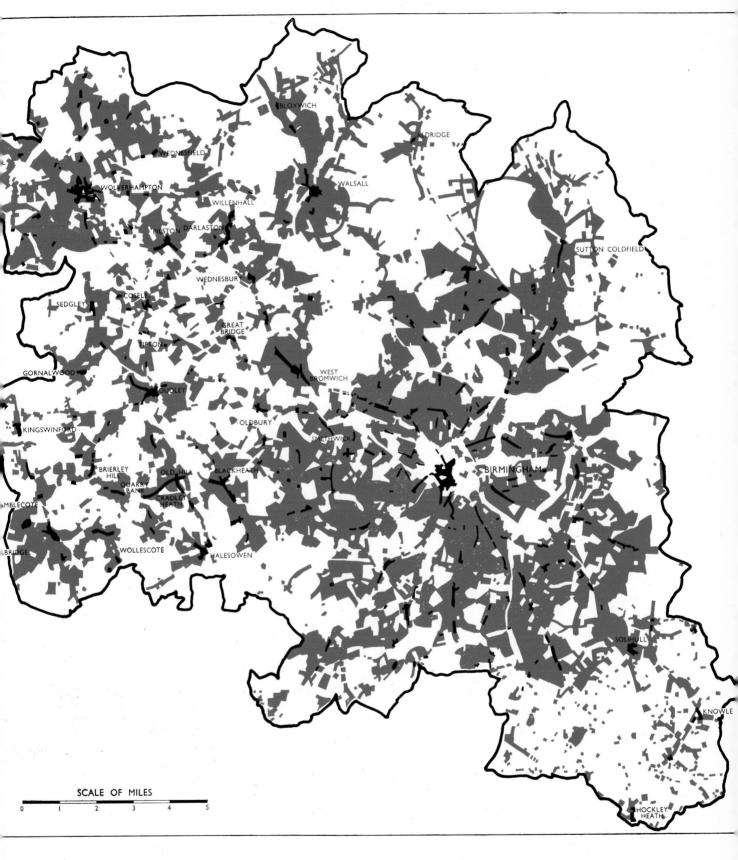

BLOXWICH

WEDNESFIELD

ALDRIDGE

WOLVERHAMPTON

WALSALL

WILLENHALL

BILSTON DARLASTON

SUTTON COLDFIELD

WEDNESBURY

SEDGLEY

COSELEY

GREAT
BRIDGE

TIPTON

GORNALWOOD

WEST
BROMWICH

DUDLEY

OLDBURY

KINGSWINFORD

SMETHWICK

BIRMINGHAM

BRIERLEY
HILL

OLD HILL

BLACKHEATH

QUARRY
BANK

CRADLEY
HEATH

MBLECOTE

SOLIHULL

BRIDGE

WOLLESCOTE

HALESOWEN

KNOWLE

HOCKLEY
HEATH

SCALE OF MILES

0   1   2   3   4   5

HOUSING   MAIN SHOPPING AND COMMERCIAL CENTRES

(The map shows distribution of principal shopping centres only. Single shops, public houses, offices and sub-sidiary centres of less than six separate premises have generally been omitted).

Public Buildings

No adequate survey has been made of existing social centres and public buildings from which it would be possible to draw recommendations for future planning. It was shown in Chapter IV (Local Government) that the complexity of the area for administrative purposes, and the artificial lines of the local government boundaries, necessitate a regrouping of different parts of the area for certain functions of regional administration and planning. A social survey to discover the character, interests and natural social centres of each local area would be of great value in helping to determine the right boundaries for this reorganization. Certain aspects—for example, the distribution of main places of entertainment such as cinemas—have been investigated by the Group, but the findings are not sufficiently complete to warrant publication.

Transport

The transport information shown on the Surface Utilisation Map merely gives existing lines of communication—road, rail and waterways—in order that they can be seen in relation to industrial and residential development. Regional lines of transport, and future recommendations for improving communications between the Conurbation and other parts of the country are described and illustrated in Chapter VI.

Conclusions

The principal fact which emerges from the Surface Utilisation Survey is the aggregate of open land—" undeveloped ", derelict and public open space—contained within the Conurbation. The area of 97,000 acres, or 56 per cent of the total area, which is not built-up or used for industry, is a major asset in planning the whole area. Whatever problems of planning the Conurbation presents, therefore, can find their solution within the limits of its present area. The amount of open land allows room not only for the loosening up of urban development, but is an all-important factor in providing temporary accommodation for building during the re-development periods. Broadly speaking, the problem of redevelopment is not complicated by the need to relieve congestion by wide dispersal, as in the case of London, Clydeside and other urban concentrations. Planned redevelopment in the Black Country will be directed towards the creation of more compact and economical groupings. The diagrammatic map, Redevelopment and Population Density (Figure 39), illustrates the validity of this approach. The Black Country is usually thought of as an almost continuous area of occupied territory, and this impression is encouraged by the sprawling lines of past development. What this diagram reveals is that a consistent policy of integrating the present settlements, and of zoning industry, could produce a group of separate compact townships each divided from the others by a clear and fairly wide strip or wedge of open space or agricultural land. An integral part of such a policy would be the rehabilitation of a portion of the existing derelict land, not for housing or other building development, but for open space. A second major conclusion to which the Surface Utilisation Map points is that the task of planning the whole area is one that cannot be done piecemeal. The Conurbation demands an overall view if it is to be planned on lines which will avoid a continuance of present evils. In view also of the extent to which the Conurbation is expanding outwards into the surrounding areas, planning control should not stop short at the edge of the present development area, but should extend into the surrounding agricultural region (see Chapter IV).

CHAPTER XII

Land Classification around the Conurbation

EXPANSION AND AGRICULTURE

THE CONSIDERABLE increase in the area of the Conurbation over the last few decades has raised many problems of which perhaps the most serious is the extensive loss of good agricultural land to suburban housing and to other forms of land use. The emergency conditions of recent years have stressed the fact that in this country, with a comparatively small area of good agricultural land per head of population, such loss is serious. It is becoming more and more urgent that conservation of the country's good agricultural land shall be an objective of high priority in any planning programme. Figures for the total and annual loss of agricultural land to non-agricultural purposes were given for the country as a whole by the Scott Committee. During the twelve years 1927-1939, 794,000 acres of agricultural land were covered by building and other forms of urban development, an average of 66,200 acres a year. Some of this has since been returned to agricultural use, but the net average annual figure remains at 60,000 acres permanently lost. The loss to agriculture is not confined solely to the physical disappearance of land beneath bricks and mortar. The productivity of a greater area is considerably reduced by the fragmentation of holdings and by trespass and encroachment. Examples of this can be drawn from almost any area in the periphery of the Conurbation, especially from the south side between Solihull and Hagley[1].

If, in spite of the conclusions reached in the preceding chapter, it should prove necessary, in relieving congestion in the Conurbation, to expand still further into the periphery of the area, all future planning must ensure that such expansion shall take place with a minimum of dislocation to agriculture, and, so far as possible, on land of lower agricultural value. We can no longer afford the expensive and uncontrolled sprawl of the period 1919-1939. Such a policy of regulated expansion depends for success upon adequate mapping of land qualities. When the Group began its investigations such mapping was not available. The preparation of a Land Classification Map of the West Midland Region and a more detailed map of the area adjoining the Conurbation, therefore, became matters of first importance.

In order to draw up a scheme upon which land classification mapping of the region could be based, and to prepare maps of the region's land resources, a Land Classification Committee was set up early in the Group's career. Details of the Committee's membership and work are available elsewhere[2]. It is sufficient to note here that the Committee included

---

[1] A **Land** Classification Map of the area around the Conurbation discussed in this Chapter will be found on Plate 12.
[2] *Land Classification in the West Midland Region*, by the West Midland Group (Faber & Faber, 1947).

geographers, soil surveyors and other agricultural experts. The classification evolved was objective, based on site and soil features rather than on current use. Three grades of land were distinguished in the scheme of mapping ; these were defined as follows:—

Category[1] *I.* Good quality land; highly productive under good management. Land in this category has the following characteristics:—

Site—not too elevated, level, gently sloping or undulating; favourable aspect.

Soil—deep, with favourable water conditions (actual or potential); texture—mostly loams, but including some peats, sands, silts and clays.

Category[1] *II.* Land of only medium productivity even under good management. Productivity is limited by reason of the operation of one or more factors of site or soil, *e.g.*, by reason of:—

Site factors: high elevation, steepness, unfavourable aspect.

Soil factors: shallowness, defective water conditions.

Category[1] *III.* Poor quality land, defined as " land of low productivity by reason of the extreme operation of one or more factors of site or soil."

For planning purposes it is recommended by the Committee that land in Category I should be retained as far as possible for agriculture, and that since much land in Category II is of only slightly less importance, major changes in its use should not be permitted without careful consideration of its agricultural possibilities.

The Survey

When the Committee began its investigations, some basic information was available from a reconnaissance survey of parts of the area around the Conurbation carried out in 1939 and 1940 by W. G. D. Walters of the Soil Survey of England and Wales: but in order to secure uniformity of classification the whole area was re-traversed in some detail by a survey team consisting of soil surveyors and geographers. Such occasional differences of opinon as arose on the classification of any particular area were settled by *ad hoc* meetings of the whole committee at the site under discussion. The area surveyed is shown on Plate 12.

Assessment of site factors was largely visual; but the assessment of soil qualities was made on the evidence of numerous auger borings. These were made at varying intervals, and were most frequent in areas of complex topography and where geological diversity seemed likely to give rise to a variety of soil types. No attempt was made to sample individual fields except in certain controversial areas. These methods limited the scope of the inquiry. In certain areas the intermingling of Categories I and II, or of II and III, is so intimate that any attempt to map the boundaries of each category would involve an expenditure of time and effort out of proportion to the result. Such areas, of which the hummocky Pebble-bed country of North Worcestershire is typical, were therefore shown as containing a mixture of two categories, and on the map they are striped accordingly.

Geographic Basis of Land Classification Around the Conurbation

The general geographic background of the Conurbation area has been described in detail elsewhere (Chapter III). Here it is sufficient to recall the salient features. The dominating feature, which also gives a unity to the area, is the South Staffordshire Plateau. This is a rolling upland with a general elevation of some 400 feet to 600 feet, developed chiefly on Carboniferous rocks. These include the yellow-grey shales and sandstones of the Middle Coal Measures, and the red marls, sandstones and breccias of the Upper Coal

---

[1]The term " Category " is used here instead of " Major Category " as adopted in *Land Classification in the West Midland Region*.

Measures. Its general slope is eastwards or north-eastwards and in these directions it merges comparatively gently with the adjoining lowland. To the west it is terminated by a steep face, rising some 300 feet—400 feet above the lowland, and deeply embayed by the upper valley of the Stour. The fringes of two other upland areas fall within the area under discussion. These are the Trimpley-Enville upland to the west, and the plateau of East Warwickshire to the east. Both are developed largely upon red rocks of Upper Carboniferous age, but include small areas of older rocks.

Between these three upland regions are two lowlands with a north-south trend, developed on Triassic rocks preserved in the intervening downfolds. Of these lowlands, the more westerly drains to the Severn, the easterly to the Tame and the Trent. Both show a gently, undulating topography, only locally exceeding 450 feet, and both are extensively covered by glacial sands and gravels.

It will be evident that site factors are of only local importance to land classification in this area. Elevation is rarely excessive and only very occasionally, as along the bleak crest of the Clents, does it become a major limiting factor. Elsewhere, however, and particularly to the north of the Conurbation, there are considerable areas over 600 feet, and conditions are perceptibly bleaker than in the lowlands. Slope is a more important factor since this, together with the associated factor of soil shallowness, limits productivity over much of the south-west fringe of the plateau, and locally in the lowland to the west where the Worfe and other small streams flow in deeply incised courses bounded by steep valley walls. Aspect is closely linked with slope, and, except on the Clent Hills, is of only limited significance. On the Clent Hills the effect of aspect is particularly evident on south-facing slopes where the intense insolation leads to rapid drying out of the shallow upland soils. Elsewhere the site factor is of less importance, and classification is based almost entirely on soil factors. Climatic factors, with the exception of those mentioned above, are unimportant; both rainfall and temperature readings within the survey area show so small a variation that for the purposes of land classification climatic conditions may be considered to be uniform.

Soil

The broad outlines given above demonstrate the considerable variety of solid geological formations. Further extensive areas are mantled by glacial drift ranging in character from heavy stony boulder clay to light sands, and in thickness from a foot or less to several feet. Great diversity of soils, therefore, is encountered in the area. In addition to most of the series already known and described, numerous new series were encountered in the Region. For this reason a full discussion of the various soil series in the area is not practicable, and the account of soil factors is limited to a brief description of some typical soils in each of the three categories.

Some of the best agricultural land around the conurbation is to be found on soils developed on the Keele beds of the Upper Coal Measures. These soils range from light loam to heavy loam; they have considerable depth, are well drained, and are particularly responsive to good management. The extensive area of Category I land between Birmingham and Coventry coincides broadly with the area of these soils. West of the Conurbation the area classed as I and II to the east of Alveley is composed of similar soils of Upper Coal Measure derivation. The deep, fine, sandy loams derived from the Keuper Sandstone (the Bromsgrove Series) are likewise first-quality soils. Of the drift-derived soils the Flint Series, developed on Triassic boulder clay, and the fine sandy soil of the Newport Series, developed on glacial sands, are among the best.

An extensive range of soil series, inherently second-rate from the farmers' point of view, is to be found within the area. In some cases, productivity is limited by heaviness and by the restricted period for cultivation, as in the Hurcot Series and in the developed Tea-green marls and some of the heavier soils developed on the yellow-grey Middle Coal Measures. Others suffer from impeded drainage, as in the case of the lower-grade Salop or Wem Series developed on glacial drift. Excessive drainage and hungry character limit the productivity of such soils as the lighter types of the Newport Series found on sandy drifts, and the Crannymoor Series developed on Triassic sandstones.

Category III soils are few, and are found generally in adverse site conditions. In this category may be classed the thinner Crannymoor and Bridgnorth soils on areas of which parts of Kinver Edge are typical, some of the wetter alluvial soils, and the man-made " soils " on the coal-spoil areas north of the Conurbation.

Human Factors

In this area human activities have had divergent influences, the results of which are apparent on the Land Classification Map. In some cases man has improved the land, in others he has spoiled it. An example of improvement is that produced by the long-continued cultivation of some of the lighter podsolic soils. Until the beginning of the nineteenth century these soils were under heath. They have been converted into productive agricultural land by persistent tillage. This improvement may be noted in the lighter land west of the conurbation. On the other hand, considerable areas of agricultural land have been ruined in the Middle Coal Measure districts by open-cast mining and by the indiscriminate tipping of mining and metallurgical wastes, and by mining subsidence. It is probably true that much of this land was never much above second quality, but, even so, it represents a loss to agriculture. The area of II and III land immediately north of the conurbation gives some idea of the extent of this loss. Here the area of Category III land is for the most part man-made.

DISTRIBUTION OF CATEGORIES

In mapping the distribution of agricultural land in the area under consideration, the main bases of classification are the three Categories described above. In some districts, however, categories are mixed, and as the conservation of all agricultural assets is of high importance, the combinations of categories are discussed under their appropriate headings.

Areas in Which Category I Predominates

The areas of first grade agricultural land in the vicinity of the conurbation are not extensive. They are included in the area shown on the Land Classification Map (Plate 12). The area of the map is roughly that covered by the 1-inch Birmingham and Wolverhampton Ordnance Survey Sheet. It must be remembered, however, that references to the areas of the various categories are generalized. Any attempt, therefore, to apply these areas to a larger scale map will be misleading.

The map shows two major areas and one minor area of first quality agricultural land:
(1) The largest of these areas lies in North Worcestershire and stretches from the vicinity of Hagley, south-westwards towards Kidderminster. Here the soils are comparatively light—chiefly sandy loams developed on Lower Keuper Sandstone. Site factors are favourable. Elevations rarely exceed 400 feet, and topography is either level or slightly undulating. Soils are deep, easy-working and " early ". These features have encouraged the development of market-gardening, and potato and sugar beet cultivation. The area is favourably sited in relation to the consuming

centres of the West Midlands. From a planning point of view this is a critical area as it represents a productive agricultural district situated between the expanding urban areas of Stourbridge-Pedmore-Hagley and Kidderminster.

(2) The second major area of first-grade land comprises the belt of red soils derived from the Upper Coal Measures (Keele Beds) of Central and East Warwickshire. Topography is somewhat more undulating than in North Warwickshire, and soils are somewhat heavier and of a closer texture. Two major types are found; fine sandy loams derived from the sandstones, and medium-to-heavy loams developed on the heavier marl beds. The belt stretches from the vicinity of Kingsbury in the north to Berkswell in the south. It is one of the most important tracts of high-grade land in the whole of the West Midlands, but it is menaced by the rapid growth of Birmingham on the one side and Coventry on the other. Any planning scheme should give special consideration to this valuable agricultural area.

(3) The smallest area of first-grade land lies to the north-west of Wolverhampton, in the vicinity of Donington. The soils are generally deep sandy loams derived from Triassic sandstone or glacial drift. Unlike the two major agricultural areas, this district is not in immediate danger. Normal extension of nearby villages must be anticipated, but the amount of land likely to be involved is comparatively small.

Category I mixed with Category II

Category I mixed with Category II land is more extensive. In this class the Category II land represents occasional patches of excessively shallow or very light soils on steep slopes. This mixture of Categories I and II occupies approximately one-quarter of the rural land in the area of the Birmingham and Wolverhampton 1-inch sheet. Three areas may be distinguished :—

(1) A discontinuous and irregular belt lying to the west of the Conurbation and stretching from south of Shifnal to the Worcestershire boundary near Upper Arley. It is bounded on the east by an irregular line running north-south from Tettenhall to Kinver, and is broken in the vicinity of Claverley and Abbotts Castle Hill by a transverse belt of poorer soils. Topography is gently undulating, and many of the smaller knolls and ridges have patches of shallow soil.

The higher-grade soils fall into two main types: the deep sandy loams developed on Triassic sandstones, and the somewhat heavier medium loam soils derived from the Keele Beds of the Upper Coal Measures. The former predominate in the east and north of this belt. Essentially arable soils and well-suited to potatoes and vegetables, they support some of the best farming in Staffordshire. In the north-east this area of mainly high-grade land is particularly menaced by the extension of Wolverhampton.

The heavier soils of the Keele Complex occur in the south-west; they are similar to the Keele soils of East Warwickshire. As they are comparatively remote from any large centres of population they have been little affected by non-agricultural development.

Elsewhere the soils are definitely second-rate, comprising poorer heath soils and soils developed on lighter types of drift. These patches, however, are too insignificant to be mapped on a one-inch scale. As the aggregate area of these soils is so small the whole belt is classified as mainly Category I with patches of II.

(2) The second extensive area classed as I with II lies to the north-east of the Conurbation and centres on the city of Lichfield, though it includes also a small area east of the

Tame. This region, which is one of the most important market-garden areas in the West Midland Region, is characterized by soils of a light texture, chiefly deep sandy loams derived from the Lower Keuper Sandstone. It includes also some heavier soils derived from glacial drift and from the fine sandy phase of the Keuper Marl.

(3) Two areas in North Worcestershire have been classed as I with II. These are a small area east of Wolverley and a somewhat larger irregularly-shaped area around the town of Bromsgrove. In both cases, soils are typically deep sandly loams, locally varied by small areas of shallow hungry soils on steeper slopes. Of the two areas, the Bromsgrove area is the more interesting: it is an important market-gardening district enjoying the advantages of deep loamy soils and of proximity to the Birmingham market, but during the last twenty years agriculture has become increasingly encroached upon by suburban development in the Catshill area.

To sum up; land in Category I, and areas of land predominantly of Category I with occasional patches of Category II, together represent the best agricultural land of the region. In the area round the Conurbation only 25-30 per cent of the agricultural land is of sufficiently high quality to come in this combined Category of I with II. The reservation of these areas for agricultural use would be of the highest importance in any planning scheme.

Areas in which Category II Predominates

Category II land has already been described as land of only medium productivity even under good management. It has already been stated that the limiting factor to productivity of this land is usually a soil factor such as shallowness, heaviness or extremes of drainage rather than site factors. Including areas with patches of Category I and Category III land, it occupies no less than 71 per cent of the rural land in the area.

Land of Category II with some of Category I occurs in three areas :—

(1) To the east of Birmingham, forming an irregular belt ranging in width from 1 mile in the north to 5-6 miles in the south, and stretching from the vicinity of Lichfield southwards to Wroxall. This belt includes the mixed soils of North-central Warwickshire developed largely on Keuper Marl or on glacial drift over marl, and varying in character from the light, excessively drained podsolic soils of the Coleshill Heath area to the heavy, badly-drained soils of the Tanworth-in-Arden area. The occasional patches of Category I land coincide generally with the better boulder clay soils (*e.g.* Flint Series).

(2) Several areas of mixed II with I land are found in North Worcestershire. The area north-east of Hagley is locally much dissected and suffers from a certain degree of bleakness; soils are developed on the Upper and Middle Coal Measures and are generally heavy so that the greater part of the area would fall within Category II. Occasional fields, however, have deeper, light-to-medium textured soils which justify their classification in Category I.

Around Kidderminster, too, much of the land has been classed as II with I. Here the limiting factor is somewhat different. Much of the area lies below 400 feet and soils are light textured, easy working and early. Drainage is generally excessive, and the land is hungry except where occasional patches of slightly heavier and deeper soils occur. Where topography is more undulating and soils shallower, the land suffers from marked drought in summer.

(3) In North-central Worcestershire a third large area occurs where the Keuper Marl is overlaid by boulder clay and glacial sands and gravels. Topographically the area is a rolling lowland and the variation of land classification through the site

factor is negligible. Soils, however, are very variable, and while some of the fine sandy Keuper Marl soils and some of the soils derived from the deeper drift are first-rate, the bulk of the area must be classed as essentially medium quality for many of the boulder clay soils are poorly drained, and some of the soils derived from the Keuper Marl are heavy and difficult to work, especially on eroded slopes. This complex intermingling of good and medium quality land necessitates the classification of the whole belt as Category II with I.

If occasional small patches on steep valley sides be omitted from consideration, land in Category II, without any appreciable admixture of higher grade land, is found in four areas :—

(1) West of the Conurbation, and especially west of Sedgley, there is a well-marked belt of Category II land. The soils are generally light, often excessively so, and sometimes shallow, and are developed either on thin patches of glacial sands and gravels or on Triassic sandstones (predominantly Bunter Pebble Beds). Much of this area has been reclaimed from heathland, and the continued presence of extensive areas of heath and birch scrub points unmistakably to its marginal quality.

(2) To the north, also, the Conurbation is fringed by an extensive belt of second-class land. Here elevation is somewhat greater and the area suffers from bleakness, as well as from smoke drift from the Black Country to the south and south-west. Soils are variable and range from light sandy soils in the west to heavier boulder clay and Middle Coal Measure soils in the east. There is a general deterioration in land quality eastwards caused by increasing human interference, *i.e.*, disturbance of the original land surface by dumping and mining subsidence, and in this direction a gradual transition occurs to a II with III area.

(3) In the Tamworth-Wilnecote area a belt of Category II land occurs north of the high-grade soils of the Keele Complex. Soils are typically shallow loams developed on the sandstone beds, with heavier soils, often impeded, on the intervening clays and shales. Sporadic mining development further reduces the agricultural value of the land, particularly in the north around Polesworth and Fazeley.

(4) South of the Conurbation a belt of rather heavy land extends west from the main Birmingham-Warwick road towards the Lickey Hills. Soils are derived either from boulder clay or from Keuper Marl; they are generally heavy and frequently show signs of impeded drainage at no great depth. In the south-east near Lapworth and in the west near Weatheroak Hill, unfavourable topography reduces productivity since many of the slopes are unsuited to arable cultivation and soils are sometimes shallow and eroded.

The complex of Category II with III occurs in parts of the worked-over mining district of South Staffordshire, in the hummocky Pebble Bed country round Hints and Hopwas, and more extensively to the west of Kidderminster. In this latter district the dissected parts of the Wyre Forest with diverse Coal Measures soils and the light " blow-away " sands and bare rock surfaces of the Habberley Valley—Devil's Spadeful district, are included in this Category II with III land.

Areas in which Category III Predominates

Category III land occupies 0.3 per cent of the rural land shown on the 1-inch Birmingham-Wolverhampton sheet.

The upland areas of Clent and Lickey have been classed as predominantly III; here will be found almost all the limiting factors of site and soil—elevation, steep slopes, local bad aspect, poverty and shallowness of soil.

SUMMARY AND CONCLUSIONS

1. Fruitful land use in the areas around the conurbation will depend ultimately upon the harmonious adjustment of the apparently conflicting claims of townsman and countryman. The wise adjustment of interests is not likely to be easy, but if adequate data is available on human needs and the potentialities of the land, there is no reason why a reasonable and economic adjustment should not be achieved. The aim of this land classification survey has been to give an objective picture of the potentialities of the agricultural land in this critical area.

2. The land classification make-up of the rural areas falling within the 1-inch Birmingham-Wolverhampton sheet is summarized below. For the purposes of this map the area within the limits of concentrated urban development in the Conurbation has been regarded as lost to agriculture, and all land, developed and undeveloped, outside these limits, has been classified.

LAND CLASSIFICATION OF THE AGRICULTURAL AREA AROUND THE CONURBATION

TABLE XXXVII

Category	Percentage* of Area Surveyed
Category I	12·3
Category I with patches of II	16·3
Category II with patches of I	22·9
Category II	36·9
Category II with patches of III	11·3
Category III with patches of II	0·0
Category III	0·3

*Percentages are proportionate to the *agricultural* area surveyed, *i.e.*, the area shown by the Land Classification Map (Plate 12) excluding the main built-up areas of the Conurbation.

3. The areas of Category I and I with II comprise the best agricultural land in the whole area. Much of it is threatened by urban sprawl. *Other things being equal, it is in the interest of both the nation and the West Midland Region that further encroachment on these areas should be strongly discouraged or even prohibited and that development should be directed to land of lower agricultural value.*

4. These areas of good quality agricultural land include a considerable range in soil textures. These are important to the agricultural needs of the Conurbation which range from market garden crops to dairy produce.

5. Certain areas have been classed as predominantly II with patches of Category I. Further detailed work is necessary to delimit the areas of Category I land. This is an essential preliminary to any projected development schemes in such areas.

6. The development of second-grade soils for market garden purposes raises a special problem. This is dealt with in the Appendix to this chapter.

7. Broadly speaking, it is suggested that further extension of the Conurbation to the south-west, north-west or north-east is undesirable. The area of soils of the Keele Complex, to the east of Birmingham, should be specially safeguarded.

8. From the point of view of agriculture, permissible lines of expansion of the built-up area (on to areas of land which are inherently of limited productivity) are as follows :—

(*a*) Due west from the Sedgley area on to light, second-rate soils;

(*b*) Due south from Birmingham on to heavy marl and boulder-clay soils;

(*c*) North from Wolverhampton on to light, second-quality soils;

(*d*) North-west from Walsall.

9. The areas of Category II with III and of Category III land include some of the most attractive scenery in the vicinity of the Conurbation. The rolling, pine-dotted country around Hints, the pine- and birch-covered heaths of South Staffordshire and North Worcestershire, and the Wyre Forest, are examples of land almost useless from an agricultural point of view but entitled to consideration for their scenic value in any rural planning scheme.

10. The land classification boundaries shown on the map are land boundaries and take no account of the boundaries of farm units. In areas of complex land quality, the average farm unit will frequently include patches of good and poor land. To avoid fragmentation it may often be found necessary to reserve for agriculture considerable areas of second quality land.

FIGURE 38

INTENSIVELY CULTIVATED AREAS IN THE WEST MIDLAND REGION

EACH DOT REPRESENTS
10 ACRES UNDER
MARKET GARDEN CULTIVATION

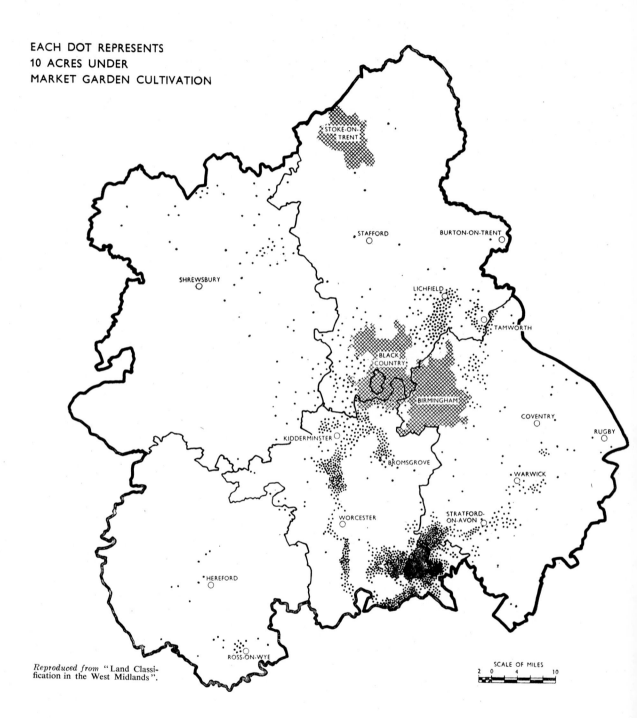

Reproduced from "Land Classification in the West Midlands".

SCALE OF MILES

Although most of the agricultural land around the Conurbation is of medium quality, a high proportion of the Region's market garden crops is grown on it.

APPENDIX TO CHAPTER XII

Horticultural Development around the Conurbation, and its relation to the Land Classification Map

Before leaving the question of land classification, it is of interest to glance briefly at the problem presented by the horticultural development of certain areas adjoining the conurbation.

The very considerable horticultural output of areas adjoining the heart of the West Midlands is not generally realized. Yet in 1937, a normal pre-war year, no less than 22 per cent of the Region's vegetable acreage was concentrated within some eight miles of the limits of Birmingham and the Black Country. It will be seen from the following table that approximately one-fifth of the 22,629 acres under market garden crops[1] in the West Midland Region is situated within eight or ten miles of the limits of the Conurbation.

TABLE XXXVIII

	Acres (approximate)	Percentage of Regional acreage under Market Garden Crops
Lichfield	1,856	8·2
Kidderminster-Hagley	1,267	5·6
South-west Staffordshire	704	3·2
Bromsgrove	588	2·6
North-central Warwickshire	498	2·2
Total in these five areas...	4,913	21·8

The distribution of these crops is shown in Figure 38.

It is generally accepted that, if the protective foods are to make their maximum contribution to our diet they should be produced as close as possible to the centres of consumption. This avoids unnecessary handling and loss of freshness. Clearly, therefore, the close proximity of these districts to the Conurbation is a factor of no small importance to the well-being of the urban population; it is unnecessary to dwell on the economic advantages to the grower of such a vast market, virtually on his doorstep.

Yet, if the distribution of these crops is compared with the Land Classification Map, the paradox emerges that a very large proportion of the vegetable production comes from second-grade soils. The explanation is, of course, that what the vegetable grower seeks above all is a soil of favourable texture—light, easy-working, early, and sufficiently well-drained to be workable even in wet weather. Poverty of plant foods is a small matter since nutrient status can be built up and maintained at a reasonably high level by manures; and excessive lightness, the chief factor in the down grading of these soils on the Land Classification Map, can to some extent be remedied by addition of humus. In other words, the horticultural soils around the Conurbation, as elsewhere in the Region, are to a large extent man-made.

Clearly, this is of importance in the planning of land use around the Conurbation. Certain areas have been indicated where inherent productivity is high, and these should be reserved for agricultural use. But, locally, outside these areas, there are certain soil types

---

[1] Cabbages and other green crops, peas, beans, onions and carrots, but excluding potatoes.

falling under the Committee's definition as second rate, which have shown themselves capable of conversion into highly productive soils under favourable economic and social conditions. The range of crops produced would be limited, but a strong case could be made for the reservation of many areas with these soils for market gardening purposes.

CHAPTER XIII

Redevelopment within the Green Setting

THE URBAN AREA

FOR MORE than fifty years, attacks on the urban congestion of the nineteenth century have been made in all the programmes of housing and planning pioneers. For the most part, early efforts were directed to the establishment of low densities. " Twelve to the acre " became something of a battle cry. The thinning of people on the ground was the principal objective aimed at, and the provision of house-gardens, wider roads, and parkways was the necessary corollary.

While their principles have been widened by later developments in planning, the aim of the pioneers remains valid; more space to live in, to work in, and to play in is still required. The wide acceptance which these conceptions attained for themselves is clearly demonstrated by the series of garden villages and green belt cities which were started between 1885 and 1945 in England and America. These included Bournville, Letchworth, Welwyn Garden City, Radburn, and Greenbelt. We have moved some distance from the conceptions of layout, urban design and architecture which went to make the garden cities of sixty, forty and twenty years ago, and although a clearer vision of the needs and functions of urban communities has gained acceptance for the idea of higher densities in the central areas of towns, the underlying planning conception remains unchanged.

The original arguments which the garden city planners used have been reinforced by the increasing concern with the dispersal of large centres of population. It has become clear that the strategic, social, and long-term economic consequences of the growth of London and other urban centres are harmful and dangerous. The answer, for many people, is found in the removal of certain proportions of the population and industry of overgrown cities and towns to new urban settlements. These are to be far enough away to avoid the danger of their being linked by a continuous urban development, but close enough to be able to receive some economic and social sustenance from the parent town. The most recently planned garden suburbs and cities in England and Europe have been satellite townships or " new towns ".

As a result of the interaction of all these developments there has come into being, not only in this country and in America, but all over Europe, a generally accepted conception of the lines on which cities should be planned or re-planned. It is recognizable in the published plans for the re-development of European towns as far apart as Moscow, Warsaw, Rotterdam and London. The plans aim at creating what have been called " Green Cities ". Density is to be systematically reduced, and open spaces interspersed throughout all city districts. The districts themselves are split up into zones and

199

neighbourhoods by continuous lanes and parkland, which widen as they lead out from the centre of the town to the surrounding country.

The "Green City" Principle and the Conurbation

The solution of the general planning problem presented by the Conurbation lies in the creation of a more rational pattern of urban development and open spaces. Two distinct considerations, however, modify the "Green City" principle in its application to the Conurbation.

First, the Conurbation has no centre. The two largest towns, Birmingham and Wolverhampton, are situated opposite each other, on the edge of the area.

Secondly, there is no case for dispersal of industry or population from the area as a whole. Apart from the essential consideration advanced in Chapter VIII, the Surface Utilisation Survey (Chapter XI) has shown that more than half the area of the Conurbation is unused. While it is true that a century-and-a-half of unplanned development has brought about congested conditions in limited districts of almost every town, there is no essential problem of congestion in the area as a whole. The process which the re-planning of the Conurbation requires, above all else, is a tidying-up. The Development Map (Figure 40) shows this clearly, and the looseness of the existing structure renders it possible to achieve such a tidying-up by re-grouping the areas of development within it.

The redevelopment pattern which the Group has in mind is of an *archipelago* of urban settlements, with each settlement isolated from its neighbours and set in green, open land, from which all development other than for agriculture or amenity is rigidly excluded. Seen from another aspect, the redevelopment pattern is a system of green strips running uninterruptedly through the Conurbation, with existing towns and townships shaped into tidy units, each surrounded by its green border.

The centres of industry and settlement which might eventually form the separate urban units appear fairly clearly from study of the Distribution Map of Industry and Communications (Figure 36) and the Distribution Map of Housing and Social Centres (Figure 37). Convenience, traditional usage, and evidence of a coherent social structure should determine the number and size of settlements, and after the broad pattern of development has been settled, decisions on such matters as the choice of centres and their ultimate size might be made on the merits of each individual case.

Such factors as population policy affect the general plan considerably. While the population of the whole area, through natural increase and recently some net immigration, has grown more rapidly than that of the United Kingdom, the population of the inner districts of the Black Country has fallen (Chapter V). The Group has recommended that steps be taken to maintain an equal balance between immigration and emigration in the Conurbation area as a whole; and the exodus from the inner Black Country districts should be checked, and possibly reversed by redeveloping them along lines which will make them attractive to live in. If both these recommendations are adopted by those responsible for planning the area, then the ultimate size for which the inner urban units should be planned will be larger, and the ultimate size of the outer urban units smaller than they will be if present tendencies remain unchecked.

Another factor to be considered in determining the ultimate size of the urban units is the balance of industries in certain districts recommended in Chapter VIII. This would entail allowance for the growth of such areas as, for example, Bilston and Dudley, into which factories might move.

The separate urban units would, therefore, vary as much in size as the towns

REDEVELOPMENT AND POPULATION DENSITY

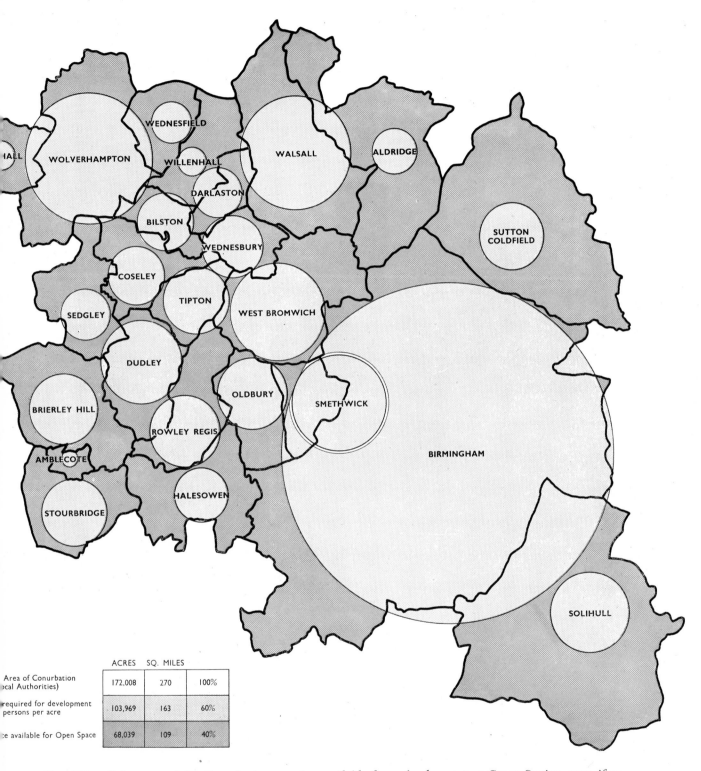

	ACRES	SQ. MILES	
Area of Conurbation ocal Authorities)	172,008	270	100%
required for development persons per acre	103,969	163	60%
e available for Open Space	68,039	109	40%

Two-fifths of the area of the Conurbation remains available for redevelopment as Green Setting, even if re-development plans allow for an overall density of twenty persons to the acre.

(This diagram has been composed on the basis of local authorities only and without reference to the individual urban units which might be developed under any plan in line with the suggestions made in Figure 41.)

FIGURE 40

DEVELOPMENT IN AND AROUND THE CONURBATION

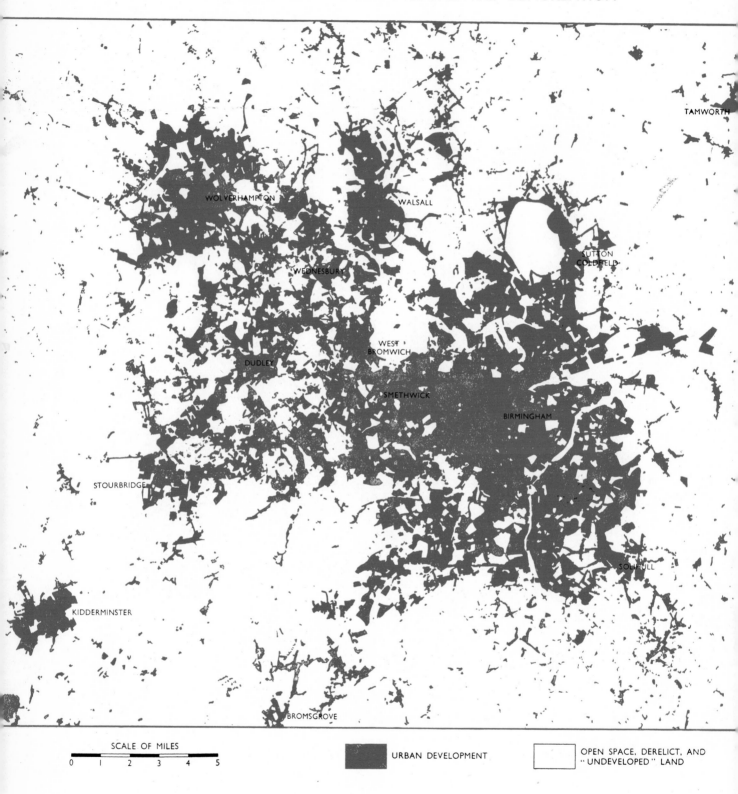

SCALE OF MILES

0   1   2   3   4   5

URBAN DEVELOPMENT

OPEN SPACE, DERELICT, AND "UNDEVELOPED" LAND

FIGURE 41

REDEVELOPMENT IN THE GREEN SETTING

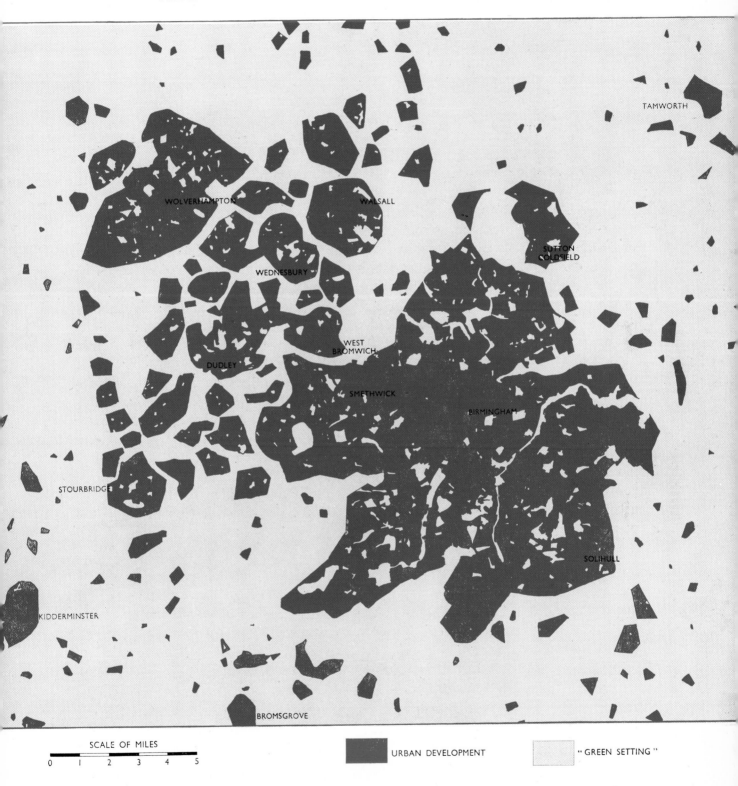

SCALE OF MILES

0 1 2 3 4 5

■ URBAN DEVELOPMENT   □ "GREEN SETTING"

Note :—Open spaces shown inside urban units are those in existence now. Areas coloured red show existing urban development and areas allowed for extensions to urban units, including open space.

of the present Conurbation. Nevertheless, the future layout of larger units such as Birmingham and Wolverhampton might be planned so that housing neighbourhoods, industrial zones, commercial centres, and so on, emerge as further islets, divided by green strips, on the same principle as in the Conurbation as a whole, but with the pattern of urban development and open space focussed on the central area of the City. Although the size of Birmingham seems to create a set of conditions separate from those of the rest of the Conurbation, there is little fundamental difference. In the Black Country the problem is to develop a continuous network of strips of open land. The main problem in Birmingham is the splitting of the central core of continuous urban development and the introduction of open space.

The existence of so much open land in the Conurbation can contribute largely to the realization of this general plan. The large areas of undeveloped and derelict land which are found even in the heart of the Black Country render it possible to effect a very considerable transformation within a comparatively short space of time. Beyond this immediate stage, further urban development should take the form of planned extensions of existing centres. A line should be drawn around each centre selected for continuance as an urban unit to act as the outside limit of development; and provision should be made for the ultimate reversion to open land of the scattered development which exists between towns. It is not suggested that recent development should be cleared immediately, but redevelopment should not be permitted on sites lying outside the "limit of development line". It would be urgently necessary to determine the general lines of the Conurbation plan at the earliest possible moment, so that Planning Authorities might prohibit building development on areas of undeveloped or derelict land falling within the open land areas. Figure 35, showing the distribution of "undeveloped" land, derelict land and open spaces, suggests in itself many of the areas which might be planned as the wedges and continuous strips which form the Green Setting (for definition, see page 210). From the map four major belts of open land already appear to exist, and it is important to prevent these more or less open lanes through the Conurbation being blocked for generations by new development unrelated to any general plan for the area. It is also necessary to begin at an early date on schemes for the rehabilitation of derelict land as open space (see Chapter XIV).

Redevelopment Map

Figure 41 shows a semi-diagrammatic outline for the redevelopment of the Conurbation. It has been drawn up to illustrate—without the loss of force which a merely diagrammatic presentation would involve—the ideas which the Group feels should lie behind such redevelopment. Figure 39 shows that the population of the whole Conurbation can be accommodated at reasonable standards of density in 163 of the 270 square miles of the Conurbation; the remaining 109 square miles could then constitute an area of open land between the towns after they had been re-formed around their centres. Though aware that many factors are involved in the planning of the area and that in some instances proposals based on the Redevelopment Map might be impracticable, the Group feels that the general principles are capable of adoption throughout the area as a whole.

OPEN SPACES INSIDE THE CONURBATION

In considering the general plan for the redevelopment of the Conurbation, it has been convenient to group together all open land—" undeveloped " land, derelict land, open spaces—inside the Conurbation. Open spaces within urban areas fulfil certain specific social functions, however, and it is necessary to examine the extent to which the areas of open space in the Conurbation are adequate to those functions.

Open spaces may be divided into two main groups, each fulfilling a different purpose in the life of urban communities. The first group consists of public parks, recreation grounds, squares and playing fields. The second group comprises private open spaces with particular uses; these serve to divide and open up urban development and so give a sense of spaciousness. Many of these spaces preserve natural and unspoilt landscapes in the town. In this second group are private parklands, woods, inland waters in private possession, all sports grounds the use of which is restricted to a limited or fee-paying public, and botanical and zoological gardens. Allotments and cemeteries comprise two other smaller groups of open spaces set aside for special purposes.

Open space is the one type of surface use which normally yields no financial return. Planning, in the sense of allocating land to different uses in accordance with the interests of the community, is of recent growth. It is only during the last two generations that increased leisure has created the demand and need for open-air activities on the part of the mass of people; and this modern need has stressed the fact that the centres of almost all our cities and towns are, by present-day standards, lamentably deficient in open space, although there are notable exceptions, such as London, Edinburgh, Dublin, and Cardiff. The inner districts of Birmingham, for example, covering an area of 3,023 acres with a population of 187,000,[1] contain only 35 acres of public open space available for recreation, a proportion of 0.2 acres per 1,000 population. Since 1909, however, five Town Planning Schemes for different sections of the outer parts of Birmingham have come into operation. The effect of these schemes has been to raise the proportion of existing public open space available for the whole population of Birmingham to 3.0 acres per thousand. If land scheduled for future public use under the above-mentioned schemes is added, the proportion becomes 3.7 acres per thousand and rises to 6.6 per thousand if all open space, public and private, is included.

Distribution of Open Space

Table XXXIX contains a full account of the 19,010 acres of open space in the Conurbation analysed according to Local Authority areas and types of use. As may be expected, there are considerable differences in the proportions of open space available in each Local Authority area. A clearer indication of the open space available is given in Figure 35, which shows the geographical distribution of open spaces and should be compared with the Distribution Map of Housing (Figure 37).

Although there are fairly wide differences in the proportions of open space available in each Local Authority area, the most significant of the figures shown in Table XL is the overall proportion of 4.1 acres of public open space per thousand population over the Conurbation as a whole. The Plan for the County of London, for example, lays down seven acres per thousand persons as an optimum, but does not hope for more than four acres of public open space per thousand of population within the county boundaries; the remaining three acres which are considered necessary to provide healthful recreation and amenity are to be situated outside the County boundary in the form of a Green Belt. Similar proportions have also been laid down in the plans for European cities as diverse in character as Rotterdam, Warsaw and Moscow.

It is interesting, therefore, to discover that the Conurbation—not counting its Green

---

[1] 1931 Census. Figures for the inner districts are quoted from *When We Build Again* (Allen & Unwin, 1941).

TABLE XXXIX

Local Authority	Acreage of Local Authority area (to nearest 10 acres)	Population (mid-year 1939)	Persons per acre	Public open space*		Private open space. All sports grounds, parkland and private water	Cemeteries	Allotments	Total Acreage
				Existing parks, Recreation grounds, reservoirs	Scheduled under Statutory Town Planning Schemes				
South-Eastern Section									
Birmingham	51,150	1,052,900	20·6	3,200	760	1,776	416	828	6,970**
Smethwick	2,490	78,290	31·4	298†		86	56	40	480
Solihull	20,190	52,260	2·6	205		923	20	92	1,240
Sutton Coldfield ...	13,980	38,260	2·7	2,292		885	34	49	3,260
Totals	**87,810**	**1,221,710**	**13·9**	**5,995**	**760**	**3,660**	**526**	**1,009**	**11,950**
Percentages				**50·2**	**6·4**	**30·6**	**4·4**	**8·4**	**100·0**
North-Western Section									
Dudley	4,070	62,100	15·3	214		169	22	45	450
Walsall	8,780	107,600	12·3	405		320	60	115	900
West Bromwich ...	7,180	83,150	11·6	164		412	42	42	660
Wolverhampton ...	9,130	147,200	16·2	294		545	53	188	1,080
Aldridge	9,280	20,420	2·2	342		444	16	8	810
Amblecote	670	2,836	4·3	8		46		6	60
Bilston	1,870	31,600	16·9	48		108	14	20	190
Brierley Hill	5,930	47,040	7·9	113		39	6	22	180
Coseley	3,290	29,640	9·0	134	‡	25	6	15	180
Darlaston	1,530	20,220	13·2	38		27	21	4	90
Halesowen	5,250	36,800	7·0	82		180	4	24	290
Oldbury	3,300	47,000	14·2	123		135	40	32	330
Rowley Regis ...	3,830	44,780	11·7	85		196	16	23	320
Sedgley	3,850	20,700	5·4	17		545	8	20	590
Stourbridge ...	4,210	35,310	8·4	169		131	37	33	370
Tettenhall	2,500	6,727	2·7	29		109	4	8	150
Tipton	2,170	37,390	17·2	65		40	18	27	150
Wednesbury ...	2,030	33,650	16·6	60		30	30	50	170
Wednesfield ...	2,520	14,540	5·8	22		10	2	6	40
Willenhall	2,830	28,320	10·0	39		6	—	5	50
Totals	**84,220**	**857,023**	**10·4**	**2,451**	**0**	**3,517**	**399**	**693**	**7,060**
Percentages				**34·7**	**0·0**	**49·8**	**5·7**	**9·8**	**100·0**
Totals for Conurbation ...	**172,000**	**2,078,753**	**12·1**	**8,446**	**760**	**7,177**	**925**	**1,702**	**19,010**
Percentages				**44·4**	**4·0**	**37·8**	**4·9**	**8·9**	**100·0**

*These figures refer to open spaces within the boundaries of the 24 Local Authorities, and do not include areas such as the Lickey Hills which, although owned by the Birmingham Corporation, lie for the most part outside the city.

†This figure includes Warley Park and Lightwoods Park, which lie in Smethwick but are owned and maintained by Birmingham.

**Of which 5,534 acres are existing open space.

‡This category of open space applies only to areas coming within Town Planning Schemes which have already received the approval of the Ministry of Town and Country Planning. The approved Town Planning Scheme for Coseley has been formally withdrawn by the Council in order to clear the way for a Scheme which will apply to the whole area covered by the Dudley and District Planning Committee.

Setting—is already provided with a total area of existing open space not far short of what is regarded as practicable for the future London. When private open spaces and scheduled public open spaces are added, the proportion of 8.1 acres per 1,000 population shows how easily the generally-accepted optimum requirements could be fulfilled. Nevertheless, although the overall proportion may be considered as satisfactory, this figure by itself would be misleading, as it takes no count of the geographical distribution of open spaces. There is a marked difference between the amount of open space in the eastern part of the Conurbation (*i.e.*, Birmingham, Smethwick, Sutton Coldfield, and Solihull) and that in the western half. In the eastern half the proportion of public open space, existing and scheduled, is 5.5 acres per thousand of population, while in the western half it is 2.9 acres per thousand. In the main, two circumstances contribute to the more favourable situation in and around Birmingham. First, Town Planning Schemes have affected the proportion of open space to population in many districts developed since 1910; and, secondly, the largest open space in the Conurbation—Sutton Park—is situated in this half, and adds nearly 2,300 acres to the total of public open space.

We have already seen that within the largest of the Local Authorities—Birmingham—the generous allowance of open space, existing and scheduled in the Outer Districts, throws into relief the congestion in the six Central Wards.

The map showing the distribution of open spaces in the Conurbation (Figure 35) makes it clear that, while the overall acreage of open space in the Black Country and the western half of the Conurbation generally is less than that in Birmingham and the eastern half, the areas in the western half are more evenly distributed. This is a natural result of the smaller size of Black Country towns and of the smaller areas of central overcrowding within those towns. The fact is that inhabitants of the Black Country have easier access to adequate open spaces than have the inhabitants of Birmingham. On the other hand, recent planning in Birmingham demonstrates the way in which, by planning for continuous open space, urban congestion may be opened up. The open spaces, existing and scheduled, in the middle and outer districts of Birmingham, as well as the Clent-Woodgate and Aldridge-Sandwell areas (see page 212), show what could be achieved by the logical pursuit of this policy. Continuous parkways of increasing width radiate outwards, breaking up the masses of urban development. In the Black Country the lack of correlation between the development of different towns is reflected in the present isolation of parks in a welter of urban development, derelict land and undeveloped land.

There are no great parks comparable with Sutton Park in the Black Country, or even adjacent to it, as the Lickeys are to the south of Birmingham. The Wren's Nest, Dudley Castle Grounds, and Turner's Hill are fairly close together and make up the largest and most attractive area of recreational space in the Black Country. Only the first of these three, however, is public open space. Sandwell Park forms a first-class recreational space serving a far wider area than its immediate surroundings. Himley Park, on the western edge of the Conurbation, is a third area which may be described as an amenity of the Conurbation rather than of a single Local Authority area.

Provision of Public Open Spaces in Local Authority Areas

Among the County Boroughs, Dudley is comparatively well supplied with open space. In free parkland and recreational grounds it has 3.4 acres per 1,000 persons; in addition there are the Dudley Castle Grounds and the golf course in Rowley Regis adjoins its boundary. Most of these open spaces, however, lie to the north of the centre of the town of Dudley, although there is a good deal of derelict and undeveloped land around Netherton, in the south of the borough.

A racetrack and golf course, together with a number of works playing-fields, account for most of the private open space in Wolverhampton, and these to some extent redress a lack of public open space which the figure of 2.0 acres per 1,000 persons indicates, since they are all serving sections of the public (in contrast to private parks and woods, school playing-fields, etc., closed to all or most sections of the public). Moreover, the distribution of open space in Wolverhampton is fairly even, many areas lying close to the town centre.

PUBLIC OPEN SPACE AND POPULATION DENSITY

TABLE XL

Local Authority	Population (mid-year 1939)	Density of persons per acre	Public open space : Parks, recreation grounds, public pools and reservoirs (acres per 1,000 persons)	Cemeteries (acres per 1,000 persons)	Allotments (acres per 1,000 persons)
Conurbation	2,078,733	12·1	4·1	0·5	0·8
Areas with Population density over 10 per acre					
Birmingham	1,052,900	20·6	3·0	0·3	0·8
Smethwick	78,290	31·4	3·8	0·7	0·5
Dudley	62,100	15·3	3·5	0·4	0·7
Walsall	107,600	12·3	3·8	0·5	1·1
West Bromwich	83,150	11·6	2·0	0·5	0·5
Wolverhampton	147,200	16·2	2·0	0·3	1·3
Bilston	31,600	16·9	1·5	0·5	0·6
Darlaston	20,220	13·2	1·9	1·0	0·2
Oldbury	47,000	14·2	2·6	0·9	0·7
Rowley Regis	44,780	11·7	1·9	0·4	0·5
Tipton	37,390	17·2	1·7	0·5	0·7
Wednesbury	33,650	16·6	1·8	0·9	1·5
Willenhall	28,320	10·0	1·4	—	0·2
Areas with Population density less than 10 per acre					
Aldridge	20,420	2·2	17·1	0·8	0·4
Amblecote	2,836	4·3	2·8	—	2·1
Brierley Hill	47,040	7·9	2·4	0·1	0·5
Coseley	29,640	9·0	4·5	0·2	0·5
Halesowen	36,800	7·0	2·2	0·1	0·6
Sedgley	20,700	5·4	0·8	0·4	1·0
Solihull	52,260	2·6	3·9	0·4	1·8
Stourbridge	35,310	8·4	4·8	1·0	0·9
Sutton Coldfield	38,260	2·7	59·9	0·9	1·3
Tettenhall	6,727	2·7	4·3	0·6	1·2
Wednesfield	14,540	5·8	1·5	0·1	0·4

Although Walsall has the much higher proportion of 3.8 acres of public open space per 1,000 persons, distribution is less even. Again, however, great opportunities are presented by the almost continuous belt of derelict and undeveloped land which separates Walsall from the rest of the Conurbation. These opportunities have been only partly realized in the narrow parkways bordering the ring road south and east of the borough.

With the highest density of population in the Conurbation—31 to the acre—Smethwick has also the highest proportion of public open space among those Local Authority areas whose population density is higher than 10 to the acre. In part, this result has been achieved by the co-operation of neighbouring Local Authorities. The City of Birmingham maintains and was partly responsible for the purchase of Warley Park and Lightwoods Park, which adjoin its boundary on the east of Smethwick. In collaboration with the borough of Oldbury to the west, a series of open spaces has been laid down running through the housing estates developed on a stretch of land running north and south and shared by both Authorities.

Stourbridge, besides being well provided with parks and recreation grounds, has its open spaces well distributed, many lying less than half-a-mile from the town centre.

The fringe areas of Amblecote, Brierley Hill, Sedgley, Tettenhall, Wednesfield, and Willenhall are notably low in provision of parks. There is, however, a large area of private open space in Tettenhall, and Sedgley is fortunate in having Himley Park within its boundaries. The low population density of these two places, and the proximity of very attractive countryside, suggest that the real needs of the areas should not be difficult to satisfy. The built-up areas of Willenhall and Wednesfield are surrounded by tracts of undeveloped and derelict land, in which their deficiences in open space could be made good.

Tipton and Wednesbury, two of the most densely populated areas in the centre of the Black Country, are together provided with 1.8 acres of public open space per 1,000 persons. This is well below the average of 2.9 for the whole of the western half of the Conurbation. The deficiency is not compensated to any extent by private sports grounds or other private open spaces.

THE SURROUNDING COUNTRYSIDE

Landscape and Planning Policy

The countryside has become increasingly important to the town dweller. Up to 1939, more and more people were spending week-ends in country areas around large towns, walking, cycling and picnicking; and if the present movement towards greater leisure is maintained the increased use of the country will continue. The countryside is now fully appreciated as a place of recreation.

On the other hand, the increasing attraction of the countryside for the town dweller has brought with it unfortunate results, not only for the farmer and country dweller but for the townsman himself. The improvement in means of transportation has made it possible for town workers to live farther and farther from their work and for their families to enjoy a country environment—during the brief period, that is, before the whole area lapses into a featureless suburb. Urban development and urban sprawl destroyed the amenities of thousands of square miles of English countryside in two decades. The effects of this escape into the countryside are very clearly shown in the Development Map of the Conurbation and the area around it (Figure 40).

Green Belt and Green Setting

Successive policies have been devised for the proper control of this expansion of the town over miles of the surrounding countryside. The most favoured was that of the Green Belt, which, in the form attempted as a practical policy by one or two large cities (notably London and Birmingham) during the 1930's, was a continuous band of countryside encircling a town and its area of probable expansion. This belt was to be fairly even in width and rigidly protected from all urban development, and was looked upon as an insurmountable fence against the speculative builder and the town dweller whose wants he served.

In practice, however, developers have not been deterred by the " fence ". Indeed, the existence of the agricultural reservations and open spaces which have been built up along part of the south of Birmingham by the efforts of the City Council and the Bournville Village Trust has probably encouraged the development of the extensive built-up areas south of the Green Belt at Barnt Green, Cofton, Catshill and Bromsgrove (Figures 40 and 42). An even clearer demonstration of this process is visible in the encirclement of Sutton Park by housing (Figure 37). Together with the tendency of manufacturers to follow the population and to move factories into this surrounding country, this jumping of the Green Belt indicates that the principle needs considerable modification if it is to achieve the right ends.

Local planning must be related to regional requirements. The Group feels that the only way to preserve the countryside is to prohibit all development, except that associated with agriculture, beyond a certain limit set around existing urban areas or new towns. This would permit the countryside to be preserved with a fair degree of safety from the threat of obliteration which the sporadic development of the last fifty years has brought. If the term " Green Belt " describes the earlier conception, the term " Green Setting " is put forward as being more nearly descriptive of this new conception in town and country planning. The term comprehends not only the general expanse of agricultural country which extends between and around the Conurbation and other areas of development, from villages to major towns, but also the continuous strips and the wedges of open space separating the re-grouped urban units inside a re-planned Conurbation.

In the opinion of the Group, it is essential that, in the rural areas surrounding the Conurbation, planned control of development and redevelopment should follow the same principles which it recommends for the Conurbation itself, *i.e.*, the creation of a pattern of nucleated development in a rural setting. The limit of development line set around each town and village could quite easily allow ample room for expansion to meet anticipated needs. It should not, however, necessarily conform to the limits of existing development, and bad urban growths and sprawls, even of the last few years, might be left in the rural Green Setting for eventual elimination. The necessary complement to the establishment of a Green Setting and the gradual elimination of urban sprawl is the regrouping of existing communities in a coherent form around their present centres (Figure 42).

The general picture, if such a plan were carried out, is presented in Figure 41. It should be emphasized that this is not advanced as a map outlining a redevelopment plan, but as a demonstration of what this general conception involves in and around the Conurbation.

Within the framework of this general plan there are other considerations which should determine the control and use of the land around the Conurbation. There are features of the countryside which have special and sometimes overriding importance in the area. Those referring to the value of land to agriculture have been dealt with in Chapter XII. Others have to do with the attractiveness of landscape and to the suitability of any area for open-air pastimes and sports. These features, which are usually termed amenity values, assume special importance in country accessible to two million town dwellers. The brief descriptions of the countryside north, east, south and west of the Conurbation have been made chiefly with regard to amenity values. Particular importance attaches to

FIGURE 42

SPRAWL AND NUCLEATION

BARNT GREEN—BROMSGROVE   BROWNHILLS—PELSALL

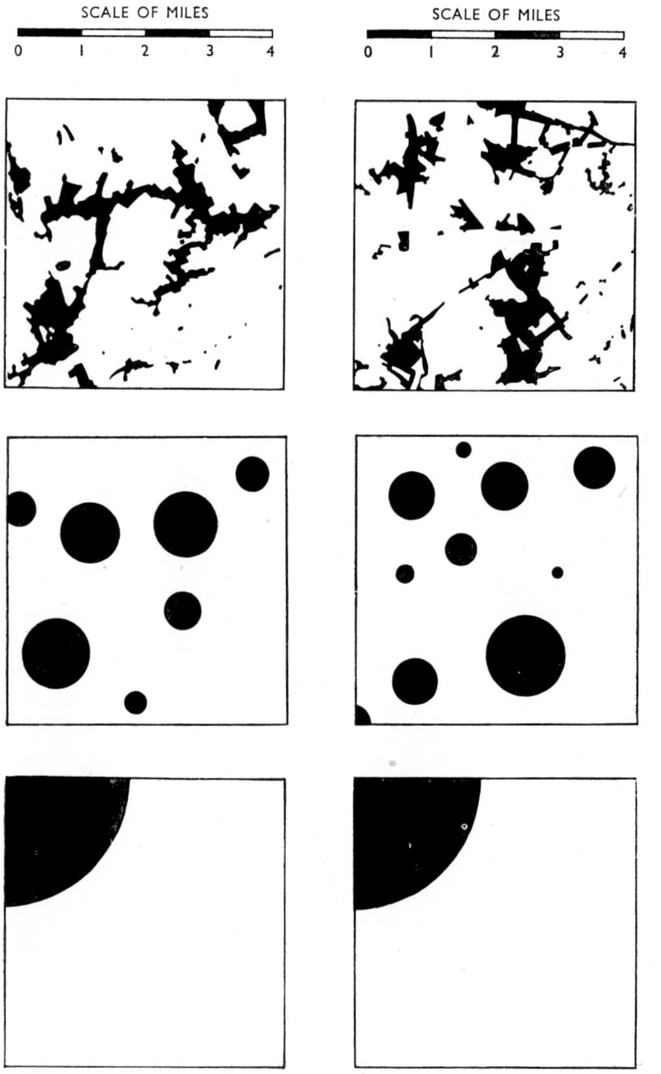

SCALE OF MILES

0   1   2   3   4

SCALE OF MILES

0   1   2   3   4

Two areas typical of those affected by ribbon development north and south of the Conurbation are shown here. The centre diagrams indicate the way in which redevelopment according to a rational pattern would help to form coherent urban units and free a large area of countryside from " urbanization ". The lower diagrams show the total amount of space actually taken up by development in the diagrams above.

the areas of countryside forming the two wedges which point towards each other across the narrow neck of urban development between Warley in Smethwick and Sandwell in West Bromwich.

General Description of Surrounding Countryside

Green Wedges:

Settlement is continuous between the major areas of Birmingham and South Staffordshire, but it extends only along a relatively narrow corridor, some $2\frac{1}{2}$ miles wide, from Sandwell to the new Birmingham-Wolverhampton Road, and much of this settlement consists of recent housing. This corridor acts as a neck separating two wedges of comparatively open country (see Chapter XI)—the Y-shaped Aldridge-Sandwell wedge in the north and the Clent-Woodgate wedge in the south. It is impossible to over-estimate their amenity value to the Conurbation as a whole or to over-emphasize the need for strict control of development in these areas in the immediate future. As already mentioned in Chapter V, these two wedges also offer natural lines for trunk roads giving access to and egress from the Conurbation to the north-east and south-west. These could run as parkways without intermediate access except at central points.

The Aldridge-Sandwell Park wedge separates the northern extensions of Birmingham from the north-eastern portion of the South Staffordshire industrial area. To the north, the open end of the wedge is divided by the town of Aldridge into two arms, the wider being on the east and including the Little Aston area. To the south, the wedge is at its widest, two miles across from West Bromwich to Hamstead. There is at present a considerable danger of its being cut by urban development in the Newton area and along the Birmingham-Walsall Road. Further north, a ribbon of eastward building from Walsall along the Streetly Road, reaching out towards southward extensions of Aldridge and western extensions of Streetly, is likely to form another barrier across the upper eastern arm of the wedge.

It is suggested that future building in the whole of this area should be controlled in such a fashion as to preserve an unbroken strip of open country from Sandwell Park out to the periphery of the Conurbation on either side of Aldridge.

Some industrial development exists at the point where the wedge is crossed by the Tame Valley Canal and there seems to be a danger of a belt of industrial development forming along a line between Newton and Walsall. The Sandwell Park Colliery, situated centrally in the wedge, and Hamstead Colliery on the eastern edge, tend to overshadow the landscape with their conical pit-heaps. (See photograph, page 278). Fairly extensive gravel pits are being worked at Hamstead and Bustleholm, between the canal and railway which cross the wedge from Hamstead to Wednesbury and Walsall. Other workings are cutting into a hillside at Queslett, on the Birmingham–Aldridge road.

Much land in the West Bromwich-Handsworth Wood area has already been, or is in the process of being, acquired by Birmingham and West Bromwich as permanent open space.

The Clent-Woodgate area forms a broad wedge between the south-westward extensions of Birmingham and the south side of the Black Country.

In general the country is pleasant and hilly, and contains in Frankley a hill (some twenty-five acres of which belong to the National Trust) overlooking much of the City of Birmingham. At its widest it is approximately three miles across, and some $4\frac{1}{2}$ miles in length from California to the Clent Hills.

Although in future planning some allowance for building will undoubtedly have to be made in this area, this should only be a marginal development and must on no account take the form of ribbons or tentacles stretching into or across the wedge. Such ribbon development already exists at Hunnington in the form of a line down the Halesowen-Bromsgrove Road, and at Romsley where the presence of good viewpoints is encouraging residential development. There is also a possibility of urban encirclement of the Woodgate Valley, which is threatened by development in the Woodgate-Moor Street area.

The Industrial North:

Most of the area to the north, especially between the Aldridge-Lichfield Road and Wolverhampton-Stafford Road, can hardly be described as countryside. For five or six miles beyond Bloxwich and Aldridge, coal workings and industrial plant are scattered over the face of a plateau some 400 to 500 feet high. This area, in which lies much of the Cannock coalfield, extends into Cannock Chase as far as Huntington and Hednesford. Around the collieries, terraces of poor-class housing stretch out raggedly, and several townships, especially along roads around Brownhills and Bridgetown, are almost linked by this 19th century ribbon development. In the extreme east of this section, at Moneymore, some four miles north of Sutton Coldfield, preparations are being made for what will be one of the largest gravel pits in Europe. The Black Country appears to be moving north.

Beyond this area lies Cannock Chase, which covers over 100 square miles of high ground rising to 800 feet, well wooded but thinning out to open moorland on the high ground. The Chase extends almost to Stafford. The valley of the Sherborne runs north through it and attracts motorists and walking parties from the Conurbation and many other towns in the Region. Between Cannock Chase and the Conurbation, however, there is very little attractive country. Only one small area, Brownhills Common, may be described as a place for recreation.

The Lowland East:

Down the east side of the Conurbation, from Tamworth in the north to Henley-in-Arden, is a stretch of very different landscape. It consists mainly of pleasant agricultural country with little contrast and few areas of exceptional scenic beauty. Like other rich agricultural districts in England, however, the pattern of fields and hedgerow trees presents a deeply satisfying sight to the townsman, and the lanes of this part of Warwickshire are often delightful. There are, too, stretches of parkland with their more formal attractiveness. Provision for its preservation must also be based on agricultural considerations, to which reference is made in the section on Land Classification. A broad belt of first-class agricultural land stretches from just south of Wilnecote in the north to to Hampton-in-Arden in the south. It is important also to preserve the substantial belt of open country which lies between the Conurbation to the west, and villages and industrial development in the East Warwickshire Coalfield to the north-east, and Coventry to the east.

Ribbon development has encroached seriously, particularly in the north-east, along the Sutton Coldfield-Lichfield Road, to the north and south of Coleshill, and along the Warwick Road in the Solihull-Knowle district. (See Development Map, Figure 40). More significant than the spread of residential development, perhaps, is the formation of an industrial belt which continues the Tame Valley industrial zone inside Birmingham (see Figure 36), and emerges about the centre of the east side of the Conurbation. This belt stretches along the railway and terminates in the electric power station at Hams Hall, whose cooling towers and chimneys dominate the landscape over an area of about fifty square miles. South of the industrial encroachment, Birmingham housing estates have been planned, extending outside the Conurbation in the areas of Castle Bromwich, Tile Cross and Marston Green.

The eastern area does contain, on the other hand, one or two examples of large villages which have escaped untidy development, notably Hampton-in-Arden.

The Hills of the South:

The character of the country south of the Conurbation differs considerably from that on the other sides. The chief feature of the landscape is the crescent-shaped range of hills running from Clent in the west to Weatheroak in the east. Much of this land has already been acquired for permanent preservation as open space, but south of the preserved areas lie Barnt Green, Cofton, Catshill, and Bromsgrove, in which uncontrolled and haphazard development has spoiled large areas of countryside. One of the finest parts of the reserved area is the extensive open space on the Lickey Hills, parts of which have been preserved since 1889.

Towards the south-east stretches a wide tract of pleasant countryside leading out to Henley-in-Arden and Stratford-on-Avon. This whole area is one of the most important " amenity outlets " for the urban population. A similar tract of country, which includes rather more attractive examples of rolling, well-wooded country, is the area due south of Stourbridge, including Chaddesley Woods, Pepper Woods and Hartlebury Common.

The Heathlands of the West:

Landscape on the west has a well-defined and individual character. From Tettenhall to Kidderminster the main Worcester-Staffordshire canal marks the present limits of urban development spreading westwards from the Conurbation. East of this only a few isolated areas of countryside—Himley Park and Rudge Hill Wood—remain between the built-up roads that stretch out from the Conurbation. Ribbon development is most pronounced in the Penn, Wombourne, and Wollaston areas. West of the canal lie large areas of the most attractive country around the Conurbation; a line of heathland and wooded hills from 500 to 600 feet high sweeps from Wyre Forest just beyond the Severn, and continues above Bewdley for twenty miles, through Arley Wood, Kinver Edge, the Sheep Walks, Enville Common, Highgate Common, Abbots Castle Hill, Rudge Heath, and Badger Dingle. The whole range forms an almost continuous crescent of pleasant uplands curving in to the west front of the Conurbation. Other heaths and wooded areas such as The Million and Blackhill (flanked by extensive gravel pits) lie closer to the Conurbation. Many parts of these pleasant areas are open to the public.

Countryside Areas of Special Value

There are a number of areas in the countryside around the Conurbation which for many reasons are of special concern. There are the important agricultural considerations to which reference has already been made, demanding the prohibition of non-agricultural development beyond the line Tamworth, Hampton, and Dorridge in the east; the rehabilitation of the market gardening area north of Bromsgrove; and the preservation of a large wedge of first-class agricultural land stretching from Hagley southward to the east side of Kidderminster.

There are also very many areas which, on account of their scenic beauty and amenity value, would profit by special attention from planners.

Playing fields devoted to games requiring a comparatively small area can be accommodated in parks and reservations. Within the Conurbation, the Green Setting and parkways between the various settlements (page 204) would offer ample space for golf courses which require a large area and to which, therefore, the public must be prepared to travel some distance. There is, however, a further type of recreational area which is exemplified in the Lickey Hills and Sutton Park. Here, large tracts of open country, comprising either natural heathland or planted woodland, are used for walking and rambling within relatively easy distance of the homes of the urban population. The Group has felt it better to delineate areas of this type rather than to classify areas of special landscape beauty or amenity value according to any absolute scale. The pattern which seems most suitable would consist of a series of large " playground " and " picnic " areas. In the main, the areas plotted on the map of Playground Areas (Figure 43) are those which have existing amenity value. It is clear, however, that to the south-east, east, and north, there is marked deficiency in areas of this sort, and new areas should certainly be reserved or laid out. Some of the areas indicated on the map are already in public ownership, others are privately owned, but in most cases the public has access to them by footpaths and bridle paths.

SUMMARY AND CONCLUSIONS

The Conurbation should be planned as a pattern of urban settlements in a Green Setting. Future urban development should be confined within specified limits around a number of existing centres of industry and settlement. Existing urban development now outside these limits should, when the time comes for redevelopment, revert to open space or agricultural use.

The development line around each defined settlement should contain within it ample space for all the expansion and redevelopment which is expected to take place, in accordance with the conditions and policy under which the plan for the whole Conurbation is formulated.

Bank Holiday at Clent.

Fine weather brings thousands of Birmingham families out by tram to the Lickey Hills.

Spring Sunshine on the Lickey Hills.

Ford at Little Packington, near Meriden, nine miles from the centre of Birmingham.

Enville Common, a fine stretch of heathland typical of the countryside west of the Conurbation. Of little agricultural value, its situation and character make its preservation as a Playground Area particularly worth while.

Kinver Edge, a precipitous ridge about a mile long, is one of the best known week-end holiday resorts in the West Midlands. The hill is National Trust property ; at its foot lies an almost continuous colony of caravans, shacks, bungalows, and converted buses.

Playground Areas (see Figure 43) is the name given in the text to stretches of open country lying within a few miles of the Conurbation which are, or should be, accessible to the public. Smaller than the Regional Parks which have been suggested in the past, sometimes of no outstanding landscape beauty, such places offer opportunities for relaxation and recreation in surroundings entirely removed from the town dweller's normal environment. Well-established playground areas such as the Lickeys and Clent (see photographs on page 215) are used by thousands of people every fine week-end.

The varied country landscape on each side of the Conurbation is revealed in this section of photographs. The lower photograph on the opposite page is typical of the attractive unspoilt Warwickshire countryside which still remains between Birmingham and Coventry. The very different landscape of the heathlands and the Severn valley, to the west of the Conurbation, is illustrated on this page. Hills dominate the rural areas to the south, much of which was acquired before 1939 by public bodies as part of the South-west Birmingham Green Belt.

The Wyre Forest, west of the Severn at Bewdley.

The Severn, above Bewdley.

The South-west Birmingham Green Belt at the point where it is crossed by the main road to Bristol, which can be seen in the middle distance.

Hopwood Dingle, Forhill, in the South-west Birmingham Green Belt.

218

Bittell Reservoir, Barnt Green.   Made to supply the Birmingham-Worcester canal, this attractive stretch of water is used at week-ends for fishing and small boat sailing.

Clent Hills.

Twentieth century country-side. On the Worcester Road at North Bromsgrove.

Belbroughton. Most of the scythes used in England are still manufactured in this small village, south of the Black Country.

Chaddesley Corbett. A street of half-timbered buildings.

So far as possible, all open space should be planned as a connected system. The future size of the towns which should emerge as isolated urban units should be determined by convenience, tradition, and their individual economic and social requirements, rather than by preconceived ideas of an optimum size.

Under this plan of redevelopment the land between the towns of the Conurbation would become a Green Setting with continuous belts of open space and agricultural land traversing the whole Conurbation and isolating each urban centre.

The larger urban concentrations within this scheme should be split by green wedges and strips of parkland penetrating to their centres, forming a continuous system of open space around neighbourhoods and other units of urban development, and leading out to the inter-urban Green Setting.

" Undeveloped " land, derelict land, and open space together make up 56 per cent of the whole area of the Conurbation. This makes it possible for immediate steps to be taken towards the fulfilment of the redevelopment plan outlined here. It is of the first importance that the green strips and belts of the Green Setting be delineated at an early stage, so that existing open land in the Green Setting may be protected from development. In the interior of the Black Country, areas of derelict land are more important in this respect than undeveloped land. As soon as possible, a start should be made with schemes and experiments for the rehabilitation of derelict land as open space.

There is no serious deficiency of open space in the Conurbation as a whole. If private open spaces were acquired and thrown open to the public, the overall proportion of open space to population numbers would exceed what is normally considered adequate in re-planned urban areas.

The central areas of most of the towns of the Conurbation are deficient in parks and other public open spaces. This deficiency is most serious in the centre of Birmingham. While, in general, the eastern half of the Conurbation is better provided than the western half with open space, those in the west are better distributed.

Local planning in country as well as in town must be related to regional requirements. The reservation of a narrow Green Belt of agricultural land and open space outside part of the built-up area has not prevented ribbon and sprawl development in the countryside beyond.

All development except that associated with agriculture should be prohibited beyond a definite limit set around existing urban areas.

Development and redevelopment in the rural areas around the Conurbation should follow the principles recommended for the area inside the Conurbation; the aim should be the creation of a planned pattern of nucleated urban development in a rural setting.

It is urgently necessary to prohibit further development in the Green Wedge areas in the neighbourhood of Aldridge and Sandwell Park, to the north, and Woodgate and Clent, to the south. Both wedges are of high value as amenities to the population of the Conurbation, and offer areas through which it might be possible to build trunk roads, laid out as parkways, approaching the Conurbation from the north-east and south-west.

There are many tracts of open country within a few miles of the Conurbation which are used by the many town dwellers for walking and outdoor activities. Still more should be made available to the public, so that the whole area of the Conurbation may be surrounded by a chain of " playground " and " picnic " areas of the type already exemplified by Sutton Park and the Lickey Hills.

FIGURE 43

PLAYGROUND AREAS

SCALE OF MILES

0   1   2   3   4   5

BUILT-UP AREAS

RURAL AREAS OF SPECIAL LANDSCAPE
BEAUTY OR AMENITY VALUE

ROADS

The areas marked green are suitable for preservation as larger recreational areas for people living in the Conurbation. Some, like Sutton Park and the Lickey Hills, are in public ownership, others are private property. It is suggested that the public should have access to all areas shown here.

THE BLACK COUNTRY SCENE

The eight photographs in this section were taken within a short distance of each other.

From Bury Hill, Oldbury. A pre-war effort at laying out a limited area of derelict land as an open space.

The ridge of hills that runs from the Lickeys in the south of Birmingham to Sedgley Beacon on the western boundary is nature's principal surviving contribution to the scenery of the Conurbation.

The edge of industrial sprawl.

THE BLACK COUNTRY SCENE

Land cannot be rendered permanently derelict; in course of time a natural covering of soil and herbage will return. This process can be speeded up and used to advantage in the re-habilitation of the Black Country landscape.

The Centre of the Conurbation.   The industrial area of Oldbury, looking towards West Bromwich.

Rows of new houses dissect a country scene already dominated by a spoil bank.

Large areas of the Green Setting are in being, despite the encroachments of housing development.

THE BLACK COUNTRY
SCENE

Land still in cultivation falls within the proposed Green Setting inside the Conurbation.

CHAPTER XIV

Two Schemes of Redevelopment

IT WAS POINTED out in the Introduction to this Report that it has not been the purpose of the West Midland Group to offer precise plans for the rehabilitation of the Black Country. Information on which such plans may be based and the recommendation of principles to be observed have been the Group's main concern.

During the Survey, however, discussion returned so often to certain problems that the Group arrived at its own definite ideas as to the best way of dealing with them. Two cases in point are the problem of derelict land and its bearing on a landscape policy for the Black Country, and the problem of surburban encroachment on areas of small holdings such as that in the Catshill district. The Group, therefore, commissioned two specialists to prepare schemes of redevelopment in which the Group's findings should be embodied. The first of these, *Derelict Land*, by Mr. G. A. Jellicoe, P.I.L.A., M.T.P.I., F.R.I.B.A., was completed in 1944, and included two Demonstration Area plans prepared by Mr. E. Lewis, A.R.I.B.A. Mr. Jellicoe's Report forms the basis of Part I of the present chapter.

The second scheme, dealing with the Catshill district—Part II of this chapter—was prepared by Mr. Thomas Sharp, M.A., L.R.I.B.A., M.T.P.I., F.I.L.A. The preservation of the Catshill area for small holdings is important to the large adjoining urban areas ; but unless the infiltration of sporadic housing development into this valuable food-producing area is corrected by a planned scheme of redevelopment, the loss of an agricultural asset of much worth is only a matter of time.

PART I

DERELICT LAND

TOWARDS A LANDSCAPE FOR THE BLACK COUNTRY

The sweep of industry over the Black Country has left behind it a much marred landscape. The original aspect of the land, partly forest and partly agricultural, was changed about a century-and-a-half ago by mining, quarrying and dumping. The period of manufacture which followed, adjusted itself as best it could to the prevailing conditions, making them neither better nor worse, but somewhat more complex. Within the area of the Black Country there are 9,300 acres of derelict land, or 12.8 per cent. of the whole. Part of this is already being reclaimed through schemes of post-war housing, but even when immediate housing needs are met, there will remain several thousand acres to which the principles of landscape planning may be applied.

PLANNING DIFFICULTIES

There are three main difficulties in formulating a landscape plan.

In the first place there are the waste lands due to excavations in clay or gravel; exhausted deep or surface coal mines; dumps formed from quarry and factory wastes; and those oddly shaped and apparently useless plots and corners which have their origin in neglect.

Secondly, many misplaced buildings have arisen in areas where planning has been conspicuously absent. These remain as blots on the landscape. Factories (more especially their chimneys), railways and ill-placed houses, all spoil the aspect of a district where no thought has been taken for appearances.

Thirdly, there are the difficulties inherent in the division of authority between several bodies of local government. Lack of co-operation between adjacent authorities results in isolated efforts which are often fatal to a continuously pleasing prospect, where Planning Authorities are numerous and their individual schemes are small. The comparatively heavy cost of comprehensive schemes is often decisive in preventing planning.

PLANNING NEEDS

The main purpose of this scheme of redevelopment is to bring back the waste areas into full usefulness. The scheme must, of course, be related to the needs of adjacent communities, and to the overall requirements of the whole area; it is in the adjustment of these two requirements that a few large Local Government Authorities would have special value. The contribution which waste lands may make to the needs of the area is threefold :—

(1) Building sites,
(2) Recreational facilities,
(3) Restoration of natural amenities such as trees and heathland.

Building Sites

In the creation of a varied landscape, sites for future building must be set aside and preserved. Houses built on raw derelict land are uninviting. The restoration of such land to some measure of attractiveness is necessary if the sites in the waste land are not to be rejected and the consequent temptation of Local Authorities to acquire land outside their own areas is to be resisted.

Recreational Facilities

Derelict land could go far towards satisfying the outdoor recreational needs of local communities in the Black Country area. Modern planning demands that schemes should be drawn up to create or preserve the following :—Public playing fields, boating, bathing, private playing fields, public gardens, parks, parkways, open-air theatres, cinemas, stadia and fairs. Areas of grass land studded with trees, and suitable for walking and similar pursuits, hereafter described as Green Setting Parkland, should also be developed and preserved.

Restoration of Natural Amenities, such as Trees

Apart from their amenity value, trees are needed as windbreaks, dust filters, soil regenerators, and for shade. On light and arid land they are particularly beneficial in retaining rainfall. Certain birds are to be encouraged, not only for song, but to assist the cycle of nature; for their well-being, adequate undergrowth is required.

ELEMENTS OF PLAN

It is generally found that when housing, factory buildings, and recreational facilities are well planned as to location, and soundly designed as to use, a general enhancement of the landscape ensues. The landscape can hardly ever be left to take care of itself.

It is far too little realized that Great Britain, from the scenic point of view, owes as much to the great landholders and planners of estates in the last few centuries as to climate and geological formation. An example of this in the Conurbation is to be found in the garden development of the Calthorpe Estate in Edgbaston, Birmingham. Here a long-term policy of planning and preservation has saved a comparatively large area near the city centre from the industrial, housing and commercial sprawl which has covered the inner suburbs in every other direction.

All other things being equal, the following are points to be observed in improving the landscape of the Black Country.

Housing

Sites should be round the perimeter of towns, off main traffic routes, and in as pleasant an environment as possible. Ugliness of outline usually means that sites are too exposed. Ground that is too high for harmony of line should be avoided.

Factories

Small, light industries may go, within reason, where they will, but with due regard to zoning regulations. Large, heavy industries should be allowed to develop only on land which cannot be otherwise utilized without excessive cost. Commercial needs will dictate location, but in so far as is possible a factory should be designed to blend with the landscape. Sometimes its function may be emphasized; it may be also harmonized with its surroundings by the addition of trees.

Playing Fields and Trees

These should also be round the perimeter of towns and on land reasonably well-drained and sheltered. Good effects can sometimes be obtained by the use of trees and shrubs foreign to the neighbourhood, even to this country, provided they are suitable to the climatic conditions and can be well tended.

Green Setting. Parkland

This should be open country, as continuous between towns as possible. Where towns are so closely linked that Parkland cannot be continuous, the barriers should be removed when buildings become obsolete. (See Chapter XIII). In the meantime much could be done by planting trees as closely as possible. Parkland might include quarries, excavations and dumps, and such natural hills and hillocks as it is undesirable to flatten. It would consist mainly of rough grassland with trees in groups or in lines, with waste waters made clean, and with planting to suit the environment. In general, these trees would be indigenous to the area. The Forestry Commission has recommended a framework of Birch, Mountain Ash and Corsican Pine for the knolls; Sycamore, Plane and Wild Cherry for the slopes; and Poplar, Willow and Alder for the level and lowland areas. Special study should be made of the accompanying " layers " of planting, *i.e.*, the undergrowth and ground carpet. A standard example of this is the three layers of oak, hazel, and bluebells and primroses; but the combination employed in each area will depend on local conditions. These Parkland areas should be intersected by pedestrian walks. The sward might be maintained by some form of grazing, if protection could be provided against dogs.

Regional Amusement Centres

These would be located in the Green Setting between urban areas. There are many sites eminently suitable for an open-air theatre, a Black Country wild park, an amusement centre, an open-air cinema, restaurants and the like.

Public Buildings

In future years sites may be found in Green Setting Parkland for colleges, churches, crematoria and other institutions requiring dignity and space.

Roads and Paths

The Birmingham-Wolverhampton Road is well-sited to become one of the finest parkways in England. Where possible, additional roads should run along the edge of Parkland rather than across it. There should be a complete system of green walking ways. Paths should pass under main roads; and where paths are broken by a built-up area the planting of trees along pavements should achieve continuity. Canal tow-paths which are not in heavy use might form part of the network by arrangement with the owners.

Odd Corners

Where there is no obvious or urgent use for small waste or derelict corners, each should be planted with trees, preferably in groves. A good example of what can be done is to be seen at the 'bus terminus at Dudley.

Agriculture has not been included in these Plan Elements, but a scheme, run on club lines, to augment allotments and private gardens, might well be encouraged. In the illustration of what might be achieved in the Bilston area (Figure 47), market gardens, orchards, allotments, and arable land have been shown. Reclamation to this extent may be out of the question for the next generation or two, but the landscape pattern shown is the sort of harmonious and satisfying whole towards which the efforts of our generation should be directed.

ECONOMICS, OUTLAY, MAINTENANCE AND RETURN

Although further study, a closer survey, and a general pooling of specialized knowledge are required before detailed plans can be evolved, there is no technical reason why these landscape proposals should not be executed on the main lines indicated, although the acquisition of top soil might be difficult. The following observations are made on the question of initial cost and maintenance.

Outlay

In considering the question of outlay, it must be borne in mind that the work, in order of basic value to general landscape, should be undertaken as follows :—

1. Tree planting
2. Ground modelling or levelling
3. Grassing
4. Drainage, paths, gates, and fences
5. All remaining proposals

The first four items belong properly to parkland. The remaining proposals are those which a Local Authority would be expected to undertake, the cost being related to the size of the community. Levelling, the acquisition of top-soil, and the creation of parkland, are the three main items which would make a landscape policy for the Black Country more expensive than a similar policy in other parts of the country. Levelling today is done with heavy machinery, and, since the proposals generally accept existing contours, the cost need not be excessive; neither need the cost of grass-seeding and the planting of small trees be great. The supply of top-soil would be the heaviest item of initial outlay.

It does not seem possible to grow adequate grass cover upon less than two inches of top-soil, and even this amount is barely sufficient on arid sub-soil. Trees, when planted small, require about one cubic foot of soil. When the trees are spaced fifteen feet apart, the proportion of soil required for grass to that required for trees is, therefore, approximately forty to one. It seems then, that the immediate production of grass in the worst areas is out of the question. A plan extending over a period of twenty-five years or more is necessary to the production of new soil. In fact, the soil plan would develop with the growth of trees.

Maintenance

In landscape activities of these proportions, the cost of maintenance may represent a larger charge on the community than the original capital outlay. Maintenance falls into the following categories:—

(a) The care of natural features such as trees, shrubs, flowers and grass. The maintenance of garden areas, which is costly, although rough grass and indigenous trees on parkland are practically self-supporting. Light maintenance may be undertaken by pensioners, and others to whom the work specially appeals; but special maintenance may be required to prevent water pollution and to safeguard wild life.

(b) Protection against wilful destruction and trespass; maintenance of buildings, paths and fences; and provision of public lavatories, lighting, etc.

(c) Supervision of special areas such as children's playgrounds, boating and bathing pools.

Return

The outstanding return would be, first, the retention within the area of a population which might otherwise live outside ; and, secondly, the consequent raising of residential site values on the perimeters of towns.

The success of Dudley Zoological Gardens and other similar ventures proves that there exists a demand for outdoor entertainments such as may be accommodated in a comprehensive landscape scheme. Returns from these would go a long way towards off-setting the total cost of maintenance and might even provide revenue to assist in meeting annual charges on capital outlay.

Interested Parties

Responsibility for the execution of a landscape plan would fall mainly on three parties:

(a) Local Authorities would be responsible mainly for housing and open spaces.

(b) Industrial firms in the area might be concerned for the amenities of their premises and for recreation areas for their employees.

(c) Private enterprise might be prepared to develop certain areas, either for houses or for entertainment for the purpose of profit, or for normal commercial development.

Initial action must necessarily be taken by the Local Authority, as it alone is able to plan on the required scale. Co-operation between all Local Authorities in the preparation of a joint plan for the Black Country is essential for a comprehensive scheme. Within that scheme individual Local Authorities, together with private landowners, would develop those amenities, which are individual to their respective areas.

The relation of children to their environment would involve Education Authorities. It has been proposed that school children should take part in the execution of the plan.

Procedure

Procedure in the drawing-up of the plan is important, as a scheme such as is contemplated here may occupy twenty-five years in active work which would come to maturity in that period. Naturally, procedure must be laid down by existing planning organizations, but in its early stages it might well comprehend the following:—

(a) The existing Joint Planning Committees to agree upon the principles of Parkland, and to set up a Joint Landscape Planning Authority.

(b) The appointment of a panel of experts to study and report upon technical problems of waste, ecology, and other matters to which this Report can only refer briefly.

(c) Preparation by each Local Authority of a detailed Physical Survey, and of a Schedule of Development.

(d) Preparation by each Local Authority of its own tentative plan.

(e) The preparation from these tentative plans of a combined Landscape Plan for the whole of the Black Country.

Execution

This combined Landscape Plan would then be executed on the following lines and would observe the following principles:—

(1) Each Local Authority to be responsible for its own area, with the exception of Parkland, the cost of which would be shared.

(2) The work to follow a twenty-five-year Development Plan. In drawing up such a Plan, those areas whose type of development is unpredictable should be specified for a return to fertility by the most economical means.

(3) One of the effects of the Town and Country Planning Act, 1947, will be to enable Local Authorities to acquire land for open space at a price determined by the existing use of the land, and not by its possibilities for speculative development. Derelict land, therefore, may become, financially as well as otherwise, more suitable for development as open space than any other land, developed or undeveloped.

(4) Each Local Authority and the industrial concerns in its area should prepare a schedule which includes the following information : the length of life of existing quarrying industries ; a list of " tipping " places where indentations may be filled ; and methods and places of the disposal of waste generally, whether liquid or solid ; the extent of privately-owned recreation areas ; an agreement on colour and camouflage ; an agreement on smoke abatement and air pollution.

(5) Orders to be placed and arrangements made for the acquisition of top-soil. Sources of supply might be found in new roads under construction, at sites where housing development is proceeding, at quarries, and at places where extractive industries are carried on.

(6) Levelling, draining, and fencing to be put in hand at once.

(7) The tree framework to be wholly planted during the first five years of the Plan. The help of schools, both in planting and maintenance, could be enlisted for this work.

(8) Approximately one-tenth of one per cent. of the total number of trees to be transplanted from elsewhere at half-size, with abundance of root soil, in key positions, to give a provisional landscape effect.

(9) Cultivation of the rough grassland to be put in hand, with the aid of imported top-soil, artificial top-soil, and fertilizers. This land should come to full fertility within twenty-five years. Nature without aid normally takes two hundred years to create top-soil. In the meantime, the planting of lupins for five years would create a dramatic landscape that would serve for a time.

(10) The main groundwork accomplished, the details of the Plan may then be filled in according to programme or expediency.

The piecemeal execution of this Plan would create a good standard of environment. The first requirement of amenity would be satisfied ; namely, that derelict and other waste areas shall become fertile and that the Black Country scene shall show a reasonable balance between town and country. A step would have been made to bring man into closer relationship with nature, and such a proximity would have far-reaching effects on the industrial and social life of the whole area.

The scope of such a Plan would be wider than anything yet attempted in this country. Yet, as indicated earlier, smaller scale precedents may be found in some of the great private parks, especially those created in the 18th century. Houses such as Chatsworth and Longleat have taken for their estate the whole valley in which they are sited, and buildings, trees, parkland and water are arranged in one great design. In such designs the more agreeable aspects of landscape are emphasized, and the undesirable suppressed. The application of the same principles, on a wider scale, is proposed for the Black Country.

The present Black Country Landscape is composed of built-up areas, separated by desolated tracts that are crossed and re-crossed by roads, railways, canals, cables, and all the threads of modern communication. These areas are spotted by indiscriminately-placed factories and houses. The two main physical features of the area are a flatness that has been disrupted by man's handiwork, and natural hills that have been added to by man's agency. In these planning proposals these two natural characteristics must be recognized and emphasized. The flat areas should have their own comeliness, and hilly districts should make their more dramatic contribution to the scene in the way that the Dudley Castle area does at present.

To illustrate this Report, two areas have been planned, according to the principles laid down in it, by Mr. Edward Lewis, A.R.I.B.A. ; one near Bilston and one near Oldbury. Each has an area of about one square mile. These two plans are illustrated by photographs taken by Mr. Roy Dixon which were subsequently treated by Mr. F. Kenwood Giles.

DESIGNS FOR OLDBURY AND BILSTON

To demonstrate how the Black Country may be restored as a green country, the Bilston site was chosen as a comparatively level area, while the Oldbury site was selected for its hills and pitted surface.

In both areas a large-scale woodland pattern has been applied as the basis of design. Into the areas between the trees fall all the main features of the new landscape. These range from broad heath and farm lands to gardens, roads, footpaths, waterways and cattle tracks, together with playing fields and all the other features set out above as essential to a rich landscape plan. The basic pattern of woodland will contrive to mask the ugly silhouettes of badly-placed houses, factories and chimneys.

For the first time in landscape history, the use of simple, large-scale painted camouflage is proposed to blend harsh factory outlines with their environment of foliage.

It has been recognized also that future designs of country (and town) must be aesthetically satisfying from the air as well as from the ground.

FIGURE 44

A LANDSCAPE FOR THE BLACK COUNTRY (I)

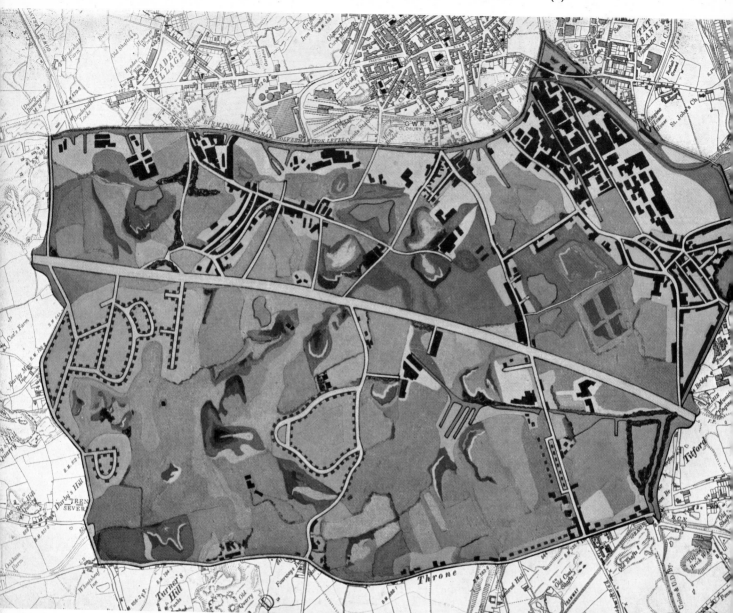

(Based on the Ordnance Survey Map, with the sanction of the Controller of H.M. Stationer

Existing landscape of an area on both sides of the Wolverhampton Road, near Oldbury.

The Birmingham-Wolverhampton arterial road runs centrally through the Oldbury site. Towards Oldbury town are factories, waste land, dumps, old housing, and a huge mound of chemical waste. On the other side of the road are old quarries, old coal workings, new housing estates, and some agricultural land. Originally three-quarters of this area was level. The remaining quarter was a hill of 700 feet, shown on the Key Plan as Turner's Heath. But the whole area is now so piled with mounds and pitted with quarries that the general effect is hilly and turbulent. From the air the area has the appearance of having been volcanically upheaved by the eruptions of industry. In planning the landscape for this difficult site, it was decided to take advantage of existing disturbances. The extraordinary confusion of hills, hollows and flats offer opportunities for creating an interesting and balanced landscape. Features which appear on the Landscape Map above (Figure 44) as liabilities can be converted into the assets for the future shown on Figure 45 (opposite).

The factory areas are treated simply. They are linked with the new landscape by a series of miniature green wedges in the form of tree-bordered car parks, lawns and walks. Next, playing fields, parkway lands, and water-gardens are designed for calmness and quiet prospects, the water-garden being adapted from the canal and its disused basins, while the nearby farmlands are extended from an existing holding. As a climax, Turner's Hill becomes Turner's Heath, a wild and magnificent retreat, crowned with a fan of great trees which merge with those that follow the skyline to Dudley. Groups and screens of birch and pine are arranged one behind the other to create an effect of space. The quarry depressions become sheltered dells into which the paths descend.

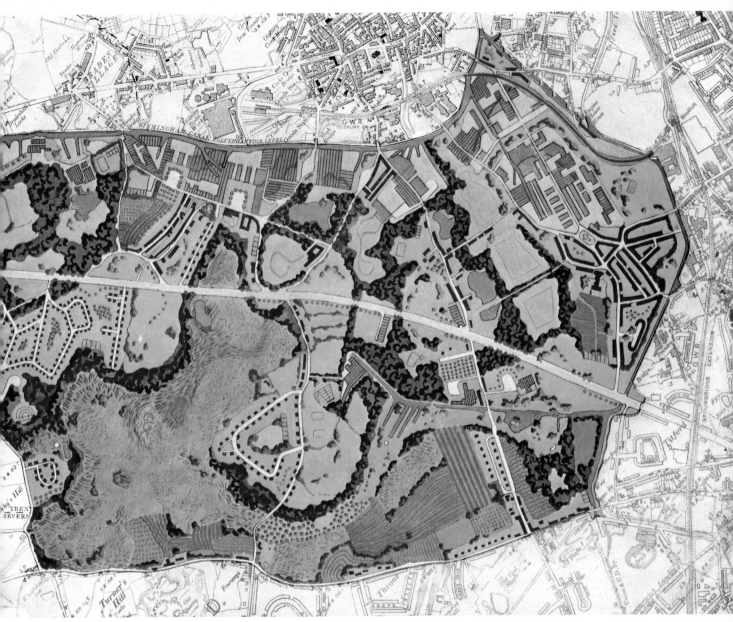

(*Based on the Ordnance Survey Map, with the sanction of the Controller of H.M. Stationery Office*)

Proposals for the treatment of the area near Oldbury.

But the main feature in the Oldbury design is the transformation of the Birmingham-Wolverhampton road into a great parkway, passing between fields, woods and gardens. Behind these comes the basic woodland pattern which runs along existing contours. Into the green clearings between the groups of trees are fitted parklands and playing fields. The tree pattern is shaped to cover unsightly land-uses (such as the I.C.I. chemical waste drainage pools and the municipal waste dump at Shidas Lane), which are likely to continue for at least another generation.

In the beautifying of this site, all the elements of landscape design are brought into play. Form, which follows land contours ; scale, which expands the confinement of houses and factories by gradations to the breadth of the heathland ; pattern, which relates in shape and size one area of woodland to its neighbours ; tone, which is achieved in the selection of vegetation by such devices as placing dark clumps of Horse Chestnut against light masses of Yellow Willow ; and texture, which results from the juxtaposition of smooth playing fields to the rougher surfaces of Mountain Ash and Corsican Pine.

Between public land, such as Turner's Heath, and private land, such as the I.C.I. estate, a network of footpaths and rights-of-way would allow the walker to roam over the whole area.

A site for an outdoor cinema is to be found in a quarry off Newberry Lane ; and an open-air theatre could be set up just below the summit of Turner's Heath where the background of the hill forms a natural setting easily accessible by road.

FIGURE 46

A LANDSCAPE FOR THE BLACK COUNTRY (III)

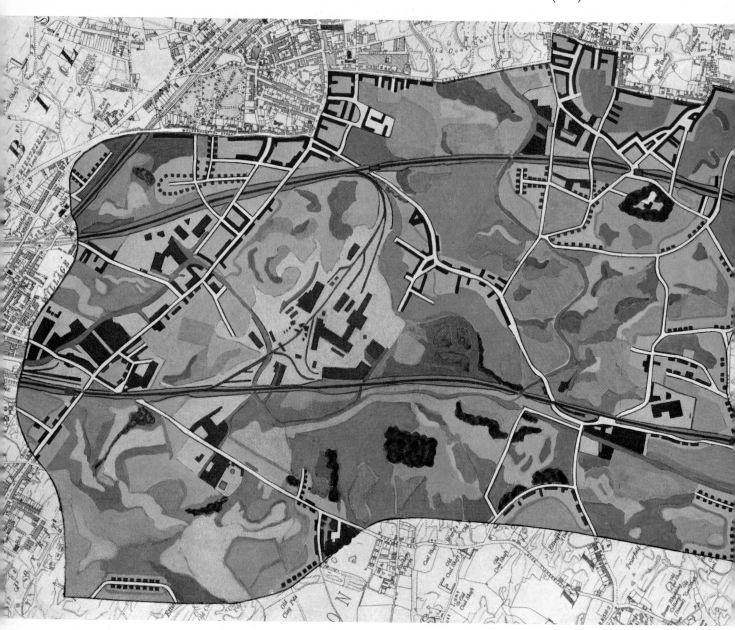

(Based on the Ordnance Survey Map, with the sanction of the Controller of H.M. Station

Existing landscape of an area at Bilston.

The Bilston site is divided into three roughly parallel strips by the L.M.S. and G.W. railway lines which are centrally linked by a branch serving the Staffordshire Steel Works. The towns of Wolverhampton, Bilston, and Coseley bound the area to the north, east and south respectively, while to the west is the land of the Parkway.

The area is marked with groups of factories and sporadic stretches of houses, chiefly along railways and canals. The intervening ground has been churned by surface coal mining into an area of scrubby dunes. The general impression is of a dismal and flat district.

The objective in planning this area was the re-integration of the disordered land with the adjacent untouched field pattern that obtains near Dudley. This implies a lay-out that would be unemotional and workaday in character. There is no call for a slavish imitation of the old field lay-out. Much preferable is a design which would harmonize with the adjacent lay-out and, at the same time, conform to the requirements of modern farming in those areas which are to be planned for agriculture.

236

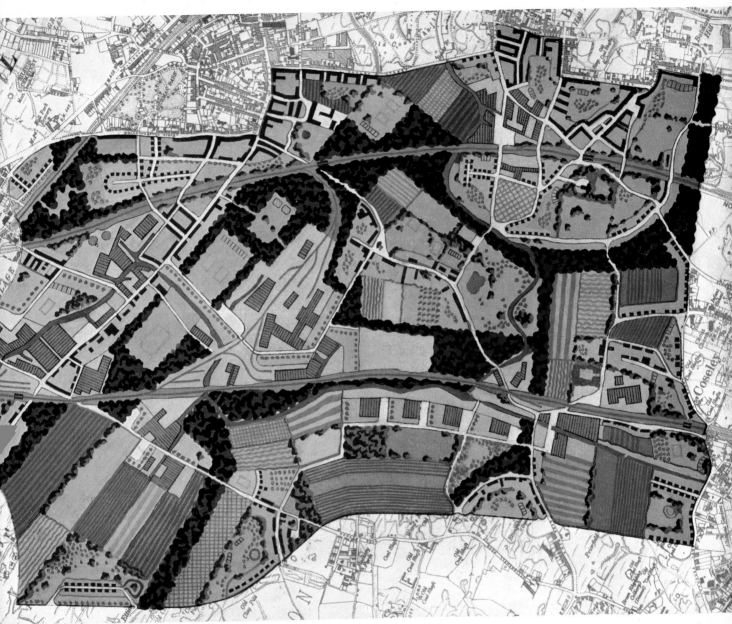

(*Based on the Ordnance Survey Map, with the sanction of the Controller of H.M. Stationery Office*)

Proposals for the treatment of the area at Bilston.

Straightforward rectilinear patterns are, therefore, prescribed for the Bilston area, these patterns to be enclosed in the basic frame of woodland. The main pattern would be sub-divided into factory and housing areas, playing-fields, horticultural strips, and fields for full-scale cultivation. As there are only minor irregularities of surface, full use could be made of modern machinery in levelling and re-soiling.

There are several distinct groups of houses based on the various factories. In the new landscape these groups are to be clearly divided from one another by the woodland pattern. This would give them individuality and privacy. The woodland pattern would also block and screen the existing vistas of factory chimneys and railways. Each of the housing groups is to be provided with its own breathing space of playing-fields, allotments and orchards, its communal garden and old-people's rest places.

This scheme accepts many present arrangements, but strives to make the best of them. Yet it is also sufficiently flexible to allow for readjustments in the future. For instance, it is suggested that suitable sites for light manufacturing industries may be found on the land to the left of the canal.

A LANDSCAPE FOR THE BLACK COUNTRY

Landscape treatment of certain areas in Figures 44 and 45. The left-hand photographs show the existing landscape. On the right are shown the same scenes as they would appear after the landscape proposals reach maturity.

Looking south across the Birmingham Wolverhampton road to Rowley Regis.

Birmingham-Wolverhampton road, near Langley; Turner's Hill in distance.

The principal effects are obtained by screening houses, factories and landscape scars with tree belts and camouflage treatment of buildings. Clumps of trees emphasize focal points so that the view is dominated by its natural features.

Birmingham-Wolverhampton road as a parkway. Hummocky land made into a grassy slope, with orchard trees. Trees and flowering shrubs screen factory sites, and punctuate the stretches of carriageway.

A LANDSCAPE FOR THE BLACK COUNTRY

Landscape treatment of certain areas in Figures 44 and 45.

Turner's Hill, Rowley Regis.

Disused canal basin, Oldbury.

Turner's Hill and the surrounding area after rehabilitation. Natural growth and soil restoration can be fostered by a carefully planned system of progressive planting.

Miles of disused waterways could be turned into one of the most attractive landscape features of the new Green Setting.

Ribbon-building along the Birmingham-Worcester road on the fringe of the
disfigured a valuable smallholdings area. Less striking examples of this type

PART II

PLAN FOR SMALLHOLDINGS IN THE CATSHILL AREA

NOTE FROM THE LAND CLASSIFICATION COMMITTEE

Reference has already been made (see Chapter XII) to the scattered development of the Bromsgrove-Catshill area. It is generally accepted that where development of this type has occurred, further planned development, aiming at the creation of a compact, closely-knit urban community, has many advantages; not the least of these is that encroachment on untouched agricultural land elsewhere is rendered unnecessary. Yet, in the Bromsgrove-Catshill area there are, it is suggested, several factors which render such continued development undesirable. These may be summarized briefly :—

1. *The area includes some of the best soils in the West Midland region, chiefly deep sandy loams derived from the Keuper Sandstone. The rolling relief of the district leads to a certain " patchiness," with occasional limited areas of shallow soil on steeper slopes ; hence the classification of the district as Category I with II. On the other hand, it is very favourable to good air drainage, and this is a factor of some importance to fruit- and vegetable-growers in the area.*

...typical of the manner in which sporadic urban development has dissected and ...y yet do more to break up holdings and reduce them to uneconomic sizes.

2. *The area is one of the more important of the small market-gardening districts of the Region, accounting for approximately one-twentieth of the Worcestershire vegetable acreage. (See Table XXXVIII). Its unique situation on the very doorstep of a vast urban market needs no stressing and is advantageous to producer and consumer alike.*

3. *It is often urged that, as a result of building development, fragmentation of holdings has proceeded to a point where agriculture is jeopardized. There is probably a measure of truth in this argument, but it should be stressed that a very large proportion of the vegetable production comes from smallholdings of 20 acres or less. In 1937, nearly 70 per cent. of the holdings in the parish of Bromsgrove were under 20 acres in size (Figure 48). These holdings, in the Catshill area particularly, seem to function efficiently within a more or less continuous girdle of housing development.*

The ultimate future of the Bromsgrove-Catshill district will depend upon a judicious harmonizing of urban and rural claims ; on agricultural grounds, however, it is suggested that any policy of extensive development which would obliterate the market-gardening areas is undesirable.

FIGURE 48   CATSHILL : EXISTING DEVELOPMENT AND FARM HOLDINGS

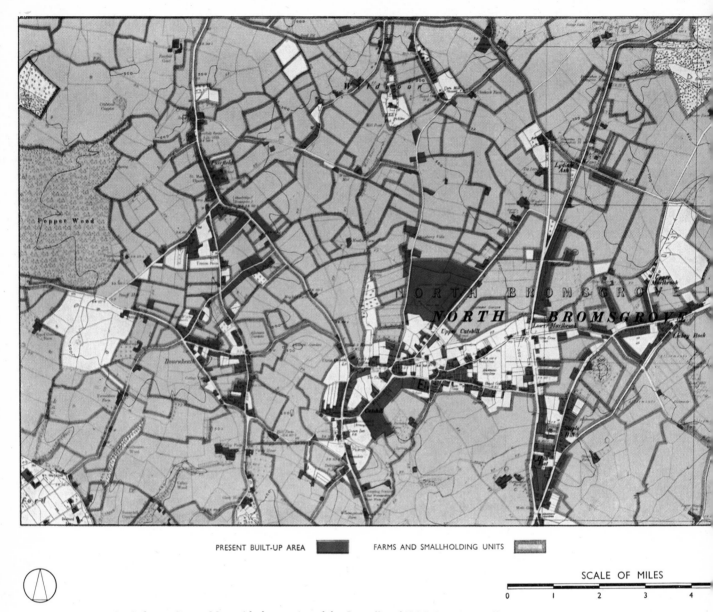

PRESENT BUILT-UP AREA ▮▮▮   FARMS AND SMALLHOLDING UNITS ▭▭

SCALE OF MILES

0   1   2   3   4

(Based on the Ordnance Survey Map, with the sanction of the Controller of H.M. Stationery Office)

DEVELOPMENT OF SMALLHOLDINGS

Round most of the great cities of England, there are extensive districts whose disordered appearance expresses, in a physical form, the conflict that has existed during the last few decades between the competing uses to which land may be put. The area about Catshill, 10 miles south-west of Birmingham, shows this conflict better than most. In a locality which is admirably suited to be one of the main market-gardening areas of the Midlands, the scattered bits and pieces of the outer suburbs of Birmingham's outer ring have encroached upon, and become intermingled with, the scattered bits and pieces which are characteristic of the smallholdings system of intensive cultivation. The result is a kind of no-man's-land.

Proper planning could have resolved this conflict. It is rather late in the day now to attempt to produce complete order out of what definitely looks like chaos at Catshill—though, perhaps, still not *too* late. Something may still be done at least to bring the conflict to an end. And, in any case, what has happened here through lack of principles

244

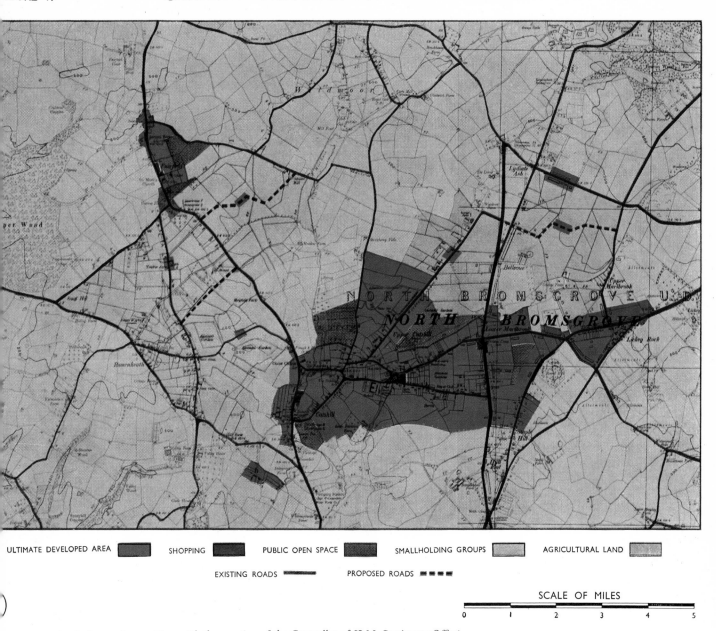

ULTIMATE DEVELOPED AREA ▮▮ SHOPPING ▮▮ PUBLIC OPEN SPACE ▮▮ SMALLHOLDING GROUPS ▯▯ AGRICULTURAL LAND ▯▯

EXISTING ROADS ▬▬▬ PROPOSED ROADS ▪ ▪ ▪ ▪

SCALE OF MILES

0   1   2   3   4   5

(Based on the Ordnance Survey Map, with the sanction of the Controller of H.M. Stationery Office)

(See Figure 50 for details of a Smallholding Group and Figures 51-54 for the new hamlets suggested in the smallholdings area)

provides an opportunity for establishing principles which may be applied elsewhere, in localities that have not yet become quite so bad as this.

Any attempt at adjustment between the claims of various uses, both for the purpose of making tidy what has already happened, and to assure the best social and economic development of the locality, must satisfy two major requirements. First, the district's value in the Regional economy as an intensively cultivated market-garden area means that it should continue in that use and be improved for it; and second, the population of the district, whether it follows urban or rural occupations, should be so grouped, and if necessary so increased, that it can enjoy the benefits of modern community life on a scale which will satisfy at least elementary social requirements.

Catshill now has a population of about 2,000. That is insufficient to call into being a good school, a shopping centre with a reasonably wide range of goods, and a cinema.

FIGURE 50

PROPOSAL FOR A PLANNED GROUP OF SMALLHOLDINGS

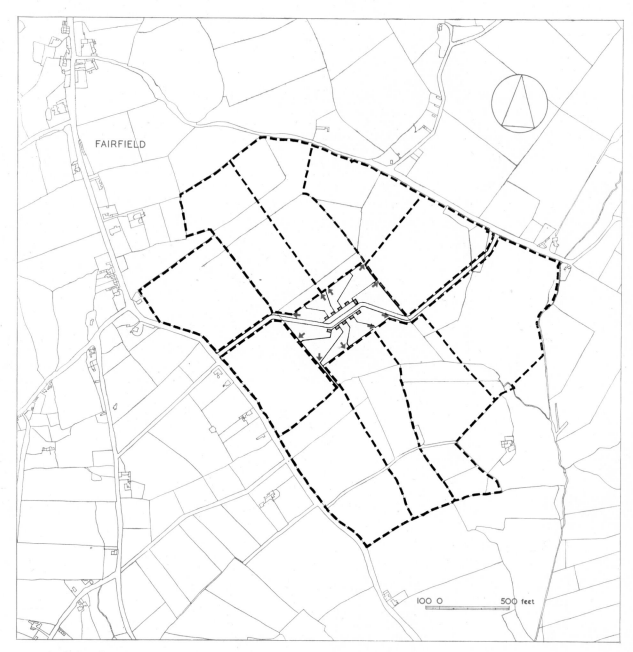

Each Smallholding Group would consist of about ten holdings, with the houses and other buildings at the centre forming a small settlement. The irregularly-shaped plot between each house and the holding attached to it may be used as private garden, glasshouse space, etc. In the Group shown here, most of the ten holdings have access to existing roads as well as to the new road which leads through the hamlet.

It is too small to enable local societies of various kinds to flourish. It should grow to something in the region of six or seven thousand. The new population can be accommodated without further undue encroachment on agricultural land, by consolidating it in the areas between the straggles and ribbons of the present sub-suburbia; and the necessary space for schools, playing fields, allotments, and other similar purposes can also be found there.

This would produce a tidy urban grouping of a reasonably satisfactory size. But if the smallholders are to live on their land, as it is held they must do, and if the scattering of

FIGURE 51

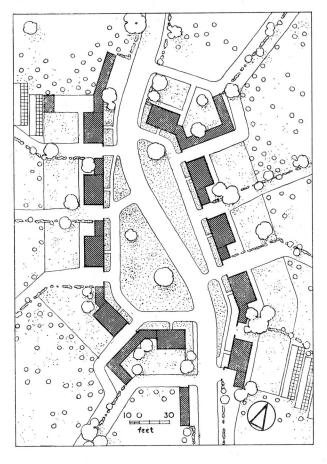

A PLANNED GROUP OF SMALLHOLDINGS (1)

The plan (above) and perspective drawing (below) show how a hamlet might be created as the centre of a residential area for a group of smallholders. It is not intended as an independent unit but as a satellite of an existing village.

FIGURE 52

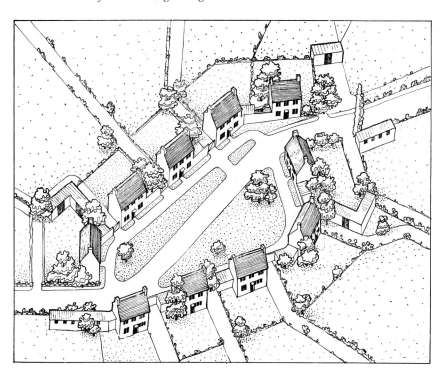

FIGURE 53

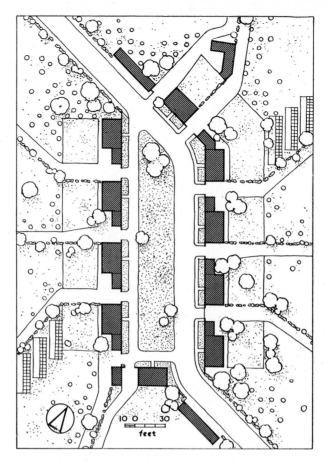

A PLANNED GROUP OF SMALLHOLDINGS (II)

This plan (above) and perspective drawing (below) offer an alternative suggestion to that shown in Figures 51 and 52.

FIGURE 54

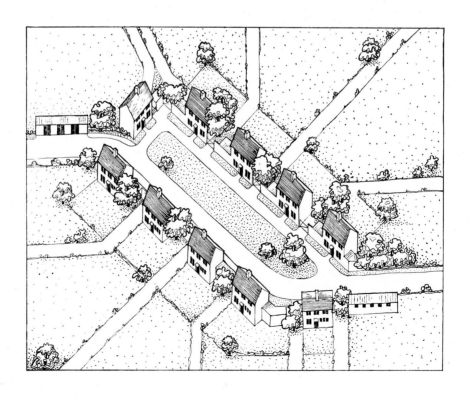

their houses along the roadsides is to be avoided, as in the interests both of landscape orderliness and sociability it certainly should be, then some special form of development outside the main grouping must be devised.

The minimum size for a smallholding on which a man can support himself in full employment is between eight and ten acres; and it is desirable that there should be some holdings of up to twenty, thirty, or even forty acres. The problem is how to lay out the holdings so that their houses can be grouped together and yet be situated on their own plots of land, such plots being of a reasonable shape for working and supervision. Probably the maximum number that can be grouped together is about ten. With this number it is possible to get the rectangular plots which tractor-ploughing demands. If the frontage of the plots is not to be more than 60 feet (and it will be difficult to get any architectural cohesion in the group if they are), it means that between the main plot and the house there must be an irregularly shaped piece of land; but this can very well be taken up by private garden, glasshouse space, and orchard. The accompanying sketch plans and sketches show the kind of hamlet that can be created by this form of grouping.

It is, of course, desirable that these hamlets should not be situated on main roads. Access to them should be by minor roads which fit into the general lay-out in such a way as not to sever any holding. At Catshill this can in fact be arranged within the existing system of side roads. Here, there could be, without any interference with the major farm units, some five or more such neighbouring hamlets, with a distance of half-a-mile between them. The hamlets would, of course, be too small to have even a shop of their own. For shopping or for schooling the inhabitants would have to go into Catshill or Fairfield, which should be built up into a rather more substantial village. For major social purposes, for the cinema and so on, everyone would have to go to Catshill. But no one would be more than a mile away from that place; thus, even while living on their own land, these fifty or more smallholders would be able to enjoy all the advantages of a full-sized " neighbourhood " community. If other layouts of this form were developed on other sides of Catshill, or round a bigger town, several hundred holdings could be established with the same advantages.

Perhaps the Catshill locality is too far gone for even these five groups to be established without great difficulty. But some such plan as this could very well be adopted in the establishment of new smallholdings elsewhere.

CHAPTER XV

Summary and Conclusions

This chapter sets out the conclusions reached by the Group as a result of its research. They are given with brief abstracts of the facts on which they are based. The sequence is not necessarily that of the chapters in the book, but the arrangement brings out the relation between the many planning problems which the Conurbation presents.

THE RESEARCH UNDERTAKEN by the Group has concentrated upon the fundamental problems facing those responsible for planning the twenty-four Local Authority areas making up the Birmingham-Wolverhampton-Black Country Conurbation.

Their researches, and their personal experience and knowledge of the area, have led to the conviction that a satisfactory solution of these problems will involve the almost total replanning and redevelopment of the whole 200 square miles. Such a plan should aim at the rehabilitation of the environment of two million people and the readjustment of the urban units with each other, with the region, and with the country as a whole.

Radical physical replanning of the whole area of the Conurbation and of the surrounding countryside is required.

THE CONURBATION IN THE ECONOMIC LIFE OF THE COUNTRY.

The enterprise and adaptability of industry in the Conurbation is a national asset of high value. The special characteristic of the Conurbation's industrial history is the vitality of the growth of new industries in areas from which minerals have been worked out by mining and quarrying, and in places which have become economically unfavourable to industries formerly established in them (pages 37-8). This vitality was evident in the relative prosperity of the Conurbation during the economic depression of the 1930's (pages 38 and 121-7).

The capacity for renewing its structure as it becomes obsolete has dissociated much of the Conurbation's industry from its original dependence on local mineral resources (pages 109 and 113). On the other hand, skill and technical ability, not limited to large concerns, have been a continuing asset and have helped to develop and attract industries dependent upon new technical processes.

The Conurbation, with its diversified but closely-linked industries, performs vitally important functions in the economic life of the country. Planning should aim at retaining and developing its characteristic industrial make-up and its capacity to respond to new industrial needs as they appear.

POPULATION

Estimates of the future growth or decrease of the country's population must, to a large extent, rest on assumptions. The Group has assumed that the tendencies which

250

were apparent over a long period of years up to 1939 will continue to determine population changes, once the abnormal conditions created by the war have disappeared. In the Conurbation, however, population increase between the years 1921 and 1939 was at a higher rate than in the United Kingdom, mainly owing to a higher natural increase, and only in the later years partly to immigration (Tables VII and IX, pages 76 and 80, and Figures 24 and 25, page 82).

To avoid the danger of congestion, the population of the Conurbation should be allowed to continue to grow only to the extent that is equivalent to the natural excess of births over deaths. Policy should, therefore, be directed to effecting an even balance between immigration and emigration.

THE PLANNING PROBLEM

If the above recommendation is made effective, the Conurbation as a whole will not present any very serious problems in relation to a national policy for dispersion. Yet the Conurbation presents one of the most difficult planning tasks in the country. In physical congestion and dereliction, in ugly slums and marred land, lies a danger to the future social life of the whole area; a danger which will persist and increase until an attempt is made to plan on a comprehensive scale.

There are heavy arrears in the improvement of conditions of living and work, in the development of a convenient and congenial urban environment, and in the expansion of social services and amenities. But the fundamental principles of planning are concerned with the future use of land and the pattern of urban development. The chief concern of the Group has been with these.

SURFACE UTILISATION

Planning should aim at achieving the most effective use of land.

Less than 45 per cent of the area of the Conurbation is built up or used for industry (Table XXXV, page 175). There is ample space for properly planned redevelopment and for carrying it out with relatively slight disturbance of the population.

The planning problems of the Conurbation can and should be solved within the broad limits of its present area.

The location of many types of development has often been decided for reasons which are no longer effective, and without regard to the interests of other land users. The long-continued contest for favourable sites has resulted in congestion and waste. Much land has been left undeveloped because its value has been reduced by neighbouring activities, or because it was an inconvenient remnant of a partly-used site. Development along roads and lines of communication (page 169), and around the periphery of old centres, has met an immediate need, but has caused waste by the irregular and sporadic use of land. Piecemeal conversion of sites from one use to another has added its own anomalies to the situation (page 140 and photograph, page 141).

Reorganization of uses of land on a more rational basis, which shall take careful account of grouping and zoning in development schemes, is an important factor in any plan which aspires to " tidy-up " the Conurbation.

DEVELOPMENT OF TOWNS

Planning should aim at grouping urban development around existing social and industrial centres. The amount of permitted development around each urban unit should be defined in relation to the specific needs of the area and the general plan for the Conurbation. The congested centres of existing towns should be redeveloped so as to make room for social, cultural and commercial facilities.

There is no serious deficiency of open spaces in the Conurbation as a whole (page 205 and Table **XXXIX**, page 206). If private open spaces were acquired and thrown open to the public, the overall proportion of open space to population numbers could exceed what is normally considered adequate in replanned urban areas.

The central areas of most of the towns of the Conurbation, however, are deficient in parks and other open spaces. This deficiency is most serious in the centre of Birmingham. (page 205). In general, the easterly half of the Conurbation has more open space than the westerly half ; but open spaces in the west are better distributed (page 207).

Steps should be taken to remedy the deficiency of open spaces in towns and to provide adequate and accessible space for play, sports and recreation.

In planning open spaces, more consideration than is normally given should be applied to the functions they are to fulfil. Spaces for recreation and amenity, for example, should be laid out so as to afford people in their vicinity a variety of sports grounds, spaces in which they can walk, play games, and enjoy pleasant scenery.

THE GREEN SETTING

A Green Setting of open land should be created between the urban areas in which all development, except for the purposes of agriculture and amenity, should be prohibited.

The Green Setting should be created by a gradual process involving the reservation of existing undeveloped land for open space or agriculture, the rehabilitation of derelict land, and the reversion of developed land to open land. Where buildings, such as houses in ribbon-developed areas, exist in the Green Setting, they should be allotted a term of " life ", and when this expires they should be eliminated (page 209).

Under the plan of redevelopment by nucleation, the land between the towns and smaller settlements of the Conurbation would become belts of open space and agricultural land, traversing the whole Conurbation, separating each town from its neighbours, and leading into the surrounding countryside.

The larger urban areas should be split by " green wedges " and strips of parkland penetrating from the inter-urban Green Setting to the centres of the towns. The Conurbation should be traversed by a continuous network of open spaces.

It is of first importance that the Green Setting be delineated at an early stage in order to protect from development the existing open land that would form part of it.

AMENITIES IN THE NEIGHBOURING COUNTRYSIDE

There are many tracts of open country adjacent to the Conurbation, or within a few miles of it, which are enjoyed by many town dwellers (Figure 43) ; but there is a deficiency of such tracts of open country to the east.

The whole area of the Conurbation should be surrounded by a chain of " playground " or " picnic " areas of the type already existing at Sutton Park and the Lickey Hills.

It is necessary to prohibit further development in the " green wedge " areas in the neighbourhood of Aldridge and Sandwell Park to the north, and Woodgate and Clent to the south. Both these wedges are of great value as amenities, and could be used also for parkway motor roads leading to the centre of the Conurbation and giving easy means of egress into the country to the south-west and north-west.

REHABILITATION OF DERELICT LAND

In the interior of the Black Country, areas of derelict land will, when restored, make as large a contribution to the Green Setting as undeveloped land.

The possibilities and opportunities which are afforded by large-scale schemes of landscape treatment and extensive tree-planting are not yet sufficiently appreciated. In the opinion of the Group, the right approach to the problem of improving the physical environment of the Black Country, is demonstrated in the schemes prepared at the Group's suggestion by Mr. G. A. Jellicoe (pages 227-242). The two areas treated in these schemes contain a high proportion of derelict land.

Schemes and experiments, on the lines described in Chapter XIV, for the rehabilitation of derelict land as open space, should be started as soon as possible.

NEW URBAN UNITS

The size of the towns should be determined by convenience and tradition, and by their individual economic and social requirements, and not by pre-conceived ideas of optimum size.

The pattern of urban development which might ultimately result from the redevelopment scheme outlined above is suggested in the diagrammatic map (Figure 41). An important feature of this recommendation is a "limit of development" line (page 204).

A limit-of-development line should be drawn around each town, which should enclose ample space for all the development expected to take place, in accordance with the plan for the Conurbation as a whole.

The task of planning urban centres should not be regarded as complete when the plans are drawn and embodied in operative town planning schemes. Good design and the resources of the applied arts should be used, and every effort made to ensure that the re-created towns shall have beauty and dignity as well as convenience and amenity.

UNIFIED PLANNING CONTROL

Physical redevelopment of the whole area of the Conurbation must be executed as a single, comprehensive scheme. This was recognized by the Government when they invited Sir Patrick Abercrombie to prepare a plan for the Conurbation and the three counties of Warwickshire, Staffordshire, and Worcestershire.

The working out of local schemes within the framework of the general plan, and the discharge of administrative functions, must be the task of the local planning authorities, working with full knowledge of the plans of their neighbours. At present a measure of co-operation has been achieved in that 23 out of the 24 Local Authorities have formed themselves into six Joint Planning Committees with executive powers.

REORGANIZATION OF LOCAL GOVERNMENT UNITS

The reorganization of Local Government units within the area is necessary in order to provide efficient machinery for the administration and detailed planning of the Conurbation. In the Group's opinion this can be most effectively brought about by the creation of a limited number of large, All-Purpose Authorities of County Borough status which together would cover the whole Conurbation. Nevertheless, having regard to the social value of the small townships in the Conurbation, the elements which make up the larger authorities should be redeveloped as units, each separated from the others by open space.

PLANNING AND THE COUNTRYSIDE

The unification of planning control over the whole conurbation should also extend into the surrounding rural areas for a sufficient depth to ensure prevention of undesirable urban spread. For this, and other reasons, there is a clear need for some extension of the boundaries of the proposed All-Purpose County Boroughs for some miles into the surrounding rural areas—not, as is sometimes imagined, to extend the area of urban development, but, on the contrary, to ensure the preservation of the Green Setting. (See footnote, page 65).

The acquisition of a narrow green belt of agricultural land and open space along part of the edge of urban development south of Birmingham during the 1930's did not prevent ribbon and sprawl development in the countryside beyond. Rural land should be regarded as a ground or backcloth upon which are set clearly-defined areas of urban development with inviolable boundaries.

Development in the countryside outside the Conurbation should follow the same principles as recommended for the urbanized area inside its boundaries. The aim should be a planned pattern of nucleated development in a rural setting.

In predominantly rural areas all development except that associated with agriculture, mineral extraction, and amenity, should be prohibited beyond the limit of a development line set around existing settlements.

AGRICULTURAL LAND AROUND THE CONURBATION

The recommendations set out above are dictated by the planning needs of the Conurbation area itself. They are reinforced by the study of agricultural land around the Conurbation.

Further development north-west, north-east, east and south-west of the Conurbation is particularly undesirable, since first-class land would thereby be lost to agriculture.

The area east of Birmingham, beyond the line Tamworth, Hampton-in-Arden, Dorridge, should be especially protected (page 191).

The reservation of areas under planning for agricultural use should have regard to existing use as well as to inherent fertility, since a great deal of production comes from second-grade soils (pages 197-8).

AGRICULTURAL AREAS AFFECTED BY UNDESIRABLE URBAN DEVELOPMENT

The most serious losses of agricultural land to urban development have not been caused by the spread of compact urban development, but by the penetration of sporadic residential development in the countryside. The Catshill area, north of Bromsgrove, clearly shows the effects of such penetration (Figure 48). The area is valuable to the Conurbation as a market-garden centre, and intensive cultivation has increased the productivity of what is inherently second-grade soil. Fragmentation and separation have caused a decrease of efficiency and much land has been taken up during the last two or three decades by ribbon and sprawl development.

In rural areas where amenities and agriculture have been injured by surburban spread, the Group recommends redevelopment schemes aimed at the creation of compact towns and villages. Houses and buildings associated with the agricultural needs of the area should, in the case of smallholding and market-garden districts, be regrouped into small hamlets. This should be accompanied by redistribution of smallholdings so that the land may be worked efficiently.

EARLY REDEVELOPMENT OF INNER AREAS

First attention in the redevelopment programme should be given to the central slum areas of the older towns, in order that the present centrifugal drift of the population may be checked. In the redeveloped centres of the old towns, space must be provided for shopping centres, hotels, restaurants, theatres, concert halls, and assembly rooms.

INDUSTRY

A number of specific conclusions were reached in the chapter on Industry with the object of achieving (a) a stable and high employment regionally, using the various capacities of the population and resulting in a high standard of living and amenities, and (b) participation in any policies that may be adopted nationally.

Stability of employment was lacking in some of the central areas of the Black Country. The areas particularly affected were Dudley, Bilston, Cradley Heath, Wednesbury and Brierley Hill. Here unemployment can be associated with high specialization in the earlier iron and steel processes and in constructional engineering, which are subject to cyclical fluctuations. Further, there is a clearly-marked decline in coal-mining and the primary processes of iron and steel smelting and rolling in the northern and western areas of the Conurbation.

Employment should be diversified by extending existing stable industries, such as clothing at Dudley, and bringing in industry from the more stable areas, such as Birmingham and Smethwick. Maintenance of high employment does not require the introduction of completely new industries into the Conurbation as a whole, but industries should be redistributed within the Conurbation to make up for the relative decline of coal-mining, and iron and steel smelting and rolling. Within the established group of metal industries, conditions favourable to rejuvenation and redevelopment, i.e., the continual opening-up and development of new branches within a given industry, should be encouraged.

It has already been noticed that one of the remarkable factors in the industrial history of the Conurbation is the diversity of small firms and the wide range of skills in the area.

Diversity of occupation and status among the employed population should be preserved, and wider technical education, including training in management, should be provided as one means to this end.

Small firms in certain trades should be assisted by the building of trading estates or, in congested areas, flatted factories; and the need for assistance by the provision of pooled technical, market, and design research facilities, should be examined.

The Group believes that the total population of the Conurbation should increase no further than its natural growth. If there is to be no net immigration this may imply the deliberate restriction or dispersal of certain industries.

The further entry into the Conurbation of large, self-contained factories owned by large firms is probably undesirable. In particular, new industries not closely linked with other industries in the Conurbation, and even factories not closely linked with Conurbation factories in the same industry should be discouraged.

When judging the mobility and dispersibility of existing industries, the alleged need for a large supply of skilled labour should be reviewed in the light of modern production methods. It may be possible to move the small staff of technicians, foremen, and toolmakers, still required under newer methods, and find unskilled labour in a new area.

SMOKE POLLUTION

The smoke pall which overhangs the Conurbation is not caused entirely by industry. The domestic chimney contributes largely (pages 153-4). Pollution of the atmosphere by smoke would mar any Green Setting the Conurbation might achieve. Smoke is harmful also to people and building fabrics. Heavy smoke pollution is unnecessary. It indicates the inefficiency of coal-burning appliances now in use (page 157).

The use of efficient coal-burning appliances should be encouraged for industrial and domestic use. The practice of washing and hand-picking coal at the pit-head should be extended.

TRANSPORT

Ports; Services and Access: The natural outlet for the Conurbation's export products is the Bristol Channel, but the shipping services and organization of the ports should be considerably extended. Extensive use is also made of the Mersey-side ports, of Hull, and of London. The shipping facilities of London and of the Mersey ports are good. The Humber is an important port of entry, but land communications with the Conurbation area are poor.

Communications with main seaports should be improved by new main roads.

Roads: Other roads are needed direct to Leicester and the Eastern Counties, and to Yorkshire and the North-east. New roads leading to the Mersey and the Humber should be linked north of the Conurbation: these would complete a ring road system surrounding the built-up area (Figure 19).

New roads, of the class of the new Birmingham-Wolverhampton road, are much needed inside the conurbation. The planning of such roads would depend on the general scheme of redevelopment.

Airports: Elmdon should be developed as a national airport.

Canals: The canals which connect the Conurbation with the rest of the country were cut when this form of transport was the most used method of carrying heavy goods. Navigable waterways connect the Conurbation with the four major ports, but the system is not now adequate for more than a small proportion of the heavy freight traffic (page 72).

The approaches to the Conurbation canal system by water should be improved by widening the rivers that feed the area. The Severn Carrying Company, the Trent Navigation Company, and the Weaver Navigation Board have drawn up schemes intended to achieve this (Figure 20, page 70).

Within the internal system of canals, improvements in lock facilities would expedite the handling of mineral freight, although the hilliness of the Conurbation area prevents the expansion of the canal system except at very great expense.

Railways: In general, railway communications between the Conurbation and the rest of the country are good. The internal network of railway lines is adequate to carry an efficient passenger service; but existing train services are poor. Three suburban lines in the Birmingham area have fallen into disuse, despite the growth of the city and the increasing pressure on road transport services (page 69).

Better train services within the Conurbation are urgently needed. It is recommended that the possibility of electrification of suburban lines be investigated.

Passenger stations throughout the whole Conurbation are out-of-date, inefficient, indifferently served and unprepossessing. A large-scale rebuilding programme for railway stations is urgently needed. At the same time, closer co-ordination of road passenger services and stations with those of the railways should be effected.

HOUSING NEEDS

In the whole Conurbation, approximately 128,000 dwellings were needed in 1947 to accommodate new families and to replace bomb-damaged houses and slum dwellings.

As soon as this immediate need is satisfied, a further 95,000 slum-borderline houses should be demolished and replaced by new dwellings.

The number of slum and slum-borderline houses which should be replaced is thus 198,720— about a third of all houses in the Conurbation.

FACTORIES

One of the main functions of any plan is the appropriate siting of industrial areas:

Under planning, newly-developed and redeveloped areas should define zones for industry. Particular attention should be paid to the accommodation of all noisy and noxious factories in zones separated from residential neighbourhoods.

While there is now adequate legislation by which Local Government Authorities may condemn slum dwellings and empower their replacement by houses which conform to recognized standards, the means of ensuring good standards of working conditions in factories are inadequate. Many factories are as unfit for working in as are slum dwellings for living in. There are no powers, however, for condemning factory buildings. Much of the legislation contained in Factory Acts is impossible to apply, and the endeavours of Factory Inspectors to establish standards are frustrated because of lack of space and sub-standard building.

Powers are needed to enforce the demolition of factory buildings in which the attainment of certain minimum standards of working conditions is not practicable. Such standards should take account of lighting, ventilation, spacing, sanitary conditions and general structure.

Standards would have to be modified in their application to certain industries. Powers to enforce standards should be in the hands of Local Authorities. Supervision of variations from general standards might be left to Factory Inspectors.

Although plans for all new buildings have to be submitted to Local Authorities, no general regulation exists by which plans for new factories must be examined by the Factory Inspectorate. At present, most of the provisions of the Factories Act can be enforced only after buildings have been erected.

Powers should be given to make it obligatory for firms engaged in certain specified industrial processes to produce certificates of approval by the Factory Inspectorate of plans for the erection of factory buildings when such plans are submitted to Local Authorities.

Conversion of premises, especially dwelling houses, into factories, should be subject to the same control as applies to the erection of new factory buildings.

Factory areas should be so laid out as to provide optimum daylight conditions for work and sufficient open space for amenities and recreation.

Appendix

The South Staffordshire and Cannock Chase Coalfields and Future Planning in the West Midland Conurbation

INTRODUCTION

THIS SURVEY of mining trends in the South Staffordshire and Cannock Chase Coalfields in and adjacent to the West Midland Conurbation was carried out in July and August, 1947, with the primary object of assessing the extent to which any future plan for the Conurbation should take into account possible developments in the coalmining industry. Efforts have been made to analyse the major influences of the physical background and to show the main stages in the growth of the industry in the Conurbation ; at the same time, an attempt has been made to indicate the probable areas in which future coalmining activities may develop, and to discuss some of the problems that may be occasioned by shifts of mining activity. It is hoped, too, that enough detail has been added to enable the reader to assess the present and future importance of the production of the two coalfields relative to the output of the nation as a whole.

Some confusion has arisen in the past regarding the nomenclature of the two coalfields. The term " South Staffordshire Coalfield " was formerly used, and is still used occasionally, to describe all the mining districts in the southern half of Staffordshire, *i.e.* south of Stafford and Rugeley. Owing to the operation of a number of physical and historical factors, however, the mining districts formerly included in that description are now divided into two well-marked regions, viz. :—

(a) The area centred on Dudley and formerly often known as the Dudley Coalfield. This includes the districts in which coalmining was first developed extensively and where the coalfield reached its maximum development about 1860. This is the area which is now usually referred to simply as the South Staffordshire Coalfield, and lies *south* of the belt of the Bentley Faults. This belt, which has important geological, historical and economic significance, extends from the north of Walsall westwards to the north of Wolverhampton (see Figure 55).

(b) The second region, now usually termed the Cannock Chase Coalfield, includes all the mining districts of the southern half of Staffordshire which lie *north* of the Bentley Faults. Development of coal working in these districts has chiefly taken place since 1860.

The presence of a coalmining industry, on even a small scale, may have an influence on town and country planning entirely out of proportion to the quantity, quality and value of the coal produced. The locations of extractive industries, the sites of mines, are, unlike the sites of most manufacturing industries, fixed within fairly rigid limits by purely

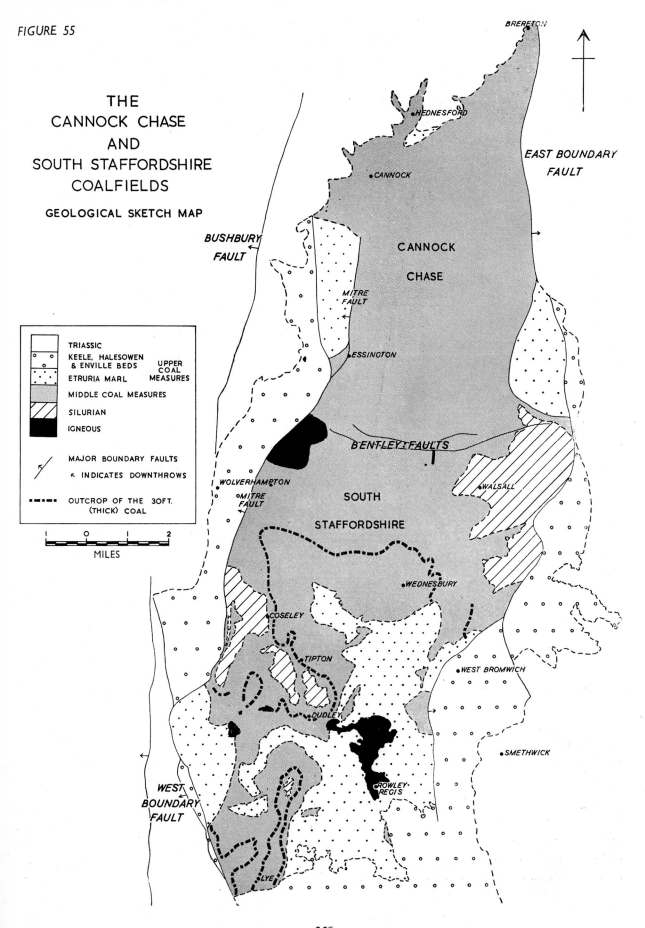

FIGURE 55

THE
CANNOCK CHASE
AND
SOUTH STAFFORDSHIRE
COALFIELDS

GEOLOGICAL SKETCH MAP

BRERETON

EAST BOUNDARY
FAULT

BUSHBURY
FAULT

HEDNESFORD

CANNOCK

CANNOCK
CHASE

MITRE
FAULT

ESSINGTON

TRIASSIC
KEELE, HALESOWEN
& ENVILLE BEDS   UPPER
                       COAL
ETRURIA MARL   MEASURES
MIDDLE COAL MEASURES
SILURIAN
IGNEOUS

MAJOR BOUNDARY FAULTS

INDICATES DOWNTHROWS

OUTCROP OF THE 30FT.
(THICK) COAL

1   0   1   2
MILES

BENTLEY FAULTS

WALSALL

WOLVERHAMPTON

MITRE
FAULT

SOUTH

STAFFORDSHIRE

WEDNESBURY

COSELEY

WEST BROMWICH

TIPTON

DUDLEY

SMETHWICK

WEST
BOUNDARY
FAULT

ROWLEY
REGIS

LYE

physical factors, which are the presence and accessibility of the mineral. It is, of course, impossible to transfer coal mines to new locations simply because the ugly pithead buildings and waste heaps form a disfigurement to an otherwise attractive landscape. The presence of Hamstead and Sandwell Park collieries in the northern " green wedge " of the Conurbation is unfortunate from the point of view of landscape and amenity, but the planner must at present accept the coal mines as necessary and formulate such plans as he can for minimizing their consequences. Even when collieries become defunct, the black pyramidal bulk of the pit heap, together with the skeletons of colliery wheels and pithead buildings, remain to overshadow the countryside.

A knowledge of mining trends is essential to those responsible for planning areas such as the Conurbation ; they must know the precise limits of those areas into which mining operations are likely to spread, and, just as important, those areas in which it is likely to cease. It may well be, for example, that an otherwise desirable regional park or " playground area " is destined in the course of a few decades to become the centre of a new mining zone. The planner should be warned, and should have in mind his alternatives or his plans for minimizing the effects of the entry of the industry by schemes for control of pithead sites and rehabilitation of the landscape. Near the West Midland Conurbation, for example, mining is gradually spreading towards and across the forest- and heath-clad slopes of the northern part of Cannock Chase, at present of great value both from landscape and amenity standpoints.

The possible attraction of a new coal producing area for industry and population is a factor to be taken into consideration. The Conurbation itself, in the first place, grew up mainly as a result of the extraction of coal and iron in South Staffordshire, and although such spectacular urban and industrial growth is not to be anticipated in the near future, the possibility that a new coalfield or a new area of a coalfield may form an attraction to industry and labour should be considered. Again, the shifting of the " centre of gravity " of a coalfield may leave a settled population in the older established mining towns and villages deprived of its major occupation—a problem of workers without industry. Are the towns and villages to move ? Are means to be found for conveying miners to the new colliery sites ? Or is the old area to be classified as one suitable for the entry of new industries ? Associated with those problems, and of immediate urgency, is the need for housing and rehousing mine-workers and for replanning and reorganizing the settlements and communities which have grown up throughout the coalfields.

Finally, the effects of surface subsidence caused by underground working of the coal seam can be disastrous to any development scheme prepared without regard for such contingencies.

It is apparent, then, that in any area in which mining has a place in the economic structure, planning must be sufficiently flexible to allow for the appearance of new mine-workings in a hitherto rural countryside. The possibility of shifts of mining centres must be kept in mind when planning for industry, when providing for housing, and when laying out the towns and villages, communities and neighbourhoods of the region. Changes in the size and shape of working coalfields are often gradual but, with very few exceptions, are effective for very long periods of time. Without careful planning and control, the decay of mining in once active areas may leave scars more lasting and disfiguring to the landscape of town and country than are produced by changes in any other single industry. Almost every square mile of South Staffordshire offers evidence of this.

The South Staffordshire Coalfield, which has played such a large part in the industrial rise of Birmingham and the Black Country, lies entirely within the West Midland Conurbation; the Cannock Chase coalfield which has, as it were, grown " out of " its now less important southern neighbour, fringes the Conurbation on its northern side. The outcrop of Carboniferous rocks, across the southern half of which the Conurbation " straddles ", extends in an elliptically-shaped band from the neighbourhood of Hednesford and Brereton in the north almost to the Lickey and Clent Hills in the south—a total distance of some 20-24 miles. The band is widest in its centre where it extends for some 11 miles from Baggeridge Wood, in the west, to Hamstead, in the Tame Valley, to the east.

Of the Carboniferous rocks, only the Middle and Upper Coal measures are present; Carboniferous Limestone and Millstone Grit are locally absent. Details of the Carboniferous rocks present are given in Table II (Chapter III).

The " *visible* " or " *exposed* " coalfield, comprising that area in which the coal seams are present at or near the surface, is cut off on both its east and west sides by boundary faults (Figure 55). It will be seen that some outcrops of Etruria Marl fall within the area enclosed by the boundary faults, and on that account, although the Etruria Marl is barren of coal, the outcrops are usually included within the " visible " coalfield. To west and east the boundary faults bring Middle Coal Measures and Etruria Marl against the barren sandstones and marls of the Keele and Halesowen beds of the Upper Coal Measures, which overlie the productive measures.

In the extreme south the Middle Coal Measures thin out and pass, finally, beneath the Upper Coal Measures, while in the north of the coalfield the coal seams disappear beneath the Triassic red sandstones and pebble-beds which form a bold southward-facing escarpment extending roughly east-west immediately to the north of Hednesford.

Those areas to the west and east of the boundary faults in which the coal seams are known to exist but are overlain by barren rocks, are regarded as belonging to the " *concealed* " coalfield. In the concealed coalfield the seams in general tend to " dip " or slope away from the boundary faults; thus, as one passes out of the Conurbation to west or east of the exposed coalfield, the seams for the most part attain greater depths. This depth is increased by the presence of faults, such as, in the West, the Bushbury Fault (Figure 55), which throws down the coal seams to the west, *i.e.*, away from the Conurbation.

The apparent continuity of the Middle Coal Measure outcrop, from Brereton and Hednesford in the north to Lye in the south-west (Figure 55), is broken along a narrow belt extending from the north of Walsall westwards across Bentley Common to the north of Wolverhampton. This is the belt of the Bentley Faults, which is usually taken as the line of demarcation between the South Staffordshire and Cannock Chase Coalfields, although in practice a very much wider zone separates the areas of each field at present actively worked.

The South Staffordshire Coalfield

This coalfield has a total area of approximately 62 square miles and is divided into two unequal sectors by the four outcrops of non-Carboniferous rocks which extend from Sedgley, through Dudley Castle hill to Rowley. The outstanding feature of the field has been the presence of the Thick or Thirty-foot coal, from the exploitation of which resulted much of the area's early prosperity. The chief seams of the coalfield, as given in the recent Regional Survey Report of the Ministry of Fuel and Power, are given, in descending order, in the following table :—

TABLE XLI

Name	Approximate Thickness
Brooch Coal	2 ft. 9 ins. – 3 ft. 6 ins.
Flying Reed Coal (where separated from the Thick Coal) ...	2 ft. – 3 ft.
Thick Coal	18 ft. – 30 ft.
Heathen Coal	3 ft. 6 ins. – 5 ft.
Sulphur Coal	4 ft. – 7 ft.
New Mine Coal	4 ft. – 6 ft.
Fireclay Coals	About 4 ft.
Bottom Coal	2 ft. – 12 ft.

In addition to coal, the field has had considerable importance as a producer of ironstone and fireclay. Most coal seams rest upon a layer of clay (fireclay or underclay), which is usually grey in colour and contains the roots and rootlets of the plants and trees from which the coal seams themselves were formed. The fireclays vary in composition but they are generally deficient in alkalies, a characteristic which renders them particularly resistant when strongly heated. In South Staffordshire fireclays are particularly well-developed in the Lye and Amblecote districts as well as near Dudley and Gornal. There is considerable variation in the type of clay over the coalfield ; the best clay has been used chiefly for the manufacture of glasshouse pots and the inferior qualities have been principally employed in the manufacture of crucibles and firebricks.

In general, exploitation of the seams has been an easier operation in the north-eastern (Tame Valley) sector of the field than in the south-western, for here the almost horizontal seams were never far from the surface, while the outcrop of the Thick Coal was extensive, passing from near Dudley through Darlaston and Bilston to Wednesbury (Figure 55). In the extreme north-east, however, between Wednesbury and Walsall, the Coal Measures have proved very much less productive. The more restricted south-western (Stour Valley) sector has presented more difficult problems. In this part of the coalfield the outcrop of Thick Coal was more limited, while much more folding and faulting of the rocks has taken place than in the north-eastern sector. To the south the Middle Coal Measures gradually thin and die out as they pass beneath the barren Upper Coal Measures, with the result that there is virtually no concealed field in the Halesowen-Stourbridge district.

CANNOCK CHASE COALFIELD

North of the Bentley Faults the Thick Coal splits, and is represented by a number of distinct seams. The classification of coal seams in this field, given in Table XLII, is essentially that of G. H. Mitchell[1], the seams being given in descending order.

Not all the coalfield area lies on Cannock Chase itself ; its southern portion includes the undulating land around Essington and Cheslyn Hay, while in the west and north-west the coalfield now extends off the Chase on to the relatively fertile valley of the Penk. Topographically the coalfield is, in general, at a higher elevation than the neighbouring area of South Staffordshire, for although the Essington area, which forms a link with South Staffordshire lies at only some 400-600 feet above sea level, the Chase rises in places to heights greater than 750 feet.

In general, the seams dip to the north-west and the angle of dip increases towards the western and north-western edges of the present worked coalfield. To the east the Eastern

---

[1] G. H. Mitchell: *Geology of the Northern Part of the South Staffordshire Coalfield (Cannock Chase Region).* (Geological Survey Wartime Pamphlet No. 43, May 1945, pp. 3 - 13).

TABLE XLII

Name	Thickness	Remarks
Top Robins Coal	4 ft. – 7 ft. 6 in.	—
Bottom Robins Coal	6 ft. – 9 ft.	The topmost coal of importance
Wyrley Yard Coal	2 ft. 6 in. – 5 ft.	Best developed in the Wyrley district
Charles Coal	Up to 5 ft.	—
Brooch Coal	3 ft. – 4 ft.	An important well-worked seam
Benches Coal...	3 ft. – 6 ft.	—
Wyrley Bottom Coal	4 ft. – 8 ft. 6 in.	Thickest in west and north-west of field where it consists of high quality coal
Old Park Coal	2 ft. 6 in. – 7 ft.	An important good quality coal
Heathen Coal...	2 ft. 6 in. – 5 ft.	An important secondary coal
Stinking Coal...	1 ft. 6 in. – 3 ft.	Of inferior value and little worked
Yard Coal	2 ft. 6 in. – 3 ft. 6 in.	A widely worked, good quality coal
Bass Coal	2 ft. – 8 ft.	—
Cinder Coal	2 ft. 4 in. – 10 ft.	An inferior coal, though now considerably worked
Shallow Coal	5 ft. – 10 ft. 8 in.	—
Deep Coal	3 ft. – 7 ft. 3 in.	Represents the Bottom Coal of South Staffordshire
Mealy Grey	2 ft. – 4 ft. 3 in.	—

Boundary Fault throws down the Coal Measures to a considerable depth, beneath Triassic rocks, while in the west the exposed coalfield is bounded by the westerly throwing Mitre Fault. An unmistakable indication of the presence of the Mitre Fault may be seen on the road between Essington and Cheslyn Hay, where, to the east, opencast mining for coal is in progress, while, immediately to the west of the road, Etruria Marl is quarried for the manufacture of bricks and tiles. In the extreme west, the coal seams are down-thrown westwards by the Bushbury Fault, to the west of which the Productive Measures have been encountered in a borehole at a depth of well over 2,000 feet. In the north of the field the coal seams pass beneath the Triassic escarpment beyond Cannock and Hednesford, and are again down thrown westwards and northwards by the Huntington and Littleworth Faults respectively. Boreholes have proved the existence of the Productive Measures beneath the Trias of the higher portions of Cannock Chase at depths greater then 1,000 feet. It will be seen then that the coal measures are present to north and west of the present worked field though at greater depths, and, in general, dipping more steeply than on the exposed and already proved coalfields.

GROWTH OF THE COALMINING INDUSTRY IN SOUTH STAFFORDSHIRE AND CANNOCK CHASE

Mining of the coal seams and ironstones has been carried on in South Staffordshire and in local areas of Cannock Chase since medieval times, and formed the foundation on which the prosperity of the iron industries of the Birmingham district arose. By the sixteenth and early seventeenth centuries, the industries were well established and Leland in 1538 was able to describe how the smiths of Birmingham had their " iron and seacole out of Staffordshire." The pits of the time were small and provided employment for only a few men or perhaps a family, while they were limited to areas where coal seams out-cropped at the surface. Wednesbury was a well known early centre. From records of collieries and pits—some sunk in the middle of the roads, to the great inconvenience of travellers—and from maps and descriptions, we have evidence of the change in the modes of life and landscape of the district, (" the south part of Staffordshire hath coles digged out of the earth, and mines of iron, but whether to their commodity or hindrance I leave to the inhabitants, who do or shall better understand it "—Camden's *Britannia*, 1610). The coalworkings and iron furnaces, set at first against a rural background, spread and multiplied, population increased and towns formed. The speed of change quickened in the eighteenth century, and the early nineteenth century displayed the full extent of the exploitation of the countryside in the smoke and grime of the fully developed Black Country.

The early coal workings were shallow. Coal was dug at the surface or from immediately under it by " bell " pits. Plot, writing in 1686, described how the miners of Wednesbury, in their open works, " rid off the earth and dig the coal under their feet and carry it off in wheelbarrows ". This, it may be noted, was an area in which the Thick Coal appeared at the surface (Figure 55).

By the early eighteenth century, production was increasing and coal was being sent by road from South Staffordshire to many parts of England, notably into Northampton-shire and Oxfordshire. Later in the century, developments in the iron industry, together with improved means of transport and technical improvements in the mines (notably the introduction of the steam engine) were responsible for large increases in production. New mines were opened and the size of many of the older ones increased. " The Proprietors of the Hoo Estate,[1]" Shaw writes at the end of the century, " have lately opened a large colliery of excellent coal, having branches of the Birmingham canal brought close to it : and there being a quantity of ironstone Mr. Addenbrooke has since erected a large furnace for the purpose of smelting that valuable commodity, which undertaking alone will consume a great part of the inferior coal."

Output continued to be drawn mainly from outcrops of the Thick and other seams and considerable quantities of ironstone were also raised—a fact which led to the erection of many blast furnaces and ironworks adjacent to the mines. Limestone was available locally—it was extensively quarried in Dudley Castle and the Wren's Nest hills—for use as a flux, while the growth of the canal network made transport of the raw materials and heavy products a comparatively straightforward matter. Fireclay was also mined over the whole field, though principally to south and south-west of the central ridge and formed the basis of the pot, crucible, firebrick and other industries of the Stourbridge district. Methods of working the coal varied somewhat from mine to mine, but, as contemporary diagrams, illustrations and descriptions attest, coal from the 30-ft. seam and others of the thickest seams was won principally by the " pillar and stall " method. By this method the coal was excavated in chambers, in size up to 50 yards square, four large pillars some 9 feet square being left to support the roof, with each chamber separated from its neighbour by a solid rib of 6-10 yards width. The whole thickness of the coal was extracted and the rock roof then allowed to fall in, but it was often possible to extract the coal remaining in the pillars and ribs by driving roads through the fallen debris of the old workings. As one would expect, accidents were common, and fatalities of frequent occurrence.

The immediate results of this undermining of the land surface were serious: it was reported to the Midland Mining Commission in 1843, for example, that a number of houses in Sedgley had, perforce, to be built with a special framework to " admit of their being screwed up into the perpendicular again, whenever they may be thrown out of it," while the lay rector of Wednesbury reported that great difficulty has been experienced in finding a site for a new Church owing to the " hollow nature of the land." The long term effects of eighteenth and early nineteenth century exploitation of the exposed coal seams, on the

---

[1] The Hoo Estate was situated near Bilston. *Vide* Shaw, *History of Staffordshire*.

Pithead gear in a South Staffordshire colliery a century ago. (From the Report of the Midland Mining Commission, 1843).

Colliery at Upper Gornal, Sedgley, in the South Staffordshire Coalfield. Pithead gear at one of the small collieries still working in the western part of the Conurbation. Lifts and cages have improved upon the simple pithead gear of the nineteenth century, and beam engines have been replaced by more efficient steam engines, but in many cases a century has produced few essential changes in mining methods and pithead equipment.

FIGURE 56

SOUTH STAFFORDSHIRE COALFIELD

COLLIERIES 1861

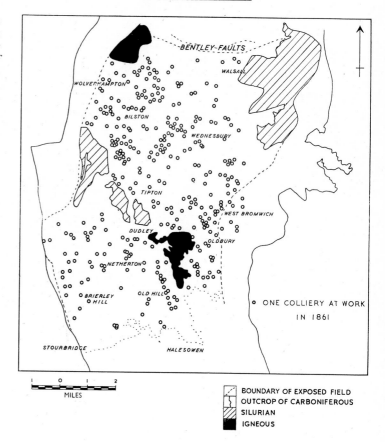

Three hundred and twenty pits have been identified on the first map (Figure 56), which shows the location of almost all the collieries in existence in 1861, at the peak period of the coalfield's productive life. Others, which would bring the total to 380, were in existence at the same date, but could not be located. There are no statistics to indicate the relative size of pits, but the average colliery was small.

The two later maps (Figures 57 and 58) show clearly the decline of the coalfield since 1861, especially during the present century. Apart from Hamstead and Sandwell Park Collieries, all workings in the centre, north and east have closed down.

present land surface, are, in certain areas, only too apparent today. In many districts of the Black Country wide stretches of abandoned, derelict land, pitted by old workings, now flooded, and scarred by broken pit banks and heaps, are the only evidence left of the former prosperity of the coal and iron mining industries.

Compared with other British coalfields, the unit of production remained small and an average mine in 1800 raised perhaps 300-400 tons weekly, though, of course, this varied from time to time with demand, and according to local conditions. During the nineteenth century production rose fairly rapidly and steadily and, though most mines remained small, larger enterprises began to raise an increasing proportion of the production. The prosperity of this coalfield reached its peak in about 1860 in which year a total output of about $7\frac{1}{2}$ million tons of coal (nearly 10% of the national total) and $\frac{3}{4}$ million tons of ironstone were raised from over 400 collieries. At this time, coal was being mined from almost every part of the exposed coalfield south of the Bentley Faults (Figure 56), but after 1860 changes in the distribution of active collieries began to take definite form.

In South Staffordshire itself increasing difficulties of drainage and exhaustion of the better seams caused gradual abandonment of much of the north-eastern sector—particularly the Tipton-Bilston-Wednesbury sector, in the prosperity of which the Thick Coal had been such a vital factor. By the turn of the century the south-western sector of the coalfield was relatively of greater importance than the north-eastern—mines in the latter were generally small and of limited life (Figure 57). The total number of mines had

FIGURE 57

FIGURE 58

SOUTH STAFFORDSHIRE COALFIELD

MINES AND WORKERS 1902

SOUTH STAFFORDSHIRE COALFIELD

MINES AND WORKERS 1945

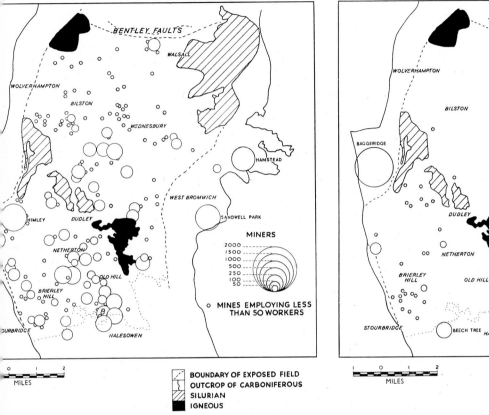

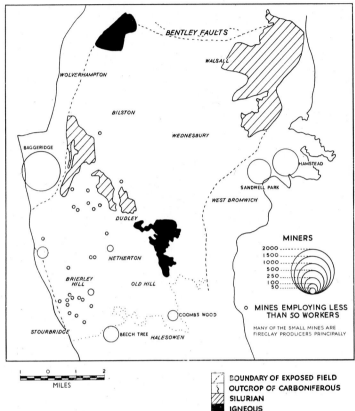

fallen to less than 300 and was decreasing year by year, the chief centres of production remaining in the Netherton-Lye-Old Hill areas of the south-western sector. Here exploitation of the coal seams had been delayed by the presence of the overlying Etruria Marl. By 1900, a shift of mining outwards, towards and on to the concealed coalfield, had taken definite form. The earliest attempts at working coal through the overlying Upper Coal Measures had been made on the eastern side of the field in the middle of the nineteenth century, and the Heath Colliery at West Bromwich had been working for some years prior to 1860. Following a number of trial borings in the Tame Valley, pits were sunk at Sandwell Park (1873) and Hamstead (1875), the Thick Coal being encountered at depths of 1,200 and 1,800 feet respectively. In the west of the coalfield, mining activity was concentrated on the fringe of the exposed coalfield where the Himley Collieries were in 1902 the largest in the coalfield, employing over 700 workers. The move on to the concealed coalfield in the western district has been a twentieth century development, the Baggeridge Colliery opening in 1912 (Figure 58).

In the north of the South Staffordshire coalfield, the second half of the nineteenth century witnessed a spread of mining northwards through Wednesfield and Bentley Common, across the Bentley Faults and on to the fringe of Cannock Chase itself. The development of coalmining in the area of the Bentley Faults had been delayed by a number of factors, among them the considerable thickness of the overlying glacial deposits. The sinking of shafts in this area now went on vigorously, and activity was carried northwards into the Wyrley, Pelsall and Brownhills areas, where the activity was clearly an extension northwards from South Staffordshire. The most intensive period of this growth of the Cannock Chase Coalfield, as it came to be known, lay in the two decades 1860-1880; collieries were opened as far north as Cannock, Hednesford and Brereton, and mining became the principal occupation throughout the area. The urban district of Cannock, for example, which in 1861 contained only 2,913 persons, increased its population to 20,613 by 1891, the population of Rushall, 2,842 in 1861, had more than trebled by 1891, while the figure of 1,628 persons for Norton was more than doubled during the same period. The spread northwards was accompanied by the growth of the elongated street villages, *e.g.*, Brownhills, Great Wyrley and Cheslyn Hay, which form so prominent a feature of the present settlement pattern. By 1880 coal production in the Cannock Chase area had reached a total of two-thirds of that in South Staffordshire, and by 1900 the totals were approximately equal, despite the fact that only some 33 mines were at work in Cannock Chase (Figure 59) as against a total of about 276 for South Staffordshire. Only eleven mines in South Staffordshire, however, employed more than 100 men underground, and only three (including Hamstead and Sandwell Park) employed more than 250 underground. Against this, Aldridge Nos. 1 and 2, typical of the Cannock Chase mines, employed 514 and 568 respectively beneath the surface, while there were at this time no less then 837 employed at Cannock Wood and 870 at Conduit Collieries. By 1913, two-thirds of the entire mining population employed in the southern half of Staffordshire were working in the pits of Cannock Chase.

Mining trends since 1905 are shown on a series of maps (Figures 59-61), and it will be observed that the progress of mining during this century has seen a virtual extinction of mining in the south of the exposed field. The pits of moderate size in the centre of the field have shown an actual decline in output and in size of labour force and a consequent relative decline in importance. Mining has tended to move to the north-west, where the increase in importance of the now comparatively large Littleton collieries since 1905 is significant, and to the extreme west, where Hilton Main commenced operations in 1924.

PRESENT PRODUCTION AND FUTURE PROSPECTS
South Staffordshire

Activity in the South Staffordshire coalfield is concentrated for the most part in one large and two moderate sized pits, all of which are working the concealed coalfield (Figure 58). On the exposed field, a number of mines are still in operation; most, however, are extremely small, eighteen of them together employing a total of only 277 wage earners, and only one colliery, Beech Tree, employs as many as 200. Total output of saleable coal is small and the active life of the majority very limited. They are situated principally in the south-western sector of the field and many of them are principally fireclay producers. One or two mines only may be worked for coal for any length of time, and for all practical purposes the exposed coalfield is dead. The chief planning problem lies in the reclamation and allocation to new uses of land left derelict following either open-cast or shallow-depth coal working or after its use for pit banks.

The three collieries working the concealed field to west and east of the boundary faults are, in the west, Baggeridge, the largest, and in the east, Hamstead and Sandwell Park in the Tame Valley. Compared with Cannock Chase, mining depths are great, over three-quarters of the output being obtained from a depth greater than 550 yards, whereas on the Chase three-quarters is mined from depths less than 300 yards. Production

Tipping at Baggeridge Colliery. The situation and shape of the tips render them comparatively inconspicuous even though the colliery is situated on the edge of Himley Park.

figures show a gradual decline and it is likely that this decline will be continued. In the east, mining difficulties are increasing, and it is likely that in the not too distant future mining will cease altogether. The total labour force involved in the two mines working the eastern side of the field is about 1,400, and the redeployment of this number should not be difficult. Mining prospects are brighter in the west of the field, where Baggeridge has a much longer potential life than either of the eastern mines. Reserves here are extensive and the possibility exists of some further extension of mining to the west, up to, perhaps, the line of the Smestow Brook.

In 1946 the total annual production of saleable coal from the coalfield amounted to 934,344 tons, a figure which represents little more than 0.5% of the national output. Production will decline absolutely and relatively.

Coal mined in South Staffordshire is suitable for domestic and industrial use. It is burnt chiefly in the Midlands and South of England.

The number of wage-earners on colliery books in 1945 totalled 4,056, of whom about 3,000 were accounted for by the three collieries on the concealed field.

Cannock Chase

During the eighty or so years of the existence of the Cannock Chase coalfield, its " centre of gravity " has shifted progressively northwards and westwards into areas of deeper seams and more difficult mining conditions (Figures 59-61).

The present position may be summarised as follows:—

(i) Deep mining has now practically ceased in the south centre and south-east of the field, *i.e.*, the area bounded to the south by the Bentley Faults and extending to the area of the present Wyrley Colliery. This area includes a number of towns and villages, *e.g.*, Aldridge, Brownhills, Rushall and Pelsall, which expanded, and in some cases began, as a direct result of the spread of mining north from South Staffordshire. This part of the coalfield is now almost worked out.

(ii) The boundaries of the area in which deep mining has ceased are likely to spread gradually into the central districts, *i.e.*, Great Wyrley, Norton and Cannock, as these areas become worked out. The cessation of mining here is not an immediate prospect, but will be rather a gradual process.

(iii) Mining activity will concentrate in the western, north-western and northern districts of the coalfield. Further development is probable to the west, in the

FIGURE 59

FIGURE 60

THE CANNOCK CHASE COALFIELD
MINES & WORKERS 1905

THE CANNOCK CHASE COALFIELD
MINES & WORKERS 1924

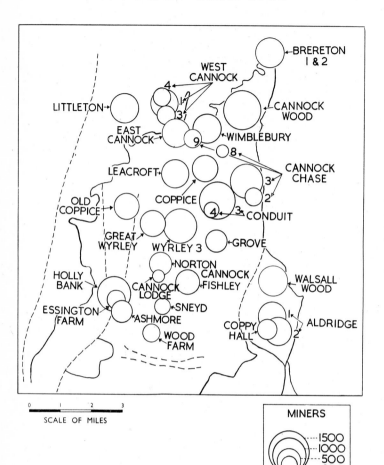

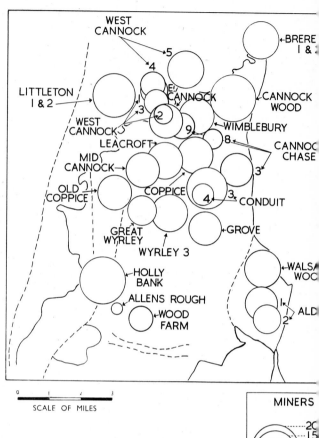

area between the exposed coalfield and the Bushbury Fault, while long-term possibilities exist for mining west of the Bushbury Fault, where the existence of coal has been proved at a depth of over 2,200 feet. An extension of the coal-mining area to the north and north-west is also probable. Numerous boreholes have proved the existence of coal beneath the Triassic rocks and although geological evidence is at present insufficient, it seems reasonable to anticipate future development of workings into this area, while the sinking of new pits is a long-term possibility.

It should be noted that future mining operations in any of the above areas will encounter increased difficulties owing to the greater depth and, probably, greater dip of the seams. They are likely to be comparatively large-scale undertakings.

A statement by the Chairman of the West Midlands Division of the National Coal Board, published on 17th November, 1947, contains an account of the plans for future development in both South Staffordshire and Cannock Chase Coalfields, and details of the National Coal Board's future policy. The published statement enables us to add some details to the outline of the present position and future prospects given in the preceding paragraphs :—

THE CANNOCK CHASE COALFIELD
MINES & WORKERS 1945

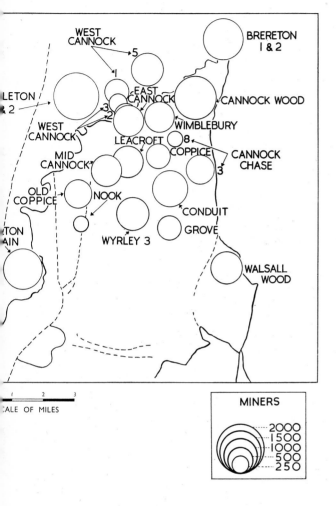

WEST CANNOCK

BRERETON 1 & 2

5

1

LETON & 2

EAST CANNOCK

CANNOCK WOOD

3

2

WEST CANNOCK

WIMBLEBURY

LEACROFT

8

MID CANNOCK

COPPICE

CANNOCK CHASE

3

OLD COPPICE

NOOK

TON AIN

CONDUIT

GROVE

WYRLEY 3

WALSALL WOOD

1 2 3
CALE OF MILES

MINERS

2000
1500
1000
500
250

These three maps (Figures 59, 60, 61) show the north-westward movement of mining operations across the Cannock Chase Coalfield during the present century. The Bentley Faults (indicated by broken lines running across the bottom of the maps) mark the southern edge of this coalfield and the northern boundary of the South Staffordshire Coalfield. Mining spread northward across the Bentley Faults in the latter part of the nineteenth century, and followed the dip of the coalfield towards Cannock Chase and beyond. The older, smaller pits in the south have now closed down and the life of the pits in the centre is limited.

All three tendencies—concentration of operations into the coalfield into a few large mines, the movement of active mining north and west, and the cessation of mining in the south, east and centre—create conditions which seriously affect the economic and social life of the area, the maintenance of an adequate number of workers for the mines, the growth, decline or re-development of many townships and villages, and the landscape of a large area of open countryside.

" *Cannock :*

" This coalfield has been heavily worked over a long period by a large number of comparatively small mines.

" The seams are believed to extend Westward and North-west and the ground will be proved by deep boreholes in order to ascertain the exact location of the seams. If sufficient quantities of coal are found the Littleton and Hilton Collieries will be completely modernised to work them.

" So far as the existing mines in the centre of the coalfield are concerned, plans are being compiled to show the exact location of remaining unworked coals, and it is hoped shortly to produce a scheme whereby one large colliery will take the place of 10 or 12 of the present pits. Whether a new shaft will have to be sunk for this purpose or whether one of the old collieries will be reconstructed cannot yet be seen. My Production Director holds the view that the Cannock Chase coalfield should consist of four large mines each producing about 1½ million tons per year, thus giving a total output of 6 million tons."

The developments and programme outlined above will necessarily occupy a large number of years before they are complete. As part of the short-term plan to improve

271

production in the immediate future two drift mines, Hewtree and Essington, have been opened up in the Cannock Chase coalfield.

The siting of new pits will be decided after consultation with the Ministry of Town and Country Planning, the Ministry of Agriculture, the Ministry of Health, and Local Authorities. " The reconstructed mines," the statement points out, " will have to have shafts deepened and enlarged, underground roads reconstructed on a new scale suitable for dealing with modern underground Diesel or electrically-driven locomotive haulage with which mine cars, capable of carrying from 2 tons to 5 tons each, in place of the small pit tubs now in use which carry only from 8 to 14 cwts., could be used."

Reorganization and reduction in the number of collieries may not necessarily mean the closing of an equal proportion of shafts. Some of the existing shafts will probably be kept working in order to provide access to different parts of reorganized pits.

The reorganizing of old collieries and the laying out of new ones provide opportunities for the design of pithead buildings and plant worthy of a great national industry. Many of the new pithead baths designed for the Miners' Welfare Committee point the way to improvement. There is no intrinsic reason why colliery buildings, if properly designed, should be excessively disfiguring to the landscape.

The shifts and possible future trends of coalmining in Cannock Chase raise a number of planning problems.

In the first place, much of the future development above ground is likely to take place on Cannock Chase itself. Disturbance of good agricultural land will thus be small and should be confined to specific areas in the Penk Valley. Of more immediate concern is the positive danger to the landscape and amenity value of the Chase that may result from the development of collieries. It was pointed out earlier that the degree to which collieries can disfigure a landscape is often disproportionate to the extent and value of the workings. The area of Cannock Chase covers about 100 square miles and the amount of land occupied by colliery buildings and tips within it is quite negligible; if the same amount of land were used for almost any other kind of development, little harm would be done to the attractiveness and amenities of the Chase. But collieries, with their tall chimneys dominating the countryside, the huddle of blackened buildings around them and, most of all, their enormous barren heaps of waste, have become almost symbolic of the dehumanised environment of the industrial worker's life which townspeople seek to leave behind them when they enter the countryside. The possibility of electrically powered mines renders the smoke stack a less inevitable part of the future scene. Better architectural design may improve the appearance of shafts and engine house. The problem of the pit bank remains. Not much can be done by re-packing unusable waste below the surface, especially as much of it comes from drifts and passages mined in order to reach the coal seams; a little may be done in certain instances by careful siting of tips; much more depends on carefully planned and fully implemented schemes to ensure orderly tipping and rehabilitation of each section of the heap as tipping is completed. Controlled tipping and rehabilitation should proceed as a continuous process in which the landscape may be altered considerably, but not spoiled.

Secondly, the gradual movement of mining centres has had, and may still have, important repercussions on the disposition of the labour force, on the character and structure of the mining towns and villages, and on the settlement pattern generally. The triangular area lying between Pelsall and Aldridge, with Brownhills as the apex, and fringing the immediate north of the West Midland Conurbation, affords many examples

Littleton Colliery. Two of the four spoil heaps. The conical shape is now usual as being more economical, but tips of this size dominate a large area of landscape. The land on the far side of the ploughed fields beyond the tips is much inferior agriculturally to that on which the tips have been sited.

Open cast workings, Heath Hayes. Cuts of this depth are made to extract seams of only a few feet in thickness. Government regulations now require top soil to be preserved and returned after working.

of the type of problem which has followed the northward spread of mining. It is an area with a character of its own which has been held, as it were, in tension between the pull of the coalfield moving to the north and the increasingly stronger pull of the Conurbation to the south, until today it is probably to be considered more an integral part of the Conurbation than of the Cannock Chase Coalfield. The problems of the area warrant an extensive survey ; some indication of them is all that is possible here. Mining in the area of Aldridge U.D., for example, ceased finally in 1936. There are, however, still many hundreds of adult colliery workers in Aldridge U.D. who travel some miles to other collieries for employment. In other words, the movement of mining out of the district has not been followed by an equivalent movement of colliery workers and their dependants. Again, the gap left by the removal of a primary industry has not been nearly filled, as a full survey would show, by the entry of new industries. The result is that many of those workers who have forsaken the coal industry following its removal, together with their sons and daughters, have found employment in the workshops and offices of the Conurbation rather more attractive. Tentative studies have shown the extent to which Walsall, for example, draws its labour force from the triangular area of the worked out coalfield to the north, while the pull of Birmingham's industries is felt as far north as Brownhills and the villages near the line of Watling Street. As coalmining activity moves northwards through and out of this area, so Walsall, in particular, has spread its " sphere of influence " northwards, closely following the retreating southern boundary of the coalfield. It may be noted that 'bus services from Walsall now radiate over the whole sector from Cannock to Brownhills and bring in to the Conurbation workers from the districts of the old coalfield. The appearance of the area remains very much the same as at the time of the decline of coalmining. The landscape presents an untidy picture of street villages, dilapidated sub-standard houses, railway junctions and sidings, brickworks belching smoke, old quarries, pit banks and derelict land. The background to all this is agriculture in the north, and suburban development outwards from the Conurbation in the south. There has been little reorganization or reorientation of industry, such as that which followed the cessation of mining in the Black Country ; brickworks still flourish in the Aldridge district, but attempts at the introduction of new industries are few and isolated.

Similar conditions seem likely to arise in the present central area of the coalfield as mining activity shifts north and west, and it seems unlikely at present that movement of mining out of this district will be followed naturally by the large scale entry of new industries. A situation is likely to arise in which the mining population still lives in the ramshackle and unsightly villages and towns of this central area, while finding employment in the newer collieries on the northern and western fringes of the coalfield.

The likelihood of this development raises the whole question of future policy in the housing of mining employees. It would seem, at first sight, desirable to group the mining population as near as possible to its place of employment. This would result in economy of travelling time and would afford an opportunity of abandoning the older, unplanned settlements of the centre of the coalfield, while creating orderly, organized communities in the newer areas. There are, however, fairly substantial arguments against such a policy. First of all, the total area is small ; the amount of time spent in travelling from existing settlements to new mines would not be great, and transport costs inconsiderable compared with the amount which new settlements would cost. New villages on Cannock Chase or in the Penk Valley would probably do more harm to the landscape and the amenities of these areas than the workings themselves, especially if careful siting, good design, and landscape treatment are employed in the development of new mines.

We have to make up our minds whether or not the " mining village " built near the pithead and tied culturally, as well as economically and geographically, to the mining industry, is a really desirable form of settlement. Bad planning and bad conditions apart, such settlements are not likely to improve the appearance of the countryside, but the effect on the miner's social status and on his relationship with the rest of society is much more important. There seems little doubt that the segregation of the mining community in mining villages has produced a sense of isolation and an " isolationist " attitude, and that these are major causes of the recurrent crises in the industry. It is high time that mining took its place as a truly national industry drawing its recruits from among the general community. This can only happen if the miner takes a rightful place as a member of a mixed and not of a segregated or isolated community. It is in the interests not only of the coal industry in particular but of the general public that we adopt and put into effect the principle of the " residence of colliery employees in the larger and mixed communities presented by normal town and village life ", laid down in the Regional Survey Report, *Coalfields of the Midland Region*, (Ministry of Fuel and Power, 1945, page 27).

It follows that in the Cannock Chase Coalfield planning policy should be directed towards the fuller development, equipment and organization of the chief existing centres of population, rather than towards the creation of new ones. The nineteenth century spread of mining has left a legacy of unplanned, ugly, undeveloped street villages which can and must be adapted to meet changed conditions, and rehabilitated to offer a fuller life for the coalfield population. The nature of many of the outstanding problems can be seen in a short journey through the area which includes Walsall Wood, Brownhills, Heath Hayes and Hednesford, but a full understanding of them can only be achieved by an investigation and planning survey—which in this area is long overdue.

Output of the Coalfield

The output of saleable coal in the Cannock Chase field in 1946 was 4,405,973 tons. This was chiefly domestic and industrial coal for use in the Midlands and south of England. Production at approximately this level (which represents about 2.5% of the national total) is likely to be maintained for some little time, but the coalfield will eventually decline both in actual and relative output. Apart from extensions of the field, technical reorganization of many of the older collieries is to be expected, but repercussions of this from a planning point of view are unlikely to be great.

The total number of wage-earners on colliery books has shown a steady decline since the 1914-1918 war, but despite this, average output has remained reasonably steady.

							Persons employed in all mines of Cannock Chase Coalfield
1920	..	..	..	..	..	..	25,107
1930	..	..	..	..	..	..	22,872
1938	..	..	..	..	..	..	19,892
1940	..	..	..	..	..	..	18,778
1945	..	..	..	..	..	..	18,158

Other Future Extensions

It should be noted finally that further long-term possibilities for coalmining exist beneath the thick covers of Triassic rocks which separate the coalfields of the Conurbation from those of Shropshire and East Warwickshire.

In Shropshire the coals already being mined in the area of Lilleshall (between Newport and Wellington) have been discovered to extend in a north-westerly direction, and the limits of the field are now being proved. Already sufficient coal for a new large mine has been found and surveys are in hand to find the proper position for the proposed shafts. In Warwickshire possibilities for extension exist towards the north-east and the south-west of the present coalfield, but the principal development here will be in the reconstruction of existing collieries. It is possible that a new shaft may be sunk in the neighbourhood of Coventry, but this will depend on the results from the borings now in progress.

Developments in Shropshire or in hitherto unexploited areas of the Warwickshire coalfield may involve rather different planning problems from those presented by the gradual movement of an existing coalfield. Apart from reducing as far as possible the disturbance of fairly high grade land which would be involved, it would be necessary to plan settlements and services for a mining community which would have to be located in a hitherto wholly rural area.

Such " new " coalfields would lie well outside the present limits of the Conurbation, but it is conceivable that they might have a decided influence on the future growth and extension of the urban fringe.

OPEN-CAST WORKINGS

Coal seams are at present being worked by open cast methods in a number of localities in the Cannock Chase coalfield, while " drift " mining operations, *i.e.* mining by shallow tunnel or " adit ", are also in progress. In both open-cast and drift-mining, operations at any one site will be only temporary, lasting in the case of drift-mining 5 to 10 years at most. Total coal production by these methods is not and will not become great, relative to that of deep-mined coal.

Planning problems in this connection are twofold :—

(a) Open-cast workings, especially, result in considerable disfigurement of the landscape (see page 273). This is not, however, a particularly serious consideration in an area such as the Cannock Chase coalfield where surface mining operations take place against an already badly scarred background and in view of the temporary nature of such workings. Conservation of surface soil and rehabilitation of sites after exploitation are now obligatory.

(b) Problems of damage to, and restoration of, the soil, though of local importance, are not as immediate or urgent as they are, for example, in the Warwickshire coalfield, by reason of the more restricted extent of the workings, and of the inferior quality of the land disturbed. Much of the affected land consists of heath or woodland while the remainder has been classified as Category II with III in the Land Classification Survey of the rural area around the West Midland Conurbation. (See Plate 12).

SURFACE SUBSIDENCE

Although generalizations about surface subsidence are notoriously dangerous, the planning difficulties arising from subsidence in the South Staffordshire and Cannock Chase coalfields do not appear to be as serious as they are elsewhere—in the North Staffordshire coalfield, for example. Much of the derelict land in South Staffordshire has resulted from the subsidence of old, shallow workings and will prove costly and difficult to reclaim. Subsidence has in the past presented serious problems to canal, railway and other civil engineers. In areas worked at present or likely to be worked, the depths of workings are great, generally in the region of 600 yards, seams are only moderately inclined, and the building density on the ground above is not particularly high. The likely degree of subsidence to be expected is small, and building in areas likely to be worked in the future is of low density per acre and usually of modern construction.

In the Cannock Chase area the effects of subsidence are widespread and the resultant loss and inconvenience has often proved serious as, for example, at Clayhanger near Brownhills (see page 278). Owing to the relatively low building density over the coalfield as a whole, however, the total amount of damage to building property, though locally severe, has not been unduly great and most buildings liable to be affected are strutted or buttressed in order to withstand the results of surface settlement. Canals have been damaged, and roads have suffered widely, as any traveller along Watling Street west of Brownhills will know, while many acres of flooded and derelict land near Brownhills, Norton Canes and in other districts mark the areas in which surface subsidence has been most widespread and severe.

Building density is low in those areas which might become important mining districts in the future. Mining depths will be greater than in the older areas of the coalfield and the problem of surface subsidence is unlikely to be of other than local importance in limiting either future mining operations or building activities.

In preparing local planning schemes in the area of the working coalfield, however, every effort should be made to assess accurately the extent to which subsidence is to be expected in the neighbourhood.

CONCLUSIONS

1. Coal mining has played an important part in the growth of the West Midland Conurbation. Future trends in the location and relative importance of the industry should be taken into account when planning for the future development of the Conurbation.

2. The importance of the output of the South Staffordshire and Cannock Chase Coalfields relative to total national production will show a steady decline during the next hundred years.

3. *South Staffordshire Coalfield*

This coalfield is dying. Possibilities of important future development lie only in the extreme west of the field, at Baggeridge and in the area of Himley and Wombourn. Pits on the eastern side, between Birmingham and West Bromwich, will probably be worked for a few years only. The pithead buildings and waste heaps of these latter pits dominate the landscape of the southern part of the Aldridge-Sandwell wedge, and their rehabilitation should be planned now.

4. *Cannock Chase Coalfield*

The south and south-east of this field, is, to all intents and purposes, worked out. Coal working in the middle of the field is declining and approaching the end of its life. Planning problems in these " older " areas are associated with the need for rehabilitation of towns and villages such as Walsall Wood, Pelsall, Shire Oak, Brownhills, Chasetown, Great Wyrley, Norton Canes and Bridgetown. The distribution and movement of industry need examination and the work-home relationship is often unsatisfactory in these areas. Settlements and settlement pattern need redevelopment and replanning, and services and amenities urgently need improvement. Some derelict land (which has lain outside the scope of previous studies of the Black Country), should be reclaimed.

Mining activity is at present concentrated in the west, north-west and north of the field

The two conical banks of Sandwell Park Colliery dominate much of the open country which makes up the wedge of open land stretching from the Aldridge area into the heart of the Conurbation.

The effects of recent subsidence in the Cannock Chase Coalfield. The road has been re-made on a causeway, but fields and houses are derelict.

An old shaft at Wednesbury. The presence of the steel plant in the background indicates how industry has remained in the area after the coal which first brought it there has been worked out.

278

around Cannock and Hednesford. Planning and redevelopment of settlements, *e.g.*, Hednesford and Huntington, are an urgent necessity. The probability of shifts north and west of the present " centre of gravity " should be taken into account in future planning, in order to avoid the development here of such a problem area as exists in the southern portion of the coalfield.

Future possibilities for mining development exist to north and west of the existing field. In addition, there are long-term possibilities in parts of the belts of agricultural land which separate the Cannock Chase from the Shropshire and East Warwickshire Coalfields.

Conflict between mining and planning may arise in areas of landscape and amenity value, *e.g.*, Cannock Chase. Every effort must be made to minimise disfigurement of the landscape by careful siting and good design of pithead buildings. The chief danger to the landscape is likely to arise from the colliery tip. More attention should be given to schemes for reducing the adverse effects of mining on the usefulness and beauty of the countryside. Control of the site, shape and extent of tips, and rehabilitation of waste heaps by systematic planting, are the principal means by which this can be done.

Apart from landscape considerations, disturbance of limited areas of good quality agricultural land is unavoidable.

The need for providing transport facilities for collieries developed in " new " fields should be recognised. There may also arise the necessity of providing for the founding of new settlements, fully equipped with services and amenities. The development of " new " coalfields may also have a direct influence on the directions of growth of the Conurbation.

Open-cast Workings

Although open cast workings and " drift " mining will result in considerable disturbance of agricultural land and spoilation of the landscape, the influence of this type of mining, if well controlled, is of a local and transient nature.

Surface Subsidence

The effects of surface subsidence have not been as disastrous as in North Staffordshire. Nevertheless, considerable damage to roads, buildings, bridges and canals has been caused. Much of the derelict land of the Black Country has resulted from the subsidence of shallow workings. Local plans in areas of past and present coalmining should be related to a careful assessment of the possible effects of subsidence.

INDEX

Note.—Plates 1-15 are inserted in the text between pages 160 and 161.

283

ACKNOWLEDGEMENTS OF PHOTOGRAPHS

The photograph on page 88 (top left) is reproduced with the permission of the Town Clerk, Bilston.

The Group is indebted to the Ministry of Town and Country Planning for permission to use the aerial photographs on pages 24, 164, 165 and 166 (bottom), 167 and 176, which have been supplied from the photographic survey in their possession.

Thanks are also due to Mr. S. H. Beaver, of the Ministry of Town and Country Planning, for permission to reproduce the photographs on pages 89 (second from top), 178 and 180 (top), and to *The Birmingham Gazette* for supplying the photographs on page 216.

The photographs on pages 20-21 (top), 100-103 (with a few exceptions), 141 (except bottom right), 142 (except middle right), 143, 144, 145 (except top left), 146 (bottom), 147, 179, 217, 220 and 242-3 were taken by Mr. Paul Redmayne, M.A.; those on pages 18 (bottom), 19 (bottom), 25 (bottom), 162, 163, 166 (top), 218 (bottom) and 219 (bottom) by Aerofilms, Ltd.; those on pages 215, 218 (top), 219 (top), 223-6, 238 and 240 by Roy Dixon, A.R.P.S.; those on pages 18-19 (top), 22-23 (top), 88 (except top left), 89 (except second from top), 141 (bottom right), 142 (middle right), 145 (top left), 146 (top), 177 and 180 (bottom) by Adcraft, Ltd.; those on pages 20-21 (bottom), 22-23 (bottom), 24 (top), 25 (top) and 100-103 (certain photographs) by Mr. A. Sewell; those on pages 265, 269 and 273 by Mr. D. W. Oliver, and those on page 278 by Mr. D. W. Oliver and Mr. M. J. Wise, both of the Department of Geography, University of Birmingham. The studies of landscape scenes on pages 239 and 241, which are based on the photographs shown opposite, are the work of Mr. F. Kenwood Giles.

The photograph which forms the frontispiece was taken by Roy Dixon, A.R.P.S.